Natalie Rogoff Ramsøy (ed.)

NORWEGIAN SOCIETY

Universitetsforlaget
Oslo - Bergen - Tromsø

C. Hurst & Company
London

Humanities Press Inc.
New York

Translated from the Norwegian by Susan Høivik in cooperation with
Dr. Natalie Rogoff Ramsøy

First published in Norway by Gyldendal Norsk Forlag A/S 1968 under
the title *Det Norske Samfunn*

The present edition is published simultaneously in Norway by Universitetsforlaget
Oslo - Bergen - Tromsø, in the United Kingdom by C. Hurst and Co. (Publishers) Ltd.,
London, and in the United States of America by Humanities Press, New York

Cover Design: Bjørn Roggenbihl

ISBN 82-00-04610-9 (Universitetsforlaget)

ISBN 0-903983-01-X (Hurst)

ISBN 0-391-00329-1 (Humanities Press)

Library of Congress Catalog Card No. 73-14885

Printed in Norway by E. Sem A/S, Halden

© Gyldendal Norsk Forlag A/S 1968

© (English version) Universitetsforlaget 1974

Translated from the Norwegian by Susan Høivik in cooperation with
Dr. Natalie Rogoff Ramsøy

First published in Norway by Gyldendal Norsk Forlag A/S 1968 under
the title *Det Norske Samfunn*

The present edition is published simultaneously in Norway by Universitetsforlaget
Oslo - Bergen - Tromsø, in the United Kingdom by C. Hurst and Co. (Publishers) Ltd.,
London, and in the United States of America by Humanities Press, New York

Cover Design: Bjørn Roggenbihl

ISBN 82-00-04610-9 (Universitetsforlaget)

ISBN 0-903983-01-X (Hurst)

ISBN 0-391-00329-1 (Humanities Press)

Library of Congress Catalog Card No. 73-14885

Printed in Norway by E. Sem A/S, Halden

Contents

Preface

More than most books, this one is an experiment in communication. Published originally in Norwegian in 1968 under the title *Det norske samfunn*, the book was designed to provide university and other students with a wealth of descriptive material concerning the major social institutions and structural features of contemporary Norway. Before this work appeared, Norwegian sociology had developed far enough to have produced original theoretical contributions, a number of excellent monographs, a flourishing social science journal, and a highly useful introductory text on the discipline (Vilhelm Aubert's *Sociology*). But still it was apparent that students needed a more detailed picture of their own supposedly well-known social surroundings, presented in such a fashion as to give them the opportunity to see how sociologists observe a society and describe it with the aid of the guiding concepts that typify the field.

However, the English language edition of the same book cannot assume the same familiarity with Norwegian daily life. So it is with some trepidation that we present the following chapters, each devoted to a major social institution, whether this is of a formal character such as the school system or the administration of justice, or of a less well recognized character, such as social stratification. The English-speaking reader may find that the particular contours of social arrangements in Norway are not always as clearly sketched as he might wish.

Many Norwegians today are experiencing these times as a period of extremely rapid social change, during which a host of overwhelming problems seriously threaten the fabric of society. Yet outsiders often look to the small, homogeneous country of Scandinavia as idyllic and happily spared the social ills besetting larger and less easily manageable societies. On the whole, this book takes a position between these extremes. As many of the authors suggest, most institutions in Norwegian society are based on egalitarianism as their basic organizing principle, yet none of them function in such a way as to achieve this ideal. While most of its inhabitants are of the same ethnic and linguistic origins, small minority groups (Lapps, immigrants from

Mediterranean or more distant countries) suffer from both discrimination and cultural estrangement.

Other problems with which Norway is now faced derive from the incapacity to resolve conflicts between values: on the one hand economic growth, on the other an equitable allocation of economic benefits among the various regions and branches of economic activity. Other conflicting values concern the high priority given to the nation's political sovereignty (Norway is a relatively new nation, having gained fully autonomous status as late as 1905) while at the same time valuing Norway's participation in the regional or worldwide community of nations, even though this impinges on its national sovereignty.

Conflicts of values and interests are inherent in all societies based on specialization and the division of labour. But societies of this type vary considerably in their capacity to resolve such conflicts and to provide their members with enough satisfaction to win their confidence and to secure adherence to basic values. Norway relies in good measure on a pattern of responsible negotiating partners as its solution to these problems – virtually all major economic, cultural, occupational, and social groups in the society are organized in nationwide voluntary associations which have been granted official status to negotiate either with the government or with their opposite numbers with regard to the distribution of rewards, privileges, and obligations. A great many things, from the price of milk to the allocation of radio and television time, broadcast in each of the two forms of the Norwegian language, are decided on through this mechanism. To be sure, the success of this pattern depends on the degree of 'responsibility' with which the parties fight for their rights, and this, in turn, requires that each organization identifies enough with the society as a whole, to keep the demands each makes within some reasonable limits. So, Norwegian society is 'conflictful', but not ridden by its conflicts.

Another theme of interest to English-speaking readers is that of Norway's status as a welfare state. Again, this is treated in the following chapters primarily as a set of aspirations and values, rather than an accomplished reality. It is safe to say that the Norwegian polity has so firmly committed itself to a host of policy decisions implied by the idea of the welfare state, that there is no turning back. Yet the implementation of these policies has given rise to a plethora of unexpected difficulties, many of them of so fundamental a character as to jeopardize basic values in the Norwegian social structure. Many of these unanticipated consequences stem from the practical difficulties of applying the general and generally accepted idea that society is to take on the responsibility of guaranteeing the economic security and well-being of those who cannot provide for themselves.

In fact change in some of these spheres is so rapid that the material presented here, compiled as it was in 1967, no longer fits the facts. In particular, the formal apparatuses in education, health, and social services – the core of the welfare state – have been so revamped that the structural descriptions given here should not be taken literally. Furthermore, the formal changes have produced a new crop of social problems and conflicts of interest, as is to be expected of so open-ended a system.

On the whole, the introduction of welfare state policies is part of a more fundamental set of social changes, in which the scale of rights and obligations between individuals on the one hand and larger collectivities on the other is increasing in balance. In Norway as elsewhere, everything costs more than it did a generation ago, including the social and psychic costs of living one's everyday life as a member of a family and of the local, national, and worldwide communities. And under such conditions, the social arrangements whereby we try to bring costs and rewards into reasonable relation with one another inevitably appear to be provisional, to be ripe for experiment, criticism, and thorough scrutiny.

So this is a book written by Norwegian sociologists who portray the social arrangements characterizing their society at a particular point in time. When presented to an international audience, it may give members of that audience new impulses, associations, and insights. It may increase the repertoire of social arrangements with which readers are familiar. It may even, through unforeseeable chains of events, bring about changes in social arrangements elsewhere.

A collective work of this scope could never have been produced without the collaboration of a great many persons in addition to the authors. Of those who have contributed their valuable services I want to mention first Arne Dolven, Anita Werner, and Mariken Vaa. As the editor's nearest collaborators during different phases of the work, they deserve credit for seeing to it that the great mass of information contained in the book was complete and correct. Many students have worked as assistants to the authors, both in searching out data and reworking available information. Among these were Liv Bøysen, Torbjørn Kalberg, Tore Semmingsen, Leif Kåre Solberg, Bjørg Åse Sørensen, and Ivar Bermann.

The editor and authors wish finally to express their thanks to the Norwegian Research Council for Science and the Humanities, which provided economic support over several years to cover the costs of preparing the Norwegian version of the book.

May 1973   *Natalie Rogoff Ramsøy*

I. Norway's Population

By Ørjar Øyen

1. INTRODUCTION

Anyone doing social investigation has many good reasons for an interest in the population, or *demography,* as the specialized study of population is called. The population comprises the very basis of a society, so its size and growth, its composition and changes, are important features for study.

In this chapter we shall first see how Norway's population has grown, and how it will probably continue to grow in the immediate future. Then we shall view its composition as to age and sex, discussing problems about fertility and mortality, and finally we shall take a look at migration tendencies in Norway.

Some of the themes usually treated under the heading of 'population' are taken up in other chapters of this book. An analysis of causes of death is given in Chapter VIII, of civil status and marriage in Chapter II, of education in Chapter V, of income and occupation in Chapter III, and of stratification in Chapter IV.

2. SIZE AND GROWTH OF THE NORWEGIAN POPULATION

Norway's population comprises only about one-thousandth of the total number of people on the earth today. For every Norwegian there are about 200 Chinese, 120 Indians, 60 Soviet citizens, 50 Americans. Norwegians are few in number and widely spread.

According to the census of 1 November 1960, Norway's total population numbers 3,591,234. The four million mark will probably be passed sometime in the early 1970s (see Table II).

The country's total land area measures some 308,000 square kilometres (119,000 square miles)[1] and in 1960 the average population density was 11.6 persons per square kilometre. This does indeed provide a certain amount of elbow room, at least as far as sports, outdoor life, and recreation activities are concerned. By contrast, in the Netherlands population density has reached almost 400 persons per square kilometre. Norway's population density is lowest in her northernmost county, Finnmark: only 1.5 per square kilometre. The density in counties around the Oslo Fjord (Oslo, Akershus, Østfold, and Vestfold, which in 1960 had 30 per cent of Norway's total population) averages around 100 persons per square kilometre.

Norway's first census was taken more than two hundred years ago, on 15 August 1769. At that time, the total population numbered 723,618, or, with some 4,000 members of the military then in garrisons excluded in that census, a grand total of about 728,000, or one-fifth the 1960 total.

We know little about Norway's population in the years and centuries before this first census, although historians and archaeologists have presented estimates that stretch far back in time. Estimates from the earliest periods are founded on archaeological findings. As to the Middle Ages, records on the 'Roman tax', for example, have provided points of departure for estimating the population size. A more thorough survey of descriptions of developments in Norway's population in the times before the first census is given in Lunde (1955, pp. 27–35).

From 1735 onwards we also have yearly reports on the number of births and deaths, reports which the early Norwegian sociologist Eilert Sundt utilized in his demographic studies made over a hundred years ago. Of these, suffice it to mention *Om Giftermaal i Norge* (Concerning Marriage in Norway), 1855, with a paperback re-issue in 1967; and *Om Dødeligheden i Norge* (Concerning Mortality in Norway), 1855, both published in Christiania, as Oslo was then called.

Norway's second census was taken in 1801, followed by a third in 1815, and then further censuses every ten years until 1875. In 1890 there was another census, and so on every ten years until 1930. Due to the war there was no 1940 census; one was held in 1946 instead; in 1950 the regular ten-year pattern was again resumed.

Table I shows the changes in total population from the first census of 1769 to the most recent in 1960. The increase is considerable. In the period 1815–1960 alone the population doubled twice; from 1870 to 1960 the increase was as great as that in all previous periods, from the time of the first human settlements in Norway.

The 1769 population figures doubled by the 1850s, tripling in the 1890s, then becoming four times as great in the 1930s and five times greater in the early 1960s.

The average growth rates in the periods between census years show some variations. In the 1920s a low point of 6.0 per thousand was reached, whereas the corresponding rate for the period 1855–1865 was as high as 13.4. However, at no time has the growth rate even approached levels as high as those found today in many developing, ex-

Table I. *Norway's population according to censuses, 1769—1960, and average yearly growth rates in the periods between censuses*

Census date		Total population	Average yearly growth rate per 100 in period since last census*
15 August	1769	723,618**	—
13 February	1801	883,487	—
30 April	1815	885,431	—
27 November	1825	1,051,318	—
29 November	1835	1,194,827	12.9
31 December	1845	1,328,471	10.6
31 December	1855	1,490,047	11.5
31 December	1865	1,701,756	13.4
31 December	1875	1,813,424	6.4
31 December	1890	2,000,917	6.6
3 December	1900	2,240,032	11.4
1 December	1910	2,391,782	6.6
1 December	1920	2,649,775	10.3
1 December	1930	2,814,194	6.0
3 December	1946	3,156,950	7.3
1 December	1950	3,278,546	9.6
1 November	1960	3,591,234	9.3

* Obtained according to the formula: $r = \left(\sqrt[n]{\dfrac{P_2}{P_1}} - 1 \right) = 1{,}000.$

where r is the yearly growth rate, P_1 the population at the beginning of the period, P_2 the population at the end of the period, and n the exact number of years between the beginning and the end of the period. The growth rate reflects the total effect of migration, fertility, and mortality. It has not been computed for the first three periods because of uncertain data.

** Some 4,000 garrisoned soldiers on active duty not included, cf. NOS XII 195, Table IV, p. 5.

panding countries: for example, in many Central and South American countries the latest growth rates surpass the 30 per thousand mark *(Population Index* 1967, pp. 138–147).

Now a constant growth rate of 10 per thousand means that it takes the population 70 years to double itself; a rate of 20, that the population doubles in 35 years; and at a rate of 30, the time needed is only 24 years. The time needed for doubling, given a certain growth rate, can be calculated by solving the equation in the footnote to Table I with respect to n, when $P_2 = 2P_1$.

In the period 1960–1966 Norway's average yearly growth rate has been about 7.8 per thousand; given this rate, the population will double again in about 90 years.

In preparing population prognoses, however, this method is less than satisfactory. It is better to try to form differentiated ideas on

Table II. *Population prognoses for Norway, 1970 and 1980, by type of municipality*

Type of municipality	1970	1980
Urban or densely settled	2,316,000	2,663,000
Rural, non-urbanized	1,579,000	1,607,000
Norway as a whole	3,895,000	4,270,000

Source: Bendiksen 1963. The prognoses have been prepared on the basis of sex and age distribution in the individual municipalities, according to 1960 census data; the following have been assumed: a) continuing age-specific fertility rates as in 1956-1959, corrected for regional variations; b) age-specific mortality rates as in 1951-1955, with a decrease per five-year period (after 1951-1955) — 10 per cent for the age group 50 years and under, 5 per cent for the age group 51-59, and 2 per cent for the age group 60 years and over; and c) age-specific migration rates (between the different types of municipalities) based on trends from the period 1957-1959, corrected for net migration from Norway. Further details are given in Bendiksen 1963, pp. 10-11).

how a series of different factors will influence increase and decrease of population, through migration, fertility, and mortality.

According to prognoses from the Norwegian Central Bureau of Statistics, the population will increase in coming years in the way presented in Table II. This estimate shows that Norway's population is to pass the 4.25 million mark by 1980.

3. POPULATION COMPOSITION

We shall here describe the population according to the two most characteristic demographic factors: age and sex. Sociologically, let us note that these seem to be the most important criteria for ascribed status in our society. Together they place us within fairly definite limits as to our interaction patterns and social activities.

3.1. *Age composition*

The best point of departure for describing the age composition of a given population is the *age pyramid,* a double histogram showing the absolute or relative number of persons from birth upwards. The vertical axis shows age, the horizontal shows number or percentage. The one side of the pyramid shows the age distribution for men; the other, for women. As to percentage, the area under the pyramid represents 100 per cent, i.e. the percentage basis is the total population.

Figure 1 shows the age composition of Norway's population by five-year groups, according to 1960 census data. The largest five-year group consists of children aged 10–14; they were born to a large age

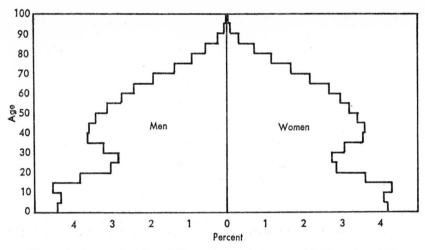

Figure 1. *Age composition of Norway's population, as of 1 November 1960.*

group of parents gradually approaching the top of the pyramid. We see a sharp decline in size when considering the age group 20–34. This is of course the most highly reproductive portion of the population; it is in these years that most people have their children. When the number of parents is small, the number of children born to them will also be small, under otherwise equal conditions – and we do see a corresponding, although less drastic decrease at the bottom of the pyramid. This will soon disappear, however, as the large youth group reaches its reproductive years.

Any irregularity in the pyramid, once started, will create waves lasting for several generations before finally being equalized. In the past century, Eilert Sundt made this wave phenomenon the subject of thorough analysis. He describes the process thus:

> If the number of children born increases suddenly and strongly, then under normal conditions, there will in time occur a corresponding increase in the number of adult persons; and of those that marry, there will also be more than previously (Sundt 1855, p. 92).

This, Sundt's Law, was also explained thus:

> The number of marriages taking place in the various age groups will, under normal conditions, generally follow the number of births in the corresponding earlier years. It varies as the water level in the rivers according to the amount of snow that has melted in the mountains (Sundt 1855b, pp. 89–90).

The form an age pyramid takes can tell us much about the general condition of the population, its productivity potential, the relationship between occupationally active and non-active portions of the population. A population rich in persons in their prime is in many ways better situated than one in which the largest groups of persons are elderly. It may well be that a population of this latter type is less adaptive to technological change (Broom and Selznick 1963, p. 316).

As we see from Figure 1, Norway's population in 1960 was poor in fresh, new blood in the occupational sector. But a new generation is on its way, having now passed through most of the educational phase and begun to fill in the open spaces in the 25-35-year-old group.

Further, the pyramid's form can indicate how the population has developed through recent generations, as well as hint at how the development will continue in the future. Moreover, it reveals much about the general standard of health and living, as we see from Figure 2, where Norway's pyramid is compared with that of a fairly typical developing country, Venezuela. Figure 2 shows the pyramids drawn with the same co-ordinates. Like other developing countries, Venezuela has high fertility and high mortality rates; the pyramid is broad at the bottom, narrowing rapidly with increasing age. The proportion of older persons is small, while that of children and babies is very high. In 1961, some 45 per cent of the population was under 15 years of age in Venezuela; the corresponding figure for Norway was 26 per cent.

Somewhat earlier in Norway's own development its population structure was similar to that of Venezuela and other countries today.

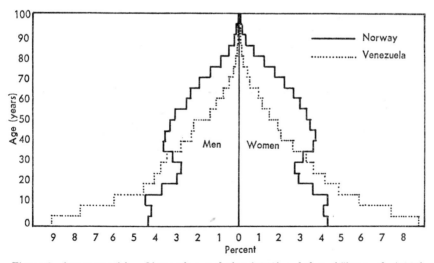

Figure 2. *Age composition, Norway's population (1960) and that of Venezuela (1961)* Source: Data for Venezuela from *United Nations Demographic Yearbook 1962*, pp. 164-165.

15

Table III. *Norway's population by age, according to census data from 1865, 1890, 1930, and 1960, and the 1980 prognoses (percentage distribution)*

Age	1865	1890	1930	1960	1980
0-14	36.0	35.5	32.1	25.8	25.4
15-59	55.0	53.4	56.9	58.0	54.1
60 and over	9.0	11.1	11.0	16.2	20.5
Total	100.0	100.0	100.0	100.0	100.0

Sources: Backer 1961, Table 7, p. 32; NOS XII 195, Table 10 and Table 11, p. 11.

Table III shows how the proportion of the population under 15 years of age has gradually decreased, while the proportion of older people has increased. If the prognoses for 1980 prove correct, the proportion of persons 60 years and over will thus have doubled in the course of these hundred-odd years.

Today, the age composition of the Norwegian population varies according to location, with the rural, non-urbanized areas having the greatest proportion of older persons. This is primarily a result of the differentiation produced by migration: a population on the move generally has a different age composition from that of one where little migration or movement takes place. A society composed of persons who have only recently moved in – be it a new suburban area, for example the new industrial town of Mo i Rana shortly after its founding in the 1950s – will have many preschool children, very few teenagers, very many persons in the 25–35 year age group, and very few older persons (Holm et. al. 1958, p. 70). Should such a population settle down there for good, the population development would be very uneven, 'wavy', indeed, and probably by no means unproblematic, with greatly varying demands for housing, schools, and old-age homes as the families move, in parallel fashion, through their life-cycles.[2]

3.2. *Sex distribution*

If men and women were equally represented in the varying strata of the population, a description of sex distribution would be superfluous. However, there exist instead large differences, with sometimes a surplus of women and sometimes of men; such differences have many kinds of consequences for society. One might be that roles highly necessary to the society are not filled, or that many persons of marriageable age remain single. It is not improbable, as Vogt has pointed out, that such variations have more subtle influences on the general social tone in relations between the sexes (Vogt 1953).

The sex ratio used here is equal to the number of men per 100

16

Table IV. *Balance points (where sex ratio = 100) according to Norwegian census data 1900-1960, and the 1980 prognosis*

Balance point (age)	1900	1910	1920	1930	1946	1950	1960	1980
(age)	18.4	14.3	18.5	19.0	34.6	41.0	48.7	56.5

Source: Computed by linear interpolation on the basis of data in *Statistisk oversikt 1948;* NOS X 178; NOS XII 195, Tables 10-11.

women. It is skewed from birth, in that more baby boys than baby girls are born. In Norway, the number of live births for boys has been about 106, compared to 100 live births for girls, in the last decades. But although the male sex is over-represented at birth, this does not mean that men always are in a majority: women live longer than men. At all age levels, men have higher mortality rates than women, although there are certain exceptions. Thus, as each year group grows up, the male surplus is gradually reduced, until a surplus of women appears, steadily increasing with age. In 1964, there were 33,969 live births of boys and 31,601 of girls, i.e. 2,368 more boys than girls, giving a sex ratio of 107.2. In the same year, the sex ratio in the 80-year plus age group was only 72.

As life expectancy has increased, the balance point (i.e. where the ratio equals 100) has moved upwards on the age scale. In 1960 the balance point was close to 50 years; Table IV shows where balance points have been in this century's census years and where it will be in 1980 if the prognoses hold true. The Table shows a drastic change indeed, and the modern male surplus is a fact which, we can be sure, will have equally drastic social consequences.

Various factors influence the proportion of men to women at the different age levels. First, the sex ratio at birth is variable: it varies with pre-natal mortality (which is inversely proportional to the sex ratio at birth), according to the proportion of first-born (because first-born are slightly more likely to be boys than are later children in the same family), and according to the mother's age (with increasing age of mother, more girl babies are born) (McMahan 1951).

Second, migration is highly selective as regards both age and sex. And third, the sex ratio is also sensitive to such outside influences as varying causes of death: e.g. war reduces the number of men; special diseases affect one sex more than the other.

Especially because of the effects of migration, sex composition is different in urban and in rural areas (see Figure 3). The differentiation is marked from the age of 15 years and upwards, with a fairly large surplus of men in rural areas and a surplus of women in urban areas. The difference is greatest in the 20–24-year age group; rural

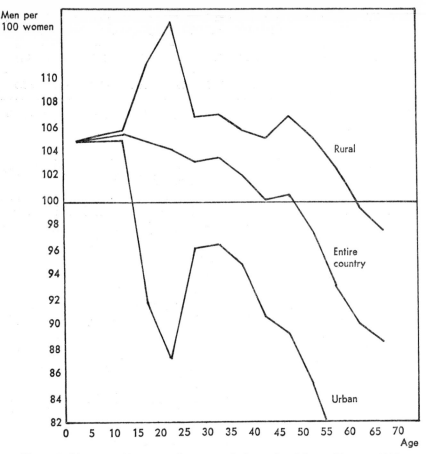

Figure 3. *Men per 100 women, by age and place of residence, Norway 1960.*

areas then have 115 men per 100 women, while urban areas have 87 men per 100 women. As it is at this age that most marriages take place, marrying chances for the sexes are quite unequal in urban and rural areas.

In rural areas this male surplus continues until the age of 65, according to 1960 data; urban areas have a surplus of women in all groups over about 15 years of age.

4. INCREASE AND DECREASE

The three main processes affecting population change are *fertility, mortality, and migration.* A population acquires new individuals in

18

two ways, either by natural reproduction (birth) or by newcomers moving in. Decrease takes place by death, or by persons moving away.

4.1. *Fertility*

4.1.1. Fertility and fecundity

The term 'fertility' refers to the population's actual reproductive patterns and behaviour, which can be observed by counting up the number of children actually born. 'Fecundity' on the other hand refers to the productive potential of the population, i.e. its maximal biological ability to bear children. The fecundity level represents an upper limit for fertility in a given population.

We may observe large variations in fertility, both over time and between different populations or population groups. But in no known society does it appear that fertility has ever approached the fecundity level. Of course, it is impossible to measure fecundity exactly, as this depends on many factors not easily observable.[3] It is therefore also difficult to decide whether fecundity generally is the same for different populations, or whether it remains constant over time.

It may be that fecundity has increased in those parts of the world that have improved their living conditions most. In such societies, the reproductive period of women has been extended, with menstruation beginning earlier and menarche occurring at a later age than before.

There is every reason to believe that in modern society fertility is so distinct from fecundity that variations in the former are fully explainable by social, economic, and cultural conditions. A valuable catalogue of factors contributing to reduce or stimulate fertility is found in Davis and Blake (1956).

4.1.2. Measuring fertility

The most common indicator of fertility is the number of live births yearly per 1,000 inhabitants. The number of births is thereby related to the total population, without correcting for its composition. This, the *gross birth rate,* is easy to compute. Especially in comparison with the gross mortality rate, computed in the same way, it can be useful, because the difference between the two yields a simple – although not always reliable – measure of the population's *natural growth,* of course disregarding the effects of migration.

But the gross birth rate can be misleading because it is highly dependent on variations in sex, age, and civil status. When a population has few individuals in their reproductive years, the rate will be much lower than in the case when there are many in their reproductive years, even though there may be no difference in the average number of children in the individual families. It is frequently necessary to adjust the rate to control the effects of such 'irrelevant' factors, by viewing the number of live births in relation to the number of women in the population, or to the number of women aged 15–44, or married women aged 15–44. Or the number of children 0–4 years of age may be viewed in relation to the number of women aged 15–44. Or, the age-specific birth rate may be computed by taking the number of live births to women in certain age groups in relation to the number of married women in these age groups. Age-specific rates can be summarized in various ways, so that fertility can be expressed by a single figure. A standardized rate of this type is the *gross reproduction rate*, which indicates the average number of live female births, under certain fertility conditions, to a woman who lives through her entire reproductive period (15–44 years of age, according to Norwegian statistics). The *net reproduction rate* indicates how many live females the average woman will give birth to in the years 15–44, under certain fertility and mortality conditions.

4.1.3. Changes in fertility

Yearly information on the number of births in Norway is available from as early as 1735, although the earliest data may be unreliable (Backer 1965, pp. 82–84). In order to compute the gross birth rate we need data on the total population in individual years; however, no census was taken before 1769. Despite this, rates have been prepared on the basis of population estimates for these early years. The number of births per 1,000 inhabitants fluctuates between 30 and 35 up to about the end of the past century. For shorter periods it was under 30 per 1,000, e.g. in the beginning of the nineteenth century (NOS X 178, Table 14).

From about 1900 and onwards, the rate decreased steadily, until 1935, when there were 14.3 live births per 1,000 inhabitants. The immediate post-war years saw high birth rates once again, with the highest, 22.6 per 1,000, in 1946. In 1965 Norway was down to 17.5 live birth per 1,000 inhabitants.

Norway's birth rates in the past decade have been among the lowest in the world. In many countries the rate is between 35 and 40: Mexico, for example, had a high of 46.7 live births per 1,000 inhabitants in 1964 (NOS XII 195, Table 396, pp. 302–303).

Figure 4 shows the main features of changes in fertility in Norway from the end of the past century up to the early 1960s. The curve represents age-specific fertility rates – computed with the total number of women in each age group. Until 1930 we have rates only for those years nearest the census years; later we have used yearly averages varying between two and five years. In the periods for which we

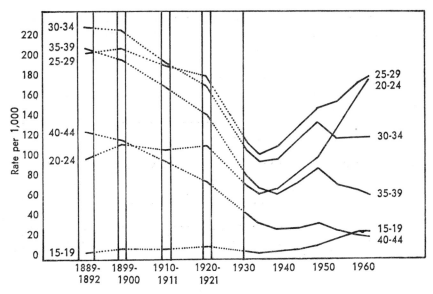

Figure 4. *Fertility by age of mother, Norway 1889-1961*

Source: *Statistisk årbok for Norge 1965*, NOS VII, 170, Table 38.

lack rates, there have probably been some fluctuations, perhaps especially around the time of World War I, but these could not be included here.

While the fertility of the oldest groups of women has been reduced, that of the youngest groups has increased considerably. As of 1960, women aged 15–19 had a fertility almost twice that of the 1890 level. During the same period, women aged 20–24 increased in fertility by some 70 per cent. On the other hand, all age groups from 25 and upwards have decreased in fertility: for example, fertility in the age group 40–44 in 1960 was only one-fifth of that in 1890. Earlier, women married at a somewhat later age, and births were more evenly distributed over the remaining years of the reproductive period. Now, as couples are marrying earlier and earlier, it is becoming more usual that children are born during the first years of marriage – which has, among other things, made age differences between generations smaller.

In order to reduce the effect of variations in age at marriage and marriage rates, we must view the number of live births in relation to the number of *married women* within the individual age groups. From 1890 to 1960 the number of live births per 1,000 married women has decreased in all age groups except that of 15–19 years. Table V shows which proportions the 1959–1962 rates formed of the 1889–1892 rates.

21

Table V. *Age-specific fertility rates (live births per 1,000 married women)*
as of 1959-1962, as a proportion of corresponding rates for 1899-1892,
by age of mother

Age of mother	15-19	20-24	25-29	30-34	35-39	40-44
Proportion	1.10	0.72	0.55	0.40	0.26	0.16

Source: NOS XII 195, Table 35, p. 26.

Thus, *married* women within each age group have decreased fertility,
except for the 15–19-year groups (the very youngest one), where it
would seem that an increase has taken place. There, however, another
factor is relevant.

This rate, number of live births per 1,000 married women, considers
all live births, whether to married women or to unmarried ones, in
relation to the total number of married women within each age group.
Therefore, these rates do not necessarily express *married women's*
fertility. In recent years, some 3 or 4 per cent of all live births in
Norway have been to unmarried women; but a full 20 per cent of
children born to women aged 15–19 are born to unmarried women
(see Table VI). In the next age group, less than 6 per cent are born
to unmarried women (Øyen 1966, pp. 48–72). In evaluating the
fertility rate for married women we must keep in mind these differences.

Family size has been decreasing steadily. From data on live
births to married women by order of birth (cf. Table VII) we see that
first and second births predominate. In 1961–1965 as much as one-
third of all births were first births, and a further one-third were
second births. Recent years show a slight increase in births of child
number three: in 1961–1965, one-fifth; twenty years ago, only one-
seventh of all births. Births of fourth and fifth children decreased in
the 1930s, but since 1940 their proportion has remained fairly constant. In the 30-year period preceding 1960 it is the number of births
from child number 6 and upwards that shows the most drastic decrease,
from 17 per cent to scarcely 3 per cent.

Table VI. *Live births to unmarried women, as percentage of all live births,*
by age of mother, Norway 1960

Age of mother	15-19	20-24	25-29	30-34	35-39	40-44
Live births	20.0	5.7	1.9	1.3	1.5	1.5

Source: NOS XII 97, Table XI, p. 65.

Table VII. *Live births to married women, by order of birth,
for selected periods (percentage)*

Child number	1929-1932	1941-1945	1956-1960	1961-1965
1	30.0	41.1	35.2	34.2
2	21.3	28.1	31.7	30.5
3	14.5	14.4	18.2	19.5
4	10.2	7.2	8.3	9.1
5	7.4	3.9	3.6	3.8
6 and upwards	16.3	5.3	3.0	2.8
Total	100.0	100.0	100.0	100.0

Source: Backer 1965, Table 50, pp. 100-09; NOS XII 218, Table 34, p. 24.

4.1.4. Differential fertility

The past two centuries' general decrease in fertility implies far-reaching changes in the social norms that control fertility behaviour. These changes have not taken place at an equal pace in all portions of the Norwegian population. And were we to view various segments of Norway's society at certain time points, we would find great differences in fertility.

It is often said that there is a correlation between social class and fertility; this is a partial truth only. It is imaginable that the change has taken place in the highly simplified manner shown in Figure 5: fertility changes starting first in the upper social levels, and then following the channels used by many other diffusion processes through the social structure. Over a fairly long period of time, the correla-

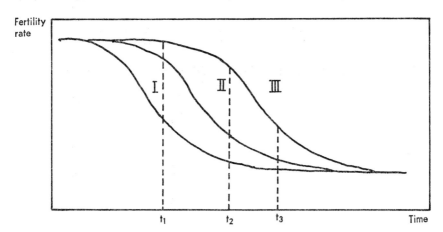

Figure 5. *Schematic diagram of possible correlation between fertility
and social class over time*

23

tion between class and fertility would appear, at t_1, t_2, and t_3. But this may be primarily because the various classes have reached different stages of the process.

Objections have been raised, however, against this way of explaining fertility changes by a model of social diffusion. Carlsson maintains that the phenomenon is more an adaptive process (Carlsson 1966).

In comparing fertility behaviour and patterns among different portions of a population, it is useful and indeed necessary to keep in mind the effects of the time dimension. Here is a real field for research and investigation. Conclusions on how the change develops and manifests itself will be of importance, for example, for specialists working on overpopulation problems in developing countries, and will help indicate where in the social structure efforts should be concentrated to achieve maximum effect.

We know little about differential fertility in Norway. Of the little we do have data on, we shall consider only some few facts here.

Table VIII shows how the gross birth rate has developed and changed in urban and rural areas from 1911 to 1960. At the beginning of this period, urban areas had a slightly higher rate than did rural ones; but then the urban rate decreased rapidly. Rural areas also saw a decrease in birth rate, but always less rapidly. Towards the end of this period, however, the urban/rural differences were no longer so great.

In other words, urbanization explains unequal proportions of fertility variations at different time points. The general pattern during the last hundred years may be said to resemble the schematic presentation in Figure 5.

It can be difficult to compare urban and rural areas, because

Table VIII. *Live births per 1,000 inhabitants in urban and rural areas. Norway 1911-1965. Yearly average*

Period	Norway as a whole	Urban areas	Rural areas
1911-1915	25.0	25.2	24.7
1916-1920	24.5	22.5	25.5
1921-1925	22.2	18.4	23.8
1926-1930	18.0	13.2	19.9
1931-1935	15.2	11.1	16.8
1936-1940	15.5	11.9	16.9
1941-1945	18.7	15.6	19.9
1946-1950	20.6	17.9	21.6
1951-1955	18.6	15.4	20.1
1956-1960	17.9	15.2	19.2
1961-1965	17.5	15.3	18.6

Source: NOS XII 195, Table 37, p. 27; NOS XII 218, Table 35, p. 24.

Table IX. *Average number of children, by father's chief occupation, in marriages of more than 17 years' duration, and where the mother married at age 20-29. Norway 1930 and 1946*

Father's occupation	Average number of children	
	1930	1946
Fisherman	5.04	3.62
Agricultural worker	4.98	2.95
Farmer	4.72	3.38
Construction worker, employed in trade, etc.	4.16	2.62
Sailor, seaman	3.95	2.55
Factory worker	3.93	2.21
Craftsman, artisan	3.92	2.36
Skilled worker	3.52	2.57
Self-employed in industry and trade	3.52	2.31
Officer (marine)	3.38	2.51
Lower civil servant	3.34	2.01
Factory owner, merchant, etc.	3.20	2.32
Office or shop workers, etc.	3.15	1.84
Self-employed, higher white-collar worker	2.73	2.31
Retired, living on inheritance/savings, no data	3.99	2.25
All groups	4.06	2.60

Source: Jahn 1952, Table 5, p. 188

geographical boundaries can have changed, and because population composition in urban versus rural areas has not remained the same. Throughout the past century urban areas had higher gross birth rates than did rural areas; but, as Julie E. Backer has observed, this is related to the fact that urban areas had a higher proportion of women in their reproductive years. Correcting for this, we find that the rates for urban areas were generally less than those for rural areas (Backer 1965, pp. 123–125).

Studies made by Gunnar Jahn help shed light on differential fertility by occupation, and over time. Using census data from 1920, 1930, and 1946, he has been able to show a distinct evening out of fertility differences between occupational groups in this period (Jahn 1952). Table IX is taken from his work.

In Table IX, agricultural workers show the greatest reduction in average number of children during this period: in 1946, they averaged two children less than in 1930. Fishermen had the largest number of children in both these years, reducing the number by 1.4 from 1930 to 1946. In 1930 the group with the lowest number was that of self-employed and higher white-collar workers, and their reduction in the 1930–1946 period, the smallest one, was only 0.4. This category had, in 1930, two children less than did farmers, in 1946, one child less. In 1930, factory workers averaged one child more than did self-employed and higher white-collar workers; in 1946 these two occupational categories were about the same.

These figures indicate the sequence of fertility changes in Norway in the brief period where the equalization process perhaps took place most rapidly. It would definitely be worthwhile to have these investigations continued with data from later censuses.

4.2. *Mortality*

4.2.1. On the study of mortality

The mortality conditions are of great importance in understanding the development and structure of a given population. Together with fertility, mortality determines the population's natural growth rate.

Changes in mortality conditions are frequently indications of changes in social conditions. Mortality patterns thus give valuable information on health conditions; indeed it is possible to evaluate the effects of health measures by studying mortality.

In trying to predict future growth in a population, we shall find mortality estimates are invaluable. This is also true if we wish to estimate population size at time points between census years.

The study of mortality has many practical applications, for example for life insurance companies who utilize mortality data in fixing insurance rates.

4.2.2. Measuring mortality

The simplest and most common measure of mortality is the number of deaths per 1,000 inhabitants. This measure, the *gross mortality rate,* has both its weaknesses and its strengths. It is, for one thing, highly dependent on the population's age composition. When older persons compose a large portion of a total population, the rate will of course be considerably higher than when there are few older persons. For Norway, mortality when measured by this rate has indeed increased in recent years.

Age-specific mortality rates are better aids, but in order to compute them, quite a bit more information is needed. We must know the number of deaths per year within each age group, as well as the number of persons alive within each group. It is usual to compute such rates separately for men and for women, because the two sexes have different mortality probabilities at all ages.

The most important instrument for thorough mortality studies are tables showing death probabilities and average number of years left to each age group. Such tables are computed on the basis of mortality data within specific time periods and present a highly compact picture of prevalent conditions.

Infant mortality is measured by counting how many children died before reaching the age of one year, within a specific year, dividing this figure by the number of live births that year, and multiplying by 1,000. This rate is thus not identical with the age-specific mortality rate for the age group under one year of age; in computing the latter it is the number of still-living individuals in the age group, by the middle of the year under study, that forms the denominator.

In detailed investigations of infant mortality other rates are also frequently employed: *neonatal mortality,* i.e. mortality within the first four weeks of life, and *perinatal mortality,* which combines the number of still births and the number of deaths within the first week of life.

4.2.3. Changes in mortality

In 1965 there were in Norway 9.5 deaths per 1,000 inhabitants: 10.3 for men and 8.6 for women. According to mortality data from 1961–1965, the average life expectancy at birth was 71.03 years for men and 75.97 for women.

We may place these figures in relief by comparing them with corresponding figures from a country with extremely different mortality conditions. As concerns those countries with extremely high mortality, we can be sure that reliable data are simply not available. There are data from Upper Volta in West Africa, where in 1960–1961 a demographic survey was undertaken on the basis of a 10 per cent population sample. The gross mortality rate was found to be 30.5; infant mortality (1960) was 174.3. According to mortality data for 1960–1961, average life expectancy at birth was 32.1 years for men and 31.1 for women (*UN Demographic Yearbook, 1962,* Tables 17 and 18).

We must go back many years indeed in Norway's own history to find mortality rates similar to those of many developing countries today. But the point of departure has probably been the same, both in Norway then and in the developing world now: a low life expectancy and an almost Malthusian 'ceiling' on population size. From 1735 up to about 1814, the gross mortality rate in Norway remained around 20. There were extreme fluctuations, because the population was highly susceptible to epidemics, wars, and bad harvest years. In the worst year from this period, 1742, almost 70 per 1,000 died, or about one out of every 14 persons. Starting with about 1814 the rates generally decline; there are still fluctuations, but they have become less and less extreme. Only in an occasional year does the rate exceed 20. The rate descends to below the 15 mark for the first time in 1901; under 10, in 1934. The lowest level yet was attained in 1951: 8.4. As mentioned earlier, the rate increases slightly from year to year due

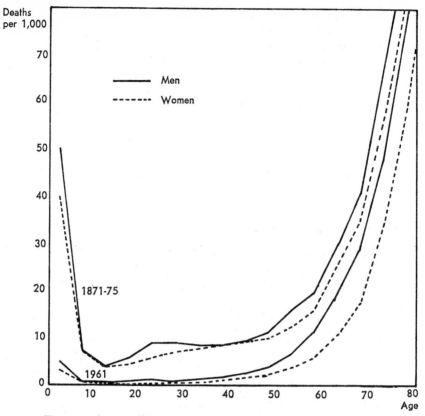

Figure 6. *Age-specific mortality rates, Norway 1871-1875 and 1961, based on data for five-year age categories*

to an increasing proportion of older persons in the population (NOS X 178, Table 14; NOS XII 218, Table 36).

Figure 6 shows age-specific mortality rates in the period 1871–1875, and in 1961. We notice especially changes in mortality for the very young: the 1961 rate for boys 0–4 years of age was only one-tenth that 90 years ago. Mortality rates for the other groups have also changed greatly: in 1871–1875 the age group with the lowest mortality rate was that from 10–14 years – about 4 per 1,000; but in 1961 all ages under 50 years had mortality rates lower than 4 per 1,000. Men aged 20–24 had in 1871–1874 a mortality rate which in 1961 corresponded to that of men of about 55 years of age. We also notice an increase in differences between mortality curves for men and women over 50 years of age: women's mortality has been reduced much more than that of men. Indeed, male mortality has increased somewhat in the higher age levels in recent years. These curves have a characteristic form:

28

Table X. *Average number of remaining years of life at selected age levels, according to mortality data in selected periods*

Period	Sex	Age (in years)			
		0	1	20	50
1831-1840	M	41.8		39.5	19.6
	F	45.6		42.4	21.4
1871-1880	M	48.3	53.4	43.1	22.5
	F	51.3	55.7	45.4	23.8
1911-1920	M	55.6	58.8	44.9	24.1
	F	58.7	61.2	47.2	25.3
1931-1940	M	64.1	66.2	49.6	24.9
	F	67.6	69.1	52.1	26.4
1951-1955	M	71.1	72.0	54.1	26.6
	F	74.7	75.2	57.0	28.6
1956-1960	M	71.3	71.9	53.9	26.2
	F	75.6	75.9	57.5	28.8
1961-1965	M	71.0	71.4	53.3	25.6
	F	76.0	76.1	57.7	28.9

Source: NOS XI 279, Table 40, p. 39; NOS XII 218, Table 44, p. 30.

high mortality in the first years of life, then declining to a low point in the 10–15 year bracket, then beginning to increase at around 20–25 years of age. According to mortality data from 1871–1875, the curve soared upwards for men of this age. From the age of 25 to about 40 years, there is little increase in mortality; then the increase becomes sharper and sharper with higher age.

Table X presents another set of data on the same changes. On the basis of mortality conditions in selected periods, from 1831–1840 until 1961–1965, the average number of remaining years of life for various age levels has been computed. The Table shows average life expectancy at birth, at one year, at 20, and at 50 years of age. Life expectancy at birth was 41.8 years for men and 45.6 for women in 1831–1840 – about the same figures as those found in a country like Burma in 1954. Data from 1961–1965 show that a newborn baby has a life expectancy of about 30 additional years today.

Once the hurdle of the first year of life has been surmounted, life expectancy is higher than it was at birth. This is true of all periods covered by the Table, although the differences were much greater earlier. In 1871–1880, a boy aged one had a life expectancy five years longer than that of a newborn baby boy. Because the dangers threatening infants in the first year of life have gradually been reduced considerably, the difference in life expectancy at birth and at one year has diminished.

As of 1831–1840 there was scarcely any difference between life expectancy at birth and at the age of 20: about 40 remaining years of life for both. Childhood and youth were the critical periods: thus, while a newborn baby could expect to live to be only about 40, a 20-year-old could expect to live to 60.

It is on the very youngest groups that improvements in health and sanitary conditions, as well as a general increase in standard of living have had the greatest effect. While from 1831–1840 to 1951–1955 newborn babies have increased life expectancy by some 70 per cent, 50-year-olds have had only a 10 per cent increase.

Life expectancy has increased fairly steadily and surely for a long period of time. However, the most recent figures indicate that this development has now reached a turning-point; indeed, male life expectancy has been reduced, for all age levels, during the period 1956–1960 to 1961–1965. Female life expectancy is still increasing, but much less rapidly than before.

4.2.4. Differential mortality

Generally speaking, women at all age levels have lower mortality than do men. However, in countries where health and sanitary standards still leave much to be desired, it is not unusual to find that men have the longer life expectancy. This is in part because women in such areas have relatively higher mortality in connection with pregnancy and child-bearing; furthermore, their generally low social status also helps bring about higher mortality. As the status of women gradually increases, their life expectancy also increases, and more rapidly than for men.

Age-specific mortality data for Norway show that girls aged 5–9 years had a higher mortality than did boys of the same age in the period 1881–1905; girls aged 10–14 had a higher mortality from the time of the earliest data up until 1925. Furthermore – in the period 1921–1925, women aged 15–19 also had higher mortality than men in the same age group. In some periods towards the end of the past century, we also find higher mortality among women aged 30–44 than among men of that age (NOS X 178, Table 21).

This over-mortality among women is probably connected with such factors as tuberculosis, which until recently was the dominant cause of death among younger persons, taking a higher toll of lives among young women than among young men. Also, women often were second in line in benefitting from general improvements in health and sanitary conditions (Backer 1961, pp. 101–102, 120–122).

That women generally live longer than men would appear to be biologically determined. Even at the pre-natal stage there are

30

Table. XI. *Age-specific mortality rates (deaths per 1,000),*
by sex for ages 30-64 years. Yearly averages

| Year | Age | | | | | | |
	30-34	35-39	40-44	45-49	50-54	55-59	60-64
A. MEN							
1946-1950	2.3	2.6	3.5	4.9	7.1	10.4	16.3
1951-1955	1.6	2.0	2.7	4.2	6.8	10.5	16.0
1956-1960	1.4	1.7	2.7	4.0	6.8	11.0	18.0
1961-1965	1.4	1.9	2.8	4.2	7.2	11.8	19.2
B. WOMEN							
1946-1950	1.6	1.8	2.6	3.6	5.2	7.6	12.4
1951-1955	1.0	1.3	1.9	2.8	4.4	7.1	11.2
1956-1960	0.8	1.1	1.6	2.6	3.9	6.4	10.6
1961-1965	0.6	1.0	1.6	2.5	3.7	6.1	10.6

Source: NOS XII 218, Table 42, p. 28.

differences in mortality. But *variations* between male and female mortality generally require consideration of environmental factors as well. As medical science is steadily reducing the number of fatal diseases not related to sex, occupational diseases and complaints, as well as other such definitely sex-determined hazards, will account for more and more deaths. Here women are favourably situated, and this is doubtless one reason why differences between male and female age-specific mortality rates are steadily increasing (see Table XI).

Increasing male mortality must be viewed in connection with the general increase of deaths due to cardio-vascular diseases. (Causes of death are further discussed in Chapter VIII, section 2.2.) But it is not so simple to ascertain exactly why these diseases have become so frequent in Norway today. One widely held hypothesis emphasizes the increased stress of living in today's world. But it is difficult to measure stress, and especially difficult to make comparisons over time.

As other death causes decrease due to improved medical knowledge and control, the selection process inherent in individuals' varying degrees of resistance to disease ceases to function as such an important factor. Also, special weaknesses and lack of resistance may be typical of the age groups with increasing mortality at present. We do know that death often occurs as a result – at least partially – of the effects of events occurring much earlier in life. It is therefore far from simple to explain all the reasons for the recent increase in mortality among men.

Table XII. *Infant mortality, Norway 1841-1965, per 1,000 live births. By sex, yearly average*

Period	Boys	Girls
1841-1850	130.5	105.5
1851-1860	121.5	101.5
1861-1870	123.0	102.6
1871-1880	122.2	102.1
1881-1890	113.1	99.5
1891-1900	105.6	92.4
1901-1905	88.2	72.5
1906-1910	76.4	63.0
1911-1915	72.6	59.8
1916-1920	68.4	55.0
1921-1925	56.8	46.3
1926-1930	55.4	43.3
1931-1935	50.6	39.0
1936-1940	44.3	34.2
1941-1945	40.6	33.6
1946-1950	35.2	26.6
1951-1955	25.3	19.8
1956-1960	22.3	17.3
1961-1965	19.2	14.9

Sources: Data previous to 1950: Lunde 1955, p. 111; after 1950: NOS XII 218, Table 35, p. 24.

4.2.5. Infant mortality

Infant mortality provides a sensitive indicator of general health conditions and standard of living. Factors affecting variations in this rate are thus an important research area.

In recent years, Norway has had one of the lowest infant mortality rates in the world: in 1966 the world's lowest rate was in Sweden, 13.3, while Norway's was 14.5 per 1,000.

Some of the world's highest registered rates are found in such countries as Gabon, Guinea, and Niger – with more than 200 deaths per 1,000 live births within the first year of life (Population Reference Bureau: World Population Data Sheet 1968).

But Norway had a higher rate previously, as we see from Table XII, which presents the general trend from 1841 until modern times. Here we must recall that only in recent years has registration become truly reliable and exact, however. The distinction between live births and still births has been a problem, and definitions have changed. Moreover, it was long the custom to register births only after baptism, so babies who died before being baptized were not included in mortality data. According to the figures, in the 1840s one out of every seven or eight boy babies and one out of every nine or ten girl babies died before reaching the age of one year. In 1961–1965, on the other hand, only one out of every 52 boy babies and one out of every 67 girl babies failed to reach its first birthday. But, as Julie E. Backer points out, mortality risks are still high for the first year of life; not until the age of about 60 is the risk so high again.

Within Norway, there have been considerable variations in infant mortality by districts; but, as the national rate has declined, so have the pronounced local differences. From Figure 7 we see some of the changes that have taken place. The extreme northern county of Finnmark has always had the highest rate: in 1911–1915, nearly 129.4 as a yearly average. Oslo had the second highest, 102.0, while the central and western counties of Oppland and Sogn og Fjordane had the lowest rates, 46.6 and 47.2 respectively in that period.

In the last 50 years the picture has changed considerably. By 1961–1965, Finnmark had reduced its yearly average rate to 24.6 (Jonassen 1964), although this still represents the highest rate in all the country (which had a yearly average of 17.1). Bergen county had the lowest rate in Norway in the period 1961–1965: 12.3 or a little less than that of its neighbouring county Hordaland, 13.5. Oslo ranked third,

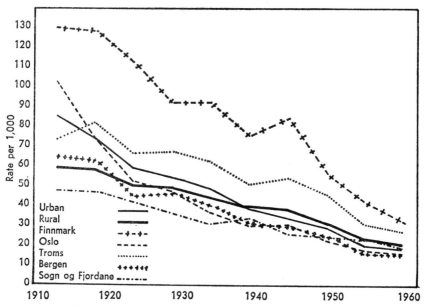

Figure 7. *Deaths in first year of life, per 1,000 of live births in urban and rural areas in Norway, and in the counties of Oslo, Bergen, Sogn og Fjordane, Troms, and Finnmark, 1911-1960*

Table XIII. *Infant mortality in urban and rural areas in Norway, 1911-1965.*
Yearly average, rate per 1,000 live births

Period	Urban	Rural
1911-1915	84.6	58.7
1916-1920	73.4	57.7
1921-1925	58.3	49.6
1926-1930	54.1	48.3
1931-1935	48.7	44.0
1936-1940	38.7	39.6
1941-1945	34.5	38.1
1946-1950	29.6	31.5
1951-1955	20.3	23.5
1956-1960	18.7	20.3
1961-1965	16.3	17.5

Source: NOS XII 195, Table 39, p. 28; XII 218, Table 37, p. 25.

with 14.8, while Sogn og Fjordane and Oppland had moved down to eighth and ninth places among Norway's 20 counties.

Infant mortality by county and over time indicates a good deal about social differentiation processes. Apparently, the fight for better living conditions and greater security has been waged with varying outcomes for the different parts of the country. However, many factors enter here. Simple physical habitat and the distance to the nearest doctor and hospital become more important as general social and sanitary conditions are improved. Further, infant mortality tends to be strongly correlated with social class and with the mother's marital status. Babies born out of wedlock have a much higher mortality risk than do babies born to married women. And the proportion of babies born out of wedlock varies considerably from county to county.

Some of the factors mentioned vary according to location – urban or rural – and the urban areas have obviously been favoured. Table XIII shows that in 1911 urban areas had a far higher infant mortality than did rural areas; but the differences decreased steadily until, by the late 1930s, the urban rate was lower than in rural areas.

4.3. *Emigration and immigration*

Norwegians have always been much on the move. In Viking times large groups of emigrants left the country for northern France and England. They colonized the Shetland, Orkney, and Faeroe Islands, and Iceland, and started farming communities on Greenland. Indeed, Norway was fortunate in being able to get rid of some of her surplus population in this way. The country's difficult geographical conditions have imposed fairly strict limits on how much the population may increase and still live comfortably.

When the population began to increase during the past century, due to the drastic drop in mortality, a whole new continent in the west – literally the New World – had been opened to emigrants from western Europe and not least Norway. Indeed, emigration to America functioned as a safety valve during perhaps the most critical phase of the enormous demographic change.

We have available a good deal of literature on the large emigration from Norway, one of the few aspects of Norway's demographic history which is well documented (cf. Backer 1965, Lunde 1955). More than *one million* Norwegians left for other continents in the period 1825–1930,[4] by far the majority of them for the USA. Emigration went in waves, with the 'peaks' in 1869, 1882, 1903, and 1923. In 1882 alone, 28,804 persons left, or 15 out of every 1,000 of the population.

The waves of emigration were connected not only with employment conditions in the USA, but also with conditions within Norway, so that we see both push and pull operating.

Throughout almost the entire migration period Norway had the second highest rate in Europe; indeed, only from Ireland did a greater proportion of the total population emigrate.

To begin with, it was the rural areas which supplied a larger share of their population, but urban areas steadily increased their contribution to the total number of emigrants. This need not mean anything else but that step-wise migration/emigration pattern started, such that many persons first left to live in urban areas, and thence emigrated to America (Backer 1965, pp. 163–164). Oppland was the county which lost the greatest proportion of its population in the period 1876–1890. In the period 1901–1910 many emigrants came from the Agder counties, in the extreme south of Norway.

Emigration was strongly age-specific. Recruitment took place primarily among the younger generation, a loss to the country's potential labour force. At the same time the departure of young people slowed down the reproductive capacity of the population.

During the last generation emigration abroad has been much more modest. In the period 1946–1960 an average of 2,327 overseas emigrants has been registered yearly, or 7.7 per 1,000 inhabitants.

With time many of the emigrants abroad have returned to Norway. According to Julie E. Backer's estimates, approximately 155,000 emigrants returned between 1891 and 1940. She supposes that a majority among them had left Norway in the period 1881–1930. Since the total number of emigrants in this period was 620,500, approximately 25 per cent have returned.

Until now the immigration to Norway from other countries has not been big enough to influence its demographic development to any appreciable degree. If international contacts and the mobility of labour across the borders continue to increase, Norway may receive many more immigrants.

The 1960 census registered 17 per 1,000 of the population as born outside Norway.[5] Of these, 28 per cent were born in Sweden, 20 per cent in Denmark, and 14 per cent in the USA (NOS XII 140, Table V. pp. 38–39).

The proportion of foreign-born was formerly somewhat higher, being 29 per 1,000 inhabitants in the year 1900. Of the foreign-born 77 per cent were born in Sweden (Backer 1965, Table 105, p. 181).

Table XIV shows migration between Norway and other countries in a single year. Of the emigrants 87 per cent were compensated for by immigration to the country. The larger part of the deficit stems from the relatively large migration flows between Norway and Denmark and Norway and Sweden. Emigration from Norway to the USA was almost completely balanced by immigration from it. It is in fact characteristic that exchange figures much more prominently than one-way traffic between Norway and other countries. As to intensity,

Table XIV. *Migration between Norway and other countries, 1964 (percentage)*

Country	Immigrants	Emigrants	Net migration (Absolute numbers)
Denmark	21.8	23.0	— 557
Sweden	15.6	22.1	— 1,220
Finland	2.2	1.5	+ 63
Iceland	1.4	0.8	+ 61
France	1.6	1.7	— 42
Italy	1.2	1.4	— 64
Netherlands	2.6	2.1	+ 27
Great Britain	9.3	8.9	— 118
Switzerland	1.8	1.7	— 21
Germany	7.3	5.9	+ 64
Austria	0.9	0.7	+ 12
Other European	4.0	3.4	+ 13
Canada	2.6	1.9	+ 51
USA	21.0	18.5	— 42
Australia	0.8	1.0	— 40
Elsewhere in world	5.8	5.0	+ 12
Not specified	0.1	0.4	— 37
Total	100.0	100.0	— 1,858
N	12,406	14,264	

Source: NOS XII 194, Table 38, p. 27.

Denmark ranks first, followed by Sweden and then by the USA. There is a considerable jump from these to Great Britain and Germany, who occupy fourth and fifth places, respectively. Closer analysis reveals that most of those moving between Norway and Denmark were Danes, while those between Norway and Sweden were Norwegians (NOS XII 194, Table 39, p. 28).

5. INTERNAL MIGRATION

More than any other demographic factor, it is the migration within Norway's boundaries that helps change the country's character. These internal migrations are a sign of the population's ability to adjust to new technological and economic conditions. At the same time, a population's willingness to move is an important factor in the success of major planning operations, or investment in new sectors, such as industry.

In 1963, some 180,000 persons moved from one municipality to another – that is, one out of every 20 persons.[6] Of these, 55 per cent were women; 47 per cent were single persons, i.e. persons who moved alone, unaccompanied by family. Accompanying family members accounted for 37 per cent, while 16 per cent were heads of family; 60 per cent were unmarried (NOS XII 171, pp. 28–34).

This migration rate has remained at between 40 and 50 per 1,000 throughout the period 1949–1963, except for the year 1960, when 52 per 1,000 changed municipality.

Migration is selective with respect to age and sex, so a population of movers or persons migrating within Norway has a composition quite different from that of the population at large. In general, persons aged 20–24 have the highest rate, both men and women. Women appear to achieve high mobility as early as 15–19 years of age: 1963 statistics show that almost one out of every eight women – or 130 out of every 1,000 – in this age group moved to another municipality. Only one out of every 21 men – or 47 per 1,000 – changed municipality of residence while in this age group. For the same year (1963) the most mobile group of all were women aged 20–24: a full 226 per 1,000 women in this age group moved – not far from one out of every four women. The corresponding figure for men was 136 per 1,000 (NOS XII 170, Table 53, p. 40).

Certain districts are distinctly more on the receiver side as to migration, while other areas experience a steady drain of certain population categories: a definite differentiation of the country's population thus comes about. At the same time as age and sex are highly important selective factors in migration, there also takes place a selection and differentiation with respect to a whole series of other factors. From a thorough study of a Swedish male population, Neymark showed how such factors as education, aptitude, social origin, and occupation influenced geographical and social mobility (Neymark 1961). A Norwegian research contribution here has been made by Solstad, who studied a group of municipalities in the northerly county of Nordland, investigating migratory trends with respect to aptitude level (Solstad 1965).

Migration goes in the direction of urban areas, with the densely settled areas surrounding the cities receiving the greatest number of new inhabitants. The cities and large towns often function as a transit station for a stream of migrants who then end up in the suburbs. The young and unmarried move to the cities; then, after having acquired an education, job, spouse, children, they move to the suburbs and settle down there. Statistics from 1963 show that the cities had a migration surplus of some 4,000 persons aged 15–24 years: but for the age group 25–44 the cities had an emigration surplus of about 2,800 persons. For married persons the corresponding figure was nearly 4,300 (NOS XII 171, p. 30).

6. SUMMARY

On a world scale, Norway's population is small indeed, comprising less than about a thousandth of the total world population. Some time around the early 1970s, the Norwegian population will pass the four million mark.

The proportion of older persons in the population is on the increase, mostly because the large parent group who in turn produced the large number of children born just after World War II, is now on its way towards the top of the age pyramid. The post-war generation is now well started in the labour force and has begun to produce its own fairly large number of children.

In the meantime the population has been acquiring an increasingly large male surplus: there are now more men than women in all age groups up to somewhere above 50 years. However, in the cities and larger towns we still find a surplus of women from age 15 and onwards.

The number of children born to Norwegian couples seems to have stabilized at an average of 2.5 per family. Couples are marrying at an earlier age, however, and it has become far more usual to complete the family within the very first few years of marriage.

Norway's mortality conditions have improved immensely in recent generations. Life expectancy at birth is nearly double that of a hundred years ago, being also among the world's highest. But in recent years male mortality has shown a tendency to increase; this holds true for all age groups, and the age-specific mortality rates increase every year, all the way down to the 30-year age group. Thus male life expectancy has begun to go down, and it is as yet unknown whether female life expectancy will follow this trend as well.

Emigration from Norway to the USA was of great importance in easing the pressures that high natural growth rates first brought with them. In recent years, migration abroad has been much more modest, consisting mainly of inter-Scandinavian movements. It is probable that further development in labour mobility between European countries and the rest of the world will, in years to come, also affect Norway's population structure and rates of change.

Each year some 5 per cent of the population is registered as having moved from one municipality to another within Norway. Geographical mobility is typical of young persons, especially women aged 15-24. The trend is in the direction of cities and larger towns, and away from isolated, thinly populated rural areas.

NOTES

[1] Svalbard, Jan Mayen Island, Bouvet Island, Peter I's Island, as well as the Antarctic territory of Queen Mauds Land are not included here.

[2] With respect to Mo i Rana, it has been calculated how age composition would develop if the town were closed to migration and further immigration for a 40-year period (see Øyen and Øyen 1959).

[3] A good discussion of problems connected with the definition of fecundity is found in Ryder 1959, pp. 414-418.

[4] The official figure is 858,196, but this is certainly too low. (See Lunde 1955, p. 218.)

[5] With respect to this there is a comparison between Norway and other countries in Chapter XII, section 4.1.

[6] Here we have utilized migration statistics from 1963 instead of from more recent years. Many municipality mergers took place in that year, and such mergers greatly influence migration statistics. In 1963, total registered migration frequency was 49.1 per 1,000, but declined to 43.5 per 1,000 in 1964 (NOS XII 218, Table 47, p. 31). This decline is due to the fact that migration within the new, enlarged municipalities was no longer registered as migration.

II. Family, Kinship and Marriage

By Erik Grønseth

1. SOME BASIC DISTINCTIONS

Nuclear family usually means 'father, mother and children'. Where one of the parents is lacking, the term 'incomplete' nuclear family is often employed, and where there is marriage but no children, 'childless family' or 'childless marriage'.

Now, the only universal function of the family – or indeed of marriage – seems to be that of providing the children with their basic social position. More precisely then, by nuclear family we shall refer to a set of social relationships (most often in the form of a group) in which one or two persons give – or have promised to give – one or more children their primary social position as determined by the child's position vis-à-vis this or these persons. In some societies these two persons are both women, in that one who is not the biological mother functions as 'social father'. The background for such definitions is further discussed in Jacobsen and Mathney (1962) and E. Grønseth (1965).

Legitimated nuclear family and legitimated marriage exist when two persons – according to the special rules of a given society – have announced, and society has approved, their position-granting obligation to the children that one or both have brought into the world, or are intending to, or whom they have adopted.

Marriage is the constitutive element of legitimated nuclear families. Incomplete nuclear families, where marriage has been dissolved through divorce or death, are also legitimated. In such cases only the position-granting obligation to the former spouse's *future* children is dissolved. In cases of death, the children are still accounted the children of the deceased person, and their social position and rights, i.e. inheritance rights and rights with respect to the deceased's relatives, are still largely determined by this relationship.

By 'family of procreation' is meant the family the individual himself has started, as opposed to his family of orientation, or parental family, into which he himself was born.

What the Norwegian Central Bureau of Statistics terms a *family nucleus* is included in the concept of the nuclear family, but is more restricted (NOS XII 151, p. 7). It includes: married couples without unmarried children, married couples with unmarried children, mothers with unmarried children, and fathers with unmarried children. This concept does not include non-legitimated, complete nuclear families; nor does it include that kind of incomplete family of orientation which consists of a married child and his single mother or father, even when these are part of the same household.

In many societies, the nuclear family is a more or less integrated part of some kind of *extended family*. In practically all societies, the nuclear family is also a part of some kind of kinship system – for example clan, lineage, or kindred. Possible exceptions are the most primitive hunting or gathering societies, e.g. of the type that formed Norway's original, prehistoric population.

By *extended family* is meant some kind of institutionalized system of joint economy, work, and residence, involving two or more related nuclear families.

The extended family can be of the *joint family* type, consisting of the nuclear families of two or more brothers and sisters, either with or without members of the older generation. Or it may be of the *stem family* type, consisting of nuclear families mutually related in directly ascending and descending lines and where only *one* of the offspring's nuclear families is allowed to remain within the fold of this type of extended family.

The concept of 'the large family', as used by Norwegian historians and ethnologists, is closely related to the concept of the stem family, but differs from it in that for one thing it includes the nuclear families of two or more married siblings. While in the stem family the older generation may transfer its authority to a younger generation, no such abdication occurs in the 'large family'. By popular usage the expression 'large family' is now being applied to all the above-mentioned kinds of extended families, as well as to what in the following we shall term 'semi-extended families'.

Depending on whether the nuclear family lives under the same roof as the husband's or the wife's parents, we have *patrilocal* or *matrilocal* extended families, respectively. When the families of procreation settle down away from the parents of both spouses, we have neo-local nuclear families. This latter family form is especially widespread in modern industrial urban societies.

Patri- og matrilocal families will generally imply, respectively, a patri- or matri*linear* kinship and descent system. However, descent can also be bilineal, with the individual counting descent from both his father's and his mother's kin. This often happens in societies with a neolocal principle of residence.

In modern society we occasionally come across households that include two closely related nuclear families (e.g. a married couple and the parents of one of the spouses), or a nuclear family and another close relative, without, however, there necessarily being any basic joint economic work relationship beyond the individual nuclear family. Here, the gainfully employed members of the household will have their separate incomes, keep separate accounts, and consider themselves primarily as financially responsible not for the whole household, but for themselves, or for that nuclear family to which they belong. Such family-and-kin-based household units we shall term *modern semi-extended families*. Also subsumed under this concept are households in which close relatives of the household head are supported by the nuclear family. Such households are not genuine extended families, since the support of the relatives does not have its outspring in any productive collectivity beyond the individual nuclear family.

Traditional semi-extended families would be, for example, farming nuclear families whose economic, work, and residential collectivity also includes relatives who do not belong to any common nuclear family within the domestic collectivity (i.e. when the relatives are *unmarried* brothers, sisters, aunts, or uncles, for instance).

The *kin family network* consists of mutually related nuclear families, principally economically independent of one another but who, on the basis of voluntary, mutual choices within the ranks of formally defined kin, form social and economic, or practical, emotional, or mutually assisting or controlling social relationships (see Sussman 1953, 1959, 1962, 1965).

The nuclear family, the extended family, and the kin family network may occur within the framework of more comprehensive kinship units such as *clan, lineage,* and *kindred.*

By *clan* is meant a descent group that is economically and residentially integrated, and unilineal, in which the genealogical relationships are not exactly known but are nevertheless socially defined.

A lineage is usually less extensive than a clan. Common residence is not a membership requisite. The unilineal kinship relation is more central than in the clan, and genealogical relationships can be determined exactly.

In most industrialized societies we find only scattered remnants of these last two types of comprehensive kinship units.

Every member of a society has his own particular *kindred* completely identical only with that of his brothers and sisters. It includes a person's blood relatives on both mother's and father's sides, for as many generations as the person himself and his society recognizes as relatives. The kindreds of relatives will partly intersect. The reference point for delimitation of kindred is always one particular person, whereas the reference point for identification of a lineage is the common ancestor of a series of persons.

A more comprehensive survey of kinship terminology is given in Zelditch (1964) and Murdock (1949).

2. FAMILY AND KINSHIP IN THE NORWEGIAN PAST AND PRESENT

2.1. *Historical development of the nuclear family's relation to kinship and social structure*[1]

For centuries, kinship structure in Norway has been marked by a patrilineal, patrilocal lineage structure. Before such specialized social institutions as the state and the occupational structure were differentiated, the nuclear family's relationship to the surrounding society consisted almost solely of its connection to the kinship structure.

In the first centuries A.D. and earlier the lineages were probably still organized in clans (Johnson 1948, p. 64, and Holmsen, personal communication). The clans consisted of extended families, in part perhaps of joint families. Due to increasing population pressures and improved agricultural techniques, the clans gradually dissolved.

When one farm (about A.D. 500) was no longer able to support the steadily expanding joint families, these began to dissolve. One or several of the married siblings on the joint farm would leave to clear a new farm, a 'homestead' or 'gard' (see Munch 1959 for a description of the Norwegian 'gard' type of farm and its social structure). Usually there would not be enough room for more than one of the married sons in the next generation, either. Thus, the others would go and clear a 'gard' for each of themselves, leaving behind only a few unmarried sisters and brothers and uncles and aunts on the 'old' farm. In this way, more and more new stem families were formed, after a first phase as a neolocal nuclear family, until the settler's eldest son married.

As a result of a beginning scarcity of available cultivable land and the accompanying differences between poor and rich lineages, an increasing number of farms gradually became too small to support even units the size of a stem family.

Probably from early Viking times, at the time of the appearance of 'large farmers', chieftains, and petty kings, the stem family pattern and the lineage structure gradually began to dissolve. Especially among the poorest small farmers, a new family system evolved quite early, one based not on the extended family and its economic collectivity, but on neo-local families. In this way, *bilateral kinship relations* became relatively more important in these groups. (For a dis-

43

cussion of the theory that bilateral kinship structure is primarily a function of a neolocal principle of residence, and not of industrialization and urbanization, see Murdock 1949, Arensberg 1962, and Mogey 1964.)

Among the self-owning peasants, however, the individual's, the nuclear family's, and the extended family's close connection to the lineage and its farm remained. This has found expression, from the days of the first laws right up to the present, in such legal institutions as *åsetes* and allodial rights.[2] Marriage, formation of nuclear families, births and burials, transfer of property, economic activity, social relations and morals, ancestor worship, and 'military' protection – all this as late as the 1100's was to serve and protect the lineage (Westrup 1943, Holmsen 1961). Neither the individual nor the individual nuclear family had any independent social existence; all were defined in relation to their position and function within the lineage.

Among the peasants the lineage kept much of its importance until modern times, especially in eastern Norway and in other areas of larger farms. In western Norway with its smaller farms and fishing, the farms were divided among the inheritors, the original farm being thus partitioned into smaller and smaller plots. In the larger eastern Norwegian farms, primogeniture was introduced in order to keep the farms intact because new land was available while alternative means of subsistence were not (Munch 1959).

However, the significance of the lineage both within society as a whole and for the nuclear families gradually became secondary in comparison with that of the new state institutions. The next blow to the lineage system was the growth of industrialization. In the rapidly expanding non-agricultural population, only tokens remained of the former lineage system. Especially among blue- and white-collar workers, the nuclear family was torn loose from the economic and social fellowship of the extended family, basing its economic provision on the husband's provider role within the new economy, and then later on the welfare state's economic controls and its social and family security programs. As a matter of fact, the families of peasants and fishermen gradually came into a new position of economic and political dependency vis-à-vis the state and the capitalist economy.

Young nuclear families were increasingly formed away from parents, relatives, and former neighbours. They often found themselves in new urban environments, which could at times contain some of their relatives. However, the individual family provider became, economically speaking, an isolated employee or worker on the new labour market, which role later became somewhat modified with the advance of the labour and trade union movement.

Both in cities and in the country, the economic and social changes

44

taking place, especially in the 1800s, made the neolocal nuclear family the dominant family pattern in Norway.

2.2. *Neolocality as the dominant pattern today*

In order to determine to what degree the neolocal pattern is in fact followed today, we would have to know how many of those who have recently started families have settled down in homes other than those of their parents. And these data we do not have. However, official statistics tell us how many of the family nuclei existing in 1960 – regardless of when they were started – had their *households* separate from the parents, and who also did not have parents on *kår*.[3] Despite several deficiencies, these data can be used to indicate the general spread of the neolocal pattern. We find that of the country's some 900,000 family nuclei in 1960, 94.7 per cent were neolocal in the above-mentioned broad sense of the term (NOS XII 151, Tables XIV and XIII). As expected, this pattern was more common among complete family nuclei (95.6 per cent) than among family nuclei with only one parent (86.4 per cent) and more common in towns and cities (96.7 per cent) than in rural areas (92.5 per cent).

If we consider families whose primary means of support is independent farming (127,999), only a small minority of these are probably neolocal in the strictest sense. When, nevertheless, as many as 83.3 per cent of these neither share household with parents nor have parents on *kår,* this is probably so because the parents are no longer living or have moved away.

3. UNILINEAL KINSHIP ELEMENTS TODAY

3.1. *Lineage and* kår

That the various lineages have now more or less disappeared does not mean that ideas and norms of the lineage era have also disappeared. There still exist some few, little-studied, informal survivals of such attitudes and norms, partly supported by official and legal institutions – for instance in legislation concerning *åsetes-* and *odels-rett,* mentioned earlier – and in legislation concerning names. A child born in wedlock must, for example, apply for special permission to use its mother's maiden name as its surname, whereas a child born out of wedlock is no longer entitled to bear its father's name. Nor does a divorced woman any longer have the automatic right to continue using her former husband's last name.

The *åsetes-* and *odels-rett* are connected with the institution of primogeniture. Today, however, it is usually maintained only on larger farms. Studies of small peasant families in a forestry community and in a mountain community in eastern Norway have shown that the eldest son's duty to take over the farm is no longer maintained. Both institutionally and behaviourally the reverse seems now to be the case: it is the *youngest* son who assumes charge of the farm because he is the one who has the shortest period to wait for the parents to stop working and step down.

According to a very old tradition, when the oldest generation in a stem family began to approach old age, or when one of the parents died, the old people 'went on *kår*'. This meant that they handed the practical charge of the farm, or a portion of it, over to another person, usually the eldest son (*odelsgutt*) or to other children of the next generation. In return the latter assumed responsibility for support of the parents (or parent) for the remainder of their lives. This was the 'old-age insurance' of the old Norwegian peasant society.

Today this older system is important for fewer and fewer older persons. One reason is of course the relative decrease in the peasant population due to the advent of industrialization and urbanization. Another reason is the introduction of public old-age insurance in 1936 and, in 1959, the removal of the requirement that aid be given according to proven need. In 1900 there were 45,000 persons on *kår;* in 1960, only 14,000. Of all independent farms in 1960, probably only about 6 per cent of the former owners were on *kår*.

The tendency of the young generation to leave the farm for other work has also reduced the upholding of the *kår* institution. This has made it necessary for the older generation to continue managing the farm much longer than was the case earlier, often, indeed, until they become ill and have to move to a home for the aged or infirm or until they die. Today, the *kår* institution is most widespread in western Norway, at any rate among the larger but more isolated and thus most traditional farms (Hornslien 1957).

3.2. *The stem family's occurrence*

Since both the lineage and the stem family institutions are closely tied to the farm, it must be on the farms – and there especially among those where the household head has farming as his chief occupation – that we should be able to find any stem families. Further, such farms would need to be those with several generations of the same family, regardless of whether the eldest members are on *kår* or not. In addition to these actually existing stem families, we must also keep in mind the possibility of *potential* stem families, ones which are for the moment in a neolocal phase, in that the youngest generation has not yet married. However, to speak with any degree of certainty about stem families even on such farms, we would first need field studies, for example, on the extent to which existence of multi-generation families on farms in fact implies the institutional content and meaning of a stem family, in accordance with traditional prescriptions – or whether it is simply a statistical coincidence, or perhaps a direct deviation from the more accepted culture pattern where the nuclear family is the expected household unit. That the latter may indeed be the case with farms in certain districts is shown by a study in Sollia in eastern Norway. Here the ideal, expected family unit was the nuclear family:

> Where the parents are still strong and active, the married son must find work elsewhere, away from the farm, and live in a distinct household, preferably elsewhere. The farm is considered the home of *one* nuclear family only (Barth 1959, p. 89).

Concerning conditions in multi-generation families that might on the surface appear as stem families, Barth says:

> The old persons in the family, grandparents still living on the farm, usually represent a difficult problem. They cannot be easily integrated into the family, since they have no role in it, and they are generally a financial burden — the small children do not need their care, nor are they strong enough to do heavy work ... If one of the surviving grandparents is living on the farm, as is nearly always the case, this will be considered quite temporary and unimportant, as he will soon die (Barth 1959, p. 89).

Now, we do not know exactly how widespread the type of family pattern found in Sollia may be in other communities. In an isolated mountain community in central eastern Norway (Femunden) we find a pattern more reminiscent of the stem family. Here, some of the younger and most passive, often parent-dependent sons usually continue living on the farm, even after marriage. They then take over the family farm when the parents finally decide to step down (von der Lippe, unpublished manuscript).

Our computations show that in 1960 some 15–18 per cent of all family households with farming as the main occupation were multigenerational; however, this need not mean they were stem families in the traditional sense (NOS XII 51, Tables IX and XVI).

Concerning the stem family and its internal relations, Dorothy Blitsen has written:

> The extended type of family persists today, particularly in rural areas. Where it does, parents tend to cling to control of family property. Their children chafe under their regulations, which often continue long past childhood and youth; if these children defect to pursue their own careers, it is seriously disturbing to both the older generations and to the young (Blitsen 1963, p. 169).

47

Also such factors as increasing life expectancy and the general better health of the aged, the tendency to marry younger, the reduction of parental authority, and the dissolution of many traditions all probably help make such conflicts more intense, or at least more open, than earlier. Nor do the modern methods of farming give the elderly the basis for useful activity, status, and authority as was the case with traditional farming. As long as the old ones can work and support themselves, the younger generation on the farm are clearly subordinated to them – a point verified by the above-mentioned investigation from a central eastern mountain community. The son who is expected to take over the farm will be especially likely to be most dependent on his parents, passively subordinated to them. And such parent–child relations lead in turn to severe tensions between the young son's wife and her mother-in-law as well as between the young wife and her husband, as he is not going to side with his wife against his mother (von der Lippe, unpublished manuscript).

In less isolated communities, on the other hand, one is today more likely to find the son siding more with his wife, defending her against exaggerated demands. To the extent that the older generation does not give up its traditional position of authority, such conditions can be expected to sharpen the generation conflict.

The tendency away from the stem family found among the farming population has several causes. First, the first-born son as well as his brothers and sisters frequently choose other occupations than farming; also, many rural girls move to towns and cities, often having no desire to become farmers' wives. And when the sons do not return home to the farm when they marry, the reason can also be that the smaller farms will not be able to support so many people or afford them a standard of living comparable to that available elsewhere. And furthermore, extended education and experience with other occupations, as well as other contacts with urban life, all tend to direct rural youth in directions other than those leading back to farming. Such tendencies, as well as the related general depopulation of the more peripheral rural communities, must be seen on the background of the lack of public and private investments in communications in public services and in local industries (cfr. Ottar Brox: *Hva skjer i Nord-Norge?* Oslo 1966).

Where the married son or daughter remains on the farm, the older generation later often chooses to move into their own apartment in the nearest town or to go to a home for the aged.

In this way, the farming stem family is cut down either 'at the root' or 'at the top' and is reduced more and more to an isolated nuclear family, whether it be an elderly married couple, perhaps with grown-up unmarried children, or a young married couple with small children.

48

Today it is perhaps misleading to speak of any unitary or general type of rural family, as opposed to an equally general type of 'town family'. Most families living outside the towns and cities are probably, in many important respects, more similar to the majority of 'town families' than to a small number of truly traditional families in rural areas. It seems more a question of gradual differences and variants of one and the same basic family pattern: neolocal nuclear families within kin family networks with an unmarried relative or two occasionally living within the nuclear family household.

4. BILATERAL KINSHIP RELATIONS

4.1. *General remarks*

Even though the older unilineal kinship pattern is in full retreat, a series of bilateral kinship relations is still of considerable importance.

Legal rules for relations between relatives concern first and foremost sexual relations, contracting of marriage, and inheritance.

As to sex, the legal incest taboo forbids marriage or sexual relations between related persons in direct ascending or descending line, between brothers and sisters, and between half-brothers and sisters, as well as 'between persons one of whom has been married to the other's relatives in direct ascending or descending line' (the marriage law of 1915, p. 8, see also Taranger 1926).

The inheritance law maintains the principle of bilateral kinship. Thus, children inherit after their father and mother, and after close relatives of both sides (Arnholm 1969, Schweigaard Selmer 1959). Direct descendants are entitled to two-thirds of the inheritance.

In modern urban societies, a person is considered as being kin (related) to persons both on his father's and on his mother's side. And through marriage he enters into a conjugal in-law relationship with the spouse's consanguine kinfolk on both sides. In general, we find a more clearly differentiating kinship terminology in rural than in urban areas. This in turn is to be seen as one of the many expressions of the more specific and extensive meaning of kinship ties in the rural communities.

Within the framework of formally defined kinship relations, much actual interaction takes place between relatives. However, most of this interaction is probably based on individual, voluntary choices, relatively independent of any institutionalized norms concerning who has which rights and obligations with respect to exactly which persons within the formal kinship structure (see Sussman 1953, 1959, 1962, 1965). In a transitional period, this has probably involved quite a bit of confusion, ambivalence, and 'kinship anomie'.

49

In addition to joint dwelling and household arrangements, kin contacts may consist in social contacts and visits – not only at family events and celebrations. They may involve financial and practical advice and aid, or emotional support. For persons just arrived in town, relatives already living there may form a kind of anchor. A young man may often find work at his father's or other relative's place of work; an older brother may help finance the education of younger brothers or sisters. Relatives may help with building a house, with baby-sitting during an illness. They can lend their sewing-machine, share their freezer, etc. Also, involvement in a relative's achievements and failures, pride in being related to well-known persons, these further indicate the continued importance of the kindred.

While no especially systematic data on the kind and extent of kinship bonds beyond the lineage based on *kår* and stem-family relations are available, we do have a few points to go on.

Here and concerning a good many other kinds of family relations we can refer especially to two family sociological studies done in southeastern urban and urbanizing areas. The 'housewives study' of 1964 included some 50 standardized interviews with non-employed housewives who lived in the stable, relatively traditional Rural Town, and an equal number of interviews both with employed and non-employed housewives in the more expansive and larger Modern Town (see B. Grønseth 1965, Holter 1966, Holter et al. 1967).

The second study, the Coast Town study, was made in 1956, based on comprehensive semi-structured interviews with 27 housewives whose husbands were at sea in the merchant marine, and with 23 matched non-seamen's wives (see Grønseth 1956, 1960, 1961).

4.2. *Families who share dwellings with relatives*

In Rural Town, Modern Town, and Coast Town, as well as in Sollia, there were more families who lived in the same *house* as a relative than families who reported sharing a *household* with a relative. Usually in these cases the 'relatives' were parents or parents-in-law. In Coast Town, as might have been expected, more of the seamen's than of the non-seamen's families lived together with parents or parents-in-law (25 per cent to 14 per cent). In the Rural Town and Modern Town, the figures for shared dwelling among the families with a non-employed wife were 27 per cent and 17 per cent, respectively; for the working wives' families the proportion was 24 per cent (B. Grønseth 1965, Table A 22). In Sollia, the corresponding figure was 35 per cent of the farms with nuclear families (Barth 1959, p. 85).

4.3. Families who share households with relatives

From Table I we see that of all Norway's nuclear families there were, in 1960, only 9.7 per cent who shared households with relatives, had relatives on *kår*, or who themselves were a nuclear family on *kår*. As expected, the proportion of those who shared households with a relative on *kår* or were on *kår* themselves was considerably greater among single parent families: 24.7 per cent.

If we ignore the *kår* cases, we find that 8.5 per cent of all nuclear families shared a household with a relative, but a full 18.5 per cent of the incomplete families and 14 per cent of all married couples without children living in the home did so, as against only 5.3 per cent of all married couples who had children in the home (NOS XII 151, Tables XII and XIII).

However, among families with children in Coast Town, there were none who shared a household with relatives, whereas in the Modern Town this was the case for 6 per cent, and in the Rural Town 10 per cent.

4.4 Multi-generational and other semi-extended families

If we take our point of departure not in the total number of nuclear families, but instead in the 881,000 family *households,* we see that some 2.3 per cent of these consist of stem families and about 4 per cent consist of other semi-extended families. Altogether, then, about 7.8 per cent of all family households are formed by genuine or semi-extended families.

4.5. Further aspects of nuclear family kinship contact

As to more special features of modern kinship relations we may mention that investigations from the USA, England, and the Nether-

Table I. *Nuclear families who share household with relatives, 1960 (percentage)*

Nuclear families that include	Married couple	Single parent	Total
Nuclear families which:			
Share household with parents, or have parents on *kår*	4.4	13.6	5.3
Share household with relative other than parents or have these on *kår*, or nuclear families who are on *kår* themselves	4.8	11.1	4.4
Do *not* share household with any relative	91.8	75.3	90.3
Nuclear families, total	100.0	100.0	100.0
N	821,740	84,333	906,073

Sources: NOS XII 151, Tab. II, VI, VII, IX, XII, and XVI.

lands have shown a tendency towards mother–married daughter relations as the dominant type of kinship relation. With the exception of the working classes, the same seems to hold true in Sweden and Finland (Sweetser 1964, 1966). However, neither the housewives survey, nor the coastal area survey, nor one from the former working class milieu in the Vika area of Oslo (Ramsøy 1967, p. 40) indicates any such tendency for Norway.

However, among the families of lower-ranking seamen on ships in foreign waters, the mother–daughter contact pattern was dominant, with respect to sharing dwelling, to social contacts, and to babysitting, etc.

Otherwise, of all the marriages in the country where the household is shared with one of the spouse's parents, we find approximately as many where it is the husband's parent(s) as the wife's (NOS XII, 151, Table XVI).

In the Oslo Vika area, both men and women had most frequent kinship contacts with their *own* relatives (Ramsøy 1967, p. 40). This also appears to be the case in the Modern 'Town' referred to earlier, especially among the families with working wives (B. Grønseth 1965, Table K. 04). On the other hand, among the typical Coast Town inhabitants there was no such tendency (Grønseth 1956, Table 61).

However, none of these investigations indicates whether husband and wife jointly generally had contacts with their own and their spouse's relatives, or whether they tended to have contacts with their own relatives, separately.

Among working-class families in traditional areas in London, E. Bott found that strong role segregations within the family and the family's openness towards relatives and neighbours were associated with a strong degree of segregation between the man's and the wife's kinship and neigbour contacts (Bott 1957). On the other hand, in newer residential areas where all the population has only recently moved in, it may be primarily the working-class families who are isolated (Gavron 1966).

As to sex-role segregation in social contacts, in Sollia the man generally had contacts with other men, the wife with other women (Barth 1959, p. 88).

The studies from urban areas in eastern Norway have shown that it was especially the *closest* relatives the married couples had contacts with, received help from, and were helping, whereas neighbours and friends came only second and third, respectively. The Vika and the Coast Town material indicate that this is also true of 'nearest' and 'most personal' contacts.

Some 90 per cent of the housewives in both Rural Town and Modern Town replied that they saw their own or their husband's relatives at least once a month. Respectively 20 and 13 per cent said they would like more contact with relatives; no one indicated a wish for less contact. In Coast Town, such contacts seem to be at least as frequent. About half the housewives saw both their mother and their mother-in-law and their sister or sister-in-law once a month or more often. Almost none of the wives ever mentioned their father or father-in-law as a social contact or as a source of assistance.

First and foremost, it is the mothers and mothers-in-law who do baby-sitting. Among working wives in Modern Town, however, more than one-third occasionally have relatives baby-sit in the evening, and about one-fourth receive such help during the day.

Also in emergencies or difficult situations it is primarily close relatives who help. For advice on difficulties concerning house, food, or children, however, housewives in both Rural Town and Modern Town turn almost as frequently to non-relatives as to their mothers.

Among the non-seamen's wives, the kind of help they themselves give goes equally often to neighbours as to relatives. However, among seamen's wives such help goes mainly to relatives.

The figures given in the Central Bureau of Statistics' 'Household Accounts 1947–1948' with respect to children's clothes, shoes, sports equipment, and recreation are so low that, when we view the actual situation, it seems reasonable to assume that a considerable portion of such expenses are borne by others – primarily grandparents.

Concerning kinship contacts in rural areas, there seems to exist even less material than for the towns and cities. The description of Sollia conditions does not exclude the possibility that there, also, contacts with relatives predominate, although far less so than one might have expected in a rural area. In Sollia formal kinship relations are carefully noted, and almost everyone in the community can trace their genealogies back to a common ancestor. However, the nuclear family's more concrete relations with 'remote relatives are few and unimportant'. Not only relatives, but also other friends are invited to baptisms, weddings, etc.

The special relations with kinfolk extend into the economic sphere; there is no patterned lending of equipment or help, not even between brothers. Kinship furthermore does not seem to influence or regulate membership in formal or informal groups (Barth 1960, pp. 89–90).

5. FAMILY AND SOCIETY

Even though the nuclear family in Norway still has connections with kin and with neighbours, such connections are hardly as strong as earlier. These 'Gemeinschaft'-type contacts have probably been dissolved, especially in the middle class, with its emphasis on 'privacy' and its closed family structure within open, loosely connected neighbourhood environments (Mogey 1964). Friendship, often based on sharing common occupation or on membership in organizations, seems to have partially taken over.

Among the family's external relations, those with economic and occupational life, and, more recently, with the growing public institutions appear to be most basic and decisive for it.

5.1. Relations with economic and occupational life

While economic production formerly took place and was controlled within the peasant family itself, it has today become mainly located in and controlled by the institutionally differentiated economic and occupational life. Whereas in the old society the majority of families lived in a subordinated, conflict relationship to the large farmers and to sheriffs and other officials, we may say that today the majority of both blue- and white-collar families, as well as of independent, 'entrepreneurial'-type families, live in a state of dependence to employers, to economic and trade union organizations and, in the final round, to big business finance and state administration (Grønseth 1972 a).

5.2. Value conflicts

Conflicts between traditional attitudes concerning family and sex life and the new societal conditions may be seen reflected in the continuing ideological debate that first started in the past century (for an analysis of central aspects of this debate, see Holter: *Rebellion against the Family* 1963).

Whereas traditional patriarchal-authoritarian value orientations seem generally to have been transferred from the older society to the industrial one, the special 'Gemeinschaft'-oriented value standards of family and kinship relations stand in conflict with the new bureaucratic, so-called 'achievement-oriented' value standards of the new economic, state, and organizational life (see Eisenstadt 1956, Ch. I and II). Psychologically compensatory values are largely oriented towards profit, prestige, and competition (Grønseth 1971).

The male family members have been drawn into this field of tension while the women have still maintained their anchoring in family and kinship relations. In addition to a sharper polarization of the sex-role division (cf. Parsons 1955, Holmberg 1966, Grønseth 1970), this has in turn had new consequences for the family as a socializing agent. The family alone has not been able to perform the functions of socialization, and the bureaucratic competition- and achievement-oriented

54

school system has taken over a considerable portion of formal child socialization. Especially as regards the boys, however, much socialization is also carried out within the solidary- and *sub-rosa*-oriented peer groups and their youth culture. Thus, a certain degree of tension exists between family values and socialization on the one hand, and that of the school and peer groups, on the other.

5.3. *Society's economic responsibility for the child's support and care*

The dissolution of the kinship-based economically productive collectivities has also meant dissolution of the kinship-based responsibility for the economic support and care of children, in which nearly all the members of the community took part, whether they had children or not. To the extent that relatives and older children lived on the farm, they helped in the care of small children as well as in the economic provision for them. Now, in the peasant community's poorer, few-person nuclear family, the farmer's wife was frequently the only person to do so: but this reflected their low social position in the class structure, not their special situation as a family with children (Grønseth 1967b).

Neither today's scant children's allowances and income tax exemptions, nor other family assistance programs, nor grandmother's help with baby-sitting, etc. constitute any satisfactory alternative (Grønseth 1967a). As a result, we have the typical situation of the husband's provider role, the wife's economic dependency, the relative social isolation of housewives in towns and cities, especially from the more comprehensive social contexts, as well as the economic discrimination against families with children (Grønseth 1970, 1971).

5.3.1. The husband's provider role

Today, not only has the relatives' contribution within the extended family to the economic support of children and of the child-carers disappeared; at the sime time, the subsistence economy value to the family represented by the housewife's work has been considerably reduced, due to the industrialization of a whole series of traditional housewifely tasks. The husband of today must pay not only for support of his children and for the services his wife performs for him; he must in addition pay her – if merely in kind – for her work in child care. And all of this is to be paid from the same salary as a single person's.

While economic production has become more collectivized, we see that child care and support have become privatized. Child care has thus, together with the remaining housewife's tasks, been left behind in a traditional subsistence economy enclave inside the otherwise modern money economy (Bonnevie 1948).

5.3.2. Lack of supplements to the mother's role in child care

The private-capitalist economy has not, even in its modern welfare-state-supplemented phase, been able to provide new arrangements for child care besides those provided by the mother herself (Grønseth 1967a). This seems to be so, since within a private profit-oriented economy it is more profitable to invest in production of consumer goods, and in their advertising. In Norway, the publicly supported kindergartens and day-care institutions cover only a fraction of the actual need, even among single-parent families and families otherwise in financial difficulties. And, only a decreasing number of better-off fathers can afford to hire a nurse or maid.

In 1966, the number of available places for children in various day-care institutions for children, forms of nurseries, preschools, day-schools, and kindergartens was about 9,000 (NOS A 191, 1967). At the same time, we can estimate the total number of children of pre-school age (0–6 years) at 442,300. Thus, for the country as a whole, there exists room in day institutions, etc. for 2.3 per cent of the child population (Ås 1966; see also Lie and Egge 1965, 1966).

For purposes of comparison we may mention that Sweden and Denmark have corresponding figures of about 8 and 7 per cent, respectively. In Oslo, coverage is 15.7 per cent. For all children of gainfully employed mothers throughout the country, the figure was 8.5 per cent (NOS A 191, 1967).

While it was estimated that at least 600 institutions would be needed in 1961, there were 259 in 1960; by 1966, the figure had risen to 303 (*Dagbladet*, January 19, 1967). In 1965, Oslo alone had 53.4 per cent of all such institutions in the whole country; other urban municipalities had 35.1; while rural municipalities had only 11.5 per cent of the total.

5.3.3. Married women and the economy

Now, only in certain, limited social groups are family finances so bad as to force both parents to work full time, leaving the children and housework to chance, or nothing. Due to reasons as yet little understood, Norway has fewer complete nuclear families in which both parents have outside employment than most other industrialized nations do. In Europe it compares with Ireland and the Netherlands. In 1960, the figure for such families was 15.1 per cent (including the 5.6 per cent where the wife had only part-time work): 18.8 per cent in towns and cities, 9.3 in rural areas. Most of these families had either a low income or a wife with education beyond the elementary school level, or they were young families with few, if any, small children at home (Vangsnes 1965). In 1968 the percentage of working married women had increased to 22 per cent; 12 per cent were working full time (Central Bureau of Statistics 1969).

As in other countries, these working women are generally employed in low-paid, subordinate jobs, with relatively poor chances of advancement or promotion, and frequently on a part-time basis.

Married women and female family providers have, moreover, a generally lower education level than do men. They are also much less permanently connected with their occupation. Their educational and occupational motivation, as well as identification with their occupational role, is usually weaker than men's; and this seems reasonable enough, considering their general economic and social position otherwise (Dahlstrøm 1967, Holter 1970). Nor has the new economic system provided possibilities for part-time work and equal salary and advancement opportunities for those married women who, despite everything, do take outside employment (Selid 1966) (not to mention that it has certainly not provided real possibilities for part-time work for men who might have been interested in having more family contacts as father and housekeeper) (See Grønseth 1972b).

Other barriers to married women's and mothers' participation in occupational life exist in the current tax and social security discrimination (Eliassen 1967), the insufficient number of kindergartens, etc., and a total lack of types of dwelling and housework rationalization that working married couples would need. The general indoctrination through school books, mass media, etc. of the pattern 'father-at-work, mother-at-home' continues as the only normal, desirable type of family, enforced by all kinds of informal barriers to women's continued education (cf. Ullern 1967, Eliassen 1967).

In addition come more general, considerably deeper-rooted considerations, such as the country's thinly spread population, combined with the relative centralization of working places of the type commonly available for women (see Lettenstrøm and Skancke 1964, Arbeidsdirektoratet 1967). Also, the perhaps especially strong identification Norwegian mothers feel with the mother role may be important here. Such considerations may help explain the notably low percentage of gainfully employed married women in Norway.

Tax and social security discrimination refers especially to married women's exemption from paying illness insurance premiums, and to tax exemptions in the husband's income reports for wives without outside employment; both of these apply, whether the wife has children at home to care for or not. Furthermore, the married woman is exempted from taxation on the income she *de facto* receives from her husband not only for taking care of the children, but also for working for him, preparing his meals, etc. Not only mothers, but also all married women without dependent children receive these benefits provided the wife/mother does not have outside employment; whereas the working mother does *not* receive them or similar advantages. In this way, society lends its support primarily not to parenthood, but to marriage. What is rewarded is being married, not the fostering of children.

These tax and social security provisions favour not only those non-employed married women who actually do have children at home under 15 years of age to care for (N: 523,100), but also those married women with neither minor children nor outside employment (N: 184,800). And those receiving the brunt of such discrimination are the group comprising nearly 9 per cent of all married women – those with both outside employment (whether full or part time) and minor children at home (Vangsnes 1965).

5.3.4. Economic discrimination against families with children

Since the family provider is to support his children and his wife or others who take care of the children on the basis of a salary no larger than that of a childless income-earner, families with dependent children are subjected to quite severe economic discrimination. Although the basis for the estimate is open to criticism, it was estimated in 1956 that a family with two children had only two-thirds the standard of living of a childless family, while a family with three had the same standard of living as did those with only old-age retirement pension to live on (Herzberg and Lindblom 1956). And since public aid to families with children has not kept pace with increases in wages and prices, the discrimination felt in 1969 was even sharper than in 1956. With the new partial shift to direct taxation (sales tax) the children's allowance was considerably increased: to 500 kroner ($ 70) per year for the first child under 16, and to 1500 kroner ($ 300) for the second child, 2000 kroner for the third and for the fourth child, 2400 kroner for each subsequent child; at the same time the income tax deduction for dependent children was abolished. Given a system of progressive taxation, this means a discontinuation of the advantages for the upper income brackets implied in tax deductions. But there is hardly full compensation relative even to the 1956 situation – and certainly not for families today with only one child under 16.

One obvious reform which would help – to the extent that the economy can in fact be of help to families with children – would be a general transfer of income both from high-profit companies and from those high-income persons who do *not* support children to those who do support children, and to introduce a general children's allowance or children's pension, large enough to cover each child's needs for material provisions and equipment, as well as for covering a salary to be paid to the person(s) taking care of the child, whether

Table II. *Average annual income* of single mothers, by civil status, Oslo 1962*

Civil status	N. kr. per year
Unwed	8,900
Separated	10,800
Divorced	12,600
Widowed	14,800

Source: Likelønnsrådet 1967, p. 11.

* Gross income minus authorized exemptions in income tax report.

the child is cared for at home, in a day institution of some kind, or both (Grønseth 1972c). For Sweden, it has been calculated that coverage in 1964, through the national budget, of only the most essential expenses of the families with dependent children involved in child-fostering, would come to about S. kr. 9 billion ($1.8 billion), whereas the national pension scheme there amounts to some 4 billion S. kr. (cf. *Radikal Familjpolitikk,* Stockholm 1965). It may be noted that in 1960 the average number of children per marriage was 2.3. (For other family demographic data see Backer 1965, Grønseth 1963, Manniche 1965, Yearbook of Nordic Statistics.)

5.3.5. Economic discrimination against incomplete families

There exists as yet no sufficient alternative to the husband's provider role, not even when there is no husband in the family. Thus, the economic discrimination against single parents and their children becomes especially severe. Hardest – and most frequently – hit are the unwed mothers (cf. Øyen 1966b, Zylberg 1967).

Table II presents the average annual income of single mothers, by civil status, in Oslo 1962.

As we have already seen, married women encounter many barriers in and are generally discouraged from taking on outside employment, away from their children, while they are infants or small and need their mothers most. Whereas some 10 per cent of all married women with one child under 15 years of age, and 6.6 per cent of all married mothers, were more than half-time gainfully employed, 58 per cent of the single mothers, and a full 69 per cent of the unwed mothers were employed.

Today's family policies – including the people's pension – primarily concentrate on helping, although scantily, the *complete* family. And this despite the fact that in 1960 there were only 41,600 single mothers, of these, some 6300 unwed. That the actual figures are so low, even when in Norway each year about 2400 children are born out of wedlock, is because the situation is so hopeless for many mothers that one-third give their children in adoption. And many of the others marry as soon as possible. How often this is not so much due to great love for the husband as to social and financial necessity, we do not know (Øyen 1966a, b). The Norwegian rate of 'illegitimacy' in 1968 was 5.5 per cent of all live births, as compared to 11.1 per cent in Denmark and to about 13 per cent in Sweden 1968 .

6. THE FAMILY'S INTERNAL RELATIONS

Despite various modifications, especially in the last 40–50 years, the husband's role as provider as well as wife's and children's economic and social dependence on him remains a fundamental and decisive characteristic of the nuclear family's internal structure, in Norway as in all other industrialized societies so far. And it is on the basis of this underlying structure that we must analyze and understand the other functional and structural aspects of the family and of the sex roles in the Norwegian society today (Grønseth 1969, 1970, 1971).

6.1. *Marriage: husband–wife relations*

In Norwegian society as elsewhere today, it is the 'official author- ity's declaration that the bride and groom are man and wife, that legalizes the marriage ... the *condition* is that they agree to wed one another' (Arnholm 1945, p. 152).

6.1.1. The basic aspect of modern marriage: monogamy

Monogamy means that no person is allowed to enter into more than one marriage at the same time. Or, in other words, no man may take upon himself full social paternity for more than one woman's future children at a time. Nor may any woman let more than one man at a time take upon himself such paternity obligations for her future chil- dren. This legal provision undoubtedly has strong support in the atti- tudes of the population in general.

6.1.2. Monopoly on the sexual relations of the spouses

In Norway, monogamy is coupled with an officially supported re- quirement, especially by church and school, that no one shall have sexual relations with anyone except one's spouse. This forms a con- trast to the case in many primitive societies, where youth has a high degree of sexual freedom – and to the case in some such societies where a high degree of infidelity is also permissible (Ford and Beach 1952). Both the civil and the religious marriage vows are vows of fidelity, implicitly sexual fidelity. Formerly, infidelity was punishable by law

60

if the offended party reported the fact. Since 1927, however, this is no longer the case, but infidelity on the part of the husband as well as on the part of the wife does give the other party the right to an immediate divorce by court decree, a provision that is, however, now under revision, so as to obliterate the 'privileged' status of adultery as a reason for divorce.

In a divorce case involving a mother's infidelity, this in itself will not appreciably decrease her chances of obtaining fairly automatic custody of the children.

To a question on how they viewed sexual relations outside of marriage, about one-fifth of the Coast Town housewives indicated strong disapproval. Altogether, about one-half considered it unconditionally wrong, while about one-fourth said they disliked the idea, but that it was not always unconditionally wrong. Almost one-third showed no blanket disapproval of extra-marital relations in general, but instead related it to the individual situation of the particular marriage.

Only one-seventh of these women felt it made a difference whether it was the man or the woman who had extra-marital relations, and only about one-tenth said they felt the situation was different for a seaman's family.

Half the women thought their husbands would get a divorce if he should find out that she had had any extra-marital relations, while one-third did not know how the husband would react. Four women answered that he would be disappointed, one furious, and three that it would depend on the circumstances.

On the other hand, fewer of the wives thought that they themselves would react by demanding divorce (about one-fourth). One-fifth said they would be very disappointed, one-sixth furious. Five of the seamen's wives and one of the others said it would depend on the circumstances (Grønseth 1956).

Divorce statistics show that of all separations registered in 1951–1955, 14.5 per cent were attained by court decision due to infidelity (NOS XI 282, p. 20). In 54 per cent of these cases it was the wife who had demanded divorce.

6.1.3. Life-long marriage

The marriage vow of fidelity is given for the rest of one's life, and in wide circles divorce seems to be considered shameful. This norm may have as one of its roots the especially poor chances women in Norway have of obtaining satisfactory jobs, and thus of economic independence. Legally, however, there exists the possibility of divorce and thereby of 'serial monogamy'. The marriage and divorce laws, just about the same as in Denmark and Sweden, allow divorce after two years of separation, and after one year when both partners agree. Perhaps the norm of life-long companionship is more deeply rooted in Norway, however, than in many other Protestant countries – Norway's unusually low divorce rate would seem to indicate something like this. In 1966, 9.7 per 100 contracted marriages were divorced, as compared with 16.2 in Denmark. And perhaps this in turn is connected with women's especially poor chances of obtaining jobs and thereby financial independence. And, perhaps Hendin and Bye are correct in saying that, for Norwegian women, the mother role and the mother's relation to her children are of especially great importance (Hendin 1967, Bye 1947). This latter point will be discussed more thoroughly below.

It may be noted that the number of marriages contracted per 1,000 inhabitants in 1967 was 7.5. Average age at first marriage in 1966 was 25.1 for males and 22.3 for females, as compared to 24.7 and 22.3 in Denmark.

Fifteen per cent of the marriages were civil marriages in 1966 as compared to 31 per cent in Denmark and 6 per cent in Sweden.

In 5.4 per cent of all marriages contracted the male was younger than 20 in 1968, and in 22.3 per cent the female was under 20, while in 4.1 per cent both partners were under 20.

Out of all 15–19-year-old men, 1.0 per cent got married in 1968, and 4.5 per cent of all women 15–19 years old (see also Moss 1964, Grønseth 1963 and 1972d).

6.1.4. Women's economic dependence in marriage

The ideal norm, as it is expressed in the marriage law of 1927, says that there shall be economic equality between the spouses. This ideal norm, however, stands in sharp contrast to the widespread *operative* norm which people both maintain and follow in practice: that the husband is to support not only his children, but also his wife. That the wife equally much as the husband – and as stated by the marriage law – shall share in the support of the children and the spouse, remains a law in form only as long as a mother's – and a father's – work with the children is not salaried independent of the husband's ordinary income and as long as married women still do not have the same income and pay opportunities as men in ordinary occupational life. Much in the Norwegian social security system is thus indeed based on the quite official and far more realistic argument that in practice not only mothers, but also married women generally, are usually economically supported by their husbands.

Thus the economic value of household chores and food preparation for the husband is minimal, something an unmarried man will frequently do himself in his spare time. The in-kind income a non-employed *childless* married woman receives from her husband for this housework for him will therefore usually far exceed normal hourly wages. And since a childless married woman today can usually support herself without special difficulties, any financial dependence on *her* part upon the husband will actually be a voluntary matter. But in periods with high rates of unemployment, such as the 1930s, married women were frequently refused jobs because 'they had a husband to support them'.

Only when we turn to the child-caring mothers, and to that portion of their daily work which consists of child care, do we confront that element in our present form of marriage which makes women economically dependent upon and supported by a husband.

For human, emotional reasons, a mother does not want to see her children suffer apparent need. Therefore she will either take care of them herself, or see that others do. In both cases she needs money: for herself, if she herself takes care of the children, or as payment to another child-carer if she takes other work. At the same time, someone must provide money for the children's support. Since in our society it is seldom possible for a woman alone – either by caring for her children or by other work – to provide *enough* money for all this (as well as since there generally do not exist sufficient numbers of alternative 'child-carers'), she is practically *forced* to seek support for herself and the children from a husband. That most women do not seem to experience this necessity as an unpleasant one – but rather, as something taken for granted – by no means makes the mother's actual economic dependence on a husband any less a necessity.

But, suppose a mother no longer loves the husband who supports her and the children. Then this necessity will often seem something forced on her. If her husband does not belong to those financially well-off in society, she will discover, should she obtain a divorce, that her economic status will sink drastically. Indeed, her social status as well. In *this* lies the married woman's and mother's basic economic dependence, and the husband's complementary provider role (Grønseth 1970, 1971).

Seen in this context, such current changes – the somewhat increased possibilities for employment among married women, their somewhat better education, the slightly increasing number of children's institutions, men's somewhat increased participation in child care and housework, or women's and mothers' greater authority within the four walls of the home – become nothing more than slight variations on a pattern which is still basically discriminatory towards women, and solidly sex-role differentiating (Bonnevie 1948, Holmberg 1967, Grønseth 1966a, 1970, 1971).

A 1952 Gallup survey showed that the population – especially the women – is also beginning to realize how the situation actually is. Of the women, 67 per cent (and 49 per cent of the men) felt that it was the woman who had to give up more of her freedom in marriage. Most of these said it was because the woman more than the man was tied to the home and children; 38 and 33 per cent, respectively, thought that the woman 'had a lot to do at home', 'less leisure', 'longest work-day'. Only 4 per cent of the women and 11 per cent of the men felt that it was the man who gave up most freedom in marrying. Considerations like the above do not of course preclude the simultaneous ill effects upon men and husbands, stemming from their old and 'new burden of masculinity' (Hacker 1957, Holter 1970). The 'over-burdened' male remains, generally, vis-à-vis even the sometimes over-protected or dominant woman, the socio-economically, independent and super-ordinate one basically.

However, no essentially more egalitarian change in these or the following aspects of the prevalent sex-role structure can take place until *women in their capacity of being mothers have gained economic independence,* partly by means of a publicly financed child-care salary, partly by full equality in occupational life, and partly by the access to fully satisfactory child-care possibilities outside the nuclear family itself (Grønseth 1967a, b, 1969, 1970, 1971).

6.1.5. Authority in the family

Taking for granted the existing, relatively isolated nuclear family, as well as married women's economic dependence on the husband, most people today seem to feel that there *ought* in general to be 'equality' and 'democratic conditions' in the family. Available studies indicate, however, that there is far from complete agreement on even these general ideas.

On the one hand, more than 90 per cent of the housewives in Rural Town and Modern Town agreed that 'in the family, both partners should have an equal say in important matters' (Holter 1966, p. 258). This was also agreed upon by white-collar employees in several Oslo firms (93 per cent of the female white-collar workers, 80 per cent of the male). However, among blue-collar workers, this was true of only 81 per cent of the women and 75 per cent of the men surveyed (Holter 1966).

And when the Oslo employees were asked whether or not 'the husband should be the one who makes decisions on important matters in the family', between 20 and about 30 per cent of even the women employees surveyed thought the husband should. This applied to 37 per cent of the male workers and 47 per cent of the male white-collar workers. Among the men asked, only 32 per cent of the workers and 41 per cent of the white-collar workers were in direct disagreement with this statement.

The picture obtained of the actual division of authority differs considerably from one to another of the few limited studies that exist, depending on such factors as which areas of authority are being investigated (see also Stephenson 1959, p. 114).

One intensive, psychiatrically oriented study claims, however, that Norwegian women tend to consider 'themselves as stronger than their husbands . . .' Also, social workers have maintained that in Norwegian marriages the women have a relatively strong position, at least psychologically, as compared with American women. They are seen as having stronger positive identification with their mothers and with the mother role. One possible reason that has been suggested, is that the men (especially along the coast) were traditionally away much of the time, fishing, hunting etc. (Lillian Bye 1947). Furthermore, these women's opportunities for gainful employment are, as mentioned, less than in most other industrialized countries.

6.1.6. Division of labour

Given the husband provider role, it is not surprising that 61 per cent of the non-employed housewives in Rural Town and Modern Town, and one-half and one-third, respectively, of male workers and white-collar workers in a sample from Oslo firms agreed that 'men should generally let housework be a matter for the housewives'. Mainly it is the working wives (in Modern Town 68 per cent) and the other working women (50 per cent of the Oslo survey's white-collar workers, 36 per cent of the workers) who disagree (Holter 1966). Several Gallup polls, and the Rural Town and Modern and Coast Town studies as well, indicate that the men generally do in fact leave housework to their wives, especially among the working class and persons with low income, among older persons, and persons in rural areas. However, among the non-employed housewives in the Rural and Modern Town surveys, 90 per cent were satisfied with the present division of labour, as were two-thirds of the Coast Town housewives.

6.1.7. Emotional and sexual relations

It is within the economic and social conditions so far considered that the partners in a marriage develop their emotional and sexual relations. With reference primarily to the modern middle-class family in the USA and in pre-war Germany, the emotional relations between husband and wife have been described as overburdened and emotionally overcharged (Parsons 1955, Reich 1945), as symbiotically clinging

65

(Fromm 1945), infantile and neurotic (Parsons 1955), sexually repressive, as well as generally life-inhibitive (Reich 1945), and also as primarily of a companionship character (Burgess 1955).

Probably Norwegian marriages also generally share these characteristics, but we have no available data on this elusive subject.

However, one Gallup survey found that only 2 per cent of the women and 4 per cent of the men considered 'companionship, friendship, cooperation' as the most important characteristics of a husband or wife, while a somewhat greater portion indicated 'companionship and mutual interests' as being most important for a happy family.

Otherwise, there seems to be evidence to indicate that Norwegian women tend – at least more so than women in Sweden and America – to identify themselves emotionally with their children more strongly than with their husbands (Hendin 1967, Bye 1947, Grønseth 1960, 1961). This is not supported, however, by a relevant, albeit highly limited question asked the housewives in Rural Town and Modern Town (B. Grønseth 1965, Table E 23).

In Coast Town, the housewives generally considered themselves quicker to be angry at their husbands than their husbands were with respect to them – but they thought their husbands more jealous than they themselves. Only a few said that they had seriously considered divorce, whereas one-third had in anger thought about divorce.

While one Gallup question indicates that married quarrels frequently concern financial matters (Gallup 1949), in Modern Town child-rearing differences appeared to predominate quarrels. (This was mentioned by about 15 per cent in the latter study, as against about 5 per cent in the Gallup poll, as being the single most important cause of quarrels.) Among working couples in Modern Town, however, quarrels most frequently concerned the partners' social contacts (13 per cent), a point scarcely mentioned in the other samples.

People's opinions about the most usual causes of divorce cannot tell us what problems people do in fact have in marriage. But such attitudes can indicate which factors people consider most serious of those difficulties that pose a potential threat to marital solidarity. One Gallup poll indicates that 'infidelity' dominates (27 per cent), followed by 'poor finances, bad living conditions' (18 per cent), and 'incompatibility, etc.' (18 per cent). Sexual problems were mentioned by only 4 per cent, drunkenness by 13 per cent, and weakness of character by 6 per cent (Gallup 1949). Unfaithfulness is also the characteristic men desired least in their wives (15 per cent), whereas it was mentioned in second place by women vis-à-vis their husbands' character (12 per cent); first place was occupied by 'too much drinking and/or smoking' (41 per cent). Other characteristics mentioned by men as being especially undesirable in women were 'entertainment-crazy, flighty' (13 per cent), as well as 'vain, fashion-crazy' (3 per cent). 'Spendthrift' was mentioned by 4 per cent (Gallup 1948).

Regarding something as emotionally charged as sexual relations, the question arises as to how valid responses are – even in unstructured interviews lasting up to four or five hours, as in the Coast Town study. From the limited material that we do have from this study, however, there seems to exist quite widespread sexual dissatisfaction and lack of sexual initiative among the wives, especially among seamen's wives.

Almost half the non-seamen's wives and about two-thirds of the seamen's wives expressed little or no pleasure in sexual relations. Nonetheless, three-fourths and one-half, respectively, also indicated that they considered the situation satisfactory, since their husbands were considerate, etc. (Grønseth 1956 and 1960).

Also among the Rural and Modern Town housewives, the overwhelming majority indicated they found their sexual relationships satisfactory. One-half of those in Rural Town and almost two-thirds of non-employed in Modern Town – as against only one-fourth of the working wives there – said they were *completely* satisfied with their sexual relations. Relatively few spoke directly of dissatisfaction. In both towns, only 14 per cent said they wished they had formerly had more information on male–female relations; 14 per cent wished more such information on sexual questions, 10 per cent as to contraceptive methods. Only 5 and 2 per cent, respectively, wished for more such information today.

A large percentage of the non-employed housewives in both Rural and Modern Town, but a smaller percentage of the working wives, said they were satisfied with their husbands, not only sexually but also with his love and consideration in general (55.8 and 33 per cent *completely* satisfied), with the husband's attitude to her leisure and personal development (43.6 and 27 per cent *completely* satisfied), and with the husband's interest in the family's welfare (69.8 and 65 per cent *completely* satisfied) (B. Grønseth 1965). Hendin found that while 'Norwegian women were inclined to complain about excessive sexual demands, they were rather indifferent to the man's sexual inadequacy or neglect' (Hendin 1964, p. 109).

When a statistically representative sample of the Norwegian population was asked in a Gallup poll to indicate what they considered important for marriage and family happiness, not only sexual satisfaction but also love was seldom mentioned. Love was mentioned by only 9 per cent as being the most important factor. Even such relatively mild, undemanding feelings as 'understanding, companionship, agreement' were mentioned by only about 29 per cent; 10 per cent mentioned 'consideration, respect', and 'trust, honesty, faithfulness' (Gallup 1952).

To a question of what was considered most important for a happy marriage, a 1954 Gallup poll showed no trend to indicate stronger positive feelings either; but both 'understanding and tolerance' and 'mutual respect' were mentioned by 87 per cent.

6.1.8. Authority, work, and emotional relations in working wives' families

Swedish studies indicate that home routines in families where the wife works are generally quite like those in which she does not (Dahlstrøm 1962). Other studies, from the USSR and the USA, for example, seem to point in the same direction. Thus, even though the wife reduces the amount of housework she does in general, and even though the husband or a paid helper takes over some of this, most of the household duties are still carried out by the wife herself.

This is also the case among working wives in Modern Town. Although they receive *somewhat* more assistance from their husbands, especially with respect to such things as bedmaking, preparing breakfast and dinner, and doing the dishes, one-fourth of these working wives felt that their husbands' participation had not increased sufficiently.

In contrast to what Swedish and American studies have found, the Modern Town working wives more frequently make decisions alone than do the non-employed wives, and this despite the formers' increased work pressures. Now, to what extent this simply means that the working wives are more independently minded than the others, or that they have not enough time to engage their husbands in all such decisions, is difficult to say (Holter 1966).

Otherwise, working wives in Modern Town were found to be more frequently dissatisfied, in various ways, with their marriages than were the non-employed wives. This is probably due in no small part to the difficulties and conflicts involved in the double roles required of working mothers. It is also possible that precisely the working wives are more independent, more problem-conscious, or they already had more difficult marriages and for this reason took outside employment. However, while Swedish studies have found a somewhat higher divorce frequency among families where the wife works, a Copenhagen survey has indicated the reverse (Dahlstrøm 1966).

6.1.9. Conflict between the family's economic provider function and its emotional and sexual satisfaction function

We have noticed above an indication of sexually and emotionally rather poor marital relationships. Both theoretically and with support in data from clinical psychology, such relations may be partly due to *the economic and social necessity of staying together.* In that society does not assume economic responsibility for children, and given the existing difficulties presented married working women today, plus the housing shortage, an economic and material tie is a necessity placed upon most marriages. Only among the financially better-off, as well as among those so poor that divorce would make little difference financially, will these economic and material ties not be decisive (Grønseth 1970, 1971).

It has been maintained that, especially for women, marriage represents a vital source of their feeling of security. This is probably true, because the woman has, at least up till now, had considerably fewer chances for developing an independent economic and social basis apart from her husband. It is true also because, for reasons of their objectively dependent position as adults, they have been reared to a corresponding psychological dependence (Raknes 1949).

The man's provider role and the woman's economic dependence seem to contribute in no small measure to the continued adherence to a pattern of limiting children's sex play and youth's safe and free sexual expression and development, since large and influental portions of the Norwegian population fear that such expression would necessarily lead to an increase in pre-marital pregnancies. And, in turn, the resulting sexual repression in childhood and youth has a tendency to bring about strong sexual inhibitions in marriage, as well as transference, to one's partner, of infantile emotional parent-fixations. The existence of such often unconscious sexual and emotional conflicts within the adult population in turn helps prevent true sexual reforms from being implemented, although such reforms would contribute to sexual freedom, health, and satisfaction for children and youth, and thereby for the adult population (Reich 1945, 1961, Grønseth 1966a, b, 1970, 1971). (Dissenting opinions are presented in Schjelderup 1940, 1964, Foss 1966.)

The neurotic solidarity of sexually unsatisfying marriages is further strengthened by moral norms, official and religious, that the partners should stay together until death, for better or worse, loving each other come what may, and not seek sexual satisfaction in other relationships. For such prescriptions, half-truths such as that children would suffer by a divorce, that marriage is no rose-coloured dream, that love presupposes willpower, etc. are popularly served as further support.

However, when divorce today does adversely affect the children, this is mainly because of the special financial, social, and psychological conditions regularly brought about by divorce in our society – conditions that could probably be avoided, given another social framework (Grønseth 1966a, b).

Thus we see that, in modern society, the nuclear family and the husband's provider role still function in opposition to what could be its potential function: to provide room for the satisfaction of primary human needs in emotional and sexual life (see also Reich 1945, 1961, Nissen 1961, 1934).

6.2. *Parent–child relations*

6.2.1. Basic institutional patterns

In Norway, as in other industrialized socities, the question of who are socially defined as parent and child is principally resolved in terms of strict biological kinship. In a few primitive societies this is not the case, for instance where all children born to one married woman are automatically considered as having her husband as their father, regardless of biological paternity. One extreme example of this formerly existed among the Nayars in India (Gough 1959).

In Norway, the rule – both in law and in most practice – is that a child's social father and mother are identical with its biological father and mother. This holds true whether the child is legitimized by the marriage between its biological parents or not. The possibility of adoption provides, however, a legal exception from this rule of identity between social and biological parenthood.

In the case of dissolved marriages of mothers, only one of the parents has a legally binding parenthood or guardianship: the parent with whom the child lives. Still, most divorces in Norway today end with the mother receiving guardianship of the children, even if these are not young. Gradually, however, more consideration seems to be paid to the father's feelings and to his importance to the children as well (Grønseth 1966a, Tiller 1958, 1960).

Also, children in so-called 'incomplete' families have a social father, because here, too, the biological father is in a certain, sometimes highly limited respect a member of the family. He is thus required to pay support to his children and to let them inherit after him. With divorce, the father usually has the right to visit his children, and – when using this – a social and emotional relationship with them. The children may use his surname as well. And although there is no longer a marital relationship between the parents, they usually continue a mutual relationship of parenthood with their children.

Children of a mother who has re-married are still members of their original nuclear family, at the same time as they have also unofficially joined the mother's new family, in which her new husband usually functions as social father, or foster father. Only if the children are adopted by the new husband is their membership in the original family discontinued.

As we have seen, the parental duty to provide for the children falls, within legitimized nuclear families, mainly upon the father, but in non-legitimized, incomplete nuclear families upon the unwed mother, since the father's contribution frequently will be the legal minimum, N. kr. 1800 per year (at present). Even though according to law unwed parents both have equal responsibility for support and inheritance to their children as do married parents, the non-legitimized child's complete equality with the legitimized remains – even economically – an illusion as long as society has not taken upon itself the economic responsibility for the child's support and care; or, alternatively, as long as the unmarried father cannot in practice be subjected to the same duties of providing for his child and its mother as is a married father.

According to law, both *married* parents have equal parental guardianship of their children. Day-to-day authority generally seems to coincide with supervision and caring for the child and is thus mostly in the hands of the mother. That this is, with certain variations, the case in the majority of families with minor children at home, has been supported by all the various studies of such conditions (see Stephenson 1959, Tiller 1960, Rodnick 1955, E. Grønseth 1956, 1964, B. Grønseth 1965). Along with one-sided dependence of children upon the father for economic provision and social position, parent–child relationships seem to be most frequently characterized by the father's socially and emotionally distant, peripheral role and the relatively one-sided and exclusive mother–child relationship. This latter situation seems due not only to the father's absorption in his provider role, but also to the lack of possibilities for play, recreation, and child-care institutions for small children, especially in larger towns (Grønseth 1963b).

6.2.2. The father's and mother's relationship with their children

The Coast Town study did not show any especially disciplinary father role in contrast to any less disciplinary mother role – indeed, rather the reverse.

To the question of who most generally disciplined, scolded, and punished the children when both parents were present, almost two-thirds of the non-seamen's wives replied that they themselves more than the husband disciplined and scolded the children, and about one-half said that they more than the husband punished them. Only one-fourth of the men were mentioned as punishing the children more frequently than the mother did. Among the seamen's wives, the mother's disciplining and the father's non-disciplining roles were even more sharply defined. And to a Gallup question, 56 per cent of the mothers, as against 40 per cent of the fathers, replied that they had spanked their children (Gallup 1947).

To questions in the Coast Town study – concerning how often mothers say to the children to wait until father comes home, or that they would tell father what had happened, or that father wouldn't approve of this or that – the answers did not indicate any especially widespread pattern of particularly strong paternal authority.

However, fathers seem to have an emotionally more distant and neutral relationship with their children than mothers do. While nearly two-thirds in both Coast Town groups said that the children had most respect for their father, less than one-fifth felt they had most respect for the mother. So, disregarding the fathers' 'instrumental' provider role and status-giving function, we seem to find that mothers are both more 'instrumental' and 'expressive' with respect to their children than are fathers.

Concerning the relationship between mother and child, Hendin (1964) has the following to say:

> The Norwegian child is not required to excel in order to win his mother's affection. The mother is usually the dominant force in shaping the child's character, and she encourages his claim to omnipotence without insisting on proof that it has been earned. Norwegian boys are not expected as they are in Sweden to excel under any circumstances. They please their mothers by being good, and good behavior means that they cause no trouble either in school or later in life (p. 131).

> The focusing of the mother's emotional life on the child is to some extent counterbalanced by this desire for an independent child. Conversely, the child's self-sufficiency does not indicate a real lack of emotional involvement on the part of the mother as it often does in Sweden (p. 143).

> She will try to derive happiness from the child's independent accomplishments and live vicariously through them. This contradiction between tying the child to her and yet wishing to have an independent child dominates Norwegian mother—child relations. On the one hand, there is the tendency to infantilize the child, ... On the other hand, the mother tends to make a relatively young child her confidant. By revealing her marital dissatisfactions to the child, she is likely to overtax his emotional strength (p. 98).

6.2.3. A modified, restrictive socialization

As soon as children enter school[4] they are no longer dominated in so one-sided a fashion by their parents and close relatives. The possibilities that slightly older children and youth have for participation outside the family itself, first in the school situation and then under relatively free conditions, probably contribute to weakening the parents' control over them. Likewise, the probably increasing uncertainty most parents feel as to traditional child-rearing and practices also acts in this same direction.

72

Although considerably dated, the following figures may be worthwhile reporting. While 54 per cent of parents over 35 years of age had spanked their children, this held true for only 37 per cent of those younger than 35. And 26 per cent of those who had spanked their children considered it wrong (Gallup 1947). Furthermore, 44 per cent felt that children today received a better upbringing than they themselves did – this was especially the case among younger town dwellers and persons from higher income groups (Gallup 1948).

Of both men and women, 41 per cent thought they themselves had received a less strict upbringing than did their parents. And one-half of those with children replied they were bringing them up less strictly and severely than they themselves had been – this especially among younger persons, city dwellers, and higher income groups (Gallup 1952). However, in response to another question, 52 per cent indicated that they felt modern upbringing lacked discipline (Gallup 1948).

The slender material available from the Coast Town study indicates that 'determination' and 'being consistent', rather than 'freedom' and 'personal fulfillment', are considered most important in child upbringing. Rodnick emphasized that children 'are allowed little choice in patterning their lives. Parents try to guide every step by making the child aware of its weakness and helplessness' (Rodnick 1955, p. 32).

He also found a marked emphasis on objective rules for good behaviour, rather than on personal authority vis-à-vis children. This would seem to agree with the more marked internalization of norms among Norwegian as compared with Italian children found by Tiller (1960), as well as with Eliot's observation about Norwegians' noticeably 'inner-directed' personality structure (Eliot 1959).

In the 'Nationalism study' made in 1951 a random sample of the adult Oslo population were asked to indicate agreement or disagreement with a series of statements (see Bay et al. 1953).

A full 88 per cent agreed completely or nearly completely that 'children nowadays have their own way far too often'. And two-thirds more or less completely agreed that 'it is more important to teach one's children neatness and cleanliness than to give them love'. Only 29 per cent expressed total or partial disagreement.

To the question of whether children aged 10–15 were asked their opinions before important decisions were made, only 23 per cent of the adult sample said 'now and then, 'often', or 'always', while respectively 46 and 19 per cent said 'never' or 'seldom'.

And to the question of whether the interviewee's children at home were allowed to criticize father or mother freely, 69 per cent replied they could not do so with either parent.

However, of the 24 nurses that Hendin interviewed in the early sixties, two-thirds said that they as children were freely allowed to be angry with their parents. And as to being angry with *other children,* Hendin found that Norwegian children until the age of 12 generally had more freedom here than did either Swedish or Danish children. They were also encouraged to fight back if they had been unjustly accused (Hendin 1964, p. 102).

A restrictive upbringing is perhaps applied even more to infants, since the basis has been laid right at birth by Norwegian doctors, midwives, and health authorities. Here the father is generally excluded from contact with his wife in labour as well as with his newborn child, no matter how strongly both he and his wife desire his presence at the birth. The painful and fear-producing delivery methods, where the general opinion is that the mother is incapable of natural childbirth methods or should not be encouraged in them by the attending midwife, tend to break spontaneous emotional and physical contact between the newborn child and his mother. This is further achieved by placing the infant in a separate room from his mother. Moreover, bureaucratic hospital schedules for nursing and mother–baby contacts, rather than promote a flexible, self-regulating feeding and contact-rhythm, set the mother–baby relation onto an unfortunate direction, as well as provoking the first, usually quite unnecessary emotional damage upon the child (Waal 1948, Ritter 1959, Read 1956, Baker 1967).

However, we do not know how many infants in private homes lie hungry and lonely, frightened and crying, nor how many have their meal-times interrupted before they are satisfied, who are met by parental disapproval or blows because they cry, suck their thumbs, spill their food, or are otherwise 'naughty'.

Nor do we know how many infants and small children are frustrated in their wish to do things by themselves, or are deprived of much self-confidence and independence by over-anxious or excessively 'correct' parents who cannot put up with untidiness or dirtiness. Neither can we know how many are more or less abruptly stopped in their sex play and interest, or are threatened that they must sit on the potty, or stay clean, and thus have their independence, their ability to fully experience pleasure and their body sensations, damaged at an early age (Raknes 1949, 1970, Ritter 1959, Baker 1967).

As earlier indicated, a family system mainly anchored in the mother's economic dependence, in the ideal of life-long monogamy, in prohibition of the sexual satisfaction of children and youth and thereby in parental sex conflicts and frustration – such a system will usually lead to the subordination of the child's individuality, independence,

74

self-expression, joie de vivre, and full ability to express love and warmth. The few, limited studies available, other than clinical psychotherapeutic experience, indicate that an upbringing that limits primary impulses and needs in these areas is in Norwegian society very widespread indeed (see Grønseth 1964, Skard 1964, Rodnick 1955).

To the question asked in the nationalism study, 'Did you, as a child, have the feeling that you could speak openly with your parents about sexual problems?', 79 per cent replied that they could not with either parent, 8 per cent would with both, 8 per cent only with the mother, and 2 per cent only with the father (Bay et al. 1953).

Yet, despite general upbringing practices which undoubtedly place serious inhibitions on life and emotional expression, it is still Hendin's opinion that, in comparison with Denmark and Sweden, Norwegians are less emotionally inhibited (Hendin 1965, p. 103).

NOTES

[1] For further presentation, see E. Grønseth 1965b, 1965c, Holmsen 1961, Jensen 1962, Johnsen 1948, and Steen 1957.

[2] The *åsetes-rett* is an inheritance right held only by the direct descendants of the owner. The *odels-rett* or 'allodial' right is the right of the direct descendants of a farm, within 20 years after its sale, to take ownership of the farm by buying it back into the lineage at a relatively low price, stipulated by a public estimate - provided the farm had been inherited within the lineage through five or more generations. (See also Grønseth 1965 and 1970.)

[3] The *kår* institution was practiced in different ways from time to time (Hornslien 1957). Essentially, a contract was signed where the son about to take over the farm stated his duty to support his parents by giving them so and so much for their material needs: food, clothes, housing, etc. Often, the old people then moved into their own small *kår*-cottage, or to one or two side rooms in the common house, where they conducted their own, independent household.

[4] In Norway, generally at the age of seven (translator's note).

III. The Norwegian Economy

By Ståle Seierstad

1. THE NORWEGIAN ECONOMY IN AN INTERNATIONAL PERSPECTIVE

1.1. *Prosperity, growth, and industrial structure*

Norway is one of the more prosperous European nations, as the national product data in Table I show.

Table I. *Prosperity and growth in selected countries*

Country	National product per capita 1960, relative figures Great Britain = 100	Growth rates GNP per capita 1950-1960
USA	184	1.6
Great Britain	100	2.2
Denmark	100	2.6
West Germany	100	6.4
Norway	99	2.5
Belgium	95	2.3
France	91	3.4
Netherlands	85	3.6
Italy	55	5.4

Source: SØS no. 12, 1965, Table 8, p. 60, and Table 11, p. 78.

The comparisons of national product per capita are not based on rates of exchange, but on European average prices as a common measurement of value for production in the various countries. This makes the comparisons fairly reliable. Sweden, while not among the nations studied, would have been located at the top of the list of European nations, with a value of perhaps 115–120 (SØS no. 12, p. 78). Norway's economic growth has been about average in relation to the other countries covered in the Table.

In a modern industrial society, a relatively small portion of the population is engaged in the primary sector – in agriculture, forestry,

Table II. *Distribution of working population by sector, for selected Western countries 1960-1961 (percentage)*

Country	Primary	Secondary	Tertiary	Not classified	Total
Norway	19.5	36.5	43.6	0.4	100.0
Sweden	13.8	45.1	40.8	0.3	100.0
Denmark	17.5	36.5	44.3	1.7	100.0
France	19.8	37.6	41.5	1.1	100.0
West Germany	13.4	48.6	37.9	0.1	100.0
Italy	28.2	39.2	29.7	2.9	100.0
USA	6.5	35.0	54.2	4.3	100.0

Source: ILO 1966 Table 2A, pp. 41-136.

fishing, etc. The secondary sector (manufacturing, mining, construction, power) and the tertiary sector (transport, trade, and other services) employ the main portion of the population. Table II shows the distribution of the working population by sector, for selected Western countries.

Generally speaking, there is a correspondence between the economic level of a country and the proportion of the working population engaged in the primary sector. For example, Norway has a considerably smaller proportion of her working population engaged in the primary sector than does economically less prosperous Italy, but a far higher proportion than do the USA and Sweden. The USA has over half her working population engaged in the tertiary sector, and it appears that other countries, among them Norway, are developing in the same general direction.

1.2. *Norway's international economic relations*

One distinctive feature of Norway's economy is its heavy dependence on world economy in general. Since 1950, export has comprised approximately 40 per cent of Norway's GNP. Because of her substantial trade abroad, variations in export and import prices are of considerable importance for her economy. If the relation between these prices – the terms of trade – were to fall 10 per cent, Norway would have to reduce her imports from abroad to a degree corresponding to 4 per cent of her NNP (Net National Product), in order to keep her balance of goods and services with other countries unchanged.

From Table III we see the geographical distribution of Norway's export and import.

Norway's foreign trade is strongly concentrated in the West European area, especially with her EFTA partners. Trade with developing countries is moderate in relation to that of other Western coun-

Table III. *Geographical distribution of Norway's foreign trade, 1960 (percentage)*

Area	Export	Import
EFTA	43.4	37.4
EEC	25.8	32.9
East Europe (including USSR)	4.6	3.2
Other European countries	4.1	2.5
North America	7.2	11.4
(USA)	(6.8)	(6.5)
Rest of the world	14.9	12.6
Total	100.0%	100.0%

Source: Klunde 1963, pp. 242-243.

tries: only one-eighth of Norway's foreign trade was with developing countries, while the corresponding figure for the EEC countries was approximately one-fifth. Great Britain and the USA have an even greater volume of trade with developing countries, respectively somewhat under and somewhat over a third of their total trade (Moyes and Hayter 1964, p. 48).

1.3. *The Norwegian welfare state*

The Scandinavian countries are often thought of as being countries with 1) a high degree of state economic planning and state intervention in the economy, 2) great social and economic equality, and 3) a highly developed system of social welfare.

Table IV. *Size of the public sector in selected Western countries around 1960*

Country	(1) Public income in % of GNP*	(2) % of population aged 15-64 employed in public sector	(3) Non-military public consumption in % of GNP	(4) Public savings % of total savings (1958-61)
Norway	40	5.9	8.8	48-58
Denmark	29	9.8	10.0	25-41
Great Britain	41	10.6	9.5	1-19
West Germany	41	7.2	10.3	32-45
France	40	7.8	8.5	36-40
USA	27	8.1	—	—5-31

Sources: Columns 1 and 2: Russett 1964, Table 16, p. 64, and Table 19, p. 70. Column 3: Johansen 1964, Table 2.22, p. 143. Column 4: SØS no. 12, Table 32, p. 138.

* 'Public income' here includes income from taxes, social insurance premiums, and incomes from public enterprises. The latter are also included under 'public sector' in Column 2.

78

Table V. *Economic importance of publicly-owned concerns in selected Western countries, 1957 (percentage)*

Country	Factor income	Public enterprises' share of: Total employment	Total investment
Norway	9	5*	14
Austria	—	8	27
Sweden	13	7	15
Great Britain	14	14	32
France	10	7	25
Denmark	5	4	12
Belgium	—	4	10

Source: UNECE 1960, Chapter V, Table 1, p. 3.

* Author's own calculations.

A society characterized by the above three features will here be called a *welfare state,* and we shall further discuss the question of whether Norway can be said to have realized the welfare state ideal to a greater degree than other European countries have done.

Norway does not distinguish herself as being a country with an especially far-reaching and important public sector, compared with other Western nations. Only with respect to public savings does Norway head the list, but West Germany and France have public savings figures not far below Norway's (Table IV).

Table V shows public enterprises' share of factor income,[1] total employment, and total investment, in selected Western countries.

Table VI. *Income inequalities in selected Western countries in the 1950s*

Country	Gini-index	% of total income earned by top 10% of population
Norway	.386	29
West Germany	.473	36
Netherlands	.431	38
Denmark	.421	31
Italy	.403	34
Sweden	.399	30
USA	.397	30
Great Britain	.366	31

Source: Russett 1964, Table 71, p. 245.

[1] Factor income equals sum of employees' wages and owners' total receipts: the latter includes both interest on outside capital and owners' compensation for own work and own capital. See NOS XII 163, 1965, pp. 21-22.

From this Table we see that Norway has no greater degree of public industrial activity than other Western countries. Various data on income inequalities are presented in Table VI.

Inequality concerns family income, before taxes. The higher the Gini-index value, the greater is the income inequality. The Gini-index is defined as follows: in calculating the difference in income between any pair of families, the Gini-index equals the average of these income differences divided by the average income of the population. (For further discussion of the Gini-index see Kendall 1948, Vol. I, pp. 42–46.)

It is very difficult to obtain reliable data on income distribution in various countries, especially because the higher income strata scarcely register their actual incomes in full. *In natura* income in the primary sector also creates difficulties. Therefore it is not easy to decide how comparable the data in Table VI are, but they seem to indicate that Norway is located near the top of the list surveyed there, as far as income equality is concerned.

However, there is little difference between Norway and other Western countries as to income inequalities: Norway's 10 per cent richest lay claim to not much less than do the top 10 per cent in other countries.

We may also study the Norwegian welfare state by a comparison of social assistance in Norway and other countries. Reliable recent

Table VII. *Social assistance in selected European countries in 1954*
(percentage of GNP)

Country	Health sector*	Pen-sions†	Family aid§	Total social assistance**
Norway	3.0	2.5	0.5	7.4
Sweden	3.1	4.3	1.3	10.6
Great Britain	3.6	3.2	0.6	9.3
West Germany	3.6	6.1	0.2	14.0
France	3.6	3.7	4.2	13.5
Belgium	2.1	4.8	2.1	12.6
Netherlands	1.8	2.6	1.6	7.5
Switzerland	2.6	2.4	0.1	6.6

Source: Dewhurst 1961, Table 12-1, p. 383; Table 12-3, p. 391; Table 12-4, p. 393; Table 12-7, p. 399.

* Includes health insurance and other public health services.

† Old-age, disability, occupational accident insurance, and widow's pensions.

§ Family allowances, and social assistance in connection with pregnancy and childbirth.

** Includes also other forms of social assistance, such as unemployment insurance, poor relief, certain administrative expenditures, etc.

80

data on this are difficult to obtain, but the information presented in Table VII helps shed light on the situation in the 1950s and is based on thorough studies.

From Table VII we see that Norway's level of social assistance in 1954 was moderate indeed compared with that of other countries. This is in part because various aid premiums frequently were lower in Norway, and in part because conditions for receiving aid differed from country to country – in West Germany, for example, most persons could receive old-age pensions at the age of 65, often at higher rates than those in force for persons over age 70 in Norway.

If we consider a more general concept of income transfer, which in addition to social assistance also includes subsidies, the result is somewhat more favourable towards Norway, as subsidies in Norway in the mid-1950s comprised approximately 4 per cent of her GNP, as against approximately 1–2 per cent for other European countries (SØS 12, p. 255, Dewhurst 1961, p. 1060). However, this only means that Norway, instead of having less than average outlays for social assistance, becomes about average as to total income transfer via social assistance and subsidies. This comparison of Norway with other relatively prosperous European countries dates from the mid-1950s, but the situation has hardly changed to any considerable extent since then.

Another thing worthwhile comparing is the degree of control which authorities have over the credit institutions in various countries. In Norway, the authorities can control the extension of credit through 1) direct public control of lending by the state-owned banks and 2) through the credit restrictions authorities have been able to place on the private credit institutions due to certain credit agreements and the credit law.

The governments in other European countries have other means of controlling the volume of credit, and it is difficult to decide where the government has most influence. For example, in West Germany municipal savings banks are very common, while in France many of the largest commercial banks are publicly owned.

In general, therefore, we may conclude that the Norwegian economy is no less capitalistic – meaning influenced by business and private capitalism – than are the economies of other European countries. The size and structure of the public sector seems for the most part to be the same in Norway as in the rest of Western Europe, nor does there appear to be any important difference in the amount of public influence on business between Norway and elsewhere in Western Europe.

Ulf Torgersen, in his article on Norwegian politics in the present volume, maintains that all the Norwegian political parties have, generally speaking, lain to the left of their corresponding parties in other

81

countries. Here we will venture to state that social equality, equalization of incomes, and social control of business have been ideals more characteristic of opinion in Norway than in most other European countries, especially the Continental ones. These ideals were also central to the Labour government's program in the years 1935–1965. Comparisons which we have made, however, show that these ideals have not led to any major differences between Norway and other Western countries as to economic 'system' or as to income distribution and size of social outlays.

Within the framework of these structural similarities we may, all the same, discern manifestations of the above-mentioned ideals in Norwegian politics. Let us only mention a few examples:

In the common program agreed upon by all political parties in 1945, one item of importance was the goal of improving income levels in agriculture, forestry, and fishing, in order to achieve more equal income distribution. The Labour Party's policies became heavily marked by this goal, and the large price subsidies for agricultural products have been one of the means of achieving such an income redistribution.

Further, Norway chose to base herself on considerably stronger government control of business decisions and of private consumption than the other European countries in the period immediately after World War II. The liberalization of economic policies which took place from 1950 has, however, brought Norwegian economic policy closer to the policies followed in other European countries. The state industrialization put into effect by the Labour Party after the war was also inspired mainly by ideas of social control of business, but state industrialization is no uncommon phenomenon in Europe.

Although Norway is far from conspicuous in amount of social assistance granted, there are interesting differences in the distribution principles used in the various countries. The various social aid systems differ from one another in 1) how large a portion of the population is covered and 2) whether the amount of assistance granted depends on income, is the same for all covered, or is distributed according to need.

In Table VIII we have characterized social assistance systems in various countries according to whether they cover all the population concerned or not, and whether or not the assistance is the same for all receiving aid as of the late 1950s.

We ought to mention that the amount of family allowance granted frequently depends on the number of children in the family, but if the assistance is otherwise granted equally to all, we have classified it as equal. Old-age pensions are different for single persons and married couples, but if the assistance is otherwise the same, we have likewise classified this as equal.

Table VIII. *Social assistance systems in selected European countries, late 1950s*

Country	Health insurance		Family allowance		Old-age pension	
	Covers total population	Cash benefits equal	Covers all children	Equal	Covers all aged	Equal
Norway	yes	no	yes	yes	yes	yes
Sweden	yes	no	yes	yes	yes	no
Great Britain	yes	no	yes	yes	yes	yes
West Germany	no	no	no	yes	no	no
France	no	no	no	no	no	no
Belgium	no	no	no	no	no	no
Italy	no	no	no	no	no	no

Source: Dewhurst 1961, pp. 375-403 and 1035-1050.

For many of the countries where the total population concerned is not covered, it is frequently the case that the system covers the great majority. Furthermore, we should mention that the retirement age is often lower in other European countries than in Norway, and this means that, for example in West Germany, the proportion of population receiving old-age pension is larger than in Norway, even though not all Germans receive an old-age pension.

Table VIII shows that the Scandinavian countries and Great Britain have employed distribution methods quite different from those used on the Continent. There is much to indicate that these differences stem from relatively fundamental cultural and ideological differences between the two groups of countries.

The British sociologist T. H. Marshall has analysed the value basis on which the British social security system is built; and since the British and Norwegian systems are so similar in this respect, it is quite possible that his conclusions are also valid for Norwegian conditions (Marshall 1965). He maintains that Great Britain's social security system has been characterized by the same ideals of equality that earlier manifested themselves in the realization of the principles of equality before the law and universal suffrage: an expansion of citizenship rights. The development of social assistance in Great Britain was meant precisely as an expansion, a further development, of these citizenship rights: *all citizens* should have the right to the *same type* of assistance. Social security systems, based on means tests or assistance according to income, treat individuals unequally and can therefore not be considered an extension of equal rights, legal and political, to the social sphere. Continental European countries appear to have been less influenced by this type of equality ideal. In these countries the social security systems build, to a greater degree, on means tests and income-scaled assistance. However, the effects of income equalization are greatest when the social security systems cover only those with a need for assistance, which indicates that it is neither equalization nor social aid which has been the main aim in Great Britain or Norway. Instead, the social security systems in these countries appear characterized by an unwillingness to treat persons unequally, or, as earlier expressed, a desire to extend citizenship rights.

We must add here that changes have taken place in the social security systems in many countries since the late 1950s. This is also true of Norway, which as of 1967 has had an income-scaled old-age pension system instead of an equal one. And this raises the question of whether the citizenship-rights ideal is not perhaps on the wane in Norway and other European countries. First, we must note that when the sums awarded within a social security system become large – as in Norway with the introduction of the 1967 'folkepension' – this can lead to certain difficulties in maintaining equality in assistance, for example that certain groups may receive a higher retirement income than what they had before. However, it is also clear, as Stein Rokkan has pointed out, that the development of an income-scaled old-age pension system was influenced, in both Norway and Sweden, by the political parties' desires to appeal to the ever-increasing, politically influential groups of white-collar workers (Rokkan 1966).

On the basis of the above, it may be interesting to speculate on whether the ideals of equality will be weakened as the proportion of white-collar workers in the population increases – an increase highly probable in the near future.

International comparisons may be summed up thus: certain political and ideological differences between Norway and most other Western, non-Scandinavian countries in the last decades have expressed themselves in differing types of economic policy, mainly in the years directly following World War II, and in differences in the forms social security systems have taken. These political-ideological differences have not, however, resulted in important differences in economic system, in size of social assistance, or in income distribution.

2. MAJOR TRENDS IN ECONOMIC DEVELOPMENT

2.1. *Economic growth*

In the course of the past 150 years, Norway has developed from an agricultural society to a highly industrialized one. Data on economic growth for the various periods are presented in Table IX. We should note that the growth rates are average figures for periods, and thus

Table IX. *Economic growth 1865-1962*

Average yearly growth rate	1895-1899	1899-1916	1916-1939	1939-1946	1946-1948	1948-1962
GDP	2.0	2.8	2.8	0.5	10.5	4.0
GDP/capita	1.2	1.9	2.1	— 0.5	9.2	3.0

Source: SØS no. 12, 1965, Table 6, p. 56.

hide business cycle fluctuations, which until World War II could be considerable. Since World War II, growth has been more stable and, as the Table indicates, stronger than earlier.

2.2. *Change in industrial structure*

The industrial structure has changed greatly (Table X). The primary sector has decreased in importance, while the secondary and tertiary sectors have increased in importance, despite the fact that personal services (e.g. domestic services) have fallen off.

In addition to the general development tendencies mentioned above, we see that the proportion of the working population engaged in the secondary sector has been stable since 1950, whereas the tertiary sector is still expanding, at the expense of the proportion engaged in the primary sector.

2.3. *Investment, savings, capital inflow*

The investment and savings' share of the total domestic product generally has a tendency to increase when the country is in a period of economic growth. Table XI shows the data on this for Norway.

We see that investments generally show an increasing tendency, as does domestic saving, although the development here has been much less even. That part of investment not financed by domestic saving has been financed by capital import. Table XI shows that the foreign-

Table X. *Distribution of working population, by economic sector (percentage)*

Sector	1865	1900	1910	1930	1950	1960
Primary	59.8	40.7	39.0	35.8	25.9	19.5
Secondary	13.6	26.3	25.0	26.5	36.5	36.5
Tertiary	20.5	30.3	32.3	37.4	37.1	43.6
No data on sector	6.1	2.7	3.7	0.3	0.5	0.4
Total	100.0	100.0	100.0	100.0	100.0	100.0

Source: SØS no. 16, 1966, Table 21, p. 54.

85

Table XI. *Net investment, saving, and foreign-financed investment in percentage of Net Domestic Product average for selected periods 1865-1960*

Period	Net investment (1)	Saving (2)	Foreign-financed investment (3)-(1)-(2)
1865-1884	6.1	6.4	— 0.3
1900-1909	6.9	1.3	5.6
1910-1919	12.1	9.6	2.5
1920-1939	9.8	7.3	2.5
1951-1960	20.1	18.3	1.8

Source: SØS no. 16, 1966, Tables 34 and 35, pp. 70-71.

financed portion of investment has been large indeed. This is clear also from Table XII, which shows the size of the foreign-owned portion of Norwegian industrial stock capital in the present century.

Direct foreign investments were of little importance to Norway's economy prior to 1895, but from that time up to World War I, foreign investment was considerable. These investments provided both financial and technological aid, as the foreign investors brought with them technological innovations of use in establishing completely new branches and in modernizing and expanding those already existing. It is possible that Norway could have managed to finance most of these new investments herself, and in this case the main importance of these foreign investments for Norwegian economic development has been technological and not financial.

The data presented in Table XI somewhat support this latter statement: in periods of high capital import, savings have been low, which may indicate that it was not the availability of domestic capital, but rather the investment possibilities (and technological ability to see and make use of such possibilities) that determined the size of investments.

The percentage of foreign-owned stock capital in industrial and

Table XII. *Foreign-owned stock capital in Norwegian mining and manufacturing firms (percentage of total stock)*

Year	%
1909	39
1919	15
1936	26
1952	12
1962	15

Source: SØS no. 14, 1965, pp. 33, 34, Exhibit 3.2., p. 47, Exhibit 4.2, p. 60.

mining concerns has varied greatly, as shown in Table XII, and was especially low immediately after World War II. Since 1952, the proportion has risen somewhat, but it is still moderate in comparison with certain earlier periods. However, many presently Norwegian concerns and corporations have previously been in foreign hands; and if we add the stock capital of presently and previously foreign firms, we find that this comprises 35 per cent of the total stock capital in manufacturing and mining firms, and 45 per cent of the stock capital in privately owned corporations in these fields (SØS no. 14, 1965, p. 207). This clearly illustrates the role foreign capital has played in the development of the Norwegian economy.

2.4. Composition of exports

Exports will often develop in the direction of greater diversity and more emphasis on highly processed goods, in the course of the process of industrialization. Less industrialized countries will mainly export raw materials from the primary sector and mining. Table XIII shows Norway's development here.

Export products from agriculture, forestry, wood and pulp industry, fishing and hunting, and unprocessed minerals are relatively unrefined, as compared with products from other branches. Norway's export is no longer dominated by these little-refined products, as it was in 1900; the main emphasis today is on highly processed and refined products, a change in composition which seems to have taken place as early as the 1920s.

2.5. Distribution of income

The changes in income distribution which have occurred in the present century are presented in Table XIV, which compares the earnings of various main occupational groups with those of industrial workers. Although Table XIV covers only a few white-collar occupations,

Table XIII. *Composition of exports, 1900-1950*

Year	Export value of products from primary sector* in % of total export of goods	Gross freight income from shipping in % of total export of goods and services
1900	80	43
1925	38	28
1950	36	42

Sources: SØS no. 3, 1955, p. 115, and NOS XII, 1959, Table 223, pp. 224-227.

* Includes agriculture, forestry, fishing and hunting, and unprocessed minerals.

Table XIV. *Selected white-collar occupations' yearly income as compared with that of industrial workers,* 1900-1965

Occupation	1900	1910	1920	1925	1930	1935	1940	1950	1965
Industrial worker	100	100	100	100	100	100	100	100	100
White collar (government employed):									
Train conductor	152	142	109	—	108	—	104	101	99†
Head, government office	443	376	208	210	255	265	212	200	206†
White collar (employed by Oslo Municipality):									
Office clerk	212	184	121	134	139	137	135	102	100
'Secretary' (head of office)	602	481	224	259	289	284	230	173	172
White collar (private):									
Bookkeeper	—	157	—	—	—	—	—	119	114

Sources: NOS XI 92, Table a, p. 11; NOS A 198, 1967, Table 5, p. 12; and *op.cit.* Table IX, pp. 53-55. SØS no. 3, 1955, Table 91, p. 181. Kjønstad, 1951. NOS A 86, 1964, Table VI, pp. 43-68. *Statistisk Årbok for Oslo 1965*, Table 99, p. 84.

* The comparison is between full-time employed in all occupations.
† The figure is for the year 1963.

more comprehensive statistics present the same picture with respect to white-collar workers. The conclusion is obvious: this century has seen a considerable equalization of income between blue- and white-collar workers.

Table XV indicates that there has not taken place any noteworthy income equalization between workers in industry, extractive industries, and shipping since the beginning of the century.

It is difficult to obtain income data concerning persons who are self-employed. However, Lee Soltow has studied individual income distribution in four towns in the county of Østfold and four towns in the county of Vestfold, on the basis of assessed income; his studies include self-employed as well, although this was not the prime focus of his work. He has measured dispersion of income in these towns by the

Table XV. *Daily earnings for various groups of workers as compared with industrial workers' average daily earnings*

Occupation	1910	1918	1932	1938	1944	1950	1965
Industrial worker	100	100	100	100	100	100	100
Mining worker	106	—	88	87	101	102	106
Agricultural worker	85	88	40	43	76	80	78
Forestry worker	72	91	35	40	75	84	87
Merchant seamen	66	65	52	51	(127)	79	—

Source: Kjønstad 1951. NOS XII 195, Table 303, p. 234, and Table 304, p. 235.

Table XVI. *Income inequality in Østfold and Vestfold towns in 1960, measured by the Gini-index*

Index average	1900	1910	1920	1930	1938	1950	1960
Four Østfold towns	0.364	0.367	0.297	0.410	0.434	0.301	0.288
Four Vestfold towns	0.438	0.428	0.391	0.406	0.430	0.341	—

Source: Soltow 1965, Exhibit 8, p. 17.

Gini-index. While the figures for assessed income are far from absolutely reliable, they may still be usable to describe *changes* in the amount of income inequality (Table XVI).

There are smaller differences in income in the towns today than at the beginning of the century. This is probably due not only to the equalization between white- and blue-collar workers, but also to that between workers and self-employed in the towns. In any case, figures from assessed income indicate that the differences in income between merchants and workers have decreased (SØS 1955, p. 185).

There has been a certain equalization of income between sectors, except with respect to the relationship between secondary and primary sectors. The relative decrease in tertiary sector income is probably due to the fact that this sector includes the free occupations and relatively more white-collar workers than the other sectors – all white-collar workers in public service and in banking and insurance are classified here, for example. These groups have regressed rather sharply with respect to relative earnings. The data in Table XVII may indicate that this has occurred in relation not only to workers, but also to farmers and fishermen.

Since the beginning of the 1950s, there have been no major changes in income distribution. Here, increases in income within the various branches of trade and industry, and for workers and white-collar workers – both private and government employed – have been very similar. This may be seen from the data we have presented here,

Table XVII. *Relation between the various sectors' factor income per member of the labour force**

Sector	1910	1930	1950	1960
Secondary/Primary	1.70	2.40	1.90	1.96
Tertiary/Secondary	1.38	1.21	1.04	1.01
Tertiary/Primary	2.36	2.90	1.98	1.98

Source: SØS no. 12, Table 112, p. 46, and SØS no. 16, Table 21, p. 54.

* For 1910, gross factor income; for later years, (net) factor income.

and is confirmed by more comprehensive statistics published elsewhere (e.g. SØS no. 12 ,1955, pp. 232–235, and *Innstilling fra Utredningsutvalget for Inntektsoppgjørene 1966,* of 22 January 1966). The income equalization process under way until 1950 has halted entirely.

Income development in the years between World Wars I and II was almost the reverse of that otherwise characteristic of the first half of the twentieth century. The differences between white-collar and blue-collar workers, and within the ranks of workers, increased considerably in the inter-war period. In particular, wages for unskilled and semi-skilled workers fell drastically. The Gini-index shows a strong increase in income inequality in the Østfold and Vestfold towns studied. Earning conditions within the primary sector were especially poor – as is obvious from Table XVII. This was true of both workers and the self-employed in this sector. Workers in agriculture and forestry saw their earnings reduced from about 90 per cent of those of industrial workers in 1918 to only about 40 per cent in 1930 (see Table XV). Whereas industrial workers experienced a certain increase in real income in the inter-war period, even full-time employed workers in agriculture and forestry saw their real income reduced by about one-third from 1920 to 1935 (SØS no. 3 1955, p. 180).

The same tendency to increased income inequality can also be seen with respect to wage differentials between groups of workers within the same branch (Soltow 1954, pp. 132–133). Table XVIII shows that the process of income equalization was under way up till 1920: from that time on, differences in income increased. All the same, the total result from 1900 to 1950 was a considerable degree of income equalization – and this was due to the extremely rapid income equalization

Table XVIII. *Wage differentials in the mechanical repair and machinery industry, and between older and younger domestic servants, 1910-1965*

	1910	1915	1920	1925	1930	1935	1940	1950	1965
Skilled workers' wages in relation to those of apprentices in the mechanical repair and machinery industry	1.40	1.28	1.17	1.18	1.20	1.21	1.20	1.11	1.15
Older domestic servants' (24-54 yrs) wages in relation to those of younger domestic servants (20-24 yrs)	—	1.17	1.13	1.15	1.18	1.18	1.10	1.09	—

Source: NOS X 178, Table 189, p. 364, and Table 192, p. 365. NOS XI 330, Tables 164 and 165, p. 161. NOS XII 207, Table 8, p. 13.

process which took place before 1920 and from the late 1930s up till 1950.

2.6. *Unemployment*

From 1900 to 1920 there was little unemployment in Norway, mainly because the considerable emigration in this period helped to stabilize the relation between supply and demand in the labour market. From 1904 to 1920, never more than 5 per cent of Norway's trade-union members were unemployed; and in the period 1911–1920, unemployment was especially low – between 0.8 and 2.4 per cent. With 1921, however, unemployment rose to a new and different level – 17.6 per cent of trade-union members – and remained very high, between 11 and 33 per cent throughout the inter-war period (aside from 1924 when the figure was 8.5 per cent) (NOS X 178, Table 187). The reasons for this high degree of unemployment were partly economic depression and partly the fact that emigration possibilities were strictly limited from the beginning of the 1920s.

The difficult employment situation also helped cause a decline in the number of women seeking employment, so that the decline in the demand for labour was even greater than the unemployment figures alone indicate (SØS no. 3, 1955, pp. 29–30). Since World War II, unemployment has again been very low, in general less than 1.5 per cent of persons employed (SØS no. 12, 1965, p. 107).

2.7. *Some comments*

Income distribution can be equalized in two ways:
1) income differences between occupations may become smaller, and
2) the occupational structure can change so that there are fewer persons employed in jobs with extremely low or extremely high incomes. This chapter has been limited to studying the former process. True, Soltow's investigations touch on both, but, comprising only towns, they do not assess the consequences for the country's total income distribution which the decline in the primary sector has produced. Furthermore, we have only used Soltow's data to shed light on income distribution by occupation.

Norwegian society has been in a process of continual change for the past hundred years, a process which shows all signs of continuing into the future as well. But in certain respects there have been few changes since 1920; 1920 marks the end of a period of rapid industrialization which laid the foundation for a modern economy. *LO* (National Federation of Labour) and *Arbeidsgiverforeningen* (National Employers' Association) were formed around the turn of the century, and the labourers' and the employers' organizations saw rapid growth up to the 1920s. One consequence of this development was that individual wage agreements between employees and employers – the usual way of settling wages until the beginning of the century – quickly gave way to wage agreements made between the respective organizations. Modern industry and influential economic organizations, in other words, characterized Norwegian society as early as around 1920. Another point worthy of note is how remarkably similar the income distribution in 1920 is to that of today – a fact obvious from Tables XIV–XVIII. In these areas, then, Norwegian society was a modern industrial society as early as in 1920.

3. THE INFLUENCE OF THE PUBLIC SECTOR

Through its economic policies, the government regulates economic activity and attempts, as far as possible, to maintain full employment, at the same time avoiding too sharp a rise in prices. With the economic instruments available to it today, and with an economic theory considerably improved since 1930, the government today is probably able to prevent large economic fluctuations, although not able to regulate production and prices in detail.

If the government is to realize its goals of full employment and high economic growth without sharp rises in prices or problems in the country's balance of payments, it must be able to influence the development of certain central ecoomic factors, or at least be able to forecast changes in these factors, so that economic policy may be adjusted accordingly. The economic factors we have in mind here are such things as *consumption* and *investment, export,* and *import.*

Consumption – both private and public – can be partly regulated and partly forecast with a fair degree of reliability by the government. As to investment, experience has shown it difficult to forecast private activities in this area. For the period 1952–1962, the national budget was not able to forecast year-to-year variations in gross investment correctly. Product-moment correlations between budgeted and realized gross investment changes from one year to the following were respectively 0.22 in 1951–1956 and – 0.50 in 1956–1962 (Seierstad 1963).

The government's difficulties in forecasting and regulating investment have at least two causes: 1) the total amount of credit extended by private lending institutions has not always been effectively regulated despite the lending restrictions imposed on such institutions by the government, and 2) a considerable portion of private investment has been financed directly by profits from private concerns. Since the end of World War II, this second type of private investment has been more prevalent than that financed by lending institutions.

The government has little control over the development of export, nor is it always easy to forecast trends in this area, since the volume of exports is largely determined by demand tendencies abroad. This lack of governmental ability to forecast and partially control certain central economic factors does mean, however, that it is difficult for the government to achieve a more exact degree of regulation of economic conditions, of production level, and of price tendencies.

Among the many problems confronting the Norwegian government in the post-war years, that of development of backward areas has been central. By means of tax reduction systems for concerns wishing to establish themselves in such areas, and by means of many other types of financial, technical, and mercantile aid and support, the government has attempted to direct concerns towards these less developed areas in Norway. In addition, the state has supported such areas by locating various state-owned concerns there.

As a result of these efforts, northern Norway's proportion of the labour force engaged in industry and mining increased from 4.8 per cent in 1952 to 5.9 per cent in 1962 – but in view of her proportion of total national population – 12.1 per cent – it is clear that northern Norway still suffers from a lack of industrial basis for her development (Brofoss 1965, p. 25). Recently there has been a certain equalization of income differences between central and peripheral areas, although the tendency cannot be said to be a strong one (Brofoss, pp. 200–202).

It is the private sector that in all essentials determines which concerns and branches shall expand and where – at any rate, within a certain region – they will be located. If a concern finds it profitable to locate in northern Norway as a result of state incentives, the concern will still decide *where within the region of northern Norway* it wants to locate. It is the already established concerns that plan and decide on matters of expansion, new establishments, and the location of new activities. We have already noted the very important role that private concerns' own saving plays in financing new activities and investments. We may also mention that more than 70 per cent of the expansion in Norwegian industry since the end of World War II has been that of already existing concerns expanding, or establishing new branches in other areas (Brofoss, p. 211).

Public authorities have limited possibilities for carrying out concrete planning of development of the various branches of trade and industry. The central government has at its disposal about the same number of employees as those employed in private banking – about 8,000 – and only a minority of these are engaged in economic affairs (Bratland 1965, p. 16). To a large degree, the government lacks the expertise necessary for such detail planning, which requires both economic and technological/commercial knowledge. A university degree in economics gives graduates employed by the central government little training in combining these types of knowledge in planning processes.

As a conclusion to these remarks we may say that the government, with the instruments and capacity and expertise available to it today, has generally little possibility of influencing the decisions made within the individual concerns and branches of trade and industry – as to which products and product variants are to be invested in, how much is to be distributed as returns to the owners, to research, to sales and promotional work, and as to prices and volume of production of the various kinds of goods. The goals and instruments of the government are more general in character; it is more a question of regulating the general level of economic activity, of preparing favourable conditions for economic growth, and of stimulating industry in the less developed areas – rather than special goals and special programs for individual lines of trade, industry, and business.

4. THE STRUCTURE OF THE PRIVATE SECTOR AND THE BEHAVIOUR OF FIRMS

It is well known that the structure of and activity in the private sector do not fit with traditional economic theory of the free-competition model. Still, it may be fruitful to study the economy in the light of two postulates that frequently form the basis of such traditional free-competition models: 1) trade and industry have many competing firms in all branches, and the volume of productions, prices, and returns are determined on the free goods and labour market; and 2) the owners have the real say as to the decisions a firm makes, and they always attempt to maximize profits.

4.1. *Competition-limiting features of trade and industry*

Free competition is characterized by many independent buyers and sellers in the market – so many that if one individual buys or sells more or less than before, this will not have any notable effect on prices. Prices and volume of trade are determined by the forces of supply and demand comprised of the aggregate of many buyers and sellers, and the individual participant must simply accept the market price as something he has no control over.

However, in reality it appears that many markets have features indicating severe restrictions on competition. These may take four forms:

1) *The monopoly or oligopoly situation.* When one particular line of trade or industry has only one or a small number of firms involved, these firms will behave differently on the market than if

there were free competition among many concerns. The monopolist is free to determine which prices he wishes to sell for.

2) *Horizontal co-operation.* Concerns within one line of trade or industry will frequently co-operate concerning prices, market shares, division of labour, and product specialization; they may also co-operate on such items as marketing, research, etc. This may take the form of official mergers and agreements, or the means and types of contact may be less formal. Sometimes, financially strong concerns with a large share of the market have been able to dominate the marketing policies of that entire branch.

3) *Vertical co-operation.* Concerns are often connected to their suppliers or purchasers through agreements or mergers – or less formally. In all such cases, a co-operative relationship different from the 'anonymity', which the free-competition model predicates as typical for the relationship between buyer and seller, arises. Vertical co-operation will frequently be profitable for one or more of the partners to this type of co-operation, and in modern economics there is a trend to merge the various steps in the production and marketing chain together into one corporation.

4) *Product specialization.* A feature characteristic of the consumer goods industry especially is that the various concerns within one branch all produce different product variants. For example, there are many makes of washing machine, and many makes of automobile. To a certain extent, these variants aim at exploiting the different purchase desires of the various types of consumers. Also, this aspect helps, in a way, to limit competition and make it more mild. For one thing, it is often difficult for a consumer to judge whether the difference in price between two product variants is unreasonable or not.

For Norway, no detailed investigations of the prevalence of these four types of limitations have been carried out. However, there is reason to assume that most branches of private trade and industry are characterized by at least one of the above.

Available data on the size structure of modern trade and business can help to some extent to shed light on oligopolic features in the various branches.

In many branches, competition is considerably limited by agreements regulating competition. For Denmark we have data showing this (*Trustkommissionens betaenkning* no. 8, 1960), but in Norway little has been done in this area.

There is also reason to assume that there exists a good deal of informal co-operation in addition to that officially registered. Further, when we consider the amount of product specialization and its effects on competition, there seems good reason to believe that there actually exists very little free competition in a modern economy.

Table XIV. *Size of firms in industry and mining, 1963 (percentage)*

| | No. employed in firms | | | |
	0-19	20-199	200 or more	Total
Percentage of total no. of. firms	84.3	14.4	1.3	100.0
Percentage of total no. employed	22.9	41.9	35.2	100.0

Source: NOS XII 208, Table V, p. 66.

This view must not be interpreted as being a statement to the effect that no kind of competition still exists. In branches that are not completely integrated or dominated by one firm, the various concerns will naturally view one another as serious competitors and will try to manoeuvre so as to strengthen their own financial positions and increase their profits. These manoeuvres, however, will seldom be based on price competition with other firms making the same product. Instead, the attempt will be made to develop distinctive product variants and to launch these products by special discount and service schemes, with a special sales and credit policy. It is by such means that economic battles are fought between concerns today (Holbaek-Hanssen 1963). These battles will, however, frequently have a certain character of gentlemanliness, as the need for security and safety often leads to the introduction of an element of co-existence and the desire to avoid major showdowns. Characteristic in this connection is the fact that firms often confidentially exchange information about forthcoming measures and decisions (Cyert and March 1964, pp. 281–282).

Also, there are great differences between market conditions in the various branches and the degree and type of competition. For one thing, there will be a big difference between branches which face competition from abroad and those which do not. In this connection it may be useful to employ a distinction introduced by the Aukrust committee report *(Aukrust-utvalgets innstilling)*, that between the competition-exposed and the shielded branches of trade and industry *(Innstilling fra Utredningsutvalget for Inntektsoppgjørene 1966)*.

The competition-exposed branches include: 1) export and 2) branches competing with foreign import – which include most of the consumer-goods industry and the investment-goods industry. The shielded branches are those producing for the Norwegian home market without competition from abroad, and include the following: service trades (except sea and air transport), agriculture, foodstuffs and beverages industry, building and construction activities, and a few others.

The competition-exposed branches operate in a harder climate than do the shielded ones, but this does not mean that concerns within these

Table XX. *Number of competition-regulating measures and large-scale concerns, 1927-1962*

Year	Mergers	Agreements and arrangements	Large-scale concerns*
1927	158	29	—
1937	239	98	—
1957	502	117	78
1962	335	153	76

Sources: Maurseth 1961 and *Bilag til Pristidende* 1963, p. VIII.

* Large-scale concerns are defined as those producing or selling 25 per cent or more of a product category.

branches always participate in some form of free competition. The world aluminium market, for example, has not been one of free competition, but has always been dominated by a few large American concerns.

There exist data on the degree of competition regulation for Norwegian industry. Table XX shows the development of competition-regulating measures in private trade and industry.

Such competition regulations consist of price and profit agreements, quota arrangements stipulating the participating concerns' production, common sales or purchasing offices, and exclusive arrangements forbidding purchase and sales to companies outside the existing arrangements and agreements.

Table XX shows that the number of such measures increased until 1957, but has since decreased slightly – mainly because since 1958 producers have not been permitted to stipulate binding prices for further sales, and since 1961 there has been a general prohibition of horizontal price and profit agreements. But there are legal exemptions from these rules; regulations have, among other things, officially recognized the right of common sales offices to enter into binding price agreements.

In the primary sector, agriculture, forestry, and fishing are especially characterized by competition-regulating measures. Farmers sell most of their products through their own co-operative organizations, and prices of the most important products are fixed by negotiations between the government and the farmers' organizations. In fishing, co-operative sales organizations handle first-hand sale of the fish, and prices are fixed mainly by means of negotiation between the fishermen's sales organizations and the organizations of merchants and fish processers. In forestry, timber prices are fixed through negotiation between the Norwegian Forest Owners' Association and representatives of the wood products industry.

The government has demanded registration of all such competition-regulating agreements and mergers, and has authority to intervene when and if it judges these to have undesirable consequences for the public, for example, if they lead to what the Prices Law terms unreasonable prices. This does not mean that the government simply evaluates such agreements and schemes negatively; in many cases, the conclusion has been that such agreements and mergers have been necessary for more efficient production and sales.

These many competition-limiting factors have severely reduced the amount of free competition in the Norwegian economy. Quite a few of the Aukrust committee's reports further support this statement. For example, after having gone through the concrete wage and price increases occurring between 1960 and 1965, the committee concluded: 'Most wage and price increases in recent years have therefore, in our opinion, been a result of the autonomous (i.e. administered) upward adjustments. The most important organs formulating such adjustments are: 1) workers' and employers' organizations, 2) the 'organs' which fix prices on those products subject to – formally or informally concluded – competition-regulating agreements between firms, and 3) the government' *(Innstilling II* from *Utredningsutvalget for Inntektsoppgjørene 1966, p. 21).*

4.2. How industrial and business concerns act – and what determines their behaviour

Recent organizational theories concerning how various firms act present a different picture from that of the free-competition model (Cyert and March 1964, Rhenmann and Stymne 1965).

These maintain that, in the first place, maximal profit is not the sole aim of company management. Other aims – such as securing and expanding the firm's activities or exploiting the maximum productivity of the firm's share of the market – are often very important. Management policies are often very much a compromise between the varying interests of different groups within and outside the firm, interests connected with the measures and decisions taken. These interest groups include both the different departments and divisions within the firm, and the external interest groups, such as owners, suppliers, lenders, customers, and in certain cases state and local authorities.

Secondly, these theories point out how complicated the situation surrounding these firms and concerns is – in part, because of the various interest groups, partly because the firms often find themselves in an oligopoly situation, partly because technological progress continually offers new production methods, new raw materials, and new products. Under such conditions, it is not possible for firms to predict which alternative course of action will give the greatest profit. Firms learn from the reaction their surroundings exhibit to their behaviour and actions. As long as the reactions are positive (i.e. as long as certain minimum requirements concerning the firm's goals are fulfilled), the same course is followed. But if these minimum requirements are not fulfilled, a new system of action must be found which will yield the desired positive reaction; and this new course will be followed until new problems turn up.

These viewpoints also represent one answer to the question of who decides how the firm is to act – in that this action, this behaviour, may be assumed to be a compromise between many varying interests. Other researchers have been more inclined to emphasize certain groups of persons as especially crucial for the decisions made and the measures taken by a firm. In modern stock companies, the owners and the management are not identical groups, and the question has been raised whether it is the stockholder or the management who has the deciding authority. In their classical work from 1932, A. A. Berle and G. C. Means maintained that power and authority were, to an ever-increasing degree, accruing to management, while stockholders were coming to wield less and less influence. One of the most important reasons for this was the great spread of shares to a large number of different stockholders – which made it impossible for the stockholders to act together with a common front and common policy. Some data on this are available for other countries (Pedersen 1965), but little has been done in Norway.

Another question is whether there exists an economic elite directing much of the activity in trade and industry in part through the influence stockholding gives, and in part by the fact of being represented in corporation management. C. H. Hermansson maintains that there does exist such an elite in Sweden, on the basis of data which indicate 1) that at stockholders' meetings in the largest Swedish corporations one or a few persons from high-finance circles will control a majority of votes, 2) that these financial circles usually have the majority on the boards of directors of the largest firms, and 3) that the directors themselves often own stock in the firms employing them and have, in general, the same social background as the dominant financial groups. There is therefore little reason to believe that any decisive shift of authority from owners to directors has taken place, or that the latter should constitute a separate group with interests different from those of the owners (Hermansson 1965).

The question of whether such an economic elite exists within the Norwegian system has not been made the subject of any thorough studies. A very modest one undertaken by P. Maurseth (1961) clearly illustrates the many links joining disparate parts of the business world together.

Of the 151 persons who, according to *Kierulfs Håndbok* for 1957, sat on the board of directors and stockholders' committees of the six major commercial banks, 111 also held positions on the boards of directors and stockholders' committees of the other concerns represented in the *Håndbok,* in the sectors of insurance, mining, transport, industry, and trade. These 111 held leading positions in a total of 128 of the 219 concerns covered in the book; and in 59 of the concerns, they held positions as chairmen of the boards.

In 16 of the 22 shipping companies of over 100,000 gross tons, we find 32 of the above-mentioned 151 persons holding 39 leading positions altogether.

Maurseth mentions that the *Håndbok,* however, by no means covers all concerns, that the criteria used for inclusion are unclear, and that all this limits the value of his study. Further, the total figures presented will, to some extent, underestimate the many ties in the business world, because such factors as family ties between leading figures in the various sectors and firms have not been considered.

There must be many such family ties in the business and trade world, judging by the results presented by Ulf Torgersen in his 1963 study of recruitment to leading positions in Norwegian trade and industry (Torgersen 1963, pp. 43–55). He found that almost two-thirds of the fathers and one-half the fathers-in-law of the leading figures in the business community were either self-employed in the secondary or tertiary sector, or higher white-collar workers in private business.

There need not be any contradiction between the view that the decisive authority in business is concentrated in the hands of an economic elite, and the view that a firm's behaviour and actions are a compromise between the interests of many groups. It is possible that major decisions concerning expansion, reduction, or alterations in production, or co-operation and mergers, are largely made by an economic elite, while the day-to-day administration is more characterized by the many considerations to be taken with regard to the many varying interest groups.

Private business seems in general to consist of a relatively stable set or number of existing firms, which largely attempt to avoid free and hard competition. Firms try rather to administer prices, sales conditions, their relations to their interest groups and to other firms, and other economic conditions, all with an eye to gaining strength, security, and large profits.

In Norway there probably exists a concentration of economic power in a few hands, and with many personal ties between the various parts and sectors in trade and industry. Exactly how important this is for the Norwegian economy is, naturally, difficult to say. However, it is likely that close connections between certain firms or branches and certain banks may influence the banks' credit policies towards various customers. This would then be of considerable importance for the finances of these customers. Further, it is not improbable that there exist such economic elite groups with good opportunities for directing capital to those branches, concerns, firms, and enterprises which they themselves wish to support and develop – elite groups which have, in this way, considerable influence on the main trends in economic development.

5. GROWTH PROCESSES

Continually increasing prosperity is created in two main ways: 1) the existing production capacity is increased and 2) technological developments lead to improvements in the production processes and capacity, to completely new methods of production, and to new and improved products.

In general, we may say that technological knowledge is common to all industrialized countries and that all countries contribute to technological development. As technological development is so decisive for economic growth, this common technological culture shared by the Western industrialized nations will tend to equalize the long-term growth rates for these countries.

Economic growth within the individual branches depends partly on technological developments within the particular sector, and partly on how consumer demands for the products of this branch develop. Increased prosperity in Norway has led to a change in the composition of personal consumption. The proportion spent on consumer necessities – for example foodstuffs – has decreased, while the proportion spent on travel, transportation, leisure activities, and education has increased considerably. Since World War II, sales of prepared and partially-prepared foods have increased; likewise, people are now buying ready-made clothing instead of cloth, thread, and yarn (SØS no. 12, 1965, pp. 161–164).

Such changes in consumer demands naturally have important consequences for the development of the various branches of industry. The stagnating demand for flour, bread, potatoes, milk, fish, and meat has created difficulties for agriculture in many countries, among them Norway.

Does this mean that consumers, by means of their choice of purchases, direct development? This may well be true to a great extent, but in several areas the interplay between consumer demands and actual development ought perhaps to be characterized differently.

First, let us mention that today certain highly valued benefits are rationed – for example, in Norway, kindergartens and nursery schools have only a limited capacity to meet a much greater demand.

Otherwise, it is not unusual to encounter views to the effect that it is production that determines demand, and not the reverse. Business creates a consumer need for its products by means of advertising – among other things, by exploiting the common tendency to obtain for oneself status symbols and to try to keep up with the Joneses in the consumer race. When the individuals' consumption is thus mutually stimulating, high consumption of such status symbols is to be expected.

Consumer choices are also characterized by certain social facts and tendencies. The increasing concentration of population in cities further increases the need for trips to the countryside, for cottages and cabins, and for automobiles in order to reach these second homes. Poor public transportation probably increases the demand for private means of transport.

True, the consumer may choose among the goods offered by private business, but in some cases it may well be that he will choose to change the social conditions that create the needs for the goods he buys.

Many things not provided by private business are taken care of by the state or municipality, for example education and health services. Production of certain other benefits, such as modern towns and residental areas, appear somewhat neglected by both the private and the public sectors. It might be interesting to speculate to what degree Galbraith's characterization of American society as a society with a prosperous private sector, but a very poor public sector, applies to Norwegian society as well (Galbraith 1959).

The development created by the interplay between the private business sector and consumer demands does not necessarily lead to a situation where all needs are satisfied – or satisfied in the most efficient way. The public sector must try to cover in part the needs which the private sector would have difficulties in covering, and otherwise attempt to adjust the imbalances which changes and developments have brought in their wake.

6. DISTRIBUTION PROCESSES

From what has been mentioned earlier, we may draw the following conclusions concerning two important aspects of Norway's economy:

1) *Economic structure.* Most business activity in Norway is more or less in private hands, and the economy is characterized by modern technology, a far-reaching division of labour, production specialization, and modern large-scale enterprises.

2) *Organization.* The economy is thoroughly organized, by means of trade and business organizations, competition regulations and laws, organizations furthering various economic interests both at home and abroad, and many other forms of organized activity.

These features of Norwegian economy probably have considerable importance for the distribution of income. A highly developed economy, for the most part private-capitalistic, will have a certain structure in which the various positions require varying types of qualifications, and the occupants varying types of power and strategic possibilities of obtaining high incomes. The 'organization society' administers the distribution of income by regulating prices and wages – if we let the term organizations include all organizations in the business and trade world, and all the formal and informal features regulating competition.

Development of labour productivity and development of prices are two decisive factors for the incomes of different industries. Industries with greater productivity increases than others will get greater increases in incomes than others – assuming that price conditions in the economy do not change. An industry will usually also get a relative income increase when its product prices rise in relation to prices of other branches. True, sales may decline as a result of price increases, but in general there will still be a net profit to be earned from such increases. This may be expressed in a different way: if an industry is to keep up with the increasing general prosperity, it must manage either to achieve the same productivity and price increase as the economy as a whole, or to compensate for a weak link in one of these areas by having a strong one in another.

Data on productivity development, and price and income development in various industries, are presented here as a point of departure for a discussion of the mechanisms governing income distribution in the Norwegian economy. Table XXI shows that the competition-exposed branches have had a productivity increase far greater than that in the shielded branches. However, real income increases in the primary sector and for wage and salary earners in the other sectors, whether exposed or shielded, have all followed the same curve since 1950. This is because the competition-exposed branches have compensated for a favourable productivity development by having a less favourable price development, while agriculture and the other shielded branches have compensated for an unfavourable productivity development by increasing their prices in relation to prices in competition-exposed branches.

More concretely, the following has probably happened. Due to great increases in productivity within the competition-exposed branches, wage and salary earners in these branches have received considerable

Table XXI. *Productivity increases in various branches, 1951-1965*

Average yearly increase in percentage of production per man year

The entire economy	3.6
Shielded branches:	
Agriculture (including dairy products)	2.2
Other shielded branches	2.4
Competition-exposed branches:	
Import-competing branches	4.2
Export branches	5.4

Source: *Innstilling fra Utredningsutvalget for inntektsoppgjørene* 1966, Table 3c, p. 16.

wage increases, without this doing much harm to the total profits reaped. Naturally, however, farmers and workers and self-employed in the other shielded branches have not been willing to lag behind in the income race. Through their organizations they have demanded and achieved a corresponding increase in real income, an increase 'paid for' by increased prices, regulated upwards by the price-regulating organs in these highly regulated, shielded branches.

The various organizations have in this way helped distribute productivity gains originally achieved in the competition-exposed branches to *all* branches of trade and industry, and have thereby also helped maintain the existing income distribution between the branches of trade or industry.

Another important effect of this distribution process is the price increases it brings with it, which, according to the Aukrust committee, are a major factor behind the steady rise in price levels since the end of World War II *(Innstilling II* from *Utredningsutvalget for inntekts-oppgjørene 1966).*

As for the fate of agriculture in the present century, until World War II, farmers frequently had difficulties in achieving the same proportion of increased prosperity as other sectors of the economy. This was because agriculture had a relatively weak productivity development, and, in the inter-war period, an unfavourable price development as well, when compared with that of other branches. Three factors were involved in creating this situation:

1) The general increase in prosperity in this century has not brought with it any noteworthy increase in demand for agricultural products, so the possibility of increasing income by increasing production – without any fall in prices – was not present.

2) Unemployment in the inter-war years helped check the decrease in agriculture's labour force, so that it was not possible to achieve in-

creased productivity and income by decreasing the number involved in producing the saleable market quantity.

3) Until the 1930s, agriculture was characterized by a far freer type of competition between producers than was the case in other branches, which helped create an undesirable price development for agricultural products in the inter-war period, with its fluctuating market conditions.

The fishing sector also experienced great difficulties in Norway in the inter-war period, partly for the same reasons as those enumerated above for agriculture. Fishing is, however, primarily an *export* industry, and its sales conditions and problems are therefore of a different type.

One natural solution to these difficulties in the primary sector in the period between World Wars I and II was to do as other branches had largely done: reduce competition within the industry. Strong market-regulating organizations were developed and expanded, with the active support of the government, in the latter half of the period.

Later, sales organizations in agriculture have – by regulating and equalizing supply to the markets and by selling surplus production abroad – managed to maintain prices at a high, stable level. In this way they have – assisted by substantial price subsidies from the state in the post-war period – managed to give farmers the same income increases as experienced by other groups in Norwegian society.

Formal and informal organizations in the economic structure have had considerable importance for the distribution of national income. Besides such organizations there are two factors which have been important for income distribution: market conditions and the general economic structure.

On the basis of data presented earlier, we may sketch, in a simplified form, the connection between income distribution and these three factors, in the present century:

From 1900 to 1920. Rapid income equalization accompanied by 1) full employment, 2) development and expansion of various labour, trade, and occupational organizations, 3) completion of the transition to modern private capitalism.

Inter-war period. Increasing income inequality, accompanied by 1) high unemployment, 2) strong organizations in the field of labour, 3) modern private capitalism.

From the late 1930s to the present. Rapid income equalization up to about 1950, later stable income distribution – this accompanied by 1) full employment, 2) the organization society imprinting itself upon economy, and 3) an economic structure still predominantly private-capitalistic.

We see that the economic activity level stands out as a central variable with respect to amount of income inequality. Despite strong workers' organizations and the bitter battles fought in the inter-war years, the workers did not succeed in defending their income position. It was especially the lower income strata that had to bear the brunt of the financial depression in those years.

The organization society also seems to have been important for income development within many groups. The organization of trade unions in 1900–1920 assisted the process of income equalization in those years, although other factors may also have played a part – e.g. full employment and the transition to a modern private-capitalistic industrial society, which in itself has increased income equality.

In addition, trade unions may also have had a braking effect on the tendency to greater income inequalities in the inter-war period, although they alone could not stop the trend. The farmers' and fishermen's very *lack* of such organization in this period must be said to be at least partly responsible for the especially difficult economic conditions these groups experienced.

Since World War II there have also been certain signs of the organization society's having modified the effects which the economic structure has on income distribution. Poorly paid groups within the working class have, since the war, generally had little wage drift, that is, wage increases above what has been obtained in collective wage negotiations. This may be interpreted to mean that poorly paid groups have a weak position in the fight for a larger share of the total income – not only in periods of depression, such as the inter-war years, but also today. Under the good market conditions in the post-war years, however, trade unions have managed to secure for these groups the same total income increases that other groups have experienced, by obtaining for poorly paid groups higher wage increases in the wage negotiations with the employers' organizations than those obtained for other groups. Further, the strong organizations in the primary sector have meant a great deal for the development of income within this sector.

Has the organization society been able to give especially preferential treatment to groups situated unfavourably economically? Naturally, it is difficult to say anything definite here, but it is possible that the increased tendency to organization in the economy has been especially advantageous for such groups. Although white-collar workers and 'capitalists' have also organized – in part as an answer to the other groups' developing and expanding their own organizations – the balance of power in the economy might be said to have changed in favour of workers, farmers, and fishermen, with the advent of the organization society in the economy.

Ideological-political factors appear to have been of little importance

106

for income distribution. Norway has long had a very strong political coalition between the workers' movement and *Arbeiderpartiet* (the Labour Party), a coalition which naturally characterized political conditions to a considerable extent in the years *Arbeiderpartiet* was in power, i.e. 1935–1965. Ideas concerning social (public) control of trade and industry have been central to *Arbeiderpartiet's* program, and ideals of equality have been generally widespread. The data on the amount of income inequality and amount of income transfer via social assistance and subsidies in Norway and other Western countries (section 1 of this article) show, however, that Norway has not come any further in the direction of income equalization than have many other countries, many of them countries considerably less influenced by labour governments or radical ideologies. Further, Norway was well on the road to achieving her present degree of income equality even before 1920, at a time when political influence of the workers' movement was far weaker, and when radical ideas were far less widespread, than in the period 1935–1965.

Therefore it appears as if economic structure, the work of economic interest organizations, and the general employment and activity level have been far more important for income distribution than have the ideological-political currents of the period. It may be mainly the full employment in the post-war years which has made income distribution relatively equal; while the influence of ideological-political factors may be fairly inconsequential in Norway's predominantly private-capitalistic, thoroughly organized economy.

Income distribution has been generally stable since the early 1950s, nor is any radical change in one direction or the other likely as long as there is full employment. Poorly paid groups' apparently weak position in the fight for higher wages may perhaps mean that it will be difficult for them to improve their relative incomes, although the organization society has thus far managed to give these groups the same income increases as others. The many organizations in the business world may perhaps administer the economy so as to stabilize income distribution. A major task for these organizations is to work so that the groups they represent achieve a 'fair' share of income. In the many conflicts which will arise concerning distribution of national income, it is perhaps unavoidable that the 'principle' of equal income development for all will be used as a key to solving conflicts concerning distribution. And this will contribute to maintaining the existing income distribution in Norway.

IV. Stratification

By Vilhelm Aubert

1. INTRODUCTION

Stratification has to do with the distribution of benefits and burdens in society. This distribution may be characterized by equality, in which case the tendency towards stratification is weak. But the distribution may also be characterized by inequality, and then a clearer social stratification arises. The inequality may be connected with various different types of benefits and burdens, and different types of norms may be used to justify the inequalities. Therefore, stratification in a society may take many varying forms. All the same, there may well exist certain basic forces in human intercourse which pull in the directions of equality and inequality, respectively.

In situations of social distribution, various considerations may result in a desire to realize the principle of *equality* (cf. Eckhoff 1966). The principle is a convenient one for whoever decides on the distribution, and provides him with protection against criticism. It further guarantees the receivers against the really bad result: getting less than the average. For those poorly situated to begin with, equality will lead to improvement. For receivers mutually dependent, who must work and live together, equality is a means of avoiding conflict and maintaining social peace.

Despite the social forces supporting the ideal of equality, all societies are characterized by a certain degree of inequality in the distribution of benefits and burdens. This is true also of Norwegian society. In part, this is because the considerations calling for equality seldom call for completely automatic equality for all. As a rule, the claim for equality applies only within categories of persons sharing some important social attribute. The claim for equal wages, for example, does not apply irrespective of qualifications or performance. The claim of equality before the law does not apply irrespective of how the individual has conducted himself. The claim of equality between regions in a country does not apply totally independently of productive capacity.

In the very formulation of equality claims, we may discern the contours of stratification: some are to be given equal access to a benefit, as opposed to those not belonging to the category to which the equality is to apply.

In addition much would seem to indicate a general regularity along the lines that for those who already have certain privileges, the chances of their receiving further privileges increase. The scarce benefits in a society are frequently found in clusters around certain groups of persons. This is just another way of saying that social stratification exists, in so far as coveted and scarce values are distributed not only unequally, but systematically unequally. The task for sociological analysis is first to define the areas where this social regularity occurs, finding, if possible, any areas where it does not occur. The next task is to find an explanation for the indicated regularity. Much of the explanation of this tendency, most clearly and concisely expressed in Matthew 13:12 ('For whosoever hath, to him shall be given, and he shall have abundance: but whosoever hath not, from him shall be taken away even that which he hath'), may be summarized in two points.

The distributors controlling the greatest amounts of scarce resources in society belong to the higher social strata. In their work of distributing – whether it be selling, making political decisions, or judging – they are dependent on communication with the receiver. Good communication possibilities will increase the receiver's chances of getting much of what is to be distributed. In this there is a general tendency for those who are like the distributor – often persons from the same social stratum – to get more than others. This does not apply as an absolute law, as many other considerations are also present. But there is reason to believe that this picture does, in the long run, apply to such a degree as to be statistically traceable.

The other point has to do with the receiver's position, independent of the distributor's status. A distributor will gain from dealing with a person of relatively high social rank, in any case, with someone who does not belong to the dregs of society. The chances of obtaining a good exchange relationship depend on the receiver's having certain resources. This is true of something as simple as the fact that a salesman will primarily direct his offers to an especially good buying public, giving precisely this public certain special advantages because it will prove profitable for him. The steady customer and the reliable payer can obtain more favourable terms than the occasional customer who is perhaps a less reliable payer. It is expensive to be poor. To the judge deciding in a criminal case it may appear sensible to place faith in someone with certain resources. A man with a home life, house, and job is 'a better bet' than one without these resources. And so it may appear more reasonable to give this former type of accused a suspended sentence. We may find similar considerations in a variety of areas. Dahl Jacobsen has shown that in the period when the Norwegian agricultural agencies were being built up, special emphasis was placed on informing and aiding the larger farms, because they were capable of putting into practice the program at which the Department aimed. They had, in other words, something to give in return (Dahl Jacobsen, 1964).

For social stratification to exist, there must be a certain degree of homogeneity in the access that large strata of the population have to vital benefits, but inequality between these strata. Traditionally, social scientists have thought of stratification, or class structure, as a situation where relatively few strata – two, or three, seldom more – are discernible in relation to one another. In modern society, however, the boundaries between strata are frequently quite flexible, and stratification resembles a stairway with many steps very close to each other. That it is at all meaningful to speak of social strata in a society where the distribution is thus shaped, is because individuals see themselves and others as members of designated, fixed social strata: the working class, middle class, upper class. The endless wealth of detail in the actual distribution of benefits is vastly simplified in the popular mind and ideology. Since such popular views do characterize the social milieu, such 'unrealistic' theories are in fact capable of making themselves come true.

The man who has worked his way up from the working class to the middle class, as measured by income and influence, may be considered an 'upstart' by the neighbourhood and thus be deprived of the prestige which accrues to a man of his means. Therefore, he actually does not become a true member of the middle class, while another who has also worked his way up, but in a more open milieu, becomes in all respects a member of the middle class.

2. A HISTORICAL PERSPECTIVE

We may ask whether stratification in a society changes in the direction of equalization or the opposite. Income distribution in Norway in the beginning of the past century and today clearly shows that these hundred-odd years have seen a considerable amount of equalization.

Sverre Steen depicts the former society as one with a small upper class of civil servants and merchants with high incomes, and a very large proletariat of small farmers, tenant farmers, servants, and workers. A clergyman earned at least ten times as much as a worker, often considerably more. A Supreme Court judge earned 60 times as much as a worker. 'No judge today earns 60 times as much as his servant girl – if indeed he has any,' adds Steen (1957, p. 247). The urban upper class of civil servants comprised, in 1825, only 0.7 per cent of the population (heads of households). True, this class was also made up of some merchants and wealthy farmers, but their numbers were small, all the same. And the difference between these groups and the common people was great, even when we consider the large farmers, subordinate officials, artisans, and lesser merchants as placed between the social extremes. At the very bottom were those classified by the official statistics as 'poor' – in the 1840s these comprised about 46,000 persons (Kristiansen, 1934).

Income distribution today gives a different impression entirely. In 1964, 72 per cent of the taxpayers earned between N. kr. 8000 and 30,000; 21 per cent earned less, but many of these also belonged to households with a total income of over N. kr. 8000 (NOS XII, 212).

A comparison of income data from the middle of the last century and today cannot in itself give much information on the changes which have taken place in the stratification structure. We must consider the distribution of other benefits, such as power and prestige. Torgersen's chapter on political institutions shows how persons situated far outside the financial upper class had the right to vote and thereby had chances for influencing political decisions. Compared with other European countries, Norway had a noticeably strong tendency towards egalitarianism as early as 1814. This is in turn related to other egalitarian tendencies in the older society. For example, there had been no true landed upper class, nor any large farming proletariat. There had been many small independent farmers, and relatively modest differences between the independent, the tenant farmers, and the crofters in many parts of the country. So at least *one* of the bases for a class distinction, and one highly important in many other European countries, was of decidedly less importance in Norway. Especially as far as relations with authorities were concerned, this is essential.

The nobility as an institution was abolished as early as 1821. Although little more than a formal confirmation of what had been a condition long in existence, this did mean the removal of the formal norms confirming the belief that highly valued social qualities are innate. The norms concerning power and prestige which were valid in the relationship between a landed aristocracy and a non-landed proletariat have found less support in Norway than in most other European countries.

On the other hand, we should not paint the situation in too rosy colours. Earlier legislation helps to indicate the power relations between employer and employee. Kristian V's Norwegian Law of 1687 had a provision concerning domestic discipline, NL 6–5–5, repealed only in 1891. It gave the master of the household authority to reprimand his 'children and serving folk' with 'stick or staff', but not with

111

'arms'. The servant's relationship to his master was such that he could refuse to carry out orders only if commanded to do something clearly illegal, or if his master attempted to obstruct the servant from carrying out duties fixed by law, such as reporting for military service. The rules concerning servants' rights and duties were dealt with in the *personretten* (lower civil courts), as were those concerning the relations between parents and children. The fact of belonging to the servant classes was considered a permanent label for a person, an ascribed and quality-oriented status.

The normative orientation so characteristic of mid-nineteenth-century stratification in Norway is apparent from the following quotation from Hanna Winsnes' widely-read book *For Tjenestepiger* (For Servant-Girls):

> The master and mistress of a household must, if they are to follow the word of God, make provision for the welfare of their servants, be solicitous in case of illness or other misfortune, caution them when they see them errant, and in all respects show them a loving disposition and good example, at the same time never placing heavier burdens on them than they are able to bear.

> Servant-girls must obey their masters and mistresses, for both their own and the Lord's sake, He who orders servants to *love and obey their masters and mistresses*. They should in all affairs promote their superiors' welfare, showing towards them a loving and obedient disposition, as that of a good and obedient child towards strict but loving parents.

> Servant-girls, your situation in life entails much exertion and self-denial; yet you ought not to be dissatisfied, as you may be certain that the Lord has allotted to each of us that situation in life for which we are best suited, to test us and lead us on to His Kingdom (Winsnes, 1868, p. 2).

The subordinate's status was ascribed ('the Lord has given to each of us . . .') and quality-oriented ('showing towards them a loving and obedient disposition, as that of a good and obedient child . . .'). The relationship was diffuse ('make provision for the welfare of their servants . . . caution them when they see them errant') and wide-reaching ('the Lord's sake, He who orders servants to love . . .'). On all these points the relationship between superior and subordinate is different in modern society, also as regards the ideals guiding the relationship.

Fiction and popular literature from that era clearly illustrate the psychological importance of the distinction between 'gentry' and 'common folk'. The mutual, subjective judgements between members of unequal social strata have obviously undergone great changes in the course of the past hundred years. But, it may well be the case that these subjective changes are greater than the changes which have actually taken place in the distribution of economic benefits.

Social stratification frequently, although not necessarily, expresses itself in social classes. The formation of such classes implies that those somewhat similarly situated in their access (or lack of such access) to benefits, experience this similarity, give it importance, identify themselves as fellow members of a class group, and begin to show interest in common action. This may lead to the development of organizations, centralized leadership, and common ideology. After the 1814 independence, the first manifestation of such organizational activity concerning stratification was the peasant opposition in Parliament. Due to the political system, the issue to be first articulated and take on a certain organized character was the distinction between the independent farmers on the one hand, and the civil servants on the other. The Thrane-ite movement for workers' rights in the mid-nineteenth century must be viewed as an attempt to give an organizational expression to the interests of people of humble means. This, however, was successful only at a later date. Meanwhile, Norwegian politics were dominated by the division between a conservative and a liberal viewpoint in Parliament, after 1884 organized as political parties.

But it would be incorrect to flatly define the Conservative *(Høyre)* and Liberal *(Venstre)* Parties as the political expressions of two social strata. Leading Liberal politicians often belonged to the same social strata as the leading Conservatives, and the two parties served, to a large degree, to channel other clashes of interests than those arising from stratification. Not until after the formation of the labour movement into the Labour Party *(Arbeiderpartiet)* and Labour's strong representation in Parliament (as a result of reforms in the voting franchise laws) may the political system in Norway be said to reflect an underlying social stratification. However, neither does the division between socialist and non-socialist correspond to stratification: the relations between various parts of the country, between urban and rural areas, between differing mentalities – all these influence party membership and voting, so that many 'poorer folk' vote non-socialist while many of the well-to-do vote socialist.

While we may rightly claim that the past hundred years have seen a kind of equalization in social stratification in Norway, it is more difficult to say anything definite about class conflict on the organizational level. True, political conflicts were sharper in 1884, when parliamentary government was introduced, and in 1905, when the union between Norway and Sweden was dissolved, than is the case today. But they cannot be called class conflicts. We may, however, say that class conflicts reached a climax in the 1920s and 1930s, when the controversy between socialists and non-socialists was raging, and largely along stratification lines.

We may summarize the development of class structure in Norway as having passed through three stages: feudal society, class society, welfare society. Around 1814 we may still discern many traces of the earlier feudal society. Birth was still highly decisive in defining the individual's future stratum position, and this was in part even stipulated by law. Inheritance of social status usually took place via inheriting a family occupation or trade. Political rights were in turn dependent on occupation and property ownership. Studies of recruitment to academic professions and officialdom previous to 1814 have shown that it was highly unusual for farmers' sons or others from the ranks of the common people to have access to this top stratum. Much more usual was that clergymen's sons became clergymen, and officers' sons officers.

The nineteenth century saw a consolidation in the direction of a more modern class society. Birth still played an important role, but no longer was this stipulated by law, and the connection between occupation and social rank loosened somewhat. We may take as an example the social role of servants. A 1754 ordinance decreed, under penalty of law, that all unmarried women and men of the peasant class who did not possess their own farms or tenure as crofter, should enter service for at least one year at a time (Aubert et al. 1952, pp. 26 ff.). In other words, law decreed that young persons who by birth belonged to a certain social stratum must follow a certain occupation: in this case, that of servant folk. This statutory decree was abolished in 1854, although a large portion of the unmarried women and men from peasant backgrounds still found themselves obliged to enter service as before.

Within officialdom the change in recruitment is clearly visible. Sons of farmers and workers still had diffculty in gaining entry, but within the top stratum there was a lot of reciprocal recruiting from one occupational group to another. Political rights were extended to include more and more persons; the educational system grew, eradicating illiteracy; economic life became dominated by the ideologies of liberalism and competition; and favouritism and discriminatory legislation were gradually done away with. Within the top level, power shifted from officialdom to private industry, while industrial workers came to dominate in the lower social strata.

The welfare society represents a modification of the earlier class society, but may contain the seeds of an egalitarian society. The welfare state has formed the setting for stratification structure since World War II. Birth still plays a part in determining the individual's future stratum position, although to a much lesser degree than previously – a fact illustrated by data on recruitment to higher education. Even those born with social privileges must compete in the educational system for the right to maintain their places in the stratification. The distance

114

between the various social strata has decreased, as have differences in styles of life. The expression 'the two nations', formerly indicating the great cleavage between rich and poor, is no longer a valid description. The connection between occupation, income, and politics is also less clear than was earlier the case.

3. DISTRIBUTION OF INCOME, OCCUPATION, AND EDUCATION

In a modern society income distribution is a natural indicator of stratification. But taxable income is a highly unreliable measuring stick, as the same figures may represent highly divergent social realities for different sectors of the population. A young taxpayer who earns N. kr. 15,000 and lives at home with his parents may well live very comfortably, whereas a large city-dwelling family whose bread-winner has the same income may live in real poverty. For some, taxable income is an expression of what they actually earn, while others have hidden income sources: consumption of own produce, or dwelling, travel, and car maintenance paid for by the employer.

If information were available on each taxpayer's household situation and place of residence, we could proceed from income to standard of living and consumption, thereby obtaining a general overview of the distribution of material benefits. Information on households and number of persons involved is necessary, as it tells us how many the income must support. Place of residence is important, as it tells us something about living expenses and the access to various localized benefits, such as schools, doctors, cinema, restaurants, wine and liquor stores, department stores. It is also important to know from what branch of industry or trade the income stems, because occupation and prestige are so clearly interrelated.

Unfortunately, only combined data are available for some income and occupational categories. Concerning the lowest income categories there is a 1962 survey of occupation, place of residence, and household situation (Myklebust 1966). Of the 50,000 Norwegians occupied in agriculture, forestry, and fishing, 32 per cent earned less than N. kr. 4,000 yearly, while 27 per cent earned between N. kr. 4,000 and 8,000. This income distribution differs greatly from the distribution pattern for all occupations. Here, in other words, income statistics reveal special, rather small occupational categories most unfavourably situated in the stratification structure. The group perhaps worst situated of all is that of households where the bread-winner earns less than N. kr. 4000 and where the total household income less than N. kr. 8000. Here we find the independent farmers and fishermen comprising about half of the category.

115

More general statements about the interconnection between income and occupation concern the traditional division between manual and white-collar workers. This division corresponds partly to that between the secondary and tertiary sectors on the one hand, while connected with the subjective ranking of occupations so characteristic of stratification on the other. However, the criteria and division lines have by now beome so vague that since 1960 the census no longer employs the distinction between 'worker' and 'white-collar worker'. We may, however, reconstruct this grouping from the sub-groups indicated by the census; also, many other types of empirical material still build on this distinction. We shall therefore, with the necessary reservations, continue to use 'worker' and 'white-collar worker' in this presentation of stratification.

In the 1920 census we find the following definition: 'By "worker" is meant persons whose occupations require a large amount of physical work. This category also includes inspectors and foremen, who are in large part recruited from the ranks of such workers.' The official Bureau of Statistics *(Statistisk Sentralbyrå)* recognized two groups of white-collar workers: 1) administrative and sales workers, and 2) professional workers. The first category includes all types of office workers – from the director to the unpaid trainee – as well as warehouse and storeroom employees, shop and store employees, salesmen, and travelling salesmen. The second category includes a long list of dissimilar occupations – from engineers to emissaries, ship captains to midwives. Minor civil servants are usually classified as 'workers', although there is no consistent practice on this particular point (Fivelsdal 1964, p. 4).

Seierstad's chapter on Norwegian economy states that 'In the present century there has been considerable income equalization between workers and white-collar workers', but it is also shown that inequalities still exist between the two groups.

Examining this more closely in Table I, the transport workers' monthly earnings may be taken as a rough estimate of the average income for industrial workers. We then see that certain large groups of white-collar workers earn nearly twice as much as transport workers. All white-collar groups in this survey averaged higher earnings than did the transport workers, although admittedly the difference between them was often small. If we study the monthly earnings of the youngest age group, however, we see the transport workers ranking high, considerably above most of the white-collar groups. White-collar income increases appreciably with age, which is not the case for workers.

Female white-collar workers' earnings are considerably lower than those of the men. This is in part because the women are, in general,

Table I. *Monthly earnings for various white-collar groups,*
by sex and age, 1967 (in N. kr.)

Occupation	Total monthly earnings		Monthly earnings at age 18-19	
	Men	Women	Men	Women
Municipal government employees:				
Administrative employees	2,476	1,775	1,100	1,081
Technical employees	2,134	1,879	1,200	—
Other municipal employees	1,988	1,635	1,439	1,234
Total	2,176	1,726	1,237	1,133
White-collar workers in firms belonging to NAF (Norwegian Employers' Association):				
Technical employees	2,757	1,229	953	970
Supervisors	2,407	1,635	1,933*	—
Office workers	2,449	1,448	983	917
Warehouse and storeroom personnel	1,951	1,409	1,014	—
Shop employees	1,845	1,398	982	865
Retail trade:				
Office workers	2,445	1,446	1,084	982
Shop employees	1,679	1,135	995	814
Warehouse and storeroom personnel	1,750	—	1,115	—
Sales superintendents	2,618	—	1,178	—
Bank employees	2,517	1,652	1,009	980
Insurance employees	3,156	1,757	926	961
Transport workers	1,586	—	1,284	—

Sources: NOS A 260, Table IV, p. 46; mimeo Table from Central Bureau of Statistics: 'Monthly earnings in NAF's member firms, by occupation and age, 1 September 1967'; NOS A 211, Table 4, p. 9; NOS A 215, Table 2, p. 9; NOS A 216, Table II, p. 15.

* Monthly earnings at age 20-24.

much younger than the men. At the same time, fewer of the women – even those permanently connected to an occupation – attain the higher positions. Women are less socially mobile with age than are men. It is misleading to consider the family as a unit in the stratification, as this may cover important social inequalities between spouses, inequalities which may also have repercussions on the rank relationships within the family as a social system.

Some of the inequalities visible in Table I are connected with educational inequalities. In 1950, 24 per cent of the white-collar workers had attended *realskole* (total of ten years of schooling), and 21 per cent had taken *examen artium* (total twelve years), whereas the figures for manual workers were 3 and 1 per cent (NOS XI 323, p. 25). Table II illustrates the influence of education upon income within certain special groups of white-collar workers. Within the

117

Table II. *Monthly earnings for various white-collar groups by education and sex, 1967 (in N. kr.)*

Occupation	University level		High school, commercial high school, technical school		Without such education	
	Men	Women	Men	Women	Men	Women
Municipal government employees	3,900	3,315	2,623	2,035	2,012	1,665
Bank employees	4,060		2,741	1,952	2,259	1,579
Insurance employees	3,894		2,790	1,815	2,149	1,386

Sources: NOS A 206, Oslo 1967, Table V, p. 54; NOS A 215, Table V, p. 16; NOS A 147, Table VI, p. 20.

group employed in municipal government, the most highly educated earned nearly twice as much as those with the lowest level of education. Women's earnings are generally much lower than men's, but women profit as much economically from higher education as men.

4. OCCUPATIONAL PRESTIGE

Stratification is not merely objective, concerned with the distribution of benefits and burdens. It also expresses itself in the reciprocal judgments members of a society make concerning one another. Some have more respect and prestige than others, and this prestige is related to income, occupation, and education. Concerning the relative prestige of various occupations, thorough investigations are available from many countries, Denmark for example (Svalastoga and Wolf 1963). From Norway we have only small, scattered investigations, which do not give a firm enough basis to construct a hierarchy of occupations arranged according to awarded social prestige.

An investigation of sociology students' ranking of occupational titles strengthens the impression that the conclusions reached in other industrialized countries hold true, in large part, for Norway as well. There are only a few, minor discrepancies between the ranking made by Norwegian students and that made by a representative sample of the Danish population (Øyen 1964).

Another investigation sheds light on how elementary and high-school teachers evaluate their own occupational prestige as compared with a selection of other occupations. Here too it was found that the correspondence between the various interviewees' evaluations was good, although there was a certain vacillation in evaluating occupa-

118

Table III. Elementary and high-school teachers' evaluation of their own occupational prestige relative to to that of others. In per cent

Evaluation of own occupation relative to others	Other occupations									
	Doctor	Office manager	High school teacher	Engineer	Architect	Lawyer	Elementary school teacher	Skilled worker	Bank assistant	Commercial traveller
Elementary school teacher evaluates other occupation as										
higher than his own	89	85	74	78	77	66	—	3	3	5
equal to his own	8	11	23	16	15	26	—	49	40	20
lower than his own	3	4	3	6	8	8	—	48	57	75
Total .... Number = 300	100	100	100	100	100	100	—	100	100	100
High school teacher evaluates other occupation as										
higher than his own	78	56	—	21	35	14	8	5	5	6
equal to his own ...	18	37	—	74	62	81	24	14	7	5
lower than his own..	4	7	—	5	3	5	71	78	88	89
Total .... Number = 100	100	100	—	100	100	100	100	100	100	100

Source: Aubert et al. 1956.

119

tions considered to be situated near one's own on the prestige scale (see Table III) (Aubert et al. 1956).

5. SOCIAL MOBILITY

Education, occupation, income, and prestige are systematically interconnected, although it has not been possible here to indicate more than a fraction of the total pattern. There exist rather large inequalities in the distribution of these rewards even in a welfare society. However, there also exist ideologies of equality which do not necessarily reject such forms of inequality: these claim not equality in the distribution of benefits, but equal chances of obtaining the favourable positions in the stratification structure. This at once raises the question of the recruitment mechanisms and how the highly-valued, well-paid occupations are recruited. It is a question of the degree of social mobility.

The questions of changes in degree of inequality and of changes in social mobility can hardly be treated separately. As the gap between the lower and the higher strata decreases, as measured by income and prestige differences, recruitment from the lower to the higher strata increases. Increasing mobility can be seen both as the result of the fact that the 'route' between strata has been shortened and as the result of the fact that the barriers surrounding highly-valued occupations have begun to fall. They are, in other words, two sides of the same coin.

Social mobility implies that changes take place in the individual's place in the stratification structure. Here we shall discuss two types of mobility: that within the individual's life cycle, and that between two generations.

5.1. *Mobility within the individual's life cycle*

According to one view of stratification, children and young persons have low social rank. Increasing upward mobility comes with increasing age, until a certain point where rank frequently becomes stabilized, only to fall when the individual reaches retirement age. According to another view, the unit of stratification is the family, so that children and young people enjoy the same social rank as their parents. It seems reasonable to assume that the individual's rank is determined both by age and by parental rank. The division between generations seems, to some extent, to function as a difference in status or as a class division.

Due to the enormous expansion in the school and university system, young people must now spend many, many years as 'employees' – and

120

subordinate ones at that – at the country's largest 'work place'. The general social regularities concerning the relations between those in power and those subject to command and control apply in such a situation as well. We find clear tendencies towards the formation of 'pupil collectives' within a school class, for example. And in the years to come we may expect increased organized opposition, criticism, and demands from school pupils and students.

On the other hand, older pupils and students can normally count on social 'promotion' after completing their examinations. As a rule, they will end up in relatively well-paid positions in well-regarded occupations. The fact that upper-class youth were previously willing to put up with an inhumane and highly frustrating milieu – the case with the English public schools – was probably connected with the knowledge that this was a preparation for membership in an exclusive, privileged social stratum. Anticipating their high social rank, the pupils did not identify themselves with their present situation. Social equalization has, however, had an important effect here: young people at schools and universities today cannot count on automatically ending up in any such exclusive, privileged group. Competition is very strong indeed. To many it may appear as if the demands for investing time and energy in occupational preparation are immoderately great, whereas the reward is, relatively speaking, moderate indeed.

We may obtain information concerning mobility within the individual's lifetime from wage statistics by age, for various occupations and trades. Among white-collar workers there were quite notable increases in wage level with age, up to a maximum in the 50s (NOS XIII 218, p. 253, and NOS A 206, pp. 46 ff.). Whereas male office workers aged 18–19 earn scarcely N. kr. 1000 a month, white-collar workers over 40 years of age average more than N. kr. 2700. With age comes not only higher income, but also more independence, more responsibility, and more prestige. Now, such a table represents a static picture and not the shifts that took place during one and the same person's lifetime. The man who today is 50 years old and earns N. kr. 2700 a month probably had, in his youth, a lower real income than has his young colleague who today earns N. kr. 1000. While the former has ascended the wage staircase, the staircase itself has rolled upwards, expressing the general increase in real income level in society. But other interpretations are also possible. Some of the older white-collar workers with higher incomes may well have had more education than the young ones and could therefore enter the profession at a higher level from the very beginning. This would be the case with careers in the governmental bureaucracy, for example. But the opposite may also obtain – that the younger white-collar workers are better educated than their older colleagues, and that this is one reason why we see a decline in wage level at 50–60 years of age.

All in all, however, there is reason to believe that salary differences by age for white-collar workers reflect the stages of a career. A comparable sort of progress in career cannot be found among blue-collar workers. Some blue-collar workers may make a leap, for instance by becoming foremen, but wage conditions for the mass of workers improve no more, in general, than the general standard of living. Workers stand still on the wage escalator, whereas white-collar workers ascend the escalator, relative to its own movement as well. Certain groups – seamen, for example – are differently situated, in that increasing age, sometimes but not necessarily supplemented by relatively brief further schooling, results in much higher wages. This contrast in the lifetime career pattern between white- and blue-collar workers helps create notable divergences in attitude and life style. This is probably of considerable importance in the class identifications and political loyalties of members of these occupations as well.

Lysgaard has found that approximately 4 per cent of Norwegian workers expect to be promoted to the rank of foreman (Lysgaard 1965, p. 127). On the basis of estimates from the Institute for Work Management *(Institutt for arbeidsledelse)* concerning the actual need for foremen, Lysgaard concludes that this percentage does in fact closely reflect reality. Of his sample, 4 per cent indicate that they wish to become self-employed, but exactly how this corresponds to the actual possibilities is not known. In any case, we may conclude that scarcely every tenth worker, perhaps considerably fewer, can count on social mobility which will bring him out of the ranks of common workers. True, we have not taken into consideration the fact that some workers, functioning as shop stewards, union representatives, and local politicians, achieve social rank above the average. But this number is also low, and we must conclude that, without doubt, the chances of individual mobility are far greater among white-collar workers than among non-white-collar workers.

5.2. Mobility between generations

We shall measure mobility between generations by comparing the occupations (or occupational plans) of fathers and sons. One approach is to compare the distribution of fathers' and sons' occupations without regard to kinship. Table IV employs this method and also enables us to make comparisons with two neighbouring countries.

Table IV shows occupational mobility in 1950 higher in Norway than in Finland, but lower than in Sweden. Of blue-collar workers' sons, 29 per cent in Sweden, 19 per cent in Norway, and 11 per cent

Table IV. *Social mobility: Norway, Sweden, and Finland, 1950 (percentage)*

Son's occupation	Father's occupation			
	White-collar	Blue-collar	Agriculture	Total
Norway:				
White-collar	61	19	12	23
Blue-collar	35	72	30	48
Agriculture	4	9	58	29
Total	100	100	100	100
Percentage of all fathers	17	39	44	100
Finland:				
White-collar	64	11	9	17
Blue-collar	24	56	21	35
Agriculture	12	33	70	48
Total	100	100	100	100
Percentage of all fathers	12	39	49	100
Sweden:				
White-collar	72	29	23	34
Blue-collar	24	64	42	47
Agriculture	4	7	35	19
Total	100	100	100	100
Percentage of all fathers	18	36	46	100

Source: Rogoff Ramsøy 1961, p. 229.

The proportion of all sons who leave father's type of occupation is for Norway 35 per cent, for Finland 34 per cent, and for Sweden 46 per cent.

in Finland became white-collar workers. Among sons of farmers and other agricultural workers, 65 per cent in Sweden, 42 per cent in Norway, and 30 per cent in Finland changed occupations. It is not quite clear exactly what this means in terms of movement upwards or downwards in the stratification structure. But it seems reasonable to assume that the movement from primary to secondary sector, and from secondary sector to tertiary sector means more social mobility upwards than downwards. To get a total picture we must, of course, also take into consideration the movement from tertiary to secondary sector and from secondary to primary sector, but this movement is certainly not frequent. The principal impression remains, therefore, that Norway lies between Sweden and Finland as regards possibilities for upward mobility, and is situated somewhat nearer to Sweden than to Finland.

Table V is based on occupational distributions of a cohort of sons and their fathers, according to place of residence. For sons we have used occupational *plans*. According to this Table, mobility is greatest in municipalities where the primary sector is dominant, and least in the most economically developed areas (Rogoff Ramsøy

Table V. *Dissimilarity between fathers' and sons' occupational distribution, by type of municipality*

Type of municipality	Dissimilarity index*
Oslo	16.7
Other cities and large towns	20.8
Suburbs	22.1
Industrial townships	29.1
Townships with mixed livelihoods	36.5
Agricultural and forestry areas	35.1
Fishing communities	38.0
All municipalities and areas	31.7

Source: Rogoff Romsøy 1966a, Table 1, p. 220-221.

* Fathers and sons were divided into seven occupational categories. The percentage distributions were compared. The index value expresses the percentage of sons who would have to change occupation to have an occupational distribution identical with the fathers.

1966a). This seems connected with geographical mobility from the periphery in towards the centre, and must not be understood as indicating that the stratification structure in rural society is more open than that in towns and cities. Also, doubts may arise here as to which changes in rank do accompany occupational mobility. In particular there may be doubt concerning how often an individual who changes his occupation from fishing or agriculture to industrial work thereby increases his prestige. But income does increase, as a rule.

Table VI gives us an idea of social mobility in 1965. A comparison of Table VI with the Norwegian data in Table IV provides a certain basis for evaluating changes in mobility in Norway between 1950 and 1965. However, whereas the first sample consisted entirely of 19-year-olds, the second was a cross-section of the adult population; and this in itself is sufficient to create major discrepancies in the measure of

Table VI. *Own occupation according to father's, 1965 (percentage)*

| Own occupation | Father's occupation | | | |
	White-collar, independent	Blue-collar	Agriculture, fishing	Total
White-collar independent	68.2	31.7	25.7	37.6
Worker	27.9	62.4	35.2	43.9
Agriculture, fishing	3.0	5.9	39.1	18.5
Total	100	100	100	100
N	384	641	668	1,693

Source: Unpublished Tables from election survey, 1965, provided by Henry Valen.

mobility. Still, it is worth mentioning that in 1965 more sons of blue-collar workers and farmers or fishermen became white-collar workers than was the case in 1950. Further, more of the farmers' sons became workers, and fewer of them farmers. This must be connected with the expansion of the tertiary sector and the movement away from rural areas.

From two specialized surveys of white- and blue-collar workers we have data on recruitment to these two broad occupational categories. Table VII shows rather large inequalities in the social origins of white-collar workers and of workers. This is especially true of the proportion of those having middle-class fathers in the two groups, and likewise the proportion having fathers as blue-collar workers. On the other hand, there is about an equal number of farmers, fishermen, and artisans in the two sets of fathers. But it is possible that a finer classification of the material would have shown that blue- and white-collar workers have their origins in somewhat differing social strata within, for example the primary sector.

We have no data from earlier periods which we could compare with the above Tables. Therefore, any attempts at ascertaining long-range tendencies in social mobility in Norway will have to be made on the basis of data on recruitment to certain top-level groups, cabinet members and Parliament members, academic professions and business people. These elite groups have been more or less open for recruitment from other strata. While bureaucracy and officialdom, and industry and trade as well, have had the door open only a crack to sons of farmers and workers, certain leading political positions have had a brisk recruitment from precisely these social strata. But this is not to say that recruitment to the cabinet, for example, has been truly representative as regards the social background of members.

Table VII. *White-collar and blue-collar workers, by father's occupation (percentage)*

Father's occupation	White-collar workers	Blue-collar workers
Middle-class occupation	29	7
Farmers	19	22
Fishermen, seamen	5	7
Independent, artisans	7	7
Foremen, lower civil servants	13	6
Workers	26	50
No answer	1	1
Total	100	100
N	1,497	1,411

Sources: For white-collar workers: unpublished data provided by Egil Fivelsdal; for blue-collar workers: Lysgaard 1965, Table 6.2, p. 133.

Before the introduction of parliamentary government, cabinet members were recruited mainly from the ranks of bureaucracy and officialdom, both as to father's occupation and own occupation previous to becoming a cabinet member. The ranks of farmers and workers were totally without representation in the cabinet. The situation changed gradually, so that in the period between 1905 and World War II, one-third of the cabinet members came from farming backgrounds. But even after the war, under Labour governments, the working class has been highly under-represented in the cabinet – although somewhat less so than in earlier times (see Table VIII).

Table IX shows that recruitment to the Storting (Parliament) differed from recruitment to cabinet posts, from as early as 1814. Even before the introduction of parliamentary government, farmers and farmers' sons occupied a rather strong position in the Storting, and this became further strengthened in 1884. Workers, on the other hand, have always been few in number in the Storting.

Of nominations to the Storting election in 1957, workers comprised scarcely 9 per cent of all elected representatives, and 17.5 per cent of the remaining candidates on the ballots – and this despite the fact that workers made up a full 55 per cent of the total working population, according to the 1950 census. Groups statistically over-represented in the ballots and in the Storting were farmers, white-collar workers, and, to a certain degree, independent businessmen. Persons in various white-collar occupations comprised 40 per cent of Storting representatives in 1957, as against 25 per cent of the working population (Valen 1966, p. 186).

Of Storting representatives elected in 1965, only 5 per cent were workers (including foremen and employed artisans). 19 per cent were (subordinate) white-collar workers, 7 per cent journalists (including editors), 3 per cent housewives, and 9 per cent held salaried positions in political parties or related organizations. The rest, some 60 per cent, were either in independent business (including farmers) or in leading administrative or professional positions (Hernes, unpublished material).

Torgersen has made an investigation of recruitment to leading positions in trade and industry, based on data from the Norwegian Who's Who (Hvem er hvem). In three selected years – 1912, 1938, 1959 – Torgersen found about the same proportion: one half, whose fathers had the same occupation as themselves. Between 5 and 9 per cent came from farming families, and a few per cent from the working class. It would thus seem that the gate of entry to these leading positions is quite narrow, nor has it widened, according to Torgersen's findings, in the course of the period covered by his data. Between 1912 and 1959, however, a considerable change had taken place in the edu-

Table VIII. Cabinet members according to father's and own occupation, 1814–1960. In per cent

Occupation	Year when first appointed							
	1814–1883		1884–1904		1905–1944		1945–1960	
	Father's	Own	Father's	Own	Father's	Own	Father's	Own
Professional, official, other civil servant	65.7	91.5	60.3	79.7	29.5	57.5	31.4	64.6
Business, owner or leader	18.6	8.6	14.3	15.9	15.1	17.8	5.9	2.0
Private office worker, junior	14.3	–	9.5	–	6.8	–	11.8	7.8
Farmer	–	–	11.1	1.6	33.6	13.7	25.5	7.8
Teacher	–	–	1.6	3.2	3.4	3.4	3.9	–
Artisan	1.4	–	–	–	6.2	2.1	9.8	3.9
Worker	–	–	1.6	–	5.5	2.1	9.8	3.9
No information	–	–	1.6	–	–	3.4	2.0	9.8
Total	100.0	100.1	100.0	100.4	100.1	100.1	100.1	99.8
Number	70		63		146		51	

Table IX. Members of Parliament according to father's and own occupation, 1814–1945. In per cent

Occupation	Year when first elected					
	1814–1883		1884–1913		1914–1945	
	Father's	Own	Father's	Own	Father's	Own
Professional, higher civil servant	27.7	39.7	12.3	22.9	13.7	28.7
Business, owner or leader	18.5	21.2	12.5	17.7	11.8	13.5
Private office worker, junior	5.3	2.6	5.5	2.1	4.4	4.5
Civil servant, junior	4.1	5.1	3.2	5.7	1.6	4.4
Farmer	28.7	24.5	47.6	34.4	44.9	28.3
Teacher	2.5	4.7	3.1	7.0	4.2	6.0
Artisan	3.4	1.0	8.7	5.4	7.4	5.4
Worker	2.3	1.0	5.8	3.0	10.6	3.9
No information	7.1	0.1	1.1	0.4	0.2	1.1
Others	0.4	0.4	–	1.7	1.0	5.1
Total	100.0	100.3	99.8	99.9	100.0	100.0
Number	1,986		997		865	

cational level of those in the business world, which means that the channels of entry into the topmost positions have been somewhat broadened. We find that this increase in educational level is concentrated among the 'newcomers', whose fathers were not in business. Earlier, such newcomers probably were gradually promoted upwards in the firm, while they today seem to enter it higher up, thanks to a more solid educational background (Torgersen 1964).

Table X shows recruitment to all types of university and professional courses of study from 1810 to 1955. While the changes are considerable, they have taken place very gradually. Self-recruitment to the academic fields has been halved in the course of this period. The first change is not apparent until around 1870, when the sons of farmers, (elementary-school) teachers, and subordinate white-collar workers began to be better represented in academic studies. On the other hand, there was as yet no change in the representation of working-class sons. They began to appear in academic studies about the time of World War I, and their participation increased again in the 1950s.

However, we should recall that considerable changes have taken place in the frequency of the various fathers' occupations in the general population. Much of the increase in working-class sons' representation in academic studies previous to 1960 is due to the great increase in the number of industrial workers in the population during this period. The same is true of subordinate white-collar workers. On the other hand, the number of farmers in the general population has sunk in recent years, so that the tendency to enter academic studies has been somewhat higher than the constant percentage would indicate. Even the most recent figures on recruitment to higher education show that it is still far from the case that children from all social strata have the same chances of entering these highly coveted careers.

As to social mobility of the working class in the future, data concerning workers' plans for their children's education can give us some ideas. Of a nationwide sample, 9 per cent report that they only plan on the children's completing elementary school and nothing more. Of those willing to talk of their plans for their children, 48 per cent report that they have considered *realskole* (10 years' schooling) and 25 per cent mention high school (total of 12 years' schooling) (Lysgaard 1965, pp. 131 ff.). Here we may clearly discern the contours of a large and increasing inter-generational mobility, even though not all these parents' plans may be realized. The working class's traditional exclusion from lengthy schooling seems well on its way to becoming an historical phenomenon.

Table X. – Academics, engineers and officers according to father's occupation and year of graduation, 1910–1955. In per cent

Father's occupation	Own graduation in period									
	1810–1829[1]	1830–1849[2]	1850–1869[3]	1870–1889[4]	1890–1909[5]	1910–1929	1930–1939[6]	1940–1949[7]	1950–1955[8]	Total
Profesionals, etc.	52.2	48.4	52.0	38.7	33.0	30.8	27.9	27.1	23.3	31.7
Business owners	19.7	24.5	21.5	22.9	23.1	21.6	18.9	18.2	14.6	20.2
Office worker	11.7	11.5	10.8	13.5	16.1	16.5	17.7	20.2	19.9	17.0
Farmer	3.7	3.9	4.4	10.1	12.3	13.0	12.8	9.3	12.2	10.9
Teacher	2.3	2.9	1.9	3.4	5.4	5.6	7.3	7.1	6.0	5.7
Artisan	2.5	3.6	5.0	8.0	4.8	4.9	6.8	6.0	4.7	5.5
Worker	1.2	1.5	0.8	1.6	1.8	3.2	4.9	6.5	11.5	4.5
No information	6.7	3.7	3.6	1.8	3.4	4.4	3.7	5.6	7.8	4.5
Total	100.0	100.0	100.0	100.0	99.9	100	100.0	100.0	100.0	100.0
Numbers	598	1,560	1,448	2,541	5,038	7,490	5,761	6,501	3,759	34,696

[1] Theological and medical degrees from 1810, law degrees from 1815.
[2] Philological degrees reckoned from 1820.
[3] Natural science degrees from 1850.
[4] Officers (Military College in Oslo) from 1880.
[5] Engineers from 1901.
[6] Law degrees from 1940 included here.
[7] Included here are law graduates who graduated in the years 1941–55 if they had examen artium before 1943; medical graduates from years 1940–51; the period does not include officers.
[8] Here are only law graduates with examen artium from 1946 and law graduates 1950–55. Information on officers refers here only to candidates in 1950–60; the period does not include medical graduates.

6. MARRIAGE AND STRATIFICATION

Since marriage implies a certain degree of equality between partners, it may contribute to changing the former social rank of one (or both). The traditional case of the woman who married 'beneath her position' expresses the possibility of social degradation. Marriage may indeed bring mobility either upwards or downwards. But it may also be seen in a different light, in that the choice of marriage partner is interpreted as resulting from the spouses' previous social rank.

Øyen has investigated data on marriage banns published in Oslo in January 1963. The method was to compare couples with respect to their occupational titles. From this he found a strong tendency towards homogamy: marriages at the same prestige level take place far more often than would be the case with random distribution. The marriages seem, as a rule, to confirm a rank already established, instead of promoting mobility. Few sink or rise in social rank simply as a consequence of marriage (Øyen 1964).

Natalie Rogoff Ramsøy made a major survey of all marriage banns published in 1962 in which the bride or bridegroom lived in Oslo, a total of 5,000 cases. Both partners were classified according to occupation, and the results showed a high degree of occupational homogamy (see Table XI). About one-third of the couples had the same occupation before marriage. Of college graduates (male) 58 per cent married women who were either college graduates, (elementary-school) teachers, or employed in responsible office positions. By contrast, only 12 per cent of semi-skilled or non-skilled workers married women in similar occupations (Rogoff Ramsøy, 1966).

These results are in line with what Eilert Sundt found in eastern and southern Norway more than 100 years ago (Sundt 1855, 1967). He too found a widespread tendency for couples to choose their partners from within the social stratum they themselves belonged to. Sundt studied 8,933 couples married in 1851 and 1852, classifying the women and men according to which of the two broad social strata – the propertied and the working class – they belonged to. Classification was made on the basis of the person's own position, or that of the parents (father). Of all men of the propertied class, 79 per cent married women from the same class, and 88 per cent of the working-class men married women from that same class. The men married 'beneath their position' somewhat more frequently than did the women. This is probably connected with the fact that men usually do not lose rank as a consequence of marriage, whereas women assume their husbands' rank and therefore decline in social rank when marrying beneath their position. For special groups we have more detailed data concerning the tendency to social homogamy. Torgersen's investigation also

Table XI. Bride's occupation according to bridegroom's occupation, Oslo 1962. In per cent

Bridegroom's occupation	Bride's occupation						Total	Number of bride-grooms
	Academics, students	Teachers, technicians, senior office workers	Junior office workers	Sales-women	Service and manual work	No occupation		
Academics, students..........	20.1	48.4	19.3	2.2	4.9	5.1	100.0	816
Teachers, technicians, senior office workers, independent	2.5	42.1	29.3	7.2	10.2	8.7	100.0	1,047
Junior office workers	1.3	25.6	35.7	9.4	19.9	8.1	100.0	694
Skilled workers	0.3	20.5	32.2	9.5	25.0	12.5	100.0	727
Semi- or unskilled workers	0.6	11.9	26.6	11.3	32.3	17.3	100.0	1,770
No occupation	0.9	21.5	19.6	2.8	16.8	38.4	100.0	107
All occupations	4.1	27.0	27.8	8.4	20.5	12.2	100.0	5,161
Number of brides...........	212	1,394	1,438	431	1,058	628		

Source: Rogoff Ramsøy 1966b, p. 778.

covers data on the fathers-in-law of businessmen, and he says: 'In general, it seems reasonable to conclude that marriage partners are recruited from very much the same social strata as those the businessmen come from themselves' (Torgersen 1964, p. 49).

As to university graduates' marriages, we have available data which for theology and law graduates reach all the way back to about 1800 (Aubert et al. 1961). At that time, clergymen showed a very strong tendency to marry clergymen's daughters – this was the case in more than half the marriages registered. Law graduates, however, did not show the same tendency to marry daughters of older colleagues, instead frequently marrying daughters of merchants, but extremely rarely those of farmers.

As to theology graduates' marriages from 1814 to today, we find that a considerable change has occurred toward less occupational homogamy, and in general less social homogamy. More and more clergymen's wives are daughters of farmers; there are also somewhat more daughters of workers and artisans in their ranks. Clergymen's daughters and daughters of other civil servants are less frequently found as clergymen's wives. A similar development, although not so marked, is seen to have occurred among lawyers. In general, homogamy among college graduates has been decreasing. This may in part be connected with the expansion in the number of college graduates, which means that the supply of daughters of college graduates has not kept pace with the demand.

For instance, more and more occupational groups are included in the middle, and in part the upper class to which university graduates belong. And throughout the whole period more university graduates married daughters of businessmen than the number who themselves had a business background. This indicates that marriages have been marked more by factors connected with vertical stratification than with horizontal occupational specialization.

7. POLITICS, MEMBERSHIP IN ORGANIZATIONS, AND SOCIAL CLASSES

Up to now we have analysed stratification through the distribution of characteristics by categories of persons. Many of these social characteristics have clear connections with organizations. Depending on their economic interests, people will join trade unions, other associations, and political parties. When organizations thus start on the basis of stratification, a class structure is created, a social structure embracing cooperation, conflict, and leadership in society. It is generally assumed that membership in trade unions and professional and political organizations in Norway is largely decided by the individual's occupation and access to society's benefits. This popular view is for the most part correct and has been verified by those systematic investigations which have been carried out. But these also provide a few modifications to the popular view.

A 1949 survey showed the connection between various important rank indicators and political preference (Holbæk-Hanssen 1951). For the various political parties, the percentage earning N. kr. 7,000 or more was as follows: Conservative *(Høyre)* 59 per cent, Liberal *(Venstre)* 37 per cent, Communist *(Kommunistpartiet)* 27 per cent, Christian People's Party *(Kristelig Folkeparti)* 26 per cent, Labour *(Arbeiderpartiet)* 24 per cent, Farmers' *(Bondepartiet)* 10 per cent. Clearly, income level varies from party to party. But these registered differences do not reflect the traditional split between the socialist and non-socialist parties, at any rate not very clearly. One important reason for this is the considerable discrepancy in income between city/town and rural areas, a discrepancy that confounds stratification as such. *Bondepartiet* (now called *Senterpartiet*) was not a 'proletariat party' to the degree perhaps indicated by income distribution. If we study the rural areas specifically, we find that both the Labour *(Arbeiderpartiet)* and the Communist *(Kommunistpartiet)* Party voters have near-average incomes. In the urban areas, on the other hand, the socialist parties more nearly represented a lower class, as measured by income.

Another important stratification indicator is education, and this too was unequally distributed by party. The proportions with more than eight years' schooling (i.e. above elementary-school level) were for *Høyre* 71 per cent, *Venstre* 50 per cent, *Bondepartiet* 32 per cent, *Kr. Folkeparti* 30 per cent, *Arbeiderpartiet* 22 per cent, and *Kommunistpartiet* 19 per cent. Here the differences would appear to correspond more closely to the traditional split between socialist and non-socialist. *Høyre* stands out clearly: its followers differ considerably from the average population with regard to access to important social rewards, via education. From this investigation it might be tempting to conclude that all the other parties could, to some extent, call themselves people's parties. This, however, is not the case if instead of income and educational level we use occupation as a basis for analysis.

The nation-wide interview survey conducted just before the 1957 Storting elections revealed the following percentages intending to vote socialist (i.e. Labour or Communist) among various occupational groups: industrial workers 65 per cent, other workers (excluding agriculture, forestry, and fishing) 56 per cent, workers in agriculture, forestry, and fishing 57 per cent, government-employed white-collar workers 30 per cent, non-government-employed white-collar workers

26 per cent, self-employed in agriculture, forestry, and fishing 24 per cent, other types of self-employed 10 per cent (Rokkan and Valen 1964, p. 212).

Table XII shows voting patterns in the 1965 election, by occupation. The connection between voting preference and the individual's place in the stratification structure appears strong, both here and in the 1957 survey. But there are also several divergences from what we would expect if party preference were determined solely by social rank. An analysis of this material, based on the hypothesis that the socialist parties are the parties of the underprivileged, shows that the pattern is far from consistent. Workers in agriculture, forestry and fishing have lower incomes than do industrial workers. All the same, they voted non-socialist more often than did the latter, in 1957 and probably in 1965 as well. Self-employed in agriculture and fishing also are, to a large extent, persons with very low incomes. Nonetheless, in both the 1957 and the 1965 Storting elections they voted, for the most part, non-socialist. This is most likely connected with the regional differences so important in Norwegian politics.

The connection between voting preference and occupation shows differing patterns for eastern Norway, southern and western Norway, the Trøndelag region, and for northern Norway. In southern and western Norway, workers are much less likely to vote socialist than they are throughout the country as a whole. On the other hand, both white-collar workers and farmers/fishermen in northern Norway are considerably more likely to vote socialist than are these groups in the rest of the country. In northern Norway and in southern and western Norway, politics are less clearly connected with class distinctions than is the case in eastern Norway. Members of the business world are as uniformly non-socialist in northern Norway as in the rest of the country, but all other residents of that region are underprivileged, so to speak, a fact not without influence on political voting patterns. The non-socialist voting pattern found among workers in southern and western Norway is connected with the widespread evangelical missions, the temperance movement, and the *nynorsk* language movement found in these regions.

Data from the Stavanger area in western Norway show disparities between occupation and voting within the region itself. Workers in the town of Stavanger have about the same party preferences as those throughout the country as a whole, but workers in rural districts are considerably more non-socialist (Valen and Katz 1964, p. 158). Also, the white-collar workers are more non-socialist (mainly Liberal) in rural districts than in Stavanger itself. This study confirms the impression given in Holbæk-Hanssen's investigation, that the tendency to vote socialist is less pronounced at the very lowest income levels than

Table XII. Voting pattern in 1965 according to own or breadwinner's occupation. In per cent

Voted	Workers	Lower civil servants	Lower office workers (private)	Higher civil servants	Higher office workers, managers	Independent business without employees	Independent business with employees	Small holders, fisher-men*	Farmers, forest-owners	Total
Communist	1	–	1	1	1	2	–	–	1	1
Socialist Left	7	4	8	2	3	3	1	2	–	5
Labour	64	48	40	25	22	33	9	33	15	43
Liberal	8	14	13	16	12	18	15	11	6	10
Christian People's Party	5	4	2	10	6	3	6	4	8	6
Centre Party	3	2	5	10	3	6	5	29	58	12
Conservative	5	16	21	35	50	26	57	14	8	17
Local small-party coalition	–	–	2	–	–	–	3	–	–	–
Did not vote	7	12	8	1	3	9	4	7	4	6
Total	100	100	100	100	100	100	100	100	100	100
Number	694	77	120	125	127	68	81	126	180	1,562

Source: Valen 1967, p. 115.
* including combination of farmers and workers.

at the middle ones. This is true of both Stavanger and the surrounding rural districts. Probably it is the unmarried persons with low incomes – frequently women – who vote non-socialist, preferring instead the Christian People's Party (Katz and Valen p. 164).

Some data are available on how social mobility influences voting. Although workers who are farmers' sons vote socialist far more frequently than their fathers would have done, they do not vote socialist as often as do workers from workers' homes (40 per cent against 68 per cent). White-collar workers from working-class homes vote socialist much less frequently than their fathers would have done, but considerably more often than white-collar workers from farming or white-collar backgrounds (Katz and Valen p. 170). When the individual chooses standpoints and loyalties on the basis of his position in the stratum hierarchy, this is not due only to occupational and income conditions. The type of childhood home may long remain an influence, frequently life-long. Seip has maintained that 'A man's opinions are, as a rule, less influenced by where he comes from, and more by where he intends to go' (Seip 1964, p. 104). However, the Katz and Valen study indicates that social origins can be decisive as regards choice of party and can, for a while at least, dominate a person's views.

The various occupational statuses and social strata show differing degrees of support for the various political parties. But within each party there seems to be a somewhat more uniform principle dividing the passive members from the active participants. Table XIII shows how groups with higher social rank dominate as leaders in most parties, whereas workers comprise a rather large percentage of the regular voters in all parties. Even the Labour Party has almost as many from middle-class occupations in its higher positions as it has workers there. True, this Table is based on data from a local study of the Stavanger area and need not necessarily be valid for the country as a whole. But it is highly probable that the pattern shown here, which also fits in with many other observations, is also to be found throughout the nation.

Politics is one of the structures joining people together and giving them channels of influence and creating loyalties and leadership so that mutual interests – whether real or imagined – can be furthered. But there are other ways of realizing such goals. Professional and trade unions have much of the same character and are indeed sometimes intimately connected with political organs. Major studies are now available of organizational membership among Norwegian blue- and white-collar workers.

These studies confirm the impressions mentioned earlier that workers have a higher degree of participation in trade/professional organizations than have white-collar workers. The percentage of

137

Table XIII. *Occupations of party leaders, active supporters, and ordinary voters, according to party, Stavanger. In per cent*

Occupation	Labour			Liberal			Chr. People's Party			Centre Party			Conservative		
	Leaders	Active supporters	Voters	Leaders	Active supporters	Voters	Leaders	Active supporters	Voters	Leaders	Active supporters	Voters	Leaders	Active supporters	Voters
Workers	52	83	79	4	25	34	19	36	50	5	3	24	6	8	27
Office workers...	41	13	13	73	54	39	43	29	21	–	6	8	55	64	36
Farmers	–	1	3	3	13	7	19	16	22	95	91	67	3	4	6
Independent, others	7	3	5	19	8	20	19	19	7	–	–	1	36	24	31
Total	100	100	100	100	100	100	100	100	100	100	100	100	100	100	100
Number	42	116	246	26	24	143	26	31	58	19	32	63	35	25	86

Source: Valen 1963, p. 9.

138

workers in such organizations was found to be 73 per cent, a somewhat higher figure than that arrived at by experts within LO (Norwegian National Federation of Labour), their figure being 65 per cent (Lysgaard 1964). Fifty-eight per cent of white-collar workers are organized, whereof 42 per cent are in unions associated with LO (Fivelsdal 1964). The difference between blue- and white-collar workers is clear, though not striking. Also, it decreases somewhat if we consider only males.

Neither blue- nor white-collar workers are homogeneous categories – a fact also true of membership rate. In the survey of workers, the organizational rate is highest among those earning more than N. kr. 20,000 a year (90 per cent organized), sinking gradually with lower incomes, and lowest – only 42 per cent – for groups with incomes under N. kr. 11,000. Lysgaard comments: 'The highly-organized stand in the centre, the poorly-organized at the periphery within the Norwegian worker population. By the terms 'centre' and 'periphery' I mean not merely geographical location, but a more general type of placement close to or far-removed from the commonly preferred positions within a structure' (Lysgaard 1964, p. 73).

Heterogeneity is even more pronounced among white-collar workers. Seventy per cent of male government-employed white-collar workers are organized in LO, as against only 21 per cent of the privately employed (Fivelsdal 1964, p. 69). The lowest rate of organization is to be found among private office, sales, and warehouse employees. The connection between income and degree of organization among white-collar workers is also different from that among blue-collar workers. True, we also find here the largest number of non-organized persons in the lowest income groups (N. kr. 7,000–13,000 a year). The tendency towards LO membership reaches its peak in the middle-income groups (N. kr. 16,000–17,000), whereas the tendency towards membership in other unions is highest in the topmost income group (N. kr. 20,000–35,000). This pattern is about the same for national government, local government, and private employment (Fivelsdal 1964, pp. 45 ff.).

There appears to be good correspondence between upward social mobility within the working class and LO membership. This, however, does not hold for white-collar workers, and particularly not for those in privately owned firms. With high income, the tendency towards LO membership decreases greatly, while the probability of membership in non-LO unions increases. The increase in rank a white-collar worker attains in the course of his career has consequences which may easily bring him outside the circles of solidarity LO represents. This may be due partly to the fact that he find himself in the work situation on the opposite side in negotiations. Or his income

139

level may become so high that he has other reasons – progressive taxation, for example – for opposing LO's political views. While the worker's career seems limited to one social class, many white-collar workers will in the course of their careers cross the border between classes – a border symbolized by membership in various types of organizations and unions, for example.

So far, we have interpreted social class as an intervening variable, a construction that explains the connection between access to benefits and organizational or party affiliation. But workers have also been asked directly to which class they regard themselves as belonging. Here, the majority regarded themselves without reservation as belonging to the working class, but one-third had reservations or answered 'the middle class'. Both class identification and organizational affiliation influence party preference. Of the non-organized workers who regard themselves as belonging to the middle class the majority vote non-socialist.

Among non-organized workers, those of middle-class origins are divided fairly evenly into non-socialist and socialist, whereas both father's occupation and own regional location are less important for party preference among organized workers. Among the non-organized, there are especially many non-socialists in western Norway and the Stavanger region of southern Norway. This supports the findings of Rokkan and Valen that class structure in Norway is, to a certain extent, locally determined.

8. LIFE STYLES AND CONSUMPTION

Such expressions as 'working-class culture', 'fine culture', 'pop culture', and 'culture of poverty' indicate that there exist differences in life styles which are connected with stratification. Data on this are rather meagre in Norway, and those we do have refer to scattered phenomena, so that it is difficult to ascertain any clear system. The division into occupational or income groups is seldom a satisfactory one; thus the division blue-collar/white-collar worker, with all its shortcomings, is frequently the best we have to go on.

When stratification is perceived as a distribution pattern, it is reasonable to inquire how various occupational and income factors influence the individual's and the family's consumption patterns. It is well known that workers, and low-income groups in general, spend relatively more of their income on food than do white-collar workers and others with higher incomes. This is another facet of the situation that demand for foodstuffs is less elastic than the demand for clothes, for instance.

140

According to a 1958 consumer survey, working-class families spent 33 per cent of their income on food; white-collar families spent 26 per cent (NOS A 31, 1961). In absolute amount, however, white-collar households spent more than blue-collars'. The detailed expenditure figures on food budgets show that white-collar workers spent somewhat more on luxuries – such things as butter, poultry, shellfish, grapes – than did blue-collar workers,, who spent relatively more on pork, herring, margarine, and potatoes. The white-collar workers dined out more frequently. Alcohol should probably be counted as luxury expenditure, and here white-collar workers bought mostly wine and spirits, while workers had a higher consumption of beer. Some differences may also be explained on the basis of health norms: white-collar workers spent relatively more on vegetables while workers spent more on coffee.

As the differences are not large, they do not permit definite conclusions. More important is money spent on housing and other items requiring capital. Relatively, white-collar workers spent only slightly more on living accommodation than did workers (11 as against 10 per cent), but in absolute figures the difference is quite large. This indicates, first of all, a higher standard of living accommodation among white-collar workers. The fact that workers spent more on firewood and white-collar workers more on fuel oil indicates that white-collar workers' homes are more modern than those of workers. In this connection it is interesting to note that workers and white-collar workers live in different areas, with all the social consequences this situation implies. For Oslo, it has been shown that the occupational distribution varies, sometimes considerably, in the different residential areas in the city (see Table XIV). There are areas dominated by white-collar workers and self-employed tradesmen, and areas dominated by industrial workers. However, there also exist mixed areas. It appears as if the connection between place of residence and type of occupation has, within Oslo, been weakened by the housing shortage following World War II and the consequent program of building in new areas. The distinction between those living 'east' and 'west (of the Aker River) is much less pronounced today than was the case before the war (Rogoff Ramsøy and Iversen 1967, pp. 30–31).

A study made by Mathiesen, however, indicates that distinctions influencing local environment still exist (Mathiesen 1966). In this study, an upper-middle-class district on the west side of Oslo was compared with a working-class district on the east side. The comparison dealt with young boys' relations with home and friends. It was found that west-side boys spent considerably more leisure time at home than did the boys living on the east side. The latter spent more time on the streets with friends, or going for walks, than did the boys on the west

Table XIV. *District of residence according to occupation, Oslo 1962. In per cent.*

District	Academic	Admini- strative and sales	Junior office workers	Occupation Skilled workers, ancillary	Semi- and unskilled workers	No occupation	All occupations
Vestre Aker, Ullern	19.2	14.2	6.2	5.6	4.8	12.7	9.3
West	26.6	22.1	19.4	12.4	10.7	10.1	16.6
Nydalen	16.7	9.4	8.2	6.5	7.5	6.3	9.2
North-west	8.5	9.0	5.9	6.9	5.1	3.8	6.8
Central	4.6	4.9	6.9	7.2	7.2	1.3	5.8
Nordstrand	3.4	3.8	6.3	3.6	5.0	1.3	4.4
Grorud	5.6	9.9	13.3	15.3	16.1	13.9	12.7
North	3.6	6.2	9.3	11.4	11.1	13.9	8.9
Østensjø	6.5	7.0	8.8	9.7	11.0	6.3	8.9
East	6.3	13.5	15.7	24.0	21.5	30.4	17.4
Total	100.0	100.0	100.0	100.0	100.0	100.0	100.0

Source: Unpublished material made available by Natalie Rogoff Ramsøy.

side. All in all, there appears to be better contact between generations among the middle class than the working class. Mathiesen concludes that the difference may be due to differences both in living accommodation and in child-rearing norms between these two classes of society. In a totally different type of urban community, the new area of Mo i Rana, the site of a large iron and steel works built by the state after World War II, clear overlaps have developed between occupation, income, and neighbourhood residence. The residential neighbourhoods there are fairly homogeneous socially, despite the original intention of building a community without such class distinctions (Øyen 1958, pp. 98–100). High correlations between residential location and socio-economic characteristics can become highly important for the social setting, leading to sharper distinctions between the various social strata than the objective differences in access to benefits would imply. For example, children from the same residential district usually attend the same school and are thus further influenced by the occupational and income groups dominant in the area. Persons living near one another have contact socially, and marriages are not infrequent (Rogoff Ramsøy and Iversen 1967, pp. 34–36). There is reason to believe that when the individual's placement in the stratification influences his style of life, this is in part due to the above-mentioned ecological factor. Those who are relatively similar live near one another and become even more similar because of this.

One feature characterizing a social setting is use of leisure time. White-collar workers spend relatively more money on leisure time activities than do workers. For example, they spend more on dues to organizations and clubs of the non-occupational type, whereas workers spend more on dues to trade unions etc. This latter point is of course connected with the differences between workers' and white-collar workers' organizational rate, discussed previously. White-collar workers spend more on newspapers and books, workers more on magazines. Here we find an indication of the relative spread of 'fine culture' and 'pop culture' in the two groups. Likewise, white-collar workers spend relatively more on theatre, concerts, and musical instruments, while workers spend more on radio. Vacation expenditures – especially for vacations abroad – are considerably higher among white-collar workers than workers. Several Gallup polls have also shown that white-collar workers have, in general, longer vacations, and more often use them to travel away from home (Gallup 1962 and 1963).

White-collar workers get up later and go to bed later than do blue-collar workers, a difference generalizable for the daily rhythm of the upper versus the lower social strata. In 1954, 53 per cent of the workers surveyed got up before 6.30 a.m., as against only 20 per cent of the white-collar workers. Thirty-eight per cent of the workers went

143

to bed before 10 p.m., as against 20 per cent of the white-collar workers (NRK 1955, p. 53). In interpreting these data, we must also bear in mind that white-collar workers live in cities and towns more frequently than do workers.

This, together with the age factor, makes it difficult to interpret the large amount of data available on people's radio-listening preferences and habits. Lower income groups listen to the radio more than do higher groups, but this may be due to such varying factors as place of residence, age, and social rank. There is also the question of whether there exist differences between income groups in using the radio as background noise. Persons in higher income groups might be more likely to turn off the radio when not listening to the program. A reasonable hypothesis is that there is a connection between social isolation and low social rank. The lower strata are more dependent on a medium like radio that does not require social contact. Because members of the higher social strata are situated more centrally in society's network of communication and interaction, they have less time and interest for listening to the radio. And also, differences in listening patterns for the various income groups are actually rather small.

Access to radio sets shows no variation with social rank, in contrast to the case with television. Several surveys in 1963 and 1964 showed considerable inequalities in access to television sets in different income groups. In December 1963, 12 per cent of the lowest income group (under N. kr. 14,000 a year) reported having a television set in their apartment, as against 40 per cent of the highest income group (over N. kr. 20,000) (Gallup 1963).

Another type of investment connected with the individual's and the household's place in the social network is a telephone. There is a clear connection between occupation and possession of a telephone: generally speaking, the higher an occupation's rank, the higher the probability that persons in it have a telephone. In towns and cities, 79 per cent of managers and administrators have a phone, as do 77 per cent of merchants, but only 23 per cent of industrial workers (NOS XII 140, Table 16). Both financial ability and occupational need for a phone are important factors here. But in turn, having or not having a phone can also influence one's way of life.

Ownership of automobiles is also clearly connected with other indicators of social rank. Three occupations have especially high frequency of car ownership: 38 per cent of those employed in governmental or private administrative positions have a car, as do 37 per cent of military personnel and 32 per cent of persons in academic positions. (The figures would be even higher if we were able to exclude persons whose social rank is lower than that of the bulk

144

of each category.) Of a large category of industrial workers, where iron and metal, as well as wood products, dominate, 18 per cent have a car. And for persons with office jobs, the figure is 16 per cent (NOS XII 140, Table 12). The latter point is interesting in that it shows how the boundary between white-collar workers and workers has disappeared in respect to such an important consumer article as an automobile, an object which also has prestige value. But in general, the distribution of automobile ownership confirms the ranking order shown by other distribution patterns.

The description of consumer patterns just mentioned raises again the question of the connection between stratification and the individual's place in society's communications and contact network. We came across the same question in connection with workers' and white-collar workers' participation in trade and professional organizations. Galtung has developed an index precisely intended to localize the individual in relation to the communications network, by characterizing him as 'central' or 'peripheral'. The index is based on such indicators of stratification as occupation, education, and income, as well as age, sex, and place of residence (urban–rural). The supposition is that a socially and geographically peripheral position influences the individual's attitudes to certain types of questions. A further supposition is that young persons, as well as very old persons and all women, possess inherent characteristics pulling in the same direction as do socially and geographically peripheral positions.

Table XV shows how this index tends to correlate with certain general patterns connected with participation, communication, and information. As to participation in the communications network, the young, the old, and that part of the population living in remote areas seem to be in the same boat as the lower social strata, as stratification has been defined here. However, Galtung does not propose that the various items on the index pull in the same direction with regard to political questions, for example. We have already noted some conditions which may cause youth with low incomes to be more conservative than persons who have the same incomes but are somewhat older – because at least some of the young people expect to advance upwards. The geographically peripheral rural population of southern and western Norway is also more conservative (i.e. less socialist) than is the more central population in eastern Norway, holding income and occupation constant.

Using the centre-periphery index as a point of departure, various researchers have proposed hypotheses concerning a connection between position on the index and more general characteristics of the individual's way of thinking and 'social cosmology'. While the index does not provide an especially good basis for predicting concrete

145

Table XV. Validation of index of social position, 1961 data. In per cent

Index level	No participation				Interest in sport	No opinion			
	In elections	In newspaper reading	As organization member	As board member		On NATO membership	On atomic weapons in Norway	On whether occupation or atomic war is worse	On aid to underdeveloped countries
0	31	54	85	58	46	38	36	77	39
1	20	45	68	75	70	44	35	47	29
2	15	43	58	74	57	43	55	31	26
3	13	34	48	65	31	24	14	19	21
4	12	27	41	62	39	20	21	15	14
5	13	18	44	62	33	24	15	20	16
6	14	10	43	54	35	16	10	14	9
7	9	6	33	43	30	14	2	18	9
8	5	3	27	38	27	0		0	6

Source: Galtung 1964.

standpoints, it may possibly be a useful basis for a division according to underlying structural traits in opinion-formation. But thus far, the material is insufficient to warrant any definite conclusions.

9. SOME ATTITUDINAL PATTERNS

In the following we shall examine some of the questions put to the population by the various opinion research institutes, with income, occupation, or education as stratification variables: first, some attitudes concerning work and the economy, taken from various Gallup polls in 1961–1963.

White-collar workers, more often than workers, are of the opinion that: Their job is a satisfying activity and a worthwhile task, rather than merely a way of earning money. Good co-operation between employees and employer is the most important factor in assuring pleasant working conditions, more important than solidarity between colleagues. Not all strata of the Norwegian population work enough. It is wrong for two persons with the same job and with equally long seniority in a firm to have the same salary, if one of them is a better worker and thus does more. When wages in a particular branch of trade or industry are fixed by wage agreement, it is right for the especially good workers to receive a wage higher than that stipulated by the agreement. If two persons have the same type of work, but one of them produces more because he works harder, he should earn more. There is not enough difference in wages for skilled workers and non-skilled workers to encourage workers to train in skills. The state-owned iron works in Mo i Rana is operating at a loss and will continue to do so in the future: it ought to be sold into private hands.

From these attitudes we discern two separate profiles, even where the percentage difference is not great (10–20 per cent). White-collar workers feel that work is interesting; they show closer affinity with management, are less collectivity oriented, more performance oriented, and more sceptical towards state-controlled activity. This corresponds well with the dissimilarities in white-collar workers' and workers' political identification and their working conditions. These differences in attitude are not limited to areas closely related to work, but turn up in other areas as well.

A study concerning the 1963 wage settlement is especially interesting as it distinguishes between employee and employer. Forty-nine per cent of the employers felt the wage increase was too large, such that Norway's economic situation and competitive position would be weakened. Only 9 per cent of the employees shared that view. On the other hand, 38 per cent of the employees felt that even larger wage in-

147

creases would be justifiable, to which only 4 per cent of the employees agreed. About 50 per cent on each side felt the wage increase 'about right' (Gallup 1963). Here we see in skeletal form how differences in attitude between social groups arise directly from their differing positions in a conflict of interests.

It has often been maintained that white-collar workers are more willing than workers are to postpone gratification to achieve long-range goals. This has been viewed as being connected with the Protestant ethic (Lysgaard 1960). Answers to the following question may shed light on the two groups' relative evaluation of short-range and long-range rewards: 'If you were 15 years old and had to choose either to take up employment or spend eight years getting a college education, which would you choose if you or your parents had to pay for the eight years of study?' Fifty-seven per cent of white-collar workers, as against 36 per cent of the workers, chose the college study alternative. That this is not solely due to differences in financial ability is shown by a second question, identical to the first except for the provision that the individual would get a scholarship enabling him to live at a student dormitory those years. Under these conditions, 73 per cent of the white-collar workers and only 52 per cent of the workers chose the eight-year college study alternative (Gallup 1963).

Concerning attitudes to children, youth, child-rearing, and juvenile delinquency some data are available. These questions in themselves are further removed from the actual conflicts of interests between workers and white-collar workers. All the same, we find the characteristic differences between the two groups. Workers feel that young car thieves' names ought to be printed in the newspapers more often than do white-collar workers (54 per cent versus 42 per cent). Persons with high incomes are more often (56 per cent) of the opinion that female students should have easy access to contraception information and advice than are workers (41 per cent). Persons belonging to the higher income groups emphasize the importance of the child's own welfare in deciding which parent is to have custody of the child after a divorce, as against automatically granting it to the mother (69 to 58 per cent). More workers (72 per cent) than white-collar workers (56 per cent) felt that juvenile delinquency is not much of a serious problem. White-collar workers are more in favour of using television as a teaching medium in the schools than are workers (70 to 53 per cent). White-collar workers are more often critical of youth's manners and behaviour towards older persons than are workers (37 to 28 per cent).

There exist a great many opinion surveys on attitudes towards international questions. As a rule, the data are classified according to one or more rank indicators: occupation, income, or education.

148

A 1957 survey revealed that of those who had heard of NATO, 74 per cent of the white-collar group approved of Norway's membership in the organization, as against 59 per cent of the workers. Of Conservative *(Høyre)* supporters, 83 per cent also supported membership in NATO, while 62 per cent of those voting Labour *(Arbeiderpartiet)* and only 14 per cent of those voting Communist shared this view. In a 1961 survey, Galtung found that while 59 per cent of his 'top-dogs' were NATO-supporters, only 32 per cent of his 'underdogs' were; and 66 per cent of those with higher education supported NATO, as against 38 per cent of those with only the basic eight years' elementary schooling (Galtung 1961). From Stub's 1962 survey we have only a comparison of income groups: 63 per cent of the highest income bracket (over N. kr. 18,000) supported NATO membership, while 51 per cent in the lowest bracket (under N. kr. 12,000) did so (Stub 1962, p. 284). Although the figures from these various surveys are not quite comparable, we may conclude that attitudes towards Norway's membership in NATO are connected with the individual's position in the stratification structure. But it is also clear that this is only one of many different factors behind attitudes in this field.

In 1962 and 1963 the debate on whether Norway should join the Common Market (EEC) raged high. Three surveys which were conducted by FAKTA in Oslo – in January, April and June of 1962 – show the correlations between attitude towards the Common Market and income, occupation, and education. Many of the answers were 'Don't know', especially among women. Taking the men separately, then, we see that in January 2 per cent of those with an income under N. kr. 12,000 were *for* Norway's joining the Common Market, whereas the figure for those with incomes higher than N. kr. 18,000 was 40 per cent. In April, only 12 per cent of those with incomes under N. kr. 12,000 were *for*, and 35 per cent of those with incomes over N. kr. 18,000. In June the figures were 20 and 44 per cent, respectively.

According to other opinion surveys published by the Norwegian Gallup Institute in November 1961 and March 1962, opinions concerning the Common Market were divided in all political parties except the Communist Party. Within the Conservative Party, there was a clear majority in favour of joining the Common Market, and within Labour, a somewhat less overwhelming majority. In the three other non-socialist parties, and in the newly-formed Socialist People's Party (SF), there was a clear majority opposing Norwegian membership in the Common Market. This may indicate that those who felt they had an active share in either political or financial power in society stood on the one side, whereas those with little or no say in these matters stood on the other.[2]

Thirty-eight per cent of the workers as against 19 per cent of the white-collar workers surveyed accepted the protest of 'the 143' against Norway's joining the Common Market.[3] Some months later, 53 per cent of white-collar workers surveyed and 33 per cent of workers answered that they were in favour of Norway's negotiating for full membership in the Common Market. One week afterwards, 34 per cent of the white-collar workers and only 23 per cent of the workers opposed an advisory plebiscite on the matter. When Great Britain cut off her negotiations on joining, and Norway's basis for joining thereby fell away, 43 per cent of the white-collar workers and 31 per cent of the workers surveyed felt this was disadvantageous for Norway. The differences are not great, but their general trend confirms the supposition that attitudes towards the Common Market have been, to some extent at least, connected with the individual's occupaional position and all the other factors occupation has been found to go with.

Besides the surveys on NATO and the Common Market, there are also investigations concerning other international problems.

Some Norwegian surveys indicate that white-collar workers are at least as positively disposed to the question of international organs and actions as are workers. Eighty-eight per cent of the white-collar workers surveyed in a nation-wide sample felt that the UN does a good job, as did 78 per cent of the workers; 62 per cent of the white-collar workers, as against 39 per cent of the workers, felt that the UN ought continually to have command of a military unit large enough to prevent armed conflicts. Seventy-four per cent of the white-collar workers as against 59 per cent of the workers said that the UN should have command of a permanent security force. Sixty-eight per cent of the white-collar workers versus 49 per cent of the workers surveyed in 1953 felt it was right of Norway to give aid to economically under-developed countries; 72 per cent of the white-collar workers versus 58 per cent of the workers answered that Norway's program of aid in India was proper. That white-collar workers have a view of international developments at least as optimistic as that of workers is indicated by a 1963 survey concerning the probability of a rapprochement between the USA and the USSR: 65 per cent of the white-collar workers as against 55 per cent of the workers thought such a rapprochement probable. Also, there is in general more support of the Norwegian Peace Corps among persons with high social rank than among those with lower rank (Galtung and Seierstad 1962).

Is it possible to discern any systematic pattern in the distribution of international attitudes between groups variously situated in the stratification structure? An old notion is that workers are more international in their attitudes than are the higher social strata, which are presumably more nationalistic. Some findings may be interpreted as

150

supporting this view. Workers and socialists in general are more opposed to nuclear weapons and NATO – an opposition corresponding closely to the traditional view of internationalism as such.

While we do find this form of internationalism most strongly represented by the working class, other expressions of internationalism are more weakly represented among workers than white-collar workers and others with higher social rank. This is true of attitudes to certain aspects of the UN's activity and aid to developing countries. The working class's stronger opposition to the Common Market must also be in part an expression of similar scepticism towards certain forms of international co-operation. The pattern discernible from the Norwegian surveys is not unlike that found in American opinion surveys: an ambiguous and disparate relationship between social rank and attitudes towards internationalism.

Let us first consider some reasons why the working class might be more international in its attitudes than are white-collar workers and employers. One conspicuous reason is the traditional connection between socialism and internationalism in the programs of the various socialist parties. The individual who has identified himself with a socialist party on domestic issues has his chances increased of accepting other parts of its political program which to begin with perhaps seemed less appealing.

But there also exist other reasons for this connection, reasons more directly related to position in society. Relatively speaking, the worker has been less privileged than the higher-ranking white-collar workers and employees, for example. In general, he is more loosely joined to the network of resources, influence, prestige, and information forming the society's structure. The national interests – as defined and interpreted by the top strata in society and translated into evaluations and political platforms – reach him with weakened strength and less binding power than they do groups higher on the social ladder.

Thus, the worker stands, in a sense, freer in relation to efforts to further the national interests as interpreted by political leaders. The worker's lack of social status implies less commitment to the evaluations and choices made by the leaders. His underprivileged status leads to desires for certain changes in the distribution of economic benefits and in economic power. Sympathy and solidarity with others in similar situations in other countries can have an internationalizing effect on his attitudes. In addition to this general factor is the special constellation between the potential enemy — at the same time the native country of socialism — and the current ally — at the same time the stronghold of capitalism. A different international situation would have created other nuances in the relationships between social rank and

151

international attitudes, but would hardly have erased the general connection we have mentioned.

Let us take a look at some conditions which would seem to indicate that the working class is less international in its attitudes than are higher white-collar workers and business persons. High social status in the national society implies, to a degree, high status in the international society as well. High social rank means, as a rule, a good acquaintance with foreign languages, travels abroad, foreign friends and acquaintances, colleagues, reading of foreign literature, etc. All of this makes the world more available for persons of high social rank, makes it less strange or 'foreign' and frightening — at least, in certain respects.

The chief reason why the expected connection between low social rank and internationalism does not hold as a general law is probably to be found in the relations between stratification in national and international society. The way upwards and in towards the centre in the modern nation-state does not lead away from the global society: on the contrary, modern national society is to a large extent based on a world culture and not a primarily national one. As a result of this we have, for example, the paradox that leaders of new nations stand in danger of losing contact with those things which are national, native, and unique. The fact of belonging to the leading stratum in these countries also means having very strong connections with international culture and with an international contact network of diplomacy, alliances, and exchange.

In Norway, the fact of rising to the top as a politician, businessman, or expert has not these same drastic consequences. Once Norway was led by men who came from abroad themselves or whose ancestors had foreign origins. Today the basis for high social rank is different. But, at the top, there is a tendency for the setting to become internationalized, whether in business, politics, administration, or science and research. It is probable that high social rank in a modern national society in itself creates certain types of international loyalties.

The above material raises the general question of the connection between the working class, the workers' movement, and the creation of new values in society. Lipset feels that there is a definite tendency towards 'Working Class Authoritarianism' (Lipset 1963, pp. 87 ff.). If such an attitude can be demonstrated, this must be because the working class has less access to education and the communications network in society in general. It is from science and research and from the arts that much of that which is new and 'progressive' comes – and the workers are more removed from these institutions than are the higher social strata. Therefore, workers will tend to be more conservative on certain points. The accepted general connection between social status and radicalism/conservatism has probably always been a myth. Suffice it to point out that the one group most responsible for bringing about changes in technical and production fields, with radically innovating consequences – the leaders of business, trade and industry – have always counted themselves conservatives.

10. THE LAPP MINORITY IN THE STRATIFICATION STRUCTURE

If we study world society and the various large nation-states we find that many of the most important stratification problems arise in connection with differences in race, culture, and language. In Norway there are relatively few such minority groups: Lapps, Finns *(kvener)*, Jews, gipsies, Central European refugees from World War II, and recently arrived workers from Southern Europe. From the point of view of stratification, the most important of these are the Lapps *(samer)*, especially because they have lived so long, probably thousands of years, on what today is Norwegian territory (cf. Vorren and Manker 1958, Nesheim 1961, and Paine 1957, 1965).

The approximately 20,000 Norwegian Lapps stand out primarily with respect to their language, which belongs to the Finno-Ugric group. Almost one-tenth of these Lapps are also discernible from the majority population of Norway because of their occupation – the keeping of reindeer – and their nomadic way of life. The great majority of Lapps today, however, are engaged in typical Norwegian occupations, especially as small farmers and fishermen.

It is generally assumed today that the Lapps enjoy full judicial equality with other Norwegian citizens. To the extent that this is the case, the Lapps are situated similarly to other groups with low social rank. Their relatively low access to society's rewards comes as a result not of their legal standing but of other distribution mechanisms. However, legislation especially concerning Lapps shows that the principle of equality was applied to them much later than to other groups. As late as the 1950s there were in force various laws placing Lapps in a less favourable position than other citizens.

The most serious weakness of Lapps' legal position is that the rights of nomadic Lapps to their pasture land have never been clearly defined or agreed upon. In the preliminary work to the present law of 1933 concerning reindeer herding, the way in which Lapp interests were to be evaluated is clearly set out: 'A conflict of interests such as that which necessarily must take place between the farmer and the nomadic Lapp cannot, under conditions such as ours, which do not permit the setting of boundaries, be solved by applying a principle of absolutely equal regard for the interests of both parts ... As long as the nomadic Lapp's occupation enjoys legal protection, it has the right to be offered such conditions as may help it to continue existence. But because its position is much that of historical survival, one which to no little degree hinders the development of more legitimate and appropriate social interests, the limits on its claims are set. And these limits must, due to the very nature of the situation, be yielding' *(Utkast til lov om reindriften* (Draft of the law concerning reindeer herding), p. 43).

In other areas as well, there has existed until recently legal inequality in the treatment of Lapps. This is connected with such factors as the colonization policies enforced in the province of Finnmark during the close of the past century and the beginning of this one. Such policies were backed by state and national interests, the desire to secure and protect the northern borders, and in part the desire to make full rational use of the area's natural resources. Typical of this kind of policy was the law of 1902 concerning sale of unregistered, state-owned land in Finnmark. The sale of land titles must, according to this regulation, take place only to Norwegian citizens; the law further specifies that 'special consideration must be taken to further settlement, cultivation, and general development of a district by well-suited persons who can speak, read, and write the Norwegian language and who use it in daily parlance' (Ot.prp. no. 20, 1901–1902, p. 12). The obvious purpose of these regulations was to make the area Norwegian.

Language policies were also marked by the desire to make Norwegian prevail and to assimilate the Lappish minority group. The most important provision is to be found in the official instructions from the Ministry of Church and Education, 1898, which specify: '§ 3, The teaching in the schools is to be conducted in the Norwegian language. The Lappish or Finnish (kven-ish) language is to be used solely as an auxiliary instrument to explain what the children do not understand ... § 4, Even if, in a particular district, the majority of the children do not understand Norwegian, the teacher should always keep in mind the above-mentioned regulations and thus consider it vital to avoid regular use of the Lappish or Finnish language, employing it only to that degree which is absolutely necessary.' These regulations were still in effect when the Lapp Commission's Recommendation was presented in 1959, although they have now been annulled.

The Lapps' actual inequality before the law has affected relations between them and the majority group, contributing to the present situation where so many Lapps have low social rank. But the conditions which today are of prime importance in maintaining the Lapps'

154

low placement in the Norwegian stratification system are of a different type. In order to localize the Lapps in the stratum structure we must study their access to various types of rewards, relative to other social groups. From this point of view, the most striking characteristic of the Lapps is that they average a very low income level and a correspondingly low standard of living. Disproportionately many Lapps must be classified as poor. In the township of Kautokeino in Finnmark, studies made a few years ago show that average income per capita was about one-third that of the national average. Also, it has been estimated that only 35 per cent of the reindeer owners in Finnmark have a herd large enough to support a family. However, many of the poor Lapp families are not connected with the keeping of reindeer, but are farmers and fishermen instead.

Not only income data, but also available data concerning dwelling standards, sanitary conditions, and child mortality indicate that the typical poverty symptoms are far more common among Lapps than among the rest of the Norwegian population, also in the northern provinces.

Among nomadic Lapps, the population pressure in reindeer herding is an important reason for the low income level. From 1949 to 1964 the population of nomadic Lapps increased by 98 households, or 455 persons. The scarce natural resources, which do not expand, must suffice for a population which is greatly expanding. This growth is due, among other things, to the large number of children born to nomadic Lapp families. The average number of children among the latter is 3.8, more than 50 per cent higher than the nation-wide Norwegian average. In the towns of Kautokeino and Karasjok, 45 per cent of the population of nomadic Lapps is under 17 years of age, while the nation-wide average is scarcely 30 per cent. The growth in population is not offset by migration. Whereas many counties in northern Norway have long had decreasing populations, the typical Lappish counties show an increase of 100 per cent. In Kautokeino, the number of males aged 20–29 increased by 41 per cent from 1950 to 1960, while the corresponding average for the nation was a 17 per cent decrease (Christoffersen 1963).

This accumulation of population in typically Lapp areas is due in part to language problems and in part to fear of the prejudice a Lapp still encounters from the Norwegian population in general. But poverty is in itself an important reason why so few choose to emigrate. The level of education is low, experiences with non-Lapp modern society few and often unfavourable, and many Lapps lack the minimum of capital necessary to establish themselves and their families in a new, unfamiliar setting.

Scarce natural resources of the area are a main cause of Lapp

155

poverty. Swedish nomadic Lapps settled in Norwegian fjord districts, which were still unoccupied because the means of subsistence were considered so meagre. In other places, coastal Lapps were ousted by Norwegians and forced to settle in less favourable, even peripheral areas.

Certain aspects of national economic and social policies can help explain Lapp poverty. Most important is that the authorities are reluctant to invest in the outermost periphery – precisely where many Lapps live. In Norwegian welfare programs there is an unmet need where aid to large families with difficult finances is concerned. Aside from state family allowances, such poor families are forced to seek aid from local municipalities – and these families are concentrated in the poorest municipalities. More than any other group it is the Lapps who are hardest hit by this lacuna in welfare policy.

Education is a usual prerequisite for well-paid work today. This has created new difficulties for Lapps, difficulties they did not have fifty years ago. Language is a barrier. The large distances, which make boarding away from home a necessity even for elementary school pupils, are a great hindrance. And the fact that many Lapp children are so totally unconditioned for schooling is a third difficulty. For example, many arrive at school without having any home experience with paper and pencil. And this is true not only of nomadic Lapp children. When, in addition, children are given a teacher who has no command of their native language – as is frequently the case – schooling is of dubious value.

On the basis of 1961–1963 investigations in the Finnmark towns of Kautokeino, Polmak, and Nesseby, Hoem found 'that the average pupil in this area has, in the period after 1950, left elementary school with a level of knowledge under the minimum stipulated by the Ministry of Church and Education, ... that pupils whose native language is Lappish have left the seven-year elementary school with a level of knowledge corresponding to that stipulated for the first three years of schooling, ... that the disparity in level of knowledge – both between nomadic Lapps and resident Lapps, and between pupils with Lappish and pupils with Norwegian as their native language – increases with number of years of schooling' (Hoem 1967, p. 63).

Preliminary studies on the junior high-school *(ungdomsskole)* level seem to indicate this same trend. Here pupils are sorted according to type of curriculum chosen. The least-demanding curriculum normally excludes the pupil from further high education. In 1964, 60 per cent of the pupils in Karasjok, 77 per cent in Nesseby, and 85 per cent in Polmak chose the least-demanding curriculum in Norwegian, whereas only 20 per cent of the pupils in the country as a whole did so (Hoem 1967, p. 64). With such results in elementary schooling and such

156

choice of junior high-school curriculum, it is not surprising that only a small perecntage of Lapp young people today have a chance of doing well in the educational system. And yet, it is within the school sector that most progress has been made in recent years.

The distribution of rewards in a modern society is largely the product of a great, complicated apparatus of making claims and negotiating. The result is decided by the strength the various sides have at their disposal to back up their demands. The Lapps have little organizational strength, among other things because they are so few in number, are scattered, and have, in part, conflicting interests.

This lack of power and means of sanction is perhaps central if we should attempt to predict anything concerning the Lapps' future stratification positions. Of course some Lapps will probably, due to better schooling, have increased chances of social mobility. But as a group, the remaining Lapps will have difficulties in keeping pace with the general trend towards social equalization, unless they can somehow manage to increase their power resources.

V. Education in Norway

By Tore Lindbekk

1. INTRODUCTION

The educational institution is one of the most important unifying factors in society. In its capacity of passing on skills, knowledge, and values to new generations, the school enters a child's life at an early stage of his development, supplements the family as a factor in the child's upbringing, and, outside of the family itself, becomes the child's most important fixed point. At the same time, the school and the entire educational system are in active exchange with professional life and the whole social system, in this way helping to determine what place the individual will take in society. Economic, political, and religious institutions contribute to determining the character of the school and what values and ideas it shall pass on.

In one distinct way, the Norwegian school system differs from that of other Western countries: in Norway in this century, there has been no private general educational system paralleling that of the national-municipal system (Berge 1960, pp. 281–293). In the school year 1963–1964, 99 per cent of the country's elementary school pupils attended public schools; the same applies to 96.5 per cent of secondary school pupils.

Under the system of public education in Norway up to about 1960, the seven-year compulsory elementary school *(folkeskole)* provided a common elementary education available to all strata of the population. The most highly motivated pupils continued on for three or five years in the 'higher' schools, i.e. *realskole* (age approx. 14–16) and *gymnasium* (age approx. 16–19). Just as in the elementary schools, secondary education was the same for all; it ignored the social, religious, etc. differences of society.

The other types of schools, technical schools, vocational schools, universities, colleges, etc., have been tied to the general system of public education in that each grade of a vocational school corresponded to a specific level in the general system as a basis of recruiting. This picture of a unified school system, with conditions the

Table I. *Children in elementary schools in 1964-1965 in urban and rural areas by type of school (percentage)*

School type	Rural	Urban	Total
Undivided	0.76	0.04	0.80
Two-grade	3.97	0.40	4.37
Three-grade	4.68	0.79	5.47
Four-grade	9.38	1.16	10.54
Five-grade	3.89	0.71	4.63
Six-grade	10.41	6.27	16.68
Seven-grade	36.64	22.90	57.54
Total	67.73	32.27	100.0
N	279.78	133.260	413.041

Source: NOS A 133, Table 7, p. 13.

same for all groups within the population, however, is not completely valid.

As Table I shows, in 1964–1965, 58 per cent of elementary school pupils attended seven-grade elementary schools in which all the pupils were divided into seven grades, or classes, according to their age. Twenty-one per cent attended four-grade schools or schools with fewer grade divisions. Comparing the figures for town and country, we find that 7 per cent of urban pupils attended four- or fewer grade elementary schools, as against 28 per cent of rural pupils.

Table II shows how these figures are connected with the fact that in rural areas there existed many small schools. While there were *twice* as many pupils in rural areas as in urban areas, there were *seven* times as many schools in rural areas.

Table II. *Elementary schools in 1964-1965 in urban and rural areas, by type of school, absolute figures*

School type	Rural	Urban	Total
Undivided	326	19	345
Two-grade	805	61	866
Three-grade	487	36	523
Four-grade	613	53	666
Five-grade	174	19	193
Six-grade	248	64	312
Seven-grade	582	196	778
Total	3,235	448	3,683

Source: NOS A 133, Table 2, p. 8.

Table III. *Elementary schools, average number of pupils, and percentage of many-grade schools 1958-1969*

School year	Percent of pupils in six- and seven-grade schools	Number of schools	Average number of pupils per school
1958-1959	56.3	4,836	91
1960-1961	59.7	4,526	94
1963-1964	65.3	3,871	108
1965-1966	76.2	3,508	117

Source: NOS A 97, p. 39; NOS XII 195, p. 270.

However, developments have been such that the many-grade school, up to now considered typical of urban areas, is becoming more and more typical of the country as a whole, while schools are also becoming larger. Table III shows that this development has in the last seven years resulted in the reduction of the total number of schools by 1,328, a reduction which applies entirely to rural areas, as the number of urban schools has increased.

Such geographical differences are not the only complicating factor, however. Another is the transition to a nine-year school, a transition begun in the early 1960s. This involves setting up three-year 'compulsory secondary schools' *(ungdomsskoler)* to provide instruction from the seventh through the ninth grade. In the school year 1965–1966, there were 192 compulsory secondary schools in operation; 27 per cent of all seventh-grade pupils were attending such schools.

The introduction of these particular schools will bring about far-reaching changes in the educational system, but, as yet, only little is known about how the new structure will work when put into practice. (However, in 1965, the present author began an investigation of social differentiation in the nine-year school system.) Our present analysis of the Norwegian school system must therefore be based on what we know about the old system, even though it is now in the process of changing. In the discussion below, we shall primarily be considering conditions so basic in nature that new developments can scarcely affect them in any way.

First, we shall take up the system of values on which the Norwegian public school is based, discussing in connection with this selected aspects of the internal school structure which bear on the public school's mediatory effect.

Thereafter, we shall analyse the relationships between the different types of school in Norway and the decisive role the school plays in a pupil's choice of profession and career. Finally, we turn to *recruitment* for higher education, i.e. *who* benefits from the knowledge the school passes on, and what significance this has for an individual's future career. In general, we shall be concentrating on obligatory and secondary schooling, mainly because of the lack of sociological research on other types of schools. (An exception is G. Nørstebø's work (1957) on the *folkehøgskole*.)

2. THE SCHOOL AS A SOCIALIZING AGENT

The function of the school is to 'socialize', to pass on to a new generation a social heritage of ideas, values, and knowledge. According to usual sociological thinking, this socializing function is a replacement for and a supplement to that of the family.

The concept 'social heritage' is by no means unambiguous. Unless more closely defined, it must stand for the entire scale of ways of life, values, and points of view existing in the various groups and strata of society. Obviously the school cannot handle all that; a choice must be made. But, by making such a choice, the school risks becoming an agent in the battle between different groups and cultures in society.

The Norwegian school system implies two things: first that one common organizational pattern applies throughout the country, and second that certain official regulations concerning curricula, teaching plans, etc. also apply to the whole country. In such a situation, the choice of subject matter is of special importance. The school can no longer be simply a substitute for the parents; it can no longer be maintained that the school exists to guide and teach children solely on behalf of parents, passing on those values and that knowledge which the parents themselves accept and prize.

A choice must be made between the different parent cultures from which the pupils are drawn, or, possibly, a compromise must be found. According to Norwegian school legislation, this choice is to be made by society's political organizations. Choice of curricula, approval and choice of textbooks, appointment of teachers, and the setting-up of the entire educational system belong in part to individual school boards, but first and foremost to the Ministry of Church and Education and to Parliament. In this way, the school is screened from direct parental influence; thus parents can exert lawful influence only through their votes in municipal and parliamentary elections. In Norway, as a rule, no political party has made education a special issue in its platform, so that if a voter desired a particular type of school organization he could not express his wish by voting for any particular party. In practice, therefore, parents have been unable to exercise any influence on the school itself and on the teaching their children will receive. Their choice, in the main, has been limited to what type of secondary education their children should go on to – whether they should continue on to *realskole* or further to *gymnasium*, or simply take no further education.

Even today, we do not know to what extent this viewpoint of the parents' relationship to the school is right; nor do we know whether this policy favours certain parent groups more than others. But it is certain that the school has been able to affect every one of its pupils by cutting across all other influences, even that of the parents. The school can reach children at an earlier age than other means of mass communication, and can exert its influence by means which other methods of mass communication would be hard put to attain – an aspect of the school's activity well known to those now working with the school's problems. In 1958, Bishop Karl Martinussen expressed the opinion that the school ought 'to give youth a moral and Christian education and work to make them useful people, both mentally and physically' (1958, pp. 22–26). In 1959, a bill for new school legislation stated as its purpose that the school ought 'to make the pupils good citizens' (Ot. prop. 30, 1958). Countless other opinions on what the school ought to accomplish were expressed in parliamentary debates that same year. The opinion most often heard was that the school is a means of communicating ideas and values, and that it ought to 'make' pupils into *this* or *that*.

In Parliament, the Government's bill was amended to include that the school *along with the home* ought to work to promote the various values then under debate. However, this does not solve the problem existing in those cases where there is no active family participation in what the school is trying to accomplish, or, indeed, where the family is in active opposition. These problems have in recent years come to the fore in connection with the language problem, and occasionally in connection with attempts to introduce dancing as a school subject.

3. THE SCHOOL AS A CONVEYOR OF VALUES

To the school, pupils represent a continuous stream of newcomers to be led through a fixed sequence of instruction and other activities. By this, the socializing effect is attained; the children are to be put in possession of those facts, insights, and attitudes that society wants them to have.

The influences on pupils can be classified most simply under two main headings: 1) the school 'itself' and 2) the joint activity among the pupils within a class and in the school. Both of these elements exercise a meaningful influence on the individual's understanding of the school and affect his attitude towards it and behaviour in it.

3.1. *The internal organization of the school*

The most obvious characteristic of the school system is its dividing of the pupils into grades, each of which has a comparatively stable membership, and its placing the classes in definite 'levels', each of which is succeeded by a higher grade. This implies that the highest level of the elementary school leads to the lowest of the secondary school where, in turn, the highest level leads to the lowest level of whatever further education one may choose.

In elementary school, the first year is characterized by a relatively loose organization of subject matter and teaching. At this point, little is done to delineate subjects, and all activity is centred around a teacher whose social function within the class is at least as important as her actual teaching. She is 'the teacher'; she takes the mother's place for this group of children, as yet too young not to need protection and care.

As children climb the ladder of grades in the elementary school, however, there is an increasing specialization of subject matter. Subjects are separated from one another. At the same time, there is a change in the role of the teacher. After many grades with only one teacher, the children now have several, each with his own field. To an increasing extent, definite demands are made on the individual pupil to contribute from his specialized knowledge – contributions which are subjected to objective evaluation; by the giving of marks and in other ways, sanction is given to these efforts, and everyone realizes that those who are proficient are rewarded.

This upward movement, with its increasing specialization of subject matter, with its growing demands on the pupils to contribute factual knowledge for which they will be evaluated and ranked by objective criteria, does not take place without creating problems for the teachers. Two requirements are opposed to each other throughout the entire elementary school: on the one hand, there is the requirement that not all school activity be centred around pure subject matter – the most important thing being that the individual pupil should be able to develop himself harmoniously at his own pace; on the other hand, there is the fact of examination results, a judgement of the pupil's efforts by objective standards, which are decisive for the pupil's acceptance by a secondary school. From this comes the fact that, as the pupil draws nearer and nearer to the transition from elementary school to secondary school, attention is focused more and more on marks and examination results.

The child's movement within this structure can be analysed in diverse ways. From the point of view of pedagogical research, it is natural to raise such questions as these: What forms of activity in the

163

school will best foster the child's own purely personal development and well-being? What objective demands for factual knowledge and skills can one realistically expect from the different grades, taking into account the average pupils in them? How can a defence of these demands for factual knowledge be reconciled with the demands for respect of the individual's personal development and well-being in the school? What teaching methods are most efficient?

Sociologically this upward movement through the school grades is interesting because it can be considered as training for independence from the parents and because it gives practice in evaluating oneself in relation to other people – which anticipates the pupil's introduction into adult society where demands for efficiency, the will to compete, and the ability to compete will be made.

The school is a mediator between society at large and the family from which the child comes. The school's task is to help the family in its endeavours to make the child a good member of society; it helps the family and supplements it. At an early stage, the school takes the place of the family, and the teacher assumes the parents' authority. A process of development is introduced which will make the child more and more independent of parental authority and gradually independent of parent substitutes as well.

This development in the child's authority relationships is accomplished, in part, by the role the teacher plays. For the first three or four years of school, there is only one teacher of the class – usually a woman. This brings about a transference to her of the child's need for protection and care, a need previously fulfilled by the mother. The teacher is expected to play this role, accepting the child's demands for protection and care. Gradually, however, she helps the individual to see himself as one of several, each of whom has relatively equal rights. An understanding of the relationship between teacher and pupil is built up and is a mutually accepted fact. This understanding means not only that this relationship has a quite common meaning and applies to every member of the class, but that it also involves the growing away from a situation in which one female teacher was for several years *the* teacher, to one in which there are several teachers, both male and female, who divide up subjects and class hours among themselves. From this comes an entirely generalized concept of the teacher.

In this way, the school brings about an emotional re-orientation from the home situation – where, as opposed to the school situation, the child's existence was unique and was subject to parental authority in a completely personal and particularistic form – to a society in which the child's status is that of one of many, with equal rights and equal duties, and in which the child is subject to authorities whose powers derive from nothing so personal as the intricate relationship between child and parents. These new authorities often exist visibly only in laws, rules, and prescriptions.

Thus, the school creates a basic understanding of the concept *equality*, preparing the individual for a form of society in which equality has rooted itself in a majority of the institutions: in the judicial system and the law, in democratic civil rights, in wages and salaries, etc. A basic understanding of what equality implies is created at the same time – reinforcing the idea of equality as a *social value*.

In the classroom, children from various families and social strata are brought together, under conditions in which they are on equal footing and of the same age and are treated in the same way by the teacher. They are brought together for the purpose of acquiring those definite skills and insights which are considered worthwhile. The learning process requires that the teacher reward and encourage the will to learn and likewise punish those who neglect to show such willingness. Unavoidably, this positive and negative sanctioning must to a great extent be based on pupils' achievement, which is indicative not only of motivation but also of ability to learn. This situation is emphasized when marks enter the picture, as these are purely an expression of classwork evaluation without taking into consideration what the individual pupil's abilities suit him for. Such classwork becomes, increasingly, evaluated against completely objective norms.

As the pupil climbs the ladder of grades and approaches the time when marks may determine his acceptance by other educational institutions, he becomes more and more aware that both the school and society evaluate him on the basis of work and proficiency. He learns to understand that in school as in society there is *competition*, and he learns to accept the idea that in this competition he who contributes the most gets the most and, not only that, has a *right* to it. Thus, children learn in school that, in addition to the basic equality of people, there also exist well-defined forms of *just inequality*.

In this way the pupil gradually approaches a competitive society; at the same time, he learns to accept this system, even in those cases where he himself will be among the losers in the competition.

The school also passes on other values closely connected to these and relevant to the child's adjustment to later schooling and adult society. Here I shall mention only three: to prize knowledge for its own sake, to be punctual, to be a disciplined worker. It would be difficult to overestimate the meaning of these three things to the individual's adjustment to society and his personal advancement in it.

At the same time, such virtues as punctuality, discipline, knowledge, equal treatment, and self-assertion through competition are important requirements of our modern industrial society, which must support its system of division of labour and its complicated co-operative relationships.

3.2. *The school's official purpose and system of values*

Concerning the values discussed above, the school is seldom called upon to perform any direct propaganda function, nor is any such activity discussed in the laws which govern the school. An orientation towards such values, however, is an important prerequisite if the school is to reach the goals to which it aspires. The teacher is aware of this.

However, it can be interesting to examine more closely the school's nominal areas of responsibility to a certain extent prescribed in its teaching plans, and to investigate their implications in a broader social context, particularly the system of values with which the school is duty bound to operate.

According to the Act of Parliament passed in 1959, the aim of the nine-year school is as follows:

> It is the task of the school, together with the home, to make pupils into good members of society. It shall help to give pupils a *Christian and moral education*, develop their abilities and talents, and furnish them with good basic knowledge, so that they become useful people, both mentally and physically (Act pertaining to the Elementary School, 10/4 1959, § 7).

It is difficult to find anything concrete here as to attitudes or how to approach the world and social problems. However, we can draw certain conclusions from the more clearly-defined goals for the social sciences – history, social studies, and geography – which are set forth in *The Teaching Plan for the Experimental Nine-Year School* (Harbo 1960, p. 7). Three of seven points deal with considerations of the pupil's personal development, ability to co-operate with others, and study techniques. The remaining four are: 4) help instill a democratic attitude in the pupils and give them insight into the organization of our democratic society; 5) develop tolerance and respect for people of other colours, languages, beliefs, customs, and social reforms; 6) help form a feeling of comradeship with other people and teach the pupils the value of international cooperation and of peace between nations; 7) give the pupils a sense of history and of the values of earlier cultural epochs and help them to understand our own era in terms of its historical development.

In practice, it is difficult to fasten onto what point 7 means unless we analyse closely what the textbooks and teachers actually say about historical development and the values which different eras of history embody. Points 4, 5, and 6, however, can be considered as clear directives to teachers and textbook authors to work towards forming a democratic attitude, tolerance, general respect for people, and international cooperation – in short, all the things that come under the heading of a *liberal attitude towards people and society.*

The school also has other duties. It is to bring about insight into Christianity and in this way may also try to influence the pupils' view of life (Act pertaining to the Elementary School 1959, p. 14). Through its activities and forms of organization, the school is to work to form ties and comradeship between people from differing social backgrounds (Harbo 1960, pp. 57 and 71).

Statements about the school's goals contain no reference to other generally accepted values. For example, the press has often demanded that the school influence opinion on Nordic cooperation, aid to developing countries, and a positive attitude towards Norwegian military defence policy. However, we do not have the material necessary to clarify the extent to which such demands actually affect the school's activity.

For all of these questions, it is obvious that to define the school's position we must go farther than teaching plans and the public statements of the authorities. We must examine textbooks, to elucidate the attitudes really articulated. Some years ago, D. Haakonsen conducted an investigation on what the textbooks actually said about the Catholic Church – and found that the picture presented was far from balanced (Haakonsen 1951). At the various times, certain textbooks have been the cause of general public debate, which once again has brought up the question of what kind of picture textbooks give of events and conditions that can be interpreted in more than one way, and what attitudes they thus instill (see, for example, the debate in *Morgenbladet*, August 15–September 14, 1960, on S. Høst's and S. Kjeldstadli's textbook *Verdens historie for gymnasiet*, Oslo 1959).

3.3. *The social localization of the school's system of values and the teachers*

At this point, let us pick up the thread of the introductory paragraph, in order to locate the social basis of the values with which the school operates. The school 'socializes' pupils, but according to which social group's 'ideology' does it do so?

No investigations in this country have dealt with this question. However, data from the USA indicate that the ideas of competitiveness, equality, and high regard for knowledge and schooling are all closely connected with the way of thinking of the urban middle class (Davis 1947, Ericson 1947). Data from several other Western countries also indicate that the strong political liberalism expressed in the school's official statement of purpose and teaching plans is more characteristic of the modern urban middle class than of either the

167

working class or rural opinion (Lipset 1959, Centers 1954). We must, however, wait until Norwegian investigations have been conducted and their results published before drawing any conclusions.

It is natural to raise this question of the school's position in relationship to the viewpoints which various social groups have on things political and cultural, with special attention to the *teachers*. It is they, of course, who animate and interpret the material with which the school deals.

Several studies indicate that teaching is a typical middle-class profession (Moser and Hall 1954, North and Hatt 1949, Svalastoga and Wolf 1964, pp. 44, 66). This is the case both for teachers in the elementary school and for lecturers in the secondary school. To date, no such consistent investigation of teachers' school grouping, of the same type as those conducted elsewhere, has been conducted in Norway. In connection with an investigation of 400 Norwegian teachers in 1955, however, the teachers themselves were asked to state the position of their profession compared with other professions in society. The place Norwegian teachers and lecturers gave themselves was in agreement with that of teachers in other countries and with other investigations of the social position of their profession (Aubert et al. 1956, pp. 90–96).

Among the Norwegian elementary school teachers, there was relatively good agreement that their position was below that of physicians, executives, engineers, architects, lawyers, and lecturers; they rated themselves *above* travelling salesmen, bank clerks, and skilled workers. Lecturers, on their part, rated themselves below physicians and executives, on the same level as or below engineers, architects, and lawyers. While elementary school teachers were largely satisfied with their position in society, there was a good deal of discontent among lecturers concerning the prestige of their occupation, their salary, and how much parents value their work (Aubert et al. 1956, pp. 96–99). This bears witness to a certain insecurity among lecturers as to where they really belong in society, possibly connected with the drastic change in social status this profession has experienced in this century (Lindbekk 1967, Chapter 2).

The social stratum to which teachers and lecturers belong and with which they will seek contact, however, need not be the same in all cases. Even in 1964–1965, two-thirds of all elementary school teachers held positions in rural areas. Because of this, it was not only the urban middle class which could exercise an assimilating influence on the teachers, but also the government officials, civil servants, and well-to-do farmers, who, in a rural society, were their equals. The lecturers were relatively more concentrated in the towns, but 40 per cent of them lived and worked in rural areas.

There is also another factor which contributes to determining the stand teachers take on society's problems and values: their own social background, i.e. the environment to which they originally belonged.

The 1950 investigation referred to above showed that of 300 elementary school teachers, 20 per cent were the children of either lecturers or teachers (Aubert et al. 1956, p. 85). It can be assumed that at least one-half of these were the children of rural elementary school teachers. This means, in any case, that altogether 50 per cent of elementary school teachers came from a rural environment. It is probable that the figure is considerably higher, in that a certain number of the children of office workers, merchants, and other professions must originally have come from rural areas.

Among the lecturers who were arts and sciences graduates, the number from a rural background was much lower – although teachers' and farmers' children who studied arts or sciences took positions in the school more often than the average student (Lindbekk 1967, pp. 134–140, 209–212). In any case, the children of farmers and teachers made up a good one-third of the lecturers, as shown in Table IV.

What meaning do these environmental conditions have for teachers' and lecturers' cultural and political orientation as adults?

A closer comparison of social background and major subject chosen by arts students who were the children of farmers and teachers shows that they more often chose Norwegian as a major subject than did the other groups. A full 42 per cent of them had had one or more works published. When we investigate the subject of their writing, we find that twice as many of them wrote about Norwegian language or literature compared with the literarily productive lecturers from other backgrounds (Lindbekk 1962a, p. 59).

Table IV. *Lecturers and elementary school teachers, by father's occupation (percentage)*

	Lecturers, 1950 investigation	Lecturers of all graduates 1910-1949	Teachers, 1950 investigation
Father's occupation			
Academic	13	19	3
Businessman	18	15	9
Office worker	6	18	5
Farmer	16	18	39
Teacher	18	13	20
Worker, artisan	16	14	12
Other, unknown	13	5	12
Total	100	100	100

169

This tends to paint a picture of the group of arts graduates from farm and teaching backgrounds as a group whose orientation is to rural culture and specifically Norwegian values.

Of the arts graduates in the period 1870–1909, the number of politically organized graduates was about equally divided between the Conservative Party, on the one side, and the Liberal and Labour Parties, on the other. Among graduates in the period 1910–1949, we find that the number of Liberal and Labour Party members is six times that of Conservative Party members (Lindbekk 1962a, p. 59).

The 1950 investigation of 100 lecturers showed that 17 per cent voted Conservative, 27 per cent Liberal, and 30 per cent Labour. Taken in relation to the number of votes cast in the post-war period, the Liberal Party was over-represented in the lecturer group. This is in agreement with the common impression that the Liberal Party traditionally has been closely identified with the nationalistic movements in Norwegian society.

The 1950 investigation of teachers and lecturers also showed that there were more elementary school teachers than lecturers who wanted teaching to 'put more emphasis on developing respect for national symbols' and to include more about 'the life and work of national heroes'. In addition, the investigation showed that a full 39 per cent of the elementary school teachers were politically oriented to the Liberal Party – more than twice as many as, for example, the Labour Party, for which 14 per cent of them voted. A full 11 per cent belonged to the Christian People's Party. Altogether, of those who identified themselves with any political party, 51 per cent belonged either to the Liberal Party or to the Christian People's Party, as against 28 per cent of the lecturers (Aubert et al. 1956, p. 88).

A closer analysis of the status and personal social background of both elementary school teachers and lecturers indicates that it is not only an urban middle-class system of values which the school passes on. Particularly in the case of elementary school teachers, it can be maintained that rural society has been able to exert every bit as much influence as the urban middle class. Our data indicate that this connection with rural society has affected the subject matter and the professional activity of teachers, and that both the elementary and secondary schools deal with nationally-oriented ideologies whose social roots are to be found in rural culture.

3.4. The meaning of pupil joint activity in the class

The effect of these value and culture orientations within the school and among teachers need not in all cases be equally great. The influences which proceed from the school's internal organization, the curriculum, and the teachers are not the only influences with which the pupils come in contact. There are also the influences exerted by the pupil community itself.

The commonly held view that pupils in a school class make up a collection of individuals, whose only unifying and guiding factor is the teacher, may be valid for the first four or five years of elementary school, but not for the higher grades. With time, increasingly stable relationships grow up among the pupils. Using sociometric techniques, investigations have been conducted to elucidate more clearly the way in which groups of pupils in a school or class separate themselves from each other and how a stratification of the class and school comes about; some individuals are set apart as being especially sought after as friends, work-mates, etc. In Norway, Svein Stensaasen has conducted a series of investigations into such problems (Stensaasen 1962). Foreign investigations have given examples of how the most popular pupils form groups which exercise a certain leadership over the others. This is meaningful for the kind of activity among the pupils both in and out of the classroom, and it also affects the pupils' general attitude to the school and their ideas of desirable behaviour in general.

The way in which these groups manifest themselves has been studied in high school. This 'pupil community' clearly seems to represent an alternate authority to that of the teacher. The values this authority fosters have, under some conditions, been said to be strongly anti-school in character (Coleman 1961). As a rule the pupil community opposes achievement which is well above the average for the class (Evans 1962, pp. 48, 54, Sivertsen 1952, p. 43). Investigations conducted in Sweden by J. Johanneson, however, show positive correlations between sociometric status in the class and both I. Q. and marks (Boalt and Husén 1964, pp. 212–214).

Several different conditions may have contributed to creating this community. First and foremost of these are the difficulties attached to being an adolescent in our society. Adolescents stand at the threshold of adult society. Yet they are not accepted as adults, but they themselves are in revolt against the minority status they have. Typical of the results of this situation is a general antagonism to adult society. In the school, this antagonism is more clearly directed and more definite than in perhaps any other situation. In Norway, schooling is compulsory up to 15 to 17 years of age – in part because of official legislation, in part because of the feeling that one's parents want one to continue school. For pupils in the last years of school, the school is perhaps the most pronounced and unavoidable expression of the dependent and minor status to which adult society assigns them. Their opposition to school is intensified by the social gulf between them and the teacher in the school situation – all authority and all responsibility belong to the teachers. The status of the pupil is something else again, it is for him to receive and obey orders.

The pupil community, however, must not be considered only as the source of norms which are purely negative in the school situation. It also develops the ability to contact one's peers on a basis of equality, an ability which teachers often endeavour to develop.

3.5. The effects of socializing activity in the school

To the class, the teacher is a figure of authority – someone who knows more than the pupils, someone who will lead the class, someone who is responsible for what happens. That he is older than the pupils is in itself enough to give him the role he must play. But his position is one of leadership and responsibility also because of the expectations which parents, pupils, his colleagues, and the authorities have; as a teacher, he has and is meant to have responsibility and a position of leadership. He also has real *power* over the pupils – not only on the basis of his authority, but also because he controls the means of punishment over pupils who do not behave in class as he desires.

This position of authority and power ought to give the teacher great possibilities of exerting influence on his pupils, and of passing on the facts, ideals, and attitudes discussed above.

However, the internal structure of the pupil community makes it possible for the pupils – especially in the secondary school – to avoid to a certain extent this influence. Not only can they avoid any possible cultural and political values which the teacher imparts to them, but they can also ignore the acceptable attitudes towards higher education and competition in school and social life. In extreme cases, they can even revolt against his position of leadership in the classroom.

We must also take into account the fact that conditions *outside* of the classroom and school can influence the process of education and the teacher's authority in the class situation. One of these, for example, is the teacher's status in society at large, especially his status as compared to that of the parents of his pupils. As mentioned above, both elementary school teachers and lecturers are considered to be typical representatives of society's middle class. And, as has also been pointed out, especially in the case of elementary school teachers, it is a middle class which has a strong rural element in it.

We do not know how this influences the attitudes of pupils from different classes of society towards their teacher. Data from the USA and Sweden indicate that teachers have had special disciplinary problems with pupils from the working class and with pupils from classes above the teacher's own (Havighurst and Neugarten 1962, pp. 468–473, Boalt and Husén 1964, pp. 95, 119–121). However, no systematic data from Norway are available on this question.

172

There is also another set of factors meaningful to the pupils' reaction to the expectations and influences of the teacher and the official school system; for example, low ability or particular personality traits of the pupil concerned can make him unable to meet the general demands for effort and competition. Conditions such as these can result in school work being one long series of defeats, and in the values which teaching tries to put across losing personal meaning for the individual.

In the class situation, an interplay of different influences affects the pupil. In addition to the influences exerted by the teacher, the curriculum, and the school system itself, there are the impulses from his fellow pupils and from his environment.

Unfortunately, there have been few detailed investigations of how this interplay develops, or of the result this interplay of several factors has in the school situation.

What about the school's influence on the pupil's attitudes to political, social, and cultural questions? Several investigations, especially from American colleges, have shown the formative influence the college environment – including both teachers and student community – has had on students' attitudes to political questions, race relations, etc. These investigations have shown how the effect of these influences depends on exposure to the college milieu, for example whether the student lives at home or at the university, and how the transfer from one college to another with a different ideological orientation gradually brings about a change in attitudes (Lipset 1956, Newcomb 1958, Sims and Patrick 1958).

From these investigations, however, we cannot draw any conclusions about what general direction the influences from the university and school will take, nor predict how varied these influences will be.

From Norway we have some data indicating a general connection between higher education and a positive orientation to international co-operation (Galtung 1961, p. 77 b). Another investigation has shown that persons with higher education are on the whole more in favour of treatment – as opposed to punishment – of criminals than are persons with a lower level of education (Næss 1963). In neither of these investigations has social position been taken into account.

In his article 'Democracy and working class authoritarianism' (1959), Lipset deals with the attitude to democratic values found in the different social classes of society. His material, collected from several Western countries, shows that there are clear differences, on an educational basis, concerning tolerance of minority groups and support of a multiple-party system as a value in itself. Certain differences between social classes also exist: in general, members of the middle class take a more positive stand on these democratic values than do members

173

of the working class. But in all social classes, education brings about marked differences, to a certain extent greater differences than found between the social classes themselves. In a Norwegian study, the answers to political questions were correlated with the scores on an index of 'social position', of which education was a factor. The relationships were clear and showed the same tendencies as in Lipset's data. This indicates that Lipset's point of view is also valid for Norwegian society, even though further data might be desirable (Galtung 1961).

Taken altogether, these investigations from Norway and other countries give us ground to believe that exposure to the school's system of values does influence the pupil's own attitudes towards politics and society. The results show a tendency to tolerance, which colours attitudes towards minorities, other countries, and democratic values. Even though the main tendency is clear cut, there are still many uncertain sides of this question of the effect of ideological propagandizing in the school. Further research is desirable.

4. EDUCATION AS A DIFFERENTIATING AND RECRUITING FACTOR

The school and education exercise a further socializing influence, training the pupils in definite facts and skills, and aiming to instill in them definite ideals and points of view considered important constituents of our cultural and social heritage. Thereby, the school makes them socially proficient; the pupils acquire attitudes relevant for their roles in the adult world.

However, by doing this, the school has not only a training influence, but also a recruiting one; at the same time as it makes them proficient, it shows up differences in their degrees of proficiency.

This division between the more and less proficient becomes drastic if it affects admission to educational institutions where the number of those accepted is limited. The school creates a sharp distinction between those who complete such education and those who do not.

These differences are important for the children's later lives. They help determine what forms of further education will be open to the child, and what trades or professions the individual will be able to enter.

Knowledge and skills are not always the decisive and differentiating factors. Frequently, mere possession of a diploma, or the fact of having attended such and such a school, directly symbolizes the knowledge and skills and those attitudes that particular school reputedly tries to impart. The very *lack* of such a diploma or attendance at such and such a school can be tantamount to automatic exclusion from consideration.

But the school also instills attitudes as to what kind of use the individual will later make of his education. It creates definite preferences in respect both of profession and of further education.

The teachers and the institutions outside the school are important factors in the crystallization of these preferences. The student community also has an important, norm-forming influence among the pupils. Common education, however, creates a bond between the pupils which extends beyond school attendance itself. This is the case particularly in connection with some types of higher education – for example, medicine – where strong organizational bonds throughout one's later career make people of a similar educational background into a social unit, and where the profession as a whole is able to exercise considerable authority over the individual member. Earlier, the *examen artium* (matriculation examination from high school) was the basis of a feeling of belonging to a definite educational community.

Through social processes of this kind, type of school and education not only open the way to certain positions, but also determine whether one will be offered such positions, whether one aspires to and is interested in them, and thereby, in part, one's status in the stratification system.

The school also performs its differentiating function by giving marks, a differentiation which affects aspirations and possibilities and, thereby, further education and profession.

As an entity, this system implies that pupils from modest social circumstances but with the ability to assert themselves, also have the opportunity to advance themselves generally in a social respect, i.e. to positions considerably higher in prestige and income than those of their parents. The individual's education and diplomas open doors which would have been closed to him without such an education.

In this way, the educational system is a decisive factor in the very stratification system of society. An educational system characterized by different classes of society having exactly the same opportunities must, of necessity, bring about a social structure of a very *open* nature, one with great mobility between the different social classes.

But 'opportunity' in this context must not be taken to mean only formal opportunity. Economic conditions and prevailing ideologies and aspirations influence how the individual takes advantage of the available 'formal' opportunities. In cases where particular economic, geographical, or traditional conditions discourage use of formal opportunities, the *real* opportunities can scarcely be called equal. In such cases, education does not necessarily result in any tendency to open the stratification system.

4.1. The increase in educational achievement

Table V shows how the percentage of the Norwegian population who took *examen artium* has increased since the turn of the century. The increase applies to both men and women, and to those who took *realskole*, but did not go on to *artium*. The figures for men and women born between 1930 and 1940 correspond to those who took *artium* in the 1950s. The figures for 1964 (which have not been included in Table V) indicate that the percentage of those who later took *artium* or *realskole* increased considerably during the early 1960s; they also indicate that the percentage of men and women born between 1945 and 1950 who take further education *(realskole* or *artium)* will be double that of those born just before the war. In the school year 1951–1952, 26.2 per cent of all 17-year-olds were attending secondary schools; in 1966–1967, the figure was 53 per cent. Of these, 8.9 and 23.5 per cent, respectively, were attending gymnasium, i.e. the percentage of those attending gymnasium has tripled in the last 15 years (NAVF 1967a).

Table VI shows a significant increase in those who have taken vocational courses of one or more years' duration. The figures for those men and women born before 1890 were taken from the 1950 census and pertain to the number who took vocational education lasting *six months* or more. From these figures, it can be calculated that the percentage

Table V. *Percentage who went on to higher education, by sex and year of birth*

Year of birth Examen artium	Men	Women
1881-1890	2.4	0.6
1891-1900	3.3	1.3
1901-1910	5.1	2.2
1911-1920	6.3	3.1
1921-1930	10.2	6.3
1931-1940	11.0	8.0
Realskole or equivalent (excluding those who subsequently took *artium*)		
1881-1890	4.6	4.6
1891-1900	5.5	5.4
1901-1910	7.5	8.1
1911-1920	7.6	7.7
1921-1930	10.4	11.0
1931-1940	13.5	15.3

Sources: For men and women born between 1881 and 1890, figures from NOS XI 258, p. 21. For men and women born in 1891 and after, figures from NOS XII 133, pp. 16-17.

Table VI. *Percentage who took vocational courses lasting one year or more, by sex and year of birth*

Year of birth	Men	Women
1881-1890	20.3	8.6
1891-1900	21.3	12.3
1901-1910	25.1	14.5
1911-1920	30.6	18.1
1921-1930	37.4	19.6
1931-1935	38.0	23.0

Sources: 1881-1890, NOS XI 258, p. 23; the other figures from *Statistisk Ukehefte* no. 8, 1964.

with at least *one year's* vocational training would be about 19 per cent of the men and 7 per cent of the women.

In recent years, public attention has been especially drawn to the great increases in enrollment at both colleges and universities. From 1956 to 1966, the number of students at institutions of higher education more than doubled: from 6,000 – a figure very close to that of the last year before World War II – to 21,400. An additional 3,600 were studying abroad (NAVF 1967, p. 16). Applications to teachers' colleges and professional schools have also increased greatly in the post-war era (NAVF 1957).

This development must be viewed in the context of several situations: increasing prosperity which has enabled more persons to continue their education rather than interrupt it to work, improved terms for loans to finance schooling, better developed educational system, and better understanding of the importance of education for one's future.

4.2. *The relationship between general and vocational education*

In Table VII, general and vocational education are compared. The figures show what percentage of men and women from a given level in the general education system went on to take specialized education which lasted one or more years. The figures are based on information from the 1960 census.

Among those who did not continue their education beyond elementary school, vocational education was an exception; while among men who went on to *realskole* or *artium*, the majority also took some form of vocational education. Thus the differences in educational level present at the termination of ordinary schooling were further emphasized by the subsequent vocational education. Also, for each higher level of schooling the percentage of women taking specialized education deviated less and less from the percentage of men.

177

Table VII. *Percentage who took specialized education, by highest grade and sex***

	Men	Women
Elementary school	16.1	6.4
Continuation school	36.9	24.2
Realskole	60.5	41.0
Examen artium	73.9	53.9

Source: *Statistisk Årbok for Norge*, 1964, pp. 282-283.

* Commercial secondary school *(handelsgymnasium)* is considered as specialized education here.

These conditions can be explained in many ways, none of them decidedly 'most' important. It is reasonable to assume that in the higher grades, a process of selection of the most school-oriented has taken place, and that those with the lowest motivation have fallen by the wayside. However, it is also possible that long exposure to the school environment plays an independent role, i.e. the combined influence of the teachers and a pupil community, in which the non-school-oriented pupils have become fewer and fewer. This assumption seems supported by American data showing how the school orientation of pupils from otherwise similar social backgrounds was affected by the geographical location of the school and by the proportion of working-class pupils present (Havighurst and Neugarten 1962, pp. 334–336). Pupils in the higher age groups are probably more receptive to the school's views of the value of education than are younger pupils.

There were not only differences in frequency, but also in the types of specialized education according to highest level of general

Table VIII. *Type of specialized education, by level of highest ordinary schooling, for men over 15 years of age, 1960 (percentage)*

	Elementary or continuation school	*Realskole* or equivalent	*Examen artium*
University, teachers college	3.2	4.8	62.5
Business college	0.6	11.9	13.1
Commercial school	14.0	27.6	7.3
Technical school	4.6	11.3	5.0
Vocational school, apprenticeship	35.2	14.0	2.4
Seamen's school	18.5	8.8	1.1
Agricultural school	18.2	5.9	1.9
Diverse	5.7	15.7	6.7
Total	100.0	100.0	100.0

Source: NOS XII 142, p. 284.

178

schooling (see Table VIII). While male *artium* graduates preponderantly chose university or teachers' college, among male *realskole* graduates the general tendency was to go on to some form of commercial education or technical schooling. Men without higher general education chose semi-technical courses, industrial schools, seamen's schools, or agricultural schools.

4.3. *Education and choice of occupation*

Table IX shows the occupational statuses of men with different levels of general education. Over 90 per cent of those with only elementary or continuation school were employed in the primary or secondary sectors, whereas more than 90 per cent of those with *artium* were in the tertiary sector. Given the positive correlation between general and specialized education, we must also conclude that the number of those with some form of vocational education is low in the primary and secondary sectors. The 1960 census shows that 73 per cent of men without specialized education were employed in these sectors, while 58 per cent of those with such education were employed in the tertiary sector (NOS XII 133, pp. 108–119).

4.4. *Education as a source of advancement in occupational life*

Table X shows in some detail how men with different levels of higher general education were distributed over various status levels in the secondary and tertiary sectors. We see how men with only an elementary or continuation school education end up, in most cases, as workers or artisans. This is the case for a full 87 per cent of those with an elementary school education, as against 29 per cent of those with *realskole* and 16 per cent of those with *artium*. Men in the two higher

Table. IX. *Men actively employed in 1960, by highest level of ordinary education and occupational field (percentage)*

	Highest level of education		
	Elementary or continuation school	*Realskole* or equivalent	*Examen artium*
Occupational field			
I Agriculture, forestry, fishing	34.6	7.5	3.3
II Industry, crafts	56.2	23.5	4.7
III Trade, transport, services, civil service, teaching	9.2	69.0	92.0
Total	100.0	100.0	100.0

Source: NOS XII 133, Table III, pp. 24-26.

179

Table X. *Men employed in secondary and tertiary sector in 1960, by highest level of general education and position (percentage)*

Position	Highest level of education		
	Elementary or continuation school	*Realskole* or equivalent	*Examen artium* or equivalent
Independent businessman (trade)	2.1	7.1	5.6
Independent, higher white-collar employee in industry, shipping, finance	2.7	27.5	47.0
Lower white-collar worker	5.4	31.9	30.5
Teacher	2.6	4.1	1.5
Foreman, artisan, worker	87.2	29.4	15.5
Total	100.0	100.0	100.0

Source: Unpublished material made available by the Norwegian Central Bureau of Statistics.

educational categories went predominantly into administrative positions; in the case of *artium* graduates, predominantly higher administration.

4.5. *Education as a decisive factor for position and career*

The material presented above has shown that education has consequences for choice of profession, without there being, however, any unambiguous relationship between the two. Numerous examples exist of men with *artium* who ended up as farmers and workers, and of people without higher general education who climbed the ladder to positions as top executives. Can this mean that education in itself is not so decisive a factor? that people, after completing their education, drift back to the place in society from which they started, as if nothing had happened in the meantime?

These questions concern recruitment to education from different social groups. For example, 32 per cent of male *artium* graduates after 1930 came from farm, artisan, or working-class backgrounds, i.e. from those groups of the population for whom education would imply mobility away from their original classes. However, the census shows that of all male *artium* graduates actively employed in 1960, only 7 per cent were farmers, artisans, or workers. Sixty-eight per cent of *artium* graduates came from administrative, business, or academic backgrounds, while a full 93 per cent entered careers in those fields.

5. RECRUITMENT OF WOMEN TO FURTHER EDUCATION

From Table V we have seen that 5.2 per cent of women born between 1881 and 1890 took *realskole* or *gymnasium*, while the figure for men was 7.0 per cent. Only 12 per cent of these women took *examen artium*, as against 34 per cent of the men. For women and men born between 1931 and 1940, the proportion of those taking higher education increased, to 23.3 and 24.5 per cent, respectively; of these, 34 and 45 per cent, respectively, took *artium*. Although the differences have decreased considerably, men today still complete higher education more frequently than do women, and the differences are greatest at the *artium* level. In the 1950s women comprised about 40 per cent of those taking *artium*, in 1965, 43 per cent (Vangsnes 1967, p. 11).

Table VI showed the percentage of men and women with vocational education which lasted one year or more. Here too, the differences have decreased in the present century, but for those born between 1931 and 1935 they were still considerable. Women's low percentage here can be in part due to their generally lower participation in higher general education, but this is not in itself a sufficient explanation. The percentage of female *artium* graduates who began university-level studies was about half that of male graduates, and the percentage of those completing such studies was also considerably lower (see Thagaard Sem 1967).

Female students in the faculties of medicine and law very seldom received the best examination marks. Differences on this point were, however, insignificant in the faculties of the humanities and of mathematics and natural sciences (Aubert 1960, pp. 89–96, Lindbekk 1967, pp. 121–125, 203). As to research achievements and number promoted to leading positions, women seem to lag behind men in all the fields mentioned (Lindbekk 1967, pp. 130–134, 209–212).

6. SOCIAL RECRUITMENT TO THE GYMNASIUM

Table IV showed that, during the course of this century, further education became more and more usual. We found a development which indicated that more people go on not only to *realskole* and *artium*, but also to other forms of education.

What effect has this development had on the different classes and groups in the population? Unfortunately, we have detailed information on only the *artium* group, i.e. those completing *gymnasium*.

The material clearly shows to what extent *gymnasium* was originally first and foremost for society's two leading groups – academics and businessmen. As Table XI shows, 60 per cent of the *artium* graduates in the period 1870–1880 were the sons of academics or merchants. A significant number came from the very heterogeneous group composed of civil servants, executives, sea captains, etc., which taken together are designated 'administrative personnel'. A certain number also come from farming and teaching groups. The number of sons of craftsmen and workers was very low indeed, particularly sons of workers, who took *artium*, on the average, at the rate of three individuals a year.

Examining the distribution of these graduates by social groups, however, we find that those of 1910–1914 differed very little in social background from those of 1870–1880. The academic and business groups still supplied more than one-half of the male graduates, though the proportion of those from an academic background was somewhat reduced. Sons of farmers and teachers accounted for 14 per cent of the male graduates in the decade 1870–1880, and their percentage continued to increase until 1915–1919, when they formed 23 per cent of the group. In contrast, the proportion of graduates from working and artisan backgrounds remained the same as in the 1870s, not increasing noticeably until the end of the 1920s.

From the end of the 1920s on, development was rapid. In the period up to 1946, the number of graduates from an artisan background doubled, the number from a working-class background increased five-fold. The percentage of sons of farmers and teachers remained more or less the same, but the group from academic and business backgrounds was reduced to 28 per cent – nearly one half what it had been in 1910–1914.

After 1946 the distribution pattern of the different social groups stabilized. Comparing the social origins of 1946 *artium* graduates with the 1951 and 1958 figures, the only change is an increase in the proportion from an academic background, with a corresponding decrease in number from a white-collar background.

The Norwegian Research Council for Science and the Humanities has prepared figures for 1946–1963 *artium* graduates. Although employing a somewhat different occupational classification, this investigation shows that the percentage of male *artium* graduates from artisan, worker, or fisherman backgrounds remained fairly constant in the period 1946–1958. From 1958 to 1963, however, there was an increase, from 25.8 to 32.1 per cent (Vangsnes 1967, p. 53).

An attempt has been made to compare the changes which have taken place in the composition of the *artium* graduate group (see Table XII) with the changes in the composition of the Norwegian population. The estimates presented here are based on data from the census, population migration, etc.; changes in life expectancy and the age composition of different professional groups are taken into account, but it is assumed that the number of sons born to members of any one profession has remained constant during the period examined.

182

Table XI. *Male artium graduates 1870-1958, by father's occupation (percentage)*

Graduation year	Aca- demic	Business- man	White- collar worker	Farmer	Teacher	Artisan	Worker	Other	Total
1870-1879	34.6	22.0	17.6	9.0	5.4	8.2	2.0	1.2	100.0
1910-1914	28.1	22.9	20.5	11.8	7.3	5.5	1.8	2.1	100.0
1915-1919	24.4	23.8	18.2	16.6	6.5	5.4	2.9	2.3	100.0
1920-1924	22.3	23.2	19.8	15.7	5.6	6.8	4.1	2.6	100.0
1925-1929	18.4	20.4	21.5	14.7	6.7	8.8	5.6	3 9	100.0
1930-1934	22.4	20.7	22.9	11.3	7.2	8.3	5.0	2 2	100.0
1935-1939	20.1	20.1	26.1	9.9	6.7	7.7	6.3	2.3	100.0
1946	13.1	14.8	26.6	13.9	5.8	13.1	10.0	2.7	100.0
1951	16.3	15.5	23.7	14.7	6.9	11.3	9.4	2.1	99.9
1958	18.7	14.1	23.1	13.4	4.2	12.2	10.5	3.8	100.0

Source: Based on the author's own, previously unpublished material.

These estimates show an increase in the total number of *artium* graduates each year from the 1870 until the 1930s in all groups. The increase has been even for all groups with the exception of the white-collar and artisan categories. At the beginning of this century great changes took place in the composition of these groups, changes so radical that we can say the very character of the groups changed.

The corresponding figures for *artium* graduates of 1951, 1958, and 1963 are shown in Table XIII. The proportion with *artium* gradu- ates among sons of academically educated persons and higher white- collar workers changed only a little from the 1930s to the 1950s. Among the sons of farmers and artisans, and especially among the sons of workers and fishermen, there has, however, been a consider- able increase.

The frequency increased in all social categories from 1958 to 1963 – also among sons of academically educated persons, etc., a group that already had a high percentage. Here the increase was to 62 per cent, while among sons of working foremen, workers, and farmers and forestry workers the *artium* rate rose only to 10 per cent, i.e. about one-seventh of that of the increase among the academic group. The Table shows a similar levelling-out for women as well.

Natalie Rogoff Ramsøy's investigation of those reporting for first- time military duty in 1950 showed that 72 per cent of the sons of academically educated persons, teachers, and higher white-collar workers had completed *realskole* or further education, while the cor- responding figures for sons of artisans, workers, and sailors was 20 per cent, for sons of farmers, 11 per cent, and sons of fishermen, 6 per cent (Rogoff Ramsøy 1961, p. 222). Comparing these figures with the

183

Table XII. *Rate per 1,000 sons who took examen artium 1870-1939, by father's occupation*

Father's occupation	1870-1879	1910-1919	1920-1929	1930-1939
Academic	421.0	451	502	549
Tradesman	75.0	117	177	184
White-collar worker	79.0	48	85	111
Farmer	2.4	14	23	18
Teacher	74.0	194	392	363
Artisan	17.0	12	27	42
Worker	0.4	2	6	7

Source: These figures, aside from a few adjustments, were previously published in Lindbekk 1962 a, p. 253. There, artisans were classed together with workers.

artium figures for 1951 in Table XIII, we find that 74 per cent of the sons of academically educated persons, etc., who completed *realskole* also went on to take *examen artium*. The corresponding figures for sons of workers and artisans was 24 per cent, and for sons of farmers and of fishermen, 57 and 38 per cent, respectively. The social factor is apparent, with respect both to how many attend *realskole* and to how many continue to *gymnasium*. The percentage of sons of the academic group making the transition from *realskole* to *gymnasium* was more than triple that of sons of workers and artisans. For sons of farmers and fishermen, the transition rate was also lower, but stronger in affecting the proportion who attend *realskole* than how many of these continue on to *gymnasium*.

Broadening the social recruitment basis of *gymnasium* education brought about a breakdown of the close connection between *examen artium* and university level studies that previously existed. The growing proportion of women, who in general have less motivation for higher education than do men, probably contributed to this; likewise, a generally changed opinion of the advantage of an academic profession did its part. As a result, the percentage of *artium* graduates who went on to take a university degree decreased up to the end of the World War II and during the immediate post-war years, but the pattern was not the same in all the recruiting groups: for the sons of academics, it decreased the least, while, for the sons of teachers, there was a strong decrease only after the war (see Table XIV).

As a result, during the post-war period the sons of academics were definitely set apart as a group quite different from all others as to higher education. This was in part due to the fact that in the immediate post-war period, some faculties were 'closed'. This meant that many had to go abroad to study these fields – and the sons of academics had better chances of doing that. At the same time, their environ-

Table XIII. *Rate per 1,000 sons and daughters who took examen artium, by father's occupation, 1951-1963*

	Men			Women		
Father's occupation	1951	1958	1963	1951	1958	1963
Academic, teacher, higher white-collar employee	535	532	623	421	462	578
Self-employed in industry, trade, shipping, finance	197	309	396	166	271	352
White-collar worker	286	236	271	214	185	226
Self-employed in agriculture or forestry	63	75	93	35	47	68
Artisan	67	141	223	55	115	210
Foreman, worker	45	55	91	25	31	60
Fisherman	23	32	43	8	14	16

Source: Vangsnes 1967, pp. 79-80.

ment probably gave them more motivation to take a degree than did that of the average *artium* graduate (Lindbekk 1964, pp. 132–145).

Tove Thagaard Sem's study of the *artium* groups of 1946, 1951, and 1958 showed that a larger percentage began university-level studies among those from academic, lecturer, or higher official family backgrounds than among *artium* graduates from other backgrounds. Among the 1958 *artium* graduates, 75 per cent of the sons of the academics took up university-level studies, as against 58 per cent of the sons of farmers and forestry workers and 61 per cent of the sons of workers and fishermen. For women, the figures were, respectively, 38, 16, and 20 per cent: i.e. the social background factor was especially strong here (Thagaard Sem 1967).

Table XIV. *Rate per 1,000 male artium graduates who completed university-level education, by father's occupation and year of artium*

	Year of taking *examen artium*				
Father's occupation	1870-1879	1910-1919	1920-1929	1930-1939	1946-1951
Academic	741	565	675	485	445
Businessman	653	489	395	362	275
White-collar worker	520	481	376	324	266
Farmer	775	485	417	404	270
Teacher	566	542	398	511	295
Artisan	584	486	422	329	202
Worker	656	759	483	395	246

Sources: Figures for 1930 to 1951, Lindbekk 1964, p. 134; remaining figures are from unpublished material.

Social background was also related to university examination results, amount of original research done, and promotion to higher positions after completion of university education. The effects always tended in the same direction, so that the sons of the academic group did better than those from other backgrounds (Lindbekk 1967a, pp. 120–155, 203–213).

7. GEOGRAPHICAL FACTORS IN RECRUITMENT TO FURTHER EDUCATION

From Table IX we have seen that great differences exist between urban and rural areas with respect to further education. This is partly because persons with further education tend to take up employment in towns and cities. However, Vidkun Coucheron-Jarl Thrane's study of draftees reporting for military service in 1947–1949 showed significant differences in the percentage of those with *realskole* and *gymnasium* coming from urban as against from rural areas. The *artium* frequency for Oslo was 30 per cent here, as against only 3 per cent for young men from predominantly fishing, or combined fishing and agricultural areas.

Natalie Rogoff Ramsøy's study of the 1950 draftee group revealed differences between the various types of municipality, when father's occupation is also held constant. In municipalities where the main

Table XV. *Percentage of male draftees 1947-1949 with realskole or examen artium, by type of home municipality*

Place of residence	Realskole or equivalent	Examen artium or equivalent	Total with higher education
City			
Oslo	19	30	49
Bergen	16	25	41
Other city	17	20	37
Other types of municipalities			
Urbanized area	16	25	45
Industrialized area	12	12	24
Combination industry and agriculture	10	8	18
Combination agriculture and forestry	9	6	15
Combination industry and fishing	9	7	16
Fishing, or combination fishing and agriculture	7	3	10

Source: Coucheron-Jarl 1953, Table 17.

Table XVI. *Percentage taking examen artium, by geographical region and father's occupation. Men, 1963*

Father's occupation	Geographical area				
	Øst-landet	Sør-landet	Vest-landet	Trønde-lag	Nord-Norge
Academic, teacher, higher white-collar employee	70.0	52.9	49.7	57.6	38.2
Self-employed in trade or industry	41.3	49.5	31.6	36.2	30.4
White-collar worker	27.1	25.8	22.6	22.9	22.7
Artisan	25.0	25.6	18.4	26.1	9.9
Foreman, worker	7.3	8.6	8.2	7.9	7.5
Farmer	10.9	9.5	7.7	6.3	3.1
Fisherman	3.9	—	3.2	—	2.7

Source: Vangsnes 1967, pp. 81-83.

source of income was from agriculture, forestry, and fishing, the *real-skole* or *gymnasium* percentage for sons of artisans and skilled workers was 8–9 per cent, as against 17 per cent for more urbanized municipalities, for sons of farmers and unskilled workers, 2–5 per cent, as against 8 per cent (Rogoff Ramsøy 1961, p. 225).

Table XVI shows the variation in *artium* rate in 1963 for different geographical regions of Norway and between categories of occupation. The geographical factor seems to have influenced the rate within the majority of occupational categories, in such a way that the rate was lowest in western Norway *(Vestlandet)* and northern Norway *(Nord-Norge)*. The differences were especially large for sons of academics, teachers, and higher white-collar employees. For the sons of this group in eastern Norway *(Østlandet)* we find the percentage as high as 70.

These categories may differ somewhat from region to region, and similar objections may be raised to the draftee study of 1950. Therefore, neither Rogoff Ramsøy's material nor Table XVI can be said to present sufficient evidence of regional effects on school attainment.

The notably low *artium* frequencies among sons of northern Norwegian farmers and fishermen is connected with the region's ethnic composition, as well as its economic structure, difficulties in transport and communication, and an insufficient school system. As of yet no one has studied educational achievement level of children from the Lappish-speaking and Finnish-speaking minorities found there, despite the recognized fact that Lappish-speaking youth often have difficulties in adjusting to Norwegian society, including the Norwegian school system (Hoem 1963).

187

8. CAUSES OF THE LARGE DIFFERENCES IN LEVEL OF EDUCATION

In explaining why women less frequently take some form of further education, it is natural to draw attention to some aspects of the role of women in our society – i.e. what is expected of women (as opposed to men) in various connections. Because most women will be able to count on being supported by someone else for most of their life, any comprehensive effort to prepare for an occupation is often seen unnecessary.

Rural youths' especially low frequency of further schooling is due to several factors. First, there is the social (and ethnic) composition of the population involved; second, there are difficult practical conditions, such as that the school system is insufficient in that area, with institutions for further education located far away, which means either long journeys or boarding away from home (Solstad 1965, pp. 88–121). While most expenses connected with school transportation and boarding are refunded today, this is true first and foremost of the compulsory schooling, and not the *realskole* or *gymnasium*. Thus, financial considerations force many to give up further education.

Financial considerations are also relevant in explaining why *social factors* were so important. *Realskole* and *gymnasium* education involved expenses for textbooks – often also for tuition, transportation, and boarding. At the same time, the pupil had to postpone the time at which he would be earning his own living. Such factors must have been of greatest importance to youth from poorer families, effectively putting a brake on further education. Gradually the general level of welfare has increased, so that today this second factor should be of less importance than earlier.

Another possible factor concerns *ability*. Sigmund Stangvik's investigation from Vestfold showed an over-representation of workers' children among those classified 'not yet ready for school' in first grade (Stangvik 1967, pp. 205–221).

In an investigation of one school cohort in Stockholm, Boalt found a correlation of 0.32 between social background and marks in four-year elementary school (Boalt and Husén 1964, p. 137). An investigation conducted in Malmö by Hallgren showed a corresponding difference in the average scores on IQ tests. Boalt's investigation, however, showed that the correlation between social group and transition rates to secondary school was 0.71, i.e. double the correlation of social group to marks. Another investigation from Stockholm, dealing with those accepted by the secondary schools in 1955, showed that on each level of intelligence the number of pupils who sought admission to gymnasium was higher for pupils from the higher social classes.

Boalt also investigated recruitment from *realskole* to *gymnasium* schools. In the *realskole,* the correlation between social background and examination marks was completely insignificant. However, the correlation between social background and the number who went on to the *gymnasium* was 0.45. Because of this, the differences in *gymnasium* applications must be attributed to differences other than intellectual ability.

Norwegian studies of *examen artium* marks have not shown any tendency to poorer marks for sons of workers, for instance; in fact, a slight tendency to the contrary has appeared (Vangsnes 1967, p. 2, Skard 1964, Lindbekk 1967, p. 155). That youth from academic backgrounds more frequently continue on to university-level studies cannot, therefore, be due to better performance in the *gymnasium.*

9. MOTIVATION AND LEVEL OF EDUCATION

A Norwegian Gallup poll, published 5 April 1954, showed that 36 per cent of workers sampled wished their sons would take a university education – as against 47 per cent of the white-collar workers interviewed. Another Gallup survey, published 2 September 1960, showed that 23 per cent of those with 'low' income hoped their sons would enter an occupation which required university education – as against 30 per cent of those with 'high' income.

Sverre Lysgaard's and Egil Fivelsdal's studies from the early 1960s showed that of a sample of workers whose children were still in school, 25 per cent planned to have them take *artium* – as against 65 per cent of the white-collar workers in the same situation (Lysgaard 1965, pp. 136–141). The important thing to note there is that the percentage planning *gymnasium* studies was consistently lower among workers and those in the lowest income groups.

These questions have been especially examined by English researchers studying school selection. A comprehensive investigation from London showed that working-class children consistently differed from pupils from the middle class in attitudes to attendance and school work. Fewer of them thought that good marks would have any meaning in their future lives. And there were fewer of them, who, when faced with the choice of going to a party or preparing for an examination, chose preparing for an examination. The teachers also considered them to be less responsible in their school work; they were less industrious and behaved more badly at school (Himmelweit 1959, pp. 145–151). Working-class children thought less of school, and, at the same time, the teachers considered them less worthwhile pupils. There are indications that they were also often evaluated below the other

189

pupils and that they took little part in activities organized by the other pupils (Jackson and Marsden 1962, pp. 105–112, Havighurst and Neugarten 1962, p. 246, Evans 1962, pp. 46–50).

In 1952, F. M. Martin interviewed all of the parents in one English school district whose children were to take the 11-plus examination that year. The investigation showed that the parents who belonged to the group 'unskilled workers' were very little interested in their children's school attendance and the impending examination. They had little feeling that further education would have any special meaning for the children, and they were rather indifferent as to whether the children were accepted for grammar school or not. Only 1.5 per cent of the unskilled workers wanted to send their children to another type of school in the event that they did not pass the examination, while 49.4 per cent of the parents belonging to the professional groups wanted to do so (Martin 1954).

However, the situation was not only that the home was little concerned with education as an important means of social advancement and that it had little insight into how school attendance, in general, could be useful; some investigations indicate that the working-class system of bringing up children has some characteristics which have prompted the development of deep-seated traits which oppose both the general aptitude for persistent effort and the investment of energy and emotion in mastering tasks (Davis 1958, pp. 139–150, Ericson 1958, pp. 494–501). American researchers have made up personality tests which attempt to measure general 'achievement motive'. Marked differences in scores have been shown between working-class and middle-class children (McClelland 1953, S. Rosen 1961).

It has been proposed that the reason for the failure of working-class children is to be found in the *language* which the working class use, since the IQ tests in part measure proficiency in the use of the language of the middle class (Bernstein 1961, pp. 188–314). Other

Table XVII. *Parents' preferences in secondary education, S. W. Hertfordshire (percentage)*

Father's occupation	Preferred grammar school	Had thought a great deal about secondary education
Professional, specialist, etc.	81.7	82.7
White-collar worker	77.8	70.2
Independent, foreman	60.7	62.0
Skilled worker	48.2	50.5
Unskilled worker	43.4	35.3

Source: Martin 1954

190

studies have emphasized the fact that the very nature of the problems contained in the tests has consistently favoured middle-class children whose environment has prepared them for such problems (Nisbet 1961, pp. 273–287).

However, we lack comparable data from Norway. The above-mentioned investigations do give us some ideas about how to interpret the differences found in applications for further education. How valid these ideas are, we do not yet know.

10. THE SCHOOL AS AN EXPONENT OF A FOREIGN CULTURE

It is as yet too soon to take a stand on which of the above-mentioned explanatory factors should be given most weight. However, they all have one trait in common: they all seem to point to the existence of a comprehensive system of life, thought, and values peculiar to the working class and clearly different from that of the middle class. Their language, the usual problem areas, the low achievement motivation, the virtual lack of interest in the skills which the school teaches and the opportunities it presents – all of these must be considered as parts of the *culture* of the working class, and not just random factors.

This need not be the only decisive factor. It can be that working-class children have consistently had weaker hereditary abilities, or that economic conditions have made it more difficult to keep children in school. But, in any case, the situation brings us back to the fact discussed above – that the school has overwhelmingly received its characteristics and goals from the middle class and can be considered an instrument for the propagation of middle-class culture.

Because of this, there is a true deep-seated cultural conflict which interferes with working-class children's attempts to fulfil the demands the school makes on them. When a boy from a working-class background protests against the school, it is not only because he is a teenager going through a stage of adolescent opposition to the adult world, but also because the school's system of values is not the one he knows in his working-class world; it is not the one to which he is more or less consciously aspiring. For him, further education will isolate him from his peer group, that group of his mates who are beginning their working lives, i.e. becoming adults, in contrast to himself.

The middle-class boy finds himself in an entirely different situation. His parents definitely want him to have an education. He makes his friends at school, and the manners he has learned at home make it easier for him to establish contact with the teacher. His friends

191

are at school, and he knows that for a boy of his age there is basically no alternative to school, and that *not* to go to school will isolate him from his friends.

We must assume that the same conditions that affect working-class youth affect rural youth and account for the low level of education we find in rural areas, though the situation may be more complicated in such an area. Hoem's investigation of Lapp problems may be similarly interpreted to other specific groups (Hoem 1963).

11. THE REBELS

Neither 'farmer' nor 'worker' is an unambiguous concept. Especially in the case of workers, several investigations have been conducted which have brought to light the very important differences existing between the various sub-categories of workers – differences which, among other things, affect the level of education sought. In England, for example, skilled workers differ from unskilled workers in that the former are more interested in their children's education (see Table XVII), their children's level of intelligence is often higher, and many more of their children go on to grammar school (Glass 1954, p. 22).

Martin's investigation showed that this was bound up with the differences in level of education between skilled workers and the other workers; there was a direct connection between the parents' level of education and their interest in the children's schooling (Martin 1954).

Ramsøy's Norwegian material shows a similar tendency. The percentage of working-class children who took *realskole* and *artium* was doubled in those cases where the *father* had *realskole* or more (Ramsøy 1957, p. 68).

That a worker has higher education can be taken to indicate that he himself has status ambitions unusual for workers. His education indicates that he has neither been nor wanted to be an ordinary worker, and it is reasonable to assume that all this has also affected his ambitions for his *children*. He himself has stood on the threshold of breaking out of the working class; his children's education will give them the opportunity to achieve that which he himself has not.

From this point of view, working-class children would take further education particularly in those cases where the parents themselves were not *typical* workers, i.e. where the parents were actually in a position somewhere between the working class and the middle class.

Jackson and Marsden's study of 88 working-class children who went to grammar school revealed that 34 of them were connected with the middle class, either in that their parents had earlier held middle-class jobs or in that they had close family in the middle class. In the

192

cases of some of the other children in the group, several of the parents had gone to grammar school or the father was a foreman – in other words, the parents were not ordinary workers. In the cases of only 21 of the 88 children was there no form of affiliation with the middle class (Jackson and Marsden 1962, p. 55).

Several researchers have shown that there is another factor, *size of family*, which affects continuing education, level of intelligence, and achievement motive. Working-class children from small families usually do better than the other children. Such differences are not noticeable in children from the middle class (Himmelweit 1954, Nisbet 1961, Rosen 1961). These factors cannot be completely explained only by referring to biological heredity and economic conditions. Nevertheless, family size in itself can be considered a form of middle-class infiltration since it expresses middle-class values and views. There is reason to assume that small working-class families have in general been more middle class and mobility oriented than the average working-class family. They are also probably more education oriented, and one or the other of the parents has possibly taken secondary education.

If this is right, then we have, in the established differences in intelligence, continuation of education, etc., a new expression of how the level of schooling taken by working-class children is dependent on their parents' having departed from the typical working-class culture. It is in those cases where the parents have identified themselves with the middle class that the children will be able to take advantage of and benefit from the educational opportunities available to them.

VI. Political Institutions

By Ulf Torgersen

1. INTRODUCTION[1]

Giving a general description of Norwegian political institutions can be a risky operation; it is difficult to decide which materials to include, and hard to determine how to treat the subject. I have organized the material along two main lines: first I divided it into three sections, and, second, I chose two typically Norwegian themes and have carried them through each of the three sections.

1.1. *A formal model for analysis of politics*[2]

Talcott Parsons has constructed a model which, when combined with that of David Easton, provides us with a paradigm for describing a political system, i.e. the system relating to final political authority within a territory. Parsons and Easton distinguish between the following necessary elements in a political system: 1) generation of support, 2) generation of leadership, 3) generation of demands, 4) decision-making.[3]

Parsons' model may be interpreted in two ways, each with different results:

1) We may want to establish various dimensions for the analysis of a *system*. In this case, it is important to note that we *do not* use the model as a form for mutually exclusive classification of separate actions. A single action may, for instance, be 'fitted into' the process of generating leadership, as well as into the process of decision-making, depending on the hypotheses on which the investigation is based. Thus a question put to a politician from a voter in rural western Norway as to whether he is in favour of the temperance movement, for instance, will produce an answer relevant to all four elements of the model.

2) The model may also be regarded as a type of classification of actions according to their primary normative purposes. Usually, these actions will take place within an institutional framework (generation of leadership taking place within political parties,

generation of demands within the various organizations, decision-making within the branches of government). But if we want to describe the processes that *shape* and influence decisions, we find ourselves on uncertain ground. It will not then be a question of explicit purpose and of the 'duties' of organizations, but of processes and functions as measured against the four necessary elements of the political system.

According to the first interpretation, the model establishes four separate systems of empirical cause-and-effect-relations, in which each relation has its own end variable (the four elements), but where each link is characterized by its contribution towards this end, and not because at face value it is a part of this particular type of activity. This, however, is the main feature of the second interpretation of the model; here, actions are classified according to whether they are normatively or purposefully directed towards one of the four ends in a general sense.

Personally, I prefer the second interpretation. Not because I do not regard the first interpretation as the *goal* of research. On the contrary, it means that other analytical categories are needed to describe political behaviour which then can be tied together through hypotheses about inter-connections. Classification cannot precede investigation and analysis. This model, broadly interpreted, will be used in our presentation of the material here.

Both of these directions are found in modern political research. One approach is to *describe structure,* concentrating on the normative structures that regulate recruitment to and behaviour in roles that, by general agreement, consist in making decisions authoritative and binding on those living within the territory. The second approach is to *analyse processes;* it concentrates on the processes involved in maintaining, in strengthening, or in the deterioration of institutions. The first tendency is towards analysis of existing norms, while the second seeks to describe the functioning of the system, i.e. the processes relating to introduction of new individuals into the political system, to renewal of loyalty to the system, to recruitment of personnel to leadership roles, and to the making of new decisions. Historically, concentration on this second type of research has also led to analysis of structures and systems not immediately recognized as parts of ordinary authority structures. Recent research studies indicate empirically (in politics), however, that these 'secondary' systems are so closely connected to the ordinary authority structures that it is no longer practical to exclude them. A distinction of that which is 'political', therefore, must itself be a result of considerable knowledge about politics; there will probably always be general agreement on certain elements constitutioning a 'hard core' of the subject but doubts on how far to proceed beyond this central core.

In any case – and this is a typical feature of sociological orientation the political system cannot be said to stand by itself. There must always be some form of renewal if the system is to continue functioning. Contrary to a juridical analysis, which concerns itself with the study of whether or not a given system is legitimate, the sociological orientation will concentrate on problems concerning the very existence of a system (here, a political system): studying the conditions for the necessary minimum renewal of loyalty, renewal of personnel, and continuous flow of new decisions. Rather than regarding the political system as a chair standing solidly on the floor until someone overturns it, the sociological approach studies the system as a living plant as hardy perhaps as a cactus, yet always requiring a minimum supply of nourishment.

This approach is not merely a theoretical device. From experience we know that political systems (like other social systems) have a limited lifespan, that they sometimes collapse or disintegrate, and that they pass through various types of crises. It may be convenient to use the question of legitimacy as a point of departure. To what extent has the Norwegian political system been able to establish and maintain the necessary degree of legitimacy? Have crises occurred, and if so, how have they been overcome by the system? Such problems will be taken up in section 2.

In section 3 we will discuss political personnel, participation, and recruitment, as well as generation of demands, and in section 4 we will discuss some salient features of decision-making within the system.

1.2. A dominant theme: egalitarian values and absence of a politically strong upper class

It will be particularly important to emphasize that the absence of conflict has been a constant feature in/of the development of political institutions in Norway over the last 150 years. This is a central theme in section 2, where some of the factors leading to this situation are described. The first of these appears to be the *social stratification structure* and the value system attached to it, especially such values as *equality* and *achievement*.

These factors, moreover, have had obvious consequences for the participation level and for the recruitment process and its results, as well as noticeable effects on decisions made within the political system.

1.3. A second dominant theme: 'Norway is a small country'

A second factor leading to absence of conflicts is found in the very *political-administrative structure* in a country of Norway's limited size and resources. We shall see that these conditions, together with the egalitarian values just mentioned, have led to distinctive types of approach within the system and to definite solutions to the problems of self versus collectivity and specificity versus diffuseness.

The various factors, of course, are closely interconnected. But mainly for pedagogical reasons I have chosen to view the egalitarian values as products of social stratification, and the orientation towards the collectivity and responsible all-inclusiveness ('diffuseness') as an integral part of problems prevalent in the administrative and organizational configuration in Norway. The co-ordination and fusion of these two features (as well as the conflict between them) – one rooted in social stratification and the other linked to the political-administrative structure and its internal demands – are, in my opinion, a unique feature of Norwegian political institutions throughout their development and existence.

1.4. The separation of politics from society at large

This deliberate distinction between values issuing from social stratification and values flowing from the political-administrative structure underlines the problematic nature of the politics/society configuration. Even though political institutions do 'reflect' society as a whole, the political-administrative system has its own, distinct set of problems. Because these problems are tied in with the acquisition and exercise of power, they do not allow the same values to appear in the same way or with the same importance that they would in other circumstances. The political system will often function somewhat removed from the general value system – outside and beyond it. More explicitly: in a society as small and transparent as the Norwegian, where the exercise of power is so much disliked, where equality is a dominant feature, and where evaluation on the basis of individual merit is avoided so consistently, the politics/society configuration can present serious problems.

This does not mean that power is not exercised, but characteristically the process is a difficult one. Because the use of power runs against the grain of deep-rooted values, careful planning is required. Swift improvisation and expedient exercise of power are difficult to justify. Prime Minister G. F. Hagerup's tardiness in 1905 (due to his desire to handle the conflict with Sweden through the normal, slow-moving party procedures) and the passivity of Prime Minister Johan Nygaardsvold in the period shortly before the 9 April 1940 German invasion stand as interesting demonstrations of how difficult it can be for the average political leader to move swiftly and authoritatively. That Gunnar Knudsen's dictum 'We have the power and we shall use

197

it', could cause so much sensation, is also deeply indicative of the peculiar Norwegian attitude.

Our double approach, therefore, evolves from a specific perspective best illustrated by the phrase 'partial dependence of the political system on other social institutions and its partial autonomy'. This perspective, originally opened by Max Weber and subsequently developed by Reinhard Bendix (1960), indicates that, by and large, politics and political institutions reflect human relations as they appear in other social situations. In order for them to have any real weight, norms of political behaviour must be based upon society's general system of values. One can hardly imagine the existence of a political system that had its own norms of behaviour *completely* separate from that of society at large, or that did not extensively resort to traditional reactions specific to the national culture. The existence of such a system would require exceptional ability to hold the various institutions apart from each other; this, again, would require specialized training far beyond that normally possible.

Yet true as this may be, this specific perspective also has its definite limitations. Politics *does* call for a type of behaviour not particularly prevalent; in some of its aspects, its exercise of public power is rather unique. Governing does have its own set of rules. Particularly important here is the relationship between the various high-status actors within the political system.

Accordingly, there is no reason to expect any complete overlapping of 'general' culture and political culture; problems prevalent in the 'general' culture are simply not identical with those in the political culture. Instead, it will be the strains and pressures that develop in the meeting between general culture and political culture that call for special attention; the main issue will be how and to what degree activities within these two spheres are interconnected – or regarded as being so.

1.5. *Some minor apologies*

The approach chosen, together with the way in which it is followed, has had consequences for the selection and exclusion of materials presented here.

One consequence in particular should be mentioned, even though it is due as much to space limitations as to the special approach: only brief mention will be made of the vast mass of empirical data on *elections*. Those who are interested in this matter should consult specialized treatises (see Valen and Katz 1965). It would be difficult to discuss these data in this brief presentation, hence the omission. Furthermore, formal aspects of the government structure (number of ministries, etc.)

are excluded, and very limited attention will be paid to public administration.

One limitation, due not to space problems but rather to the approach itself, is the scant discussion of the interplay between 'public' and 'private' forces. If our theme had been power instead of politics, we would have needed an entirely different type of approach, one describing either the power structure (see e.g. Mills 1956) or the power game (see Ortmark 1967). We must, however, emphasize that this is *not* our purpose in this chapter. Therefore, we perhaps offer little to the reader interested in knowing where the power lies in Norway; nor do we treat Norway's real dependence on other countries.

This lack of balance in material content is connected with a similar imbalance between 'facts' and 'interpretations'. We have organized the presentation around a few main themes even though this imposes definite limitations. Detailed documentation, therefore, dominates less than interpretative comment. The presentation, however, cannot be all-inclusive; several approaches are possible, and the choice here has been deliberate.

2. PROBLEMS OF LEGITIMACY AND INSTITUTIONAL CHANGE

2.1. *Minor legitimacy crises*

Simply stated, Norway was established as an independent nation in 1814. We shall not question legitimacy prior to that date but shall limit our inquiry to the following: Has there, after that date, been any serious challenge to legitimacy, any event or conflict that could cause any group or groups to seriously doubt the legitimacy of the system?

In general, we can state that legitimacy has remained undisturbed. Only rarely, and then for very limited periods only, have conflicts occurred involving doubts as to the validity of the rules of the game or threats of upheaval. In general, the characteristic feature is one of absence of serious legitimacy crises. Conflicts were not totally non-existent, but they were not serious enough to present a direct threat to the system, or they were given outlets which posed no threat to the system.

When compared with similar situations in other countries, the distinct impression of internal placidity in Norway is further strengthened. With exception made for Denmark and Sweden, whose fate has been quite similar to that of Norway, legitimacy crises have been the order of the day on the European continent.

Nevertheless, these four critical phases can be distinguished: 1) the first period after 1814, when the Norwegian state was young, subject to external pressures, and when the farmers had not yet realized the opportunities offered by the new political system; 2) the conflict in 1884, when bitterness generated by the parliamentary struggle and impeachment of the (Conservative) Cabinet drove the conservative forces close to a coup d'état; 3) the conflicts around 1920, when the radical section of the Norwegian Labour Party (DNA) withheld its loyalty to the system; 4) the war years 1940–1945, when the combination of external occupation and internal collaboration caused a temporary crisis of legitimacy.

In none of these crises was there any *large* group of angry and uncompromising dissidents. The crises, furthermore, were quickly resolved without leaving irreparable wounds.

The first crisis was not very important. It occurred at a time when the political system was not yet solidly established and did not last very long.

In the 1884 constitutional crisis, there was a question of the strategy the conservatives should follow in the conclusive political battle and the course to be pursued afterwards. In this case, the moderate line was victor, whereupon the conservatives without serious protest sought to gain power within the new parliamentary system, a system that was accepted without further ado.

The third crisis (1920) issued from the radicalization of the Norwegian Labour Party (DNA). It is common knowledge that DNA took a more radical position than did labour parties in most other countries, yet it gave hardly any indication of an inclination towards unconstitutional means and methods. DNA spoke and wrote revolution but was not specific on the *kind* of revolution, and the whole campaign remained on the verbal level. De-radicalization of the party took place in short order. No thorough study has been completed on these events, but material collected by Hans Stokland for a university dissertation strongly suggests that the victorious radical wing in 1918 represented a complicated conglomeration and that only a small group held anti-parliamentarian attitudes. Stokland also emphasizes the widespread pacifism within the party, which had hardly any relation to anti-parliamentarism (see also Langfelt 1961). In my opinion, non-socialist politicians had fully realized that Labour presented no threat at all to the parliamentary system even before 1926 when DNA was reunited after the schism. That these politicians found it to be in their interests to present a different opinion to the voters, however, is quite a different matter.

The fourth crisis (1940–1945) occurred in connection with World War II, and I will make no comment beyond a reminder about the swift and smooth reorganization of the political system as soon as the German occupation was brought to an end. No comparative study has been made, but, from Thomas Wyller's *Frigjøringspolitikk* (1963), one can hardly imagine any swifter reversion to normal conditions. Even superficial knowledge about the post-war normalization process in other countries gives us every reason to believe this.

2.2. Painless development of institutions: one aspect of legitimacy

We stated above that the *same* system has remained unscathed from 1814 to the present. This statement will have to be modified. Quite important things have happened to the Norwegian political system in this period, and in certain respects the system has changed beyond recognition. The absence of legitimacy crises does not mean that no changes have been made, but rather that the changes did not lead to any serious rupture in the system. To understand these events better, let us make further comments on the changes and the manner in which they were introduced.

Such revisions were not made in Norway only, but took place, *mutatis mutandis*, in most Western societies. Institutional development in most of the countries in Western Europe followed a common pattern along these general lines:

1) Extension of the franchise according to the principle 'one man, one vote, and equal weight to every vote'. As distinguished from political systems where political authority and the right to vote are tied to other social qualifications, such as economic status, literacy, or other criteria, there are now no other requirements for the right to vote than that one be a citizen of the country and of voting age.

2) Development of political parties that formulate policies and demands. There is a wide range of party types and forms in the various countries, but there is no doubt about the universal character of the political party system as a means for selection of parliamentary representatives.

3) Continuous growth in government activity due to the manifold demands for such activity, mostly a result of general and widely accepted demands on the state, but also due in part to the special demands of political movements 'on the left' in the various countries.

4) Definite growth of public bureaucracy and a shift of bureaucracy towards control by 'laymen' and/or 'technocrats' rather than by lawyers only.

5) Strengthening of the executive at the cost of the legislative branch of government.

201

6) Expansion of the role and functions of voluntary organizations.
7) Elimination of the relatively autonomous high-status political institutions.

These changes – which generally have produced a system characterized by general franchise, strong political parties, a strong state, a bureaucratic system, a high degree of centralization, and voluntary organizations ,plus a lack of conservative guarantees – have taken place in most West European countries. Description of this general development, however, only serves as a preliminary orientation – it is not difficult to point to a wide range of national differences; even cursory newspaper reading reveals significant variations from country to country, with respect to the institutional framework of political activities, as well as with regard to the attitudes and emotions that flow through the institutional channels and, at times, breach the dikes. The question is: How does the Norwegian system differ from the general pattern in Western society, and what are the causes of the differences that do exist?

Generally speaking, the differences between past and present were less dramatic and led to fewer complications than in many other countries. The predominant theme in this context is that of a flexible and yielding right wing.

1) *Extension of the franchise.* Today, the right to vote in Norway is universal. Every adult who is neither insane nor a notorious criminal may vote in national and municipal elections, and close to 80 per cent of the electorate do so. This has not always been the situation.

In 1814 the right was given to only a third of the adult male population; the franchise has been gradually expanded, primarily by the reforms of 1884 and 1898.

Less known is the fact that even in 1814 the franchise was quite wide in Norway. True, women could not vote, and men could acquire the right only at the age of 25, as against 21 today. However, the percentage of the adult male population qualified to vote in 1814 amounted to some 30 per cent or possibly more; this was an exceptionally large proportion at that time.

Subsequent extensions of the franchise also came at an earlier date in Norway than in most other similarly developed countries. It is generally correct to state that in initial position and subsequent development, the franchise was advanced indeed in Norway.

2) *Development of political parties.* The first political parties, Conservative and Liberal *(Høyre* – 'Right', and *Venstre* – 'Left', respectively), were organized on a national basis in 1884, while local party groups had already been in existence for some time. Subsequently other parties were organized. These have varied widely in structure

and tightness of organization, as well as in their level of activity. Typical for all has been that they have had a *national convention* which has elected an *executive committee* and adopted an election program. More recently, a smaller group has been interposed between the national convention and the executive: a *national committee* (with delegates from the various districts). Party programs almost uniformly have been transmitted to grass-roots organizations. There have been varying levels of continuous activity, with DNA (Norwegian Labour Party) the most effectively organized. The parties have been quite articulate in their representation of special interests – a normal feature in multi-party systems. They also perform another important task, that of nominating candidates for general elections. Political careers in Norway generally go through the political parties.

3) *Continuous growth in government activity.* Government participation in common activities in society has constantly changed. This is probably one of the most universal developmental features of modern industrial societies. It is hardly possible to state that Norway has been particularly 'socialistic' with respect to government activity – a question further discussed in Chapter III. Changes, however, may have occurred with less conflict in Norway than in other countries, because the upper class was largely composed of public officials, civil servants, who, because of their very position, had a high degree of good will towards public activity. And if they generally supported a laissez-faire philosophy, they applied it with moderation if at all.

4) *Growth of public bureaucracy.* It is essential to any advanced industrial society to have an administrative apparatus where appointment and promotion are made on the basis of merit, where the political attitude of public officials is not decisive, and where officials have security in office. This system existed in Norway from 1814, while Great Britain and the United States, for instance, have only gradually moved in this direction by eliminating vast areas of the patronage and spoils system.

As distinguished from the points discussed above, the growth of bureaucracy in Norway was not seriously resisted by any high-status groups; indeed, if there were any enemies of the bureaucracy's autonomy, they were normally found in low-status groups.

5) *Strengthening of the executive.* It is quite clear that an ever-increasing number of functions have been turned over to public administration or to the government. From one point of view, this implies that the executive has increased its strength, while the legislature has lost power.

This general expansion in executive functions as against the legislative functions is often connected with a certain type of conflict between the political right and left wings. Yet a definite pattern can

203

hardly be discerned; to a rather large extent all groups and classes in Norway have contributed to this development. However, even though the problem cuts across party lines, right wing groups deplore more strongly the end result of the development than do other groups.

6) *Growth of voluntary organizations.* Voluntary organizations, too, draw support from all groups and classes. General popular movements and economic interest organizations are probably most important in this connection. The temperance movement, the Norwegian language movement, the religious lay movement, the sports movement, and the women's movements are examples of the first. As economic interest organizations should be mentioned, the Norwegian Farmers' Union (1896), the Norwegian Small Farmers' Union (1913), the Norwegian Association of Industries (1886), and the Norwegian Crafts' Association (1919). The two last organizations were originally organized as one group, the Norwegian Joint Association of Crafts and Industries (1886). Other important organizations are the Norwegian Employers' Association (1900), and the Norwegian National Labour Organization (LO) (1899). The development of this network of organizations has been quite painless, largely due to the fact that it has always been possible to establish new organizations, provided that the purpose was legal. Norwegian employers, furthermore, recognized at a very early stage the right of labour to organize. These two factors may not be unique in Norway, but they do indicate that the modern institutional structure was created without the occurrence of serious conflict.

7) *Elimination of autonomous institutions that represented social upper classes.* Elimination of more or less autonomous institutions with a tendency to support the upper classes also took place relatively early in Norway. Abolition of the special prerogatives and functions of the executive as a conservative institution and erosion of the role of the legislative upper house has been a general tendency all over Europe. Norway was in a unique position in this respect because the legislature (the Storting) had no separate second chamber even when it was established in 1814. Apart from the attempts of a few romantics during the conflict over the royal veto (1880–1884), no serious effort has ever been made to introduce an upper house. The king, furthermore, has never had the right to dissolve the legislature. The powers of the Storting, on the other hand, were exceptionally widely defined by the Constitution of 1814.

The only exception was found in the king's right to choose his own ministers. After a long conflict – but one where some bitterness became evident only in the final stages – this royal prerogative was abolished in 1884. This change came earlier in Norway than similar reforms in Denmark and Sweden, and the victory of the Norwegian radicals was far more thorough than subsequent results in the other

Scandinavian countries. In view of the fact that additional conservative guarantees existed in Denmark and Sweden, the situation in Norway was unique.

There is only one minor example of another conservative institution in Norway: for a very short period the Supreme Court acted, although only to a very limited extent, as a brake on legislation. Basing itself on the principle that it should have the right to review the constitutionality of legislative enactments, the Supreme Court staged a number of probing attacks against a few provisions in legislation regulating the sale of liquor and in legislation controlling so-called 'vested rights'. Determined action by the Liberal Party *(Venstre)* with respect to judicial appointments and a few proposals to amend the Constitution, however, put an end to this political adventure on the part of the judiciary.

Very important in this context is that Norway has never had a more or less independent military structure in close alliance with the executive power. Throughout the nineteenth century, Norway was united with Sweden, and the country long remained a second-rate power. It was a common Norwegian attitude to think of Sweden as a hotbed of anti-democratic tendencies. At the same time, Norway's role as the weaker party in the union kept such non-democratic institutions as a strong army, the diplomatic corps, the royal court, etc., located largely outside Norway's borders. The Norwegian military apparatus was composed of personnel who had hardly ever seen any kind of military action, and this proved important for attitudes of the political 'right' *(Høyre)*. Institutions that in other countries were dominant conservative factors, were non-existent in Norway.

Most of the changes mentioned above were initially opposed by the Norwegian upper classes, who resisted extension of the franchise in 1884 and 1898 and deplored the development of political parties and other institutions related to the growing power of non-privileged groups. Yet there was in the Norwegian upper classes a marked tendency to resign in the face of these events, as well as a willingness to accept and adjust to the new situation.

It is often a typical feature of a modern society that political movements appear as 'under-dog' movements. The reason is easy to understand: a person living in a modern industrial society will normally subscribe to achievement values; he will be part of a very large organization and motivated towards doing his very best in society. Normally, too, he will feel that he does not quite live up to expectations; if he has made some achievements, he cannot relax, but must constantly exert himself. This is in part due to a need in any person to make full use of his abilities and resources. In such a society, most individuals will feel that they 'have not quite made it'. As a consequence, the general public will have a very low degree of identification with a top stratum; most persons will feel that they do not quite 'belong'. The complacent feeling of belonging that permeated the upper classes of the past is just that – a thing of the past.

How well does this apply to Norway? It is difficult to give a definite answer, but there is reason to believe that Norway fits into this general pattern. Demands for new benefits obviously must be justified by reference to an unsatisfactory situation. The enjoyment of high status has its problems and is no longer a political asset.

2.3. Features of social stratification that condition painless change

The Norwegian upper class was a *liberal* upper class without strong conservative tendencies. The dominating belief was that society was progressing, that change led to improvement and perfection, and even the bitter conflicts around 1884 could not suppress this feeling. It seems fair to state that the Norwegian 'right' has always been well to the left of Continental conservatism. 'Measured by European standards', wrote a Norwegian conservative newspaper in 1908, 'the Norwegian *Høyre* has always been a liberal party, and it has constantly moved further in this direction. Reaction is not among its aims' (*Aftenposten*, 26 January 1908).

Likewise, the Norwegian Labour Party considered itself more radical than its Danish and Swedish counterparts. This is also true for the other political parties: the Norwegian Liberal Party *(Venstre)* is well to the left of the comparable Swedish People's Party, while the Norwegian Conservative *(Høyre)* is well to the left of its Swedish counterpart.

The basic features of social stratification in Norway surely provide one of the most important explanations of this fact. In this connection we are thinking less of the types of movements supported by the various social strata than of the actual degree of social inequality.

There have been four characteristic features of social stratification in Norway:

1) It has been relatively limited in its effects;
2) The structure was quite open, in that there were few formal obstacles between the various classes and few barriers that had to be forced. Here we shall not comment on the difficulties involved in moving from one class to another (individual mobility), or on actual mobility rates.
3) The social structure has rarely left its mark on those who have moved into a higher class, nor has it prevented relatively large groups from changing rather conclusively their position within the system.
4) These features have not been restricted to urban areas alone.

206

With a few exceptions, rural Norway has been much more egalitarian than is the case elsewhere in Europe.

These are themes that have often been commented on in Norway. The interesting thing about these comments is how much consensus they show among observers of widely differing ideological and political backgrounds.

First of all, this opinion was emphasized by the conservative 'right', by *Høyre*. Within this group there was a general feeling that in Norway, with its exceptional social equality, conflict could not possibly erupt between radicals and the 'pillars of society'; there was no room for such conflicts within so small a society that housed so little inequality.

This attitude was also predominant in the Liberal Party *(Venstre)*, which answered warnings from *Høyre* by pointing out that Norwegian Social Democrats could not possibly wreak havoc because social stratification in Norway was too moderate to produce extremist movements.

This emphasis on the egalitarian quality of the Norwegian social structure has given rise to a number of comments that further demonstrate the general consensus irrespective of the political origin of the commentator. The purpose of such comments, of course, varied. The left wing saw its interest in describing Norway as a country where equality and democracy had survived a Continental period (the union before 1814 with Denmark) challenging these values, and emphasized the need to avoid contamination from 'impure' countries. The right wing was more interested in pointing out that in Norway there was hardly any inequality at all and that the insistent democratic campaign against the little inequality that did exist (in this context the Conservatives deliberately made use of the European yardstick) was so much ado about nothing, and for dubious motives, at that.

In 1873, the conservative newspaper *Morgenbladet,* for instance, in discussing the possibilities for socialism in Norway, emphasized the absence of an aristocracy of the blood as well as of the purse, and the lack of such social inequalities as were found in the 'great cultural nations'; hence, it stated, there could be no valid basis for socialism in Norway (26 September 1873).

Documentation of the relatively high degree of social equality in Norway, as well as of the general absence of large capital holdings and dilapidated slums that existed in wealthier countries, was provided by the statistician A. N. Kiær, director of the Norwegian Central Bureau of Statistics and a moderate conservative (A. N. Kiær 1892–1893).

The group calling itself *frisinnede venstre* (moderate liberals) generally agreed in this conclusion: the newspaper *Morgenavisen,* the group's original mouthpiece, argued that Norway had no upper class

207

in the European sense (*Morgenavisen,* 27 July 1903), and Chr. Michelsen, the key founder of this party, expressed similar opinions *(Sandefjords Blad,* 28 October 1909) together with other prominent members, e.g. Arctander *(Tønsbergs Blad,* 2 September 1909), Fridtjof Nansen *(Verdens Gang,* 1 March 1909), and Wollert Konow *(Verdens Gang,* 9 February 1909).

Comments on these conditions also came from the labour movement, and an article in the Norwegian Labour Party's ideological periodical, *Det 20de Århundre,* noted 'the country's lack of an aristocracy and a traditional upper class and even *its low degree of class distinction in comparison* to most other countries . . .' (1929, p. 78).

Edvard Bull, the leading theoretician within the radical movement, deplored the fact that the Norwegian Conservative Party was dominated by hucksters and small businessmen and had not been taken over by big business; he used this to accent the unique character of the Norwegian *Høyre (Det 20de Århundre* 1927). Erling Falk deplored the fact that Norway had only a petit bourgeoisie – at least he had not found a genuine upper class (Bull 1955, p. 83).

There is every reason to believe that this is an extremely important feature of Norwegian society. Norwegian private enterprise has generally been composed of quite small units, and the label 'petty bourgeoisie' is probably quite to the point.

Yet thorough integration of the lower classes into the social fabric is only part of the story. It is also important that the original elite easily admitted into its midst the growing business elite, and that the new class of engineers was also accepted without problems. In fact, the speed with which the engineer established himself in Norwegian society was indeed remarkable. Norwegian ideology with respect to social stratification has much in common with that prevalent in the USA, but with more emphasis on *equality* and less on achievement than in the USA. Furthermore, the express emphasis on the absence of insurmountable class barriers is similar in the two societies.

Norwegian society, furthermore, is relatively free from all types of institutions that symbolize an economic or hereditary upper class. There is no Social Register, nor a society page in Norwegian newspapers, and the Norwegian royal household plays a very pale role as a focusing point for aristocratic tendencies. Norway has no aristocracy of the blood, there are very few exclusive clubs, and the annual regattas at Hankø can hardly be compared with the role played by Epsom, Henley, or the Grand National. The school system has a very high degree of universality; primary and secondary education are common to all, with a totally insignificant number of 'private' schools. Any effort to establish private schools has met heavy opposition. On the political left wing all such efforts have been interpreted as moves towards exclusivism and elitism. The fact that these attitudes are probably exaggerated does not make them less important. This does not mean that Norway is totally devoid of an elite, but that the elite is to a very large extent dominated by *public institutions*. Thus, the context in which King Haakon most frequently appeared as a guest was in meetings of *Militære Samfunn* (the Military Society), due to his role as commander-in-chief, and of *Polyteknisk Forening* (the Polytechnical Association).

It is also interesting that honorary orders have always been regarded with scepticism, and that 1912 nearly saw abolition of all orders, with 75 members in the Storting voting for their abolishment, and 47 voting against. The proposal fell because a two-thirds majority was needed. All Conservative members voted to retain orders, while only 23 of the 76 Liberal members cast a similar vote; no Labour member voted for keeping the order system. The arguments for maintaining orders, furthermore, were extremely defensive: it was desirable to have orders in an international context, so that Norwegians would be able to show something when presenting themselves and, also, that Norway would be able to reward men of foreign extraction.

3. PERSONNEL: STRUCTURE AND PROCESSES

3.1. *Introductory remarks*

In Western society there are usually three categories of personnel directly engaged in the processes of authoritative decision-making:

1) *Government bureaucrats* engaged in public administration;
2) *Elected representatives* chosen in general elections and generally recruited through the political parties.
3) *Organization representatives,* who in various types of situations make decisions that are binding upon organization members in their relationship with the government/state.

A description of the political system also requires an explanation of recruitment norms for these three types of positions, particularly of the extent to which a career leading to positions within one of the above groups is arrived at via a position in another group. It will also be important to consider the social bases of the various leadership groups.

Recruitment to public administration may be more or less closely interconnected with recruitment of elected representatives. Nomination, too, and election of representatives may be more or less intimately related to the role of political parties with respect to interest articulation. The status sequences – position movements in the power structure – that have been prevalent during the various periods from 1814 to the present are shown in Figure 1, where an arrow from one column to another indicates that persons who have held positions in one leadership group to some extent subsequently moved into another group. We should emphasize, however, that the Figure does not indicate the relative role or weight of the various movements.

We see that during the *first period* (1814–1884) there was a movement from higher education to the bureaucracy and then from the bureaucracy to the Storting, as well as one stream from low education directly to the Storting. Roughly speaking, these trends exhausted political mobility lines during that period. Persons with only primary education could be elected to the Storting, but positions in the bureaucracy were reserved for those with higher education. With few exceptions, members of the bureaucracy could also hold a seat in the Storting, a situation different from that in most countries.

In the second period (1884–1905) political parties became an intermediate and qualifying station in a career leading to a parliamentary seat, while at the same time parliamentarians gained access (though limited) to certain parts of the bureaucracy. During this period there was still quite a high ratio of recruitment from high administrative positions to the Storting.

In the *third period* (1905–1960) interest organizations played an increasingly important role within the system, in part by providing recruitment to political parties, in part by furnishing recruits to public administration.

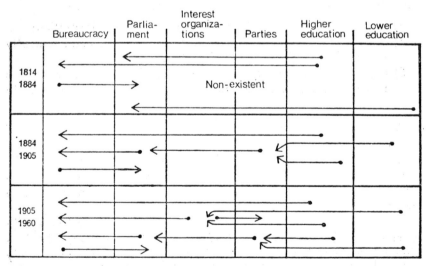

Figure 1. Channels of recruitment between the big political institutions and institutions of education at various periods of time.

210

3.2. Training and selection of administrative personnel (bureaucrats): Some consequences of the country's size

One of the consequences of Norway's limited size was that almost all education for top positions in public administration took place through one type of specialization: the study of law. This was, in a sense, a matter of numerical necessity; it would be next to impossible to train people in many fields for a limited number of administrative positions. In such a situation one would risk over-production of applicants in one field and serious under-production in another. A small society requires a high degree of personnel mobility in administrative top positions. Adaptability, common sense, and ability to co-operate are qualities of the first order. Under these conditions, broad and unspecialized training has definite advantages, whereas distinctions between personnel with more specialized – and limited – qualifications would create difficulties. Norway, therefore, has a far more flexible recruitment policy than most countries. This system of the law degree as a universal passport may not have been the only solution to the problems that existed in Norway, and it is conceivable that the same system could also be applied in other countries, possibly even with different functions. But in Norway the system was eminently suited to meet a number of basic requirements.

Norwegian bureaucrats, furthermore, were protected against dismissal, and therefore were affected only slightly by the vicissitudes of political struggle. Public officials can only be removed from office by judicial decision, and the requirements for a verdict – the burden of proof – are heavy. The officials were protected against the king (the government), against the Storting (which has little power), and against each other. But the fact that a person once appointed could not be removed also led to prudence in selection and appointment

The limited size of the bureaucracy, therefore, produced a characteristic and singular pattern of behaviour. Smallness led to a high degree of 'closeness', but the very closeness within the system frequently resulted in defensive reactions by the individual bureaucrat and in defensive norms for the administrative system. Smallness had its own problems, and protection against these was often sought through withdrawal and circumvention – a not particularly effective technique, however. Solutions to some appointment dilemmas were sought by turning them into matters of seniority, where individual evaluation could be avoided, while other problems were 'solved' by applying an equality standard as a guiding principle. The equality norm, therefore, was not only produced by the 'people', it was also a product of the dilemma of those who governed.

In this connection there is one specific feature of the educational

211

system, in the university, which deserves to be mentioned because it has been intimately related to behaviour and norms within the political-administrative structure: namely, the relationship between university students and faculty, between subordinates and superiors. It is common knowledge that a marked distance has always been kept between faculty and students in Norway. Contrary to some romantic notions, there has never been intimate contact between the two groups such as, for instance, relations in the 'Alt Heidelberg' manner or those existing at Oxford and Cambridge.

In a society where class distinctions between citizens are accepted only to a very slight degree and where the elite is small, it will be important to avoid situations that require personal evaluation and invidious comparisons. Hence, most individuals are not interested in making or in being subjected to frequent or searching evaluations of personal qualities and abilities. At the university, students and faculty were interested in avoiding such encounters as far as possible, because otherwise the precarious situation in the small academic community that in any event had to endure so many problems of mutual evaluation, would be brought to the brink of explosion. The circumstances of the situation were particularly pressing upon those students who had no connections with the families of higher officials, for these lacked a feeling of 'belonging' to the university. Consequently, professors made no effort to establish close contacts with their students, and students did not feel close to their teachers.

Because it is so different from the situation prevailing at other universities, this system deserves special interest. The French university system, based on elite schools that are extremely achievement oriented and operate on the basis of personal evaluation, *can* function in a large society living by rather inegalitarian principles. The British system, with close contact between teachers and students but also with a certain disdain for academic achievement (and where academic achievement may have little relevance for subsequent career), offers another solution in an elite-oriented society. But a *professional education* (such as the Norwegian) in a *small society* (such as the Norwegian) living by *egalitarian principles* (as does Norway) makes it mandatory to keep one's distance.

This system of keeping one's distance also has definite attractions for the students themselves. For one thing, the system would make it easy to accept the role of being a student without much ado, a role that otherwise might be difficult to reconcile with a simultaneous position of leadership in a student political movement, for instance. Such roles are played only by a minority of the students, but it is a vital minority. The limited demands for contact and close relationships made by the university enable students to be active in many

212

other fields. It is very difficult, however, to assess the effect that this system may have on the intellectual atmosphere at the university.

The small and egalitarian society in Norway leads to extremely low levels of participation in those institutions which emphasize inequality among participants. This is particularly true for institutions marked by elite participation, such as the university.

The limited size of the community also means that any person in a given position will be able to form his own 'line' to an almost unlimited degree. This has been particularly obvious within the academic community: Marcus Monrad was a Hegelian, so *that* was the philosophy taught in Norway for 30 years, no matter how un-Hegelian Norway is. When Ragnar Frisch became professor of economics, he moulded the whole study of the subject. And Arne Næss introduced logical empiricism, so that will be the main path in philosophy for 20 years, or 40 if we include the time it will take his disciples and his opponents to disprove the system (they are still working at it). But there is also another effect. Because there is hardly anyone within the field aside from those who fight each other about these matters, and even they are few indeed, it is hardly ever possible to find any kind of objective yardstick against which ideas and philosophies can be measured. There is only a belief that one's own ideas are correct, obviously correct, regardless of whether they are put into effect or not. This type of conviction is also generally manifest in the debates in Norwegian newspapers. In this connection I am not thinking of the peculiar tone in the so-called Norwegian 'culture debate' (or of the fact that the first statement in a debate is usually written as if it were the last), but rather of the apparent conviction of the writer that his statement will not be believed either by the direct opponent (who is beyond hope, anyhow) or by a presumably neutral and vaguely interested but nevertheless unengaged public. In Norwegian debates, the public will usually play the role of audience but hardly ever that of arbiter or judge. This may even be the case in more serious intellectual or scientific matters. This lack of belief in the existence of an objective yardstick also indicates a lack of belief in the possibility of making genuinely and universally valid decisions. Hence, it is extremely important to distinguish between various aspects of a value system: Justice is a Norwegian dream, but Norwegians have no belief in its existence on this earth.

But Norway's limited size has also had other effects. One of these has been the peculiar duality in the position of members of the Norwegian academic elite in their relations with each other, as well as in their relations with the general public. This duality has often been neglected, or, rather one side of it has been recognized while the other has been forgotten.

Take, for instance, a faculty member at the university in the last century. His position would usually be the following: on the one hand he was the one leading person within his field (to a large extent this is still the case) and he dominated this field without regard to his personal qualifications. This position, of course, was often highly satisfactory but represented an incredible monopoly, with all of the accompanying temptations. The most outstanding of them all, A. M. Schweigaard, was sour towards anything foreign (incidentally, he was hardly considered outstanding abroad). This, in a sense, was typical. The elite became nationalistic because they felt they owned Norway. On the other hand, members of the academic elite were lonesome within their own fields; there were few who could understand them and the limited number of available positions prevented them from encouraging students to copy them; they were in a way gods in the academic temple and the choice of a successor would be a search for the bull Apis, not a question of training several possible pretenders. They were kings in their own field, and yet the academic loneliness was so pressing that they often moved in the direction of practical work, where general recognition and a feeling of doing something sensible were strong and immediate. J. A. Seip (1945) has described this latter element, interpreting it as a concession to the legal world. I myself feel that the press from equalitarian values was more important.

At the same time, the top level was small; everyone knew everyone else, and extremely well. This made it difficult to apply any sharp qualification principles with much force, or to rigorously apply achievement criteria. Those under scrutiny always turned out to be one's friends or acquaintances. But this in turn fostered a peculiar mixture of diffuse familism combined with an egalitarian, watered-down achievement orientation. That is, within the elite, processes were at work creating egalitarian attitudes which did not spring from the peasantry alone.

However, these persons were also located in the middle of a system that required precisely these values: justice, universalistic decisions, impersonal actions. And here we have the main problem: the little Norwegian social system has required of its leaders peculiar things indeed. It asks for warmth and friendliness, but cool impartiality as well; it requires impartiality in situations conducive to the opposite. They are furthermore supposed to represent the general desire to avoid making distinctions or differentiating between persons, but as they are also leaders, they must give orders, and giving orders implies that one continually makes invidious distinctions.

These are, in my opinion, the most important characteristics of behaviour in Norway's political institutions, and the norms for these

214

various institutions. We have seen a complicated picture of the problems involved in exercising authority in a small country, a 'transparent' country, and one where there is a deep mistrust of the idea of there being differences between persons and of having some persons lead others – indeed, mistrust of the idea of its being necessary at all to have so much to do with one another.

3.3. Representation and representative: Voter-parliamentarian

As regards the second group of political personnel, the elected representatives of a geographically limited area, the mode of electing them has been revised from time to time. In the period after 1814, distinction can be made between the following groups or personnel levels in the political system:

1) *Members* and *substitute members*[4] of the Storting.
2) *Candidates* for the Storting – persons nominated by the political parties as candidates for the election of members and substitute members.
3) The various *intermediate groups* of active personnel. These groups have changed from time to time, and in the period before 1906 consisted of *electors* (since at that time Norway did not have direct election; the voters elected electors who again elected members and substitute members) and, from 1884, of *party members* and *participants in the nominating process* (persons taking part in a nominating meeting or preparation for a nominating meeting). The role, as well as the size of such groups varies.
4) *Active voters*, i.e. persons using their right to vote in elections to the Storting.
5) *Eligible voters.*

Fluctuations in the size of the above groups and their relative strength compared to the other groups have been as follows:

1) The number of members of the Storting has increased from 87 in 1815 to 155 at present (with a similar increase for substitute members).
2) Exact data cannot be given as to the number of candidates, since there was no distinctive group of candidates before 1884. However, since 1884 the number of candidates (since 1920: persons named on the ballot, i.e. the 'party list' presented by each party in each election district) has increased markedly.
3) Our knowledge about the intermediate groups of active personnel is too limited for constructing time series; shifts in the political structure, moreover, have enhanced the role of some intermediate groups, while others have disappeared. Thus, in 1815 there were

215

700 *electors* in the rural districts and 104 in the towns. In 1882 (the last election before the extension of the franchise), the number of electors was 1,051 and 367, respectively. The number of electors was tied directly to the number of eligible voters. But with the introduction of direct elections in 1906, the electors were abolished. Data on party membership are limited, but, in proportion to the number of voters, membership must have been quite high shortly after 1884, possibly as high or even higher than it is today. At present some 15 per cent of the voters belong to some political party. Also, participation in nominating meetings or in meetings preparatory to nominations appears to have been quite high in the period immediately after 1884, at least in the towns. More recently, there has been a marked reduction in nomination participation, and at present only a small fraction of the total number of voters take part in the nominating process.

4–5) The number of active as well as of eligible voters has increased dramatically. Various election reforms, with the reforms of 1884 and 1898 as the most important, vastly increased the number of persons qualified to vote (until 1898 persons qualified to vote had to register in order to be eligible to vote, similar to the present system in the USA), as well as the number of eligible voters. At the same time the proportion of eligible voters making use of their right to vote has increased. Both in relative and in absolute terms there has been a sharp increase in election participation.

The first two time series show diminishing opportunities for participation. This applies to *roles of authority* where the average citizen's chance to play an active role has decreased. The chances for reaching a position such as member of the cabinet, member of the Storting, or municipal councillor, have been drastically reduced.

Regarding the time series at the middle levels, it is difficult to draw definite conclusions, but probably the absolute numbers and almost certainly the relative numbers have been reduced and are still diminishing. This applies to party membership and active participation in the nominating process.

Third, there has been steady and unbroken growth in activity at the lowest levels: in the number of eligible voters and in election participation. This perspective brings into focus the widely varying trends at the various levels of the system. In general, there has probably been continuous growth in the volume of information on political phenomena, and we may reasonably conclude that the average level of political knowledge has improved. We must not, however, see this as an indication of increased participation and activity at all levels. The various trends are probably complementary to each other. Thus, there

216

is reason to believe that the increasing number of eligible voters has had a temporary, activating effect upon the intermediate groups of active political personnel, whereupon continuous differentiation between parties and stimulation of the electorate in turn led to some reduction of the intermediate groups, particularly relative to the number of participating voters.

In an international perspective, it is difficult to say that the situation in Norway presents any unique features. In general, Norway has had a high degree of voter participation, but this is true for most countries. It is possible that participation in the nominating process is somewhat higher in Norway than in other countries and that this is due to the absorption strategies of the political parties. This seems to be true for the period after 1880, and I do not think that this can be due to the introduction of proportional representation in a multi-party system. A fairer conclusion seems to be that continuous pressure from activists has split the parties into many factions.

3.4. *Recruitment of politicians: the standard career*
The road towards a political career in Norway is usually a gradual, step-by-step process. There are few exceptions to the undramatic pattern of gradual promotion within the system; political interest manifests itself early in the potential politician's life and leads to regular and increasingly active participation and, consequently, to gradual promotion within the political institutions. What, then, are the effects of this system?

Above all, it serves to create a great number of test situations for weighing and measuring the candidate. This means that a quick and dramatic career (a career that may give an undesired person access to the inner sanctum of policy-making) is next to impossible in Norway. This system of mutual testing and control will frequently be concentrated on making sure of the absence of negative or undesired features in potential candidates for promotion. After all, if a person is accepted, one must live with him for the remainder of his and/or one's own political life, so naturally one will want to take the necessary precautions. The mechanism, therefore, is singularly important in providing checks and guarantees in a vital matter.

The standard career of the politician, the secure position of the bureaucrat, and the manifestation of the party system as a series of interest and/or ideologically distinct parties are all mutually dependent. The politician reasonably expects to end up as a politician. He can scarcely expect to become wealthy as a Storting representative, but what he can be fairly sure of is that he will continue as a politician, never disappearing from the control of various interest groups, and always remaining sensitive to the standpoints of the voters and the opinion of the press. The bureaucrats, with their relative monopoly on administrative positions where they run programs that have been agreed upon, have thus contributed to making the parties specialists on ideas not commonly shared, i.e. controversial topics.

3.5. Political personnel and other elite groups

Finally, some comments should be made on the relationship between the political elite (represented by bureaucrats, elected representatives, and organization leaders) and other elite groups in Norwegian society.

The other elite groups important in this connection are the economic elite (represented by private enterprise leaders), the elite in the mass communications media and, specifically, in artistic and literary production, and the elite that produces and administers formalized knowledge (in academic and research institutions). We have mentioned earlier the close interconnection between the various elite groups, but the point needs to be emphasized.

In the past this close interconnection was due to *role combinations:* some members of the bureaucracy also had important roles in private enterprise, taking initiative and providing the necessary credit guarantees. Academics were the primary consumers of art and literature, and in the first period after 1814 they were also the leading producers. Because of its central position in the community, furthermore, the university was also directly involved in politics. For one thing, the establishment of a new academic chair at the university frequently was a political matter of first importance. In addition to these links came the informal contacts and relationships evolving from the existing recruitment patterns and leading to acquaintances and friendships. Such relationships, moreover, were further developed and strengthened because of the limited size of the community.

In the old system there was a tightly knit network of contacts and relations between the various elite groups. In a society with few professors, few authors, few parliamentarians, and few top-level bureaucrats, a high degree of mutual acquaintance and familiarity was inevitable. Since recruitment to the academic professions was marked by a higher degree of in-breeding than now, friendship and family ties, too, contributed to establishing and maintaining a tightly woven milieu.

These conditions, of course, have now been changed in large measure. An evaluation of the present situation will depend on the perspective one chooses: to emphasize the changes that have occurred or to stress the lines of continuity. On the one hand, it is obviously true that the various groups within the Norwegian elite have become gradually more isolated from each other; an increasing division of

218

tasks and functions has taken place at the elite level. The Bjørnstjerne Bjørnson ideal of a hyper-active, semi-intellectual jack-of-all-trades, bursting with ideas and opinions, is definitely losing its appeal, even if there are still some fighters left.

No thorough study, outside of a few minor attempts, has been made of this increasing differentiation of elite groups. In an international perspective, however, it is probably still true that Norway has a political system where the various elite groups are inter-connected to an unusual degree – a system where a medical professor may still become director of the broadcasting and television system, or minister of defence. This situation is due, at least in part, to the limited size of Norwegian society: Norway at present probably finds herself at a very interesting stage in her numerical development. Even if professional bureaucrats have had a tendency to poke fun at the politicking academic, he is just a counterpart to similar tendencies in their own midst: their great hero, A. M. Schweigaard, was *the* great professor of law at the university – he *was* Norwegian political economy and he *was* the famous parliamentarian, etc. The very chances of success are often affected by the size of the problem: because institutions frequently are so small, the road to promotion and advance within one's original field will often be closed, and success must be sought in other areas. Unfortunately, few comparative studies have been made of these problems.

4. THE POLITICAL-ADMINISTRATIVE STRUCTURE

4.1. *Responsible decisions*

Turning now to the Norwegian political-administrative structure itself and to processes connected with it, we shall take as our point of departure certain problematical conditions that, particularly when combined with egalitarian values, have set definite and unique limits for the types of norms and for the processes that could be used.

The following points will serve as a basis for my comments on the decision-making process:

1) Norway is a small country and thinly populated.
2) Norway is relatively poor in resources. Per capita statistics may show high figures, but resources are difficult to develop. (High per capita figures in road construction, for instance, do not mean much when one considers the tremendous geographical difficulties.)
3) These conditions have resulted in strong demands for government activity, intervention, regulation, and control. Public authority

has had to intervene with economic support, as co-ordinator and referee, and with initiative and counsel.

4) Solutions must be general and common to all, and they must be acceptable to all.

Various types of social organization, for instance in religion, education, and, to some extent, voluntary private organizations, have followed different organizational patterns in different countries. There are pluralistic types of organization and unitary types, and there are liberal organization forms and totalitarian patterns, just as there are public and private patterns.

In Norway, many of these institutions are publicly organized (i.e. organized by the state), they are unitary in character, yet they are also liberal in the sense that within the public and unitary organization there will be a wide variety of opinions and often bitter conflicts. Scarcity of funds has imposed co-operation; social and cultural differences support a high participation level (in part due to relative affluence and in part as a necessary defence mechanism); the liberal tradition, combined with the need to make allowances for a strong opponent, is becoming a guiding principle.

Norway has *one* school system, *one* church, *one* secondary school system (and until quite recently, *one* university), and *one* broadcasting and television system. This unitary system of organization is in large measure a result of scarcity of resources and high administrative costs. Obviously, the prevalent pattern has also been conditioned by and, in its turn, has further strengthened cultural unity. But the system has also established a pattern of collectivism and responsibility because decisions have to apply to and affect all.

The importance of the generally applicable solution can hardly be overestimated. Any thought of several parallel institutions was an economic impossibility; common decisions had to be made and common institutions established. But in so doing, a system was established where individuals and groups are of necessity frequently and intensely irritated and provoked into active participation.

In general, we may say that the processes work in this fashion: it is cheaper to try to do something within an existing institution than outside it. This requires that the organization's leadership be relatively open minded (which it is because of the institution's vulnerability and because of the common reluctance to be a 'boss'). It also means that participation may often lead to conflict and further that protests may be quickly turned into active participation and may, not infrequently, lead to a responsible position within the organization.

It is difficult, for instance, to evaluate the present status of religious conflict without considering the financial factor. The cost of main-

220

taining the State Church is covered by government appropriations. On a purely economic basis, therefore, the various Christian groups will hesitate to break away from the State Church. If they do break away, they will also leave the whole system of organizational and physical establishments and be forced to start afresh.

But the fact that there is such short distance to go before a final decision is reached has also had as a result that debate on political issues becomes 'responsible' at a very early stage. A suggestion may quickly turn into a formal proposal or bill. Norwegian political debate, therefore, is somewhat solemn and very responsible; the Norwegian system is marked by the almost complete absence of any free, theoretical discussion; the issue very quickly becomes concrete and (sometimes) personal.

This responsible attitude, which is based on a fundamental shortage of resources, limits the possibility for experimentation. There are few attempts at parallel institutions. Experiments are expensive, so it is important to know at the outset what one wants. Long experience has proved that if something has first been established (or a person elected or an official appointed), then he or it has come to stay. In any institutional change, preparation is vitally important.

This high degree of unity and responsibility is probably one reason why Norwegian 'individualism' is so frequently considered to mean withdrawal. The belief that individuality can only be exercised in isolation is probably a product of the fact that common decisions have required so much mutual accommodation and compromise that it is difficult to regard any type of social activity as an opportunity for self-assertion. This has created a distinctly ambivalent attitude towards authority and government – an attitude of strong loyalty and responsibility, combined with reactions against 'encroachment' so strong that sometimes it almost borders on the paranoid.

This sense of responsibility is also closely connected with the role of the 'judge-ideal' in Norwegian politics. And it has marked the judicial system, where the courts are so organized that counsel – the attorneys themselves – to a large extent resemble judges, and where little emphasis is put on individual opinions. The judge does not dominate the courtroom (that would violate egalitarian norms); neither does he have to be an active referee in the fashion of American or British judges. The legal profession is just not as 'party oriented' as in most countries.

This collectivistic sense of responsibility is manifest in many parts of the Norwegian political system. And the idea itself has coloured the bureaucratic elite's concept of politics as a responsible search for the common good. It has been manifest in the Norwegian teaching profession, with the teacher as the carrier of the common culture.

221

One may also discern this in the conception of authors as educators of the public (authors should be socially and politically engaged and present their opinion of the right and the just to the public – and in return for their endeavours they deserve an annual salary from public funds).

The demand for responsibility has also had some interesting effects on Norwegian political institutions. Probably one of the most interesting features is the manner in which parliamentarianism operates. It is not good political manners for the opposition to unseat a government just because it wants political power for itself; there must be a *good* reason.

This parliamentary norm has parallels in norms governing personal behaviour and other social relationships. Even social deviants and outsiders assume a 'responsible' opposing position. Sverre Lysgaard has described the so-called 'worker collective', the informal system of opposition to the plant leadership (Lysgaard 1960). The main feature of this opposition is that it is orderly and takes seriously its normative responsibilities. It is a very responsible form of deviation, a very loyal opposition. The cultural origins of this should be strongly emphasized.

In Norway even those deviants who in other societies follow other patterns display attitudes that place them on a level with those who criticize society on the basis of society's own criteria. In a study of a detention institution, Thomas Mathiesen found quarrelling over legal interpretations more prevalent than rejection of the norms (Mathiesen 1965).

4.2. *Egalitarian values and decisions*

Because of certain basic egalitarian values, Norwegians generally are not kindly disposed to the idea of leadership. The concept of leadership runs contrary to the egalitarian-populistic concepts that have dominated in Norway. The limited size of the system itself strengthens this negative attitude towards leadership.

The critical point in the analysis is the transition from the formulation of demands to the formulation of politics. Talcott Parsons has emphasized that the voter only delivers 'generalized support', and he states that 'the political supporter, in our case the voter, must not claim direct control of the consequences of his vote; if he did, political support would be reduced to a 'barter' basis and the political integration of a complex social system would become impossible' (Parsons 1959). This is generally true, but in my opinion it is also important to emphasize that there will be rather wide variations between different political systems with regard to this transition from demand to policy. A most important point is exactly how far politics is removed from this barter basis. In my opinion, Norwegian politics comes quite close to a type of barter, and the process that produces demands from the voters, and decisions from political leaders flows so quickly that there will in fact be only limited distance between the two groups and between their respective functions (presenting demands and formulating policies). There are factors in the system that counteract any clear-cut distinction between the functions and actions of leaders and of voters. One effect of the closeness of the two functions manifests itself in the general reluctance to admit that leadership performs a unique function, as well as in the defensive attitude of leadership per se and its reluctance to admit that it does have power, i.e. freedom of choice in any given situation. Hence, this is our hypothesis: in Norway there will always be a particularly strong inclination to presume that political decisions are not in the nature of free choice by the leaders between possible alternatives, but that they are, on the contrary, solutions that were there from the very outset, or that things just happened that way by their own force.

Egalitarian decisions. No systematic comparison has been made here between the situation in Norway and those in other countries, although such systematic studies should be of considerable interest. Nevertheless, we have sufficient evidence to conclude that political decisions in Norway have a strong egalitarian flavour.

The tax policy has been sharply aimed at reducing income variations. Whether or not Norway has the heaviest tax burden or the steepest progression rates in the world is probably debatable, but there is no doubt that Norway ranks very high on both counts.

Income policy has also followed egalitarian principles; differences between the salaries of public officials in high and low grades are moderate. Also, the general span between high and low income groups is far less in Norway than in most countries, including the country's closest neighbour, Sweden.

Also in *education* there is strong emphasis on equality, and very little attention is paid to outstanding students. Political demands for elimination of the grading or marking system are a further indication of this egalitarian attitude.

Checks upon high-status groups, furthermore, are often considered in order. This is particularly true with respect to price control legislation and various types of economic regulation. Also, legislation authorizing in some instances compulsory transfer and duty for physicians and dentists falls within this category.

Checks upon deviants, on the other hand, are moderate. This can probably be taken as a result of the general reluctance to give unequal treatment. Early abolition of the death penalty, the very low number

223

of actual imprisonments, and the generally mild sentences in criminal cases are apparently closely connected with egalitarian values.

4.3. *Egalitarian movements*

The relations between the egalitarian values dominant before the emergence of an industrial labour class, and the general orientation of the labour class when it had developed, need some comment. Why did Norway have a singularly radical labour movement? An extremely radical movement usually develops in a society with sharp class distinction, it has been claimed (Lipset 1960).

Even if we look for an explanation of extreme radicalism in the class structure, a second interpretation is possible. We may regard egalitarian extremism as a product of dominant egalitarian values in society generally. On this basis, we might expect to find a broad radical movement in a society where egalitarian values were strong prior to the movement. It seems reasonable to give a double explanation for the strength of the left-wing movement in Norway: it derived legitimacy from the dominant value system *and* support from a common egalitarian culture. Ordinarily, however, the typical examples of egalitarian extremism will be found in societies where equality is non-existent.

Egalitarian extremism generally takes one of two forms: a protest against *administrative* (government) authority or against an *economic upper class*. The first variation dominated the original 'left' *(Venstre* –Liberal Party) movement in its protest against administrative authority and officialdom. The second variation is found in those areas of Norway where the highest degree of stratification exists: in cities, particularly in Bergen and Trondheim with their arrogant upper class, as well as in rural districts in parts of eastern Norway, Trøndelag, and northern Norway, where social stratification is more manifest than in other areas.

A third variety exists in the religious lay movement. The lay movement found its main strength in the very egalitarian rural districts in western Norway where any farm was equal to any other and where gruelling toil was everybody's lot. But it is also true that what little authority existed in the regions was personified in the local minister and that the minister became the direct object of the movement. The egalitarian pathos of this religious movement and its pointed attack on 'the big shots' is fully at a par with socialistic egalitarian extremism in its bitter attack upon those who possess power and belong to society's 'in-groups'.

224

NOTES

[1] I am grateful to Joan Torykian for discussing and helping with the formulation of many points in this article.

[2] Readers who do not appreciate introductory remarks of a general nature may skip this section and begin with section 1.2.

[3] This is a liberal interpretation of Parsons' division into 'Generalized Support', 'Advocacy of Policies', 'Effective Leadership', and 'Binding Decision' (see Parsons 1959, Easton 1953).

[3] A substitute or alternate member takes the seat in the Storting when it is vacated by the elected members. This applies to temporary as well as permanent vacancies. Substitute members are elected together with members in the general election and are candidates from the same party as the member (i.e. candidates who did not receive enough votes to be elected in their own right). Thus there is no need for by-elections in Norway.

VII. Religion

By Thomas Mathiesen and Otto Hauglin

1. INTRODUCTION

Any sociological description of religious life in Norway will necessarily encounter various obstacles. First, there is the strong reaction from those who protest against such a personal affair as religion being made the focus of objective extrinsic research. There is, further, the ethical protest for 'privacy', which complicates practical data collection. In addition, we find the principal objection that the phenomenon 'religion' is so fundamentally different from all other phenomena as to render sociological methods inapplicable. We have indeed felt this basic doubt ourselves – a doubt which is, incidentally, discussed in Per Salomonsen's *Religionssociologi* (1966).

In addition to the above obstacles, there exist few sociological data on religion in Norway. Neither official nor privately collected statistics reveal much, and the latter are not always reliable. There have been few investigations, and the entire field lies open to research. Thus, this article will be characterized more by hypotheses and guesses than conclusions and should not be considered anything more than a rough sketch, a kind of first draft, to a presentation of the role of religion in Norwegian society.

2. SOME DEFINITIONS OF RELIGION

Most definitions of religion can be placed in one of three main categories. *Normative* definitions stating what an author thinks religion *ought* to be are frequently proposed, but such definitions are not satisfactory for the purposes of sociological analysis. In addition to the normative definitions, there are two main types of *descriptive* definitions.

The first type can be designated *functional* definitions. These specify definite social, cultural, and psychological functions and consider those ideas and actions which attempt to fulfil these functions as religious. This type of definition has relatively recently received considerable support, primarily because of the fact that Yinger uses it in his *Religion, Society and the Individual* (1957). He summarizes the ultimate functional problems which he considers as constituting satisfactory criteria as follows:

> How shall we respond to the fact of death? Does life have some central meaning despite the suffering, the succession of frustrations and trage-dies? How can we deal with the forces that press in on us, endangering our livelihood, our health, the survival and smooth operation of the group in which we live — forces that our empirical knowledge is inadequate to handle? How can we bring our capacity for hostility and our ego-centricity sufficiently under control that the groups within which we live, without which, indeed, life would be impossible, can be kept together? (p. 9)

A functional definition of religion, however, presents certain dif-ficulties – difficulties of which Yinger is quite aware. The most im-portant is that *all* the ideas and actions which attempt to fulfil the stated function must, in principle, be considered religious. This makes the questions of functional alternatives to religion meaningless, and thereby a very central sociological problem becomes blurred. Yinger attempts to resolve this difficulty by emphasizing that religion is, after all, 'a certain *kind* of effort to perform various functions' (italics ours). But here he departs somewhat from his own definitions and introduces limiting factors concerned with the content of the ideas and actions, rather than their function. Furthermore, functional defi-nitions may tempt one to make an ontological error and to take a stand as to the innermost nature and origin of religion. In addition, it becomes problematic to imagine the possibility of a functionless religion.

The other type of descriptive definition is based on the content of the ideas and actions. We may term these *content* definitions. In prin-ciple, neither an author's normative attitudes nor the function of reli-gion is included. Tylor's classical definition, 'belief in Spiritual Beings', and Wach's definition, 'the experience of the holy' (1944), belong to this category.

Naturally, content definitions also present questions and problems. For example, it is not always possible to put such definitions into prac-tice – this also applies to functional definitions. How, for instance, would Wach define 'the experience of the holy' in practice? His defi-nition requires a 'grammar of religious language', as he himself ex-presses it elsewhere. Despite such difficulties, a content definition is less fraught with problems than a functional one, in that questions as to both the function of religion and its functional alternatives remain open for speculation and investigation.

227

The strength of Wach's definition is that it introduces the fundamental distinction between the holy and the secular in human life (see Durkheim 1912). Its main weakness is that it neglects the cultic elements of religion; in fact, it is more a definition of 'religiosity' than of religion.

Against this background we shall now suggest the following definition of religion: *man's experience of the holy, as defined and regulated by cultic actions.*

3. CONTRIBUTORS TO RELIGION

The Norwegian population may be divided into two groups: 'contributors' to and 'receivers' of religious impulses. By contributor we mean here a person or social system whose main task is to exert religious influence on others. This is an admittedly narrow definition which excludes the many persons who have religious influence on others without this being their chief occupation in life; these are classified among the receivers of religious impulses.

A superficial glance at the contributor side in Norway would seem to give the impression of a lack of pluralism. The Church of Norway (*Den norske kirke*), to which the great majority of the population belong, makes the general picture appear a bit flat. If we look more closely, however, we soon discover quite sharp demarcation lines. For example, there are large variations of opinion as to what kinds of attitudes and beliefs should be disseminated. Theological disagreements and differences in working methods do exist. The largest and most volatile difference, however, is that between *official* and *voluntary* religious activity.

It has been said that the Church of Norway is the most 'state-churchly' in the world. At any rate, its official character does regulate much of the country's religious activities. But outside the framework of the Church of Norway – and, to a certain extent, within it as well – there is also a great deal of voluntary church activity. The voluntary contribution is considerable, and our picture of religious contributors would be incomplete without including it. The distinction between official and voluntary activity is decisive, and an important aim of this description will be to show how pluralistic the contributor side in fact is.

3.1. *Official religious activity*

Directly connected to the various official departments and their personnel and activities is much activity which could not without further

Table I. Church statistics for 1966 (absolute figures)

Diocese	Births	Baptisms	Confirmations	Church weddings	Civil weddings	New Church members	Officially left the Church
Oslo	16,187	14,297	10,828	5,198	1,621	172	577
Hamar	5,750	5,926	5,300	2,454	191	29	68
Tønsberg	6,079	5,615	4,909	2,310	275	68	172
Agder	6,052	5,668	4,763	2,182	242	81	303
Stavanger	5,402	4,914	3,914	1,745	163	23	105
Bjørgvin	10,717	10,684	8,925	3,772	349	48	182
Nidaros	8,598	8,615	7,398	3,342	267	21	106
S. Hålogaland	4,961	4,728	3,860	1,551	163	26	78
N. Hålogaland	4,734	4,733	3,392	1,552	102	20	76
Total	68,480	65,240	53,316	23,906	3,373	488	1,567

Diocese	Communicants	Church services	Appointments with minister	Pastoral counselling	Visits to institutions	Visits to schools	Donations and collections N.kr.
Oslo	202,824	11,135	24,841	49,763	5,028	2,248	2,196,503
Hamar	36,745	6,363	10,283	23,951	3,344	924	685,254
Tønsberg	56,207	5,570	10,858	18,957	2,545	1,032	832,041
Agder	99,473	6,652	12,309	26,950	3,727	843	1,714,337
Stavanger	60,467	3,864	6,473	17,073	4,230	839	1,101,361
Bjørgvin	129,107	9,288	14,629	45,879	5,020	1,466	2,140,313
Nidaros	64,808	7,799	17,746	31,336	3,570	821	1,090,784
S. Hålogaland	38,448	4,434	5,596	9,775	1,866	450	532,930
N. Hålogaland	44,213	3,497	3,389	10,016	1,506	339	352,073
Total	732,292	58,602	106,124	233,700	30,846	9,153	10,644,596

comment be called either official or authorized. This activity will arbitrarily be included under our designation 'official'.

That the Church of Norway is a state church means, briefly, that the king is its highest administrator, and that he, according to paragraph 16 of the Norwegian Constitution, defines and makes decisions concerning its liturgy and teachings. The ministers of the Church are for the most part civil servants, and are therefore appointed by the Cabinet. The Storting appropriates the sums needed for their salaries, etc.; in 1968 Church expenses covered by the national budget amounted to N.kr. 59,478,300, of which N.kr. 46,160,800 was for ministers' salaries. An important consequence of the fact that Norway has a state church is the religious instruction in the schools, which is directly connected to the Church and is in fact regarded as baptismal instruction.

Table I has been prepared on the basis of records from the local ministers' offices and gives a good indication of the form and extent of official religious activity in Norway.

Although the grounds for comparison are not absolutely precise, the first two columns would seem to indicate that in any given year, most people do baptize their infants (about 95 per cent). If we compare column 3 with the number of live births in 1951 (60,571 for the entire country) we see that the majority also participate in the Church ceremony of Confirmation (approximately 88 per cent). With respect to weddings, we find certain departures from this general pattern, but not drastic ones. For the country as a whole, only some 14 per cent of weddings are civil ceremonies. The great exception is the Oslo diocese, where approximately one-third are civil ceremonies. While we cannot know exactly how to interpret this finding, it seems certain that we are dealing with deliberate avoidance of religious ritual here.

The columns showing new Church members and those officially leaving the Church should be commented on. The majority of persons here either come from another confession or leave to join one; in other words, most continue to have contact with religious organizations of some sort.

The figures for 'communicants' are those for the number who received Holy Communion, not the total number of persons. Nor does the number of persons receiving Communion per church seem to be particularly large: in 1966 the average was 12.2 per church service for the whole country (figures from *Årbok for Den Norske Kirke 1967*, p. 32). As to the column concerning 'pastoral counselling', we must read it with strong reservations, as the defining criteria were not specified. There are thus great variations in what the individual ministers have included in this category, ranging from conversations in the rectory to others in homes, or after meetings, etc.

230

All in all, there would seem to be a large degree of adherence to the Church of Norway rituals connected with such important events as birth, entering adulthood, and marriage. This adherence, together with the massive, constant rate of membership in the Church of Norway (approximately 96 per cent in 1960), is frequently interpreted as tradition, habit, or lack of initiative, among the general populace. This explanation is not quite adequate, however, and, at any rate, such traditional behaviour or lack of initiative in changing such patterns demands an explanation. It would appear that belonging to the Church of Norway and adhering to its main rites of passage has certain functions for the Norwegian populace, although such functions need not be of a strictly religious character.

The Table is not complete, however. Religious instruction in the school system is perhaps the most important 'official' channel not included. The effect of this religious instruction on religious life and on society as a whole is not only a burning political question, but also one of great importance for the sociology of religion. It would also be interesting to know more about official religious influence in other non-churchly institutions – for example, the role of military chaplains, a question which has been the subject of much debate recently.

Table II. *Clerical offices and positions in Norway as of 31 December 1966*

Offices	
Bishops	9
Deans	9
Rectors	582
Vicars	160
Military chaplains	12
Minister to the deaf	1
Total	**773**

Positions	
Institution, hospital, and prison chaplains	29
Ministers to the deaf (positions)	5
Military chaplains (positions)	14
Assistant military chaplains	20
Resident curates	91
Diocesan curates	21
Assistant curates	103
Deputy pastors	10
Diocesan councillors	3
Other pastors	2
Positions for women with theological education	2
Total	**300**

Total number of offices and positions in the Church of Norway	1,073

231

Clergymen and theological candidates in institutions
and organizations

In Christian and other organizations	260
In newspapers, radio, and television	8
In schools	234
In the theology faculties	28
In other academic institutions	19
In Lutheran Churches abroad	15
Total	564

Source: *Årbok for Den Norske Kirke* Oslo 1967, p. 88.

Since the ministers of the Church of Norway act as representatives of most of Norway's religious life, it will be useful to survey the different offices and positions within the Church. Table II presents the hierarchy of the Church of Norway, and Table III presents additional information on the distribution of the clergy by educational institution and part of the country from which they come. Table III is the more interesting, showing the percentage of the clergy who graduated from the Free Theological Faculty *(Menighetsfakultetet)*, distributed by region. We investigated 223 persons who held offices or positions as listed in Reidar Bolling's *Norske prester og teologiske kandidater:* bishop, dean, rector, vicar, resident curate, diocesan curate, assistant curate, chaplain (these terms only approximate the Norwegian). Table III indicates that although clergymen educated at the Free Theological Faculty are in the majority in all rural areas, this majority is clearer in southern and western Norway *(Sør-* and *Vestlandet)* than in other parts of the country, and smallest in Trøndelag and northern Norway *(Nord Norge)*.

It is reasonable to assume that clergymen generally are drawn to places which they feel themselves suited for by education and orientation, and this helps to explain the connection between a 'low-church' educational background (the Free Theological Faculty) and a 'low-

Table III. *Proportion of clergy educated at the Free Theological Faculty, by place of assignment, 1957*

Place of assignment	Percentage	Number
Eastern Norway with Telemark county	67	108
Southern and western Norway with		
Møre and Romsdal county	79	65
Trøndelag and North Norway	56	50
Total	68	223

Source: Bolling 1958. The selection method is explained in the text.

232

church area' (southern and western Norway). However, this connection may in part be due to more complicated factors. For example, clergymen who are born and raised in southern and western Norway often attend the Free Theological Faculty, and, after completing their education, they prefer to take positions in their home areas. Also, the picture might well have been different had we included the most recent generation of theological candidates.

The information presented above and in Tables II and III gives only a static picture of same characteristics of the Norwegian clergy. Thanks to Mannsåker's (1954) investigation of the clergy in the nineteenth century and material from an investigation of academic groups underway at the Institute for Social Research, however, we now have available a great deal of information on the development of the clergy.

Table IV shows the number of clergymen, law graduates, and physicians in given years. The Table clearly indicates that the number of clergymen has increased: in 1950, there were more than twice as many ordained clergymen as in 1815. However, their number increased less in the period under consideration than did the general population (Aubert et al. 1960, p. 187).

It is of interest to compare the growth in the number of the clergy with that of law graduates and physicians. The roles of the clergyman, the lawyer, and the physician have some characteristics in common. To a large extent, the purpose of all three professions is to deal with human problems (Aubert et al., p. 185). This sets them apart from graduates in the humanities and the sciences. On the other hand, these three professions also exhibit striking dissimilarities. The

Table IV. *Number of clergymen, law graduates and physicians in given years*

Year	Ordained clergymen	Law graduates	Physicians
1815	400	329	160
1844	450	800	259
1864	567	1,250	354
1875	610	1,480	463
1885	679	1,600	610
1895	700	2,000	910
1905	720	2,400	1,210
1919	635	2,530	1,370
1930	731	3,200	1,775
1940	760	4,260	2,500
1950	828	4,807	3,754
Number in 1950 per 100 in 1815	2.07	14.61	23.46

Source: Aubert et al. 1960, p. 186.

233

roles of both clergyman and lawyer, as opposed to the physician's role, are characterized by a normative relationship with their clients. The physician typically has a non-normative, scientific relationship with his patient, although there are naturally exceptions to this in practice. The roles of lawyer and physician, as opposed to that of the clergyman, are both characterized by a worldly relationship with their clients, a relationship in which 'the holy' is in principle irrelevant. Ideally, then – each of these professions has its specific type of client-relationship: holy and normative (clergyman), worldly and normative (lawyer), worldly and scientific (physician). Which, then, of these three professional groups, whose purpose is to deal with human problems, has expanded most?

Table IV shows a much larger increase in the number of lawyers and physicians than in the number of clergymen, an increase much larger than that in the general population and, therefore, not explicable on the basis of that factor alone. In the nineteenth century, it was especially the number of lawyers which increased, the increase in the number of physicians coming somewhat later.

Aubert and his co-workers interpret these tendencies as an expression of a change in society's value system which has been taking place during the last 150 years (Aubert et al. 1960, pp. 186–187). This explanation is closely connected to the three ideal descriptions mentioned above. An increase took place first in the profession which is normative and worldly (the law), thereafter in the profession which is worldly and scientific (medicine). These developmental tendencies can be considered a result of the secularization of the academic world and society in general, and, somewhat later, of the increased influence of the sciences. Naturally, these two factors do not act independently of each other.

Table V presents information on the occupations of the fathers of clergymen. Let us first cursorily examine the period 1801–1910 as a whole. A full 28 per cent of clergymen had fathers who were also clergymen. But clergymen whose fathers were in business such as crafts, industry, trade, and transport make up a group accounting for 23 per cent of the clergy. Next come the groups whose fathers were in 'other academic' professions (17 per cent) and farmers (15 per cent). In general, we cannot say that recruiting for the clergy has been democratic; the majority of clergymen have a background in the higher strata of society.

However, it is difficult to interpret the information available on recruitment without also considering changes over time. The most important sociological changes have taken place in the portion of clergymen whose fathers were 1) small farmers, 2) academics (including officers, but not clergymen), and 3) clergymen. During the

Table V. *Distribution of clergymen by father's occupation 1801–1910 (percentage)*

Year of graduation	Clergymen	Physicians, lawyers, officers, college and secondary school teachers, higher civil cervants	Independent business men	Employees in private business, elementary school teachers	Other civil servants, professions	Farmers (large farms)	Farmers (small farms)	Workers	Total	N
1801–1820	40.1	22.8	19.1	4.4	7.4	2.5	1.2	2.5	100.0	(162)
1821–1840	27.4	26.8	27.0	3.8	6.8	4.8	2.1	1.6	100.3	(504)
1841–1860	36.2	21.7	23.3	3.8	6.7	1.3	5.8	1.2	100.0	(240)
1861–1880	30.3	12.5	24.0	8.2	6.1	3.1	13.2	2.6	100.0	(508)
1881–1900	16.9	11.0	18.4	12.6	8.8	2.3	25.7	4.3	100.0	(396)
1901–1910	29.3	6.7	15.3	15.4	8.0	4.7	19.3	1.3	100.0	(150)
Average 1801–1910	28.3	17.3	22.5	7.6	7.3	3.2	11.5	2.4	100.1	(196)

Source: Mannsåker 1954, pp. 144, 198.

period 1801–1900, there was a marked and steady increase in the percentage of clergymen whose fathers were small farmers. At the same time, there was a marked decrease in the percentage of those whose fathers were academics and clergymen.

Mannsåker's information on the clergy extends only up until 1910. In the twentieth century exact information is available on all theological candidates – not only the clergy alone. This information is presented in Table VI. This material is not completely representative of the clergy itself in this century, but the deviations are scarcely so great as to render the data meaningless for our purposes. The proportion of theological graduates recruited from a farming background continued to increase up to the decade 1930–1939, while in the 1940s and 1950s the percentage of farmers' sons was lower than before. During the same period, the percentage of graduates (candidates) recruited from sons of the clergy continued to decrease, and began to increase a little only during the last decade. It seems reasonable to conclude that these tendencies are, at least partly, also applicable to the ordained clergy.

The increase in the percentage of clergymen from groups other than the clergy itself was not caused by a decrease in the percentage recruited from clerical and academic backgrounds, but by an increasing number of clergymen recruited from other social groups – although there have been individual exceptions to the tendency.

Why did the number from other groups – especially small farmers – increase? It is reasonable to assume that the increase was due to a basic change in the system of values of Norwegian society in the nineteenth century: the development of a low-church attitude in the Norwegian Church combined with the general process of democratization that took place at that time. This low-church characteristic was a direct result of a split between liberal and conservative parties within the Church. It can also be attributed to a reaction against the secularization of society and the increased emphasis on the natural sciences.

As Pollan (1962) has pointed out, the struggle between liberalism and conservativism was more than just a theological squabble. Among other things, it included 'elements of the dispute between the official class and the agricultural class about who should appoint clergymen to livings and who had the right to become clergymen'. The play between the theological dispute and the social struggle is mirrored in the recruiting data, especially in the increased number of clergymen coming from a farming background.

The low-church party which developed represented a defence of the traditional values. The party established its footing within the Church of Norway by the founding and expansion of the Free Theological Faculty as an independent educational institution. In this connection, it is interesting that the Free Theological Faculty has always had

236

Table VI. *The occupations of the fathers of theological candidates 1800–1950 (percentage)*

	Clergy-man	Judge, senior civil servant, lecturer at university or secondary school, officer, physician, dentist, engineer, architect	Business-man, owner, or executive	White-collar em-ployee	Farmer	Ele-mentary school	Crafts-man	Worker	Other not given	Total	N
Before 1810	45.0	10.0	20.0	10.0			5.0		10.0	100.0	20
1810–1829	33.1	33.4	19.7	8.8	1.3	2.5		1.1	1.2	100.0	239
1830–1849	25.9	23.9	27.0	11.2	4.0	4.4	1.9	4.9	0.7	100.0	455
1850–1869	37.4	14.9	9.1	8.2	2.1	2.1	1.3	2.8	4.9	100.1	388
1870–1889	20.9	12.8	17.0	11.3	18.5	6.5	9.3	1.4	0.5	99.6	642
1890–1909	21.0	13.1	20.3	11.7	21.0	8.9	2.5	5.6	0.5	100.4	439
1910–1929	13.8	6.1	15.6	12.1	25.7	12.4	7.0	6.1	1.9	100.2	603
1930–1939	8.4	5.0	10.9	13.4	30.6	10.9	11.2	6.1	3.4	99.9	702
1940–1949	12.0	5.9	14.9	16.9	16.4	7.3	14.1	4.4	8.0	99.9	275
1950–1955	14.6	9.8	11.2	15.7	14.1	6.3	6.8	11.7	9.8	100.0	205

Source: Based on Aubert et al. 1960, p. 192.

more graduates with a rural background than has had the University of Oslo's Theological Faculty, a difference especially striking after 1950. At the same time, the University of Oslo has had a larger proportion of students who were sons of clergymen than has the Free Theological Faculty (Pollan 1962, p. 96). This forming of parties within the Church of Norway can, to a certain extent, be followed up to the theological debates of the 1950s and 1960s. The famous 'debate on Hell', which took place in the early 1950s and whose most important participants were Professor Ole Hallesby of the Free Theological Faculty and Bishop Kristian Schjelderup, must be considered as a continuation of party formation.

There are also conflicts over questions of belief in the Church of Norway, which are in part historically connected with the original split within the Church, although, naturally, new elements have also entered in. Today, the main issues concern opposing points of view on the Bible. Thus Professor Wisløff summarized this debate at the end of 1964:

> No one who has followed what has been said and written during the past year can doubt that the battle on biblical points of view is going to become serious . . .
> A glance at the 1964 issues of the two Church papers shows that this question has been under discussion all year long. And the questions involved are fundamental: clergymen and theologians are arguing about the Immaculate Conception and Virgin Birth of Jesus, the reality of His Resurrection, and other great and important things. In the last analysis, the debate concerns one's attitude towards the Bible. The underlying question is this: Is the Bible God's Word given to us through inspired witnesses; is, for example, the New Testament a unity expressing one message in spite of its authors' differences in style and ways of expressing themselves, or are there — as has been maintained — in the new Testament different and contradictory religious thoughts and ideas? (Wisløff 1964).

It seems reasonable, then, to conclude that pluralism in official religious activity is considerable and possesses historical roots. This is further discussed in Torgersen (1966), Flint (1960), and Flint (1964). We shall see that the picture of contributors as a whole becomes even more pluralistic when we include voluntary activity.

3.2. Voluntary religious activity within the Church of Norway
The general process of democratization that also took place within the Church was in part strongly opposed by the clergy. For this and other reasons, the increased influence given to laymen frequently found its expression in special religious organizations lying outside the sphere of the official religious hierarchy and offices (Aarflot 1967, pp. 364–

238

Name	Number of groups	Personnel	Publications	Circulation	Institutions	Camps
The Norwegian Lutheran Inner Mission Society (*Indremisjonsselskap*)	3,300	235	30	120,500	13	21
The Inner Mission of Western Norway (*Vestlandske indremisjonsforbund*)	1,300	95	11	35,000	16	10
The Norwegian Seamen's Mission (*Sjømannsmisjon*)	3,139	172	1	16,000	32	1
Oslo Inner Mission (*Oslo indremisjon*)	40	160	1	9,500	17	1
Oslo Seaman's Church (*Sjømannskirke*)	–	5	1	1,200	–	–
The Inner Seaman's Mission (*Indre Sjømannsmisjon*)	2,231	110	1	12,000	31	1
Norway's Lapp Mission (*Samemisjon*)	2,300	150	1	11,000	23	–
Norwegian Sunday School Association (*Søndagsskoleforbund*)	3,300	22	2	94,700	–	–
The Norwegian Association of Christian Youth affiliated with YWCA and YMCA (*Kristelige Ungdomsforbund*)	1,600	40	7	38,000	6	15
The Norwegian Christian Student and Secondary School Association (affiliated with IFES (*Kristelige Student- og Gymnasiastlag*)	255	21	3	23,000	–	3
Norwegian Christian Student Movement (*Kristelige Studentbevegelse*)	11	4	1	2,700	–	–
National Association for Christian Schools (*Landslaget for Kristen skole*)	37	1	1	7,000	–	–
Norwegian Blue Cross (*Blå Kors*)	525	129	1	37,500	21	2
The White Band (*Hvite Bånd*)	163	1	1	7,500	6	–
The Norwegian Mission for the Homeless (*Misjon blant Hjemløse*)	175	30	1	3,000	6	–
The Norwegian Missionary Society (*Norske Misjonsselskap*)	7,625	177	3	92,000	4	12
The Norwegian Lutheran Mission (*Norsk Luthersk Misjonssamband*)	4,317	234	15	161,000	7	16
The Norwegian Santal Mission (*Santalmisjon*)	3,500	70	2	20,000	–	4
The Norwegian Mission to the Jews (*Det norske Israelmisjon*)	2,000	15	2	16,000	–	–
The Nordic Christian Buddhist Mission (*Nordiske kristne buddhistmisjon*)	150	4	1	6,000	–	–
The Mission to the Mohammedans (*Muhammedanermisjonen*)	65	13	1	4,000	–	–

Source: *Årbok for Den Norske Kirke* 1967, pp. 48, 57. The material has been edited and rearranged by the present authors.

239

408). This historical background has been important in giving the various voluntary organizations their structure and position in the general religious picture.

Most of these organizations are ideologically Lutheran, but – with certain variations – they indicate clearly their independence and self-determination vis-à-vis the official Church. Their inner structure resembles the bureaucratic form of leadership – with a general assembly, board of directors, active secretariat, and a rational hierarchic structure with burdens and benefits well distributed. This fairly trivial fact becomes most interesting when we realize that the strongest complaint by these organizations against the Church of Norway is its lack of charismatic leadership.

However, bureaucratic tendencies are not the only form of structure. The inner structure of these organizations seems to include a mixture of bureaucracy, charisma, and tradition as well.

3.2.1. Bureaucratic features

The organizations show strong formalizing tendencies, with clear lines of command and information. In general, there is a tendency toward professionalization of those employed, with untrained, part-time workers giving way to specially trained full-time personnel. The number of personnel not directly engaged in the organization's main purpose (be it mission work, social work, etc.) seems to be increasing.

3.2.2. Charismatic features

There exist few, if any, fixed rules for advancement and promotion for personnel. Criteria for employment are seldom specified. One is usually 'called' – there is seldom the opportunity to apply for a position, and relatively few of those employed have completed training as preparation for specific positions.

3.2.3. Traditional features

The individual leader has, traditionally, a good deal of autonomy. This increases as one ascends the organizational ladder.

Because of the weaknesses to be mentioned below, it is difficult to give any exact numerical expression of religious activity in the voluntary organizations found within the Church of Norway. A general idea, however, can be formed from the figures presented in Table VII.

The first column shows the number of groups within the particular organization. The same group may well be working for several organizations at the same time, and thereby be registered here more than once. Also, the number of members varies greatly from group to group,

240

Table VIII. *Five religious organizations' schools and teachers*

	Inn. Missn. Soc.	Inn. Missn. W. Norw.	Inn. Seamen Missn.	Norw. Lapp Missn.	Norw. Assoc. Chr. Youth	Total
Schools	22	9	1	4	2	38
Teachers	212	80	3	24	10	329

Source: *Årbok for Den Norske Kirke* 1976, p. 49.

so that it is impossible to know how many *persons* are active in this field.

Column two, which gives the number of persons employed, probably presents the most correct picture of the organizations' size. However, we must recall here that 1) some organizations include office workers – i.e. personnel whose work is strictly clerical – while others do not; 2) many workers may be part time; 3) with the missions abroad, only workers within Norway are included (if the number of missionaries were included, the total number of workers would be well over 2,200); and 4) those employed in the organizations' schools are not included here. Available figures on this are given in Table VIII.

The publications, which are shown in column 3, Table VII, are mostly 'house organs'; circulation is sometimes considerable indeed (column 4). Column 5 presents information on 'institutions', charitable institutions of various types; 'business-type' activities and meeting houses (prayer meeting houses, etc.) are not included.

The effects of all this voluntary religious activity are limited by a series of geographical, social, and historical conditions, and although these organizations are, in one sense, larger than the Church of Norway (the number of those employed by private organizations: 1,688; by the Church of Norway: 1,078), their contacts with the Norwegian populace are decidedly more limited. On the other hand, however, their religious activity is probably more intense, with more interest and participation on the receiver's part.

Within both the voluntary and the official religious activities of the Church of Norway there exist considerable conflicts and disparities. The degree of 'churchly-ness' is especially important. We find the entire spectrum, from organizations clearly willing to co-operate with the official organs (here the Organization of Norwegian Missions and the Norwegian Association of Christian Youth are examples) to organizations which practise free Communion and take a highly critical attitude to the Church of Norway (for example, the Inner Mission of Western Norway and the Norwegian Lutheran Inner Mission Society). There are also disagreements on working methods – for ex-

241

ample, concerning youth activities – and comparatively little practical co-operation between the various organizations. An informal channel of inter-communication does exist in the Common Council (Organisasjonenes Fellesråd), which meets yearly, but even this Council cannot remove all conflicts.

There seems to be an important difference between official and voluntary organs concerning the use of various channels for religious work. Figure 1 has been prepared on this basis of personal evaluations and opinions, as there are very few data available here. Only those channels under organized religious direction are included: thus the school system has been excluded, despite its importance.

Channel 1: The life and death rituals are probably entirely under the direction of the official organs. To the best of our knowledge there exists no organized baptism, matrimony, or burial within the voluntary organizations. *Channel 2:* Holy Communion, however, is found to a certain extent within the voluntary groups, as 'free' and distinct from the Church of Norway practice. *Channel 3:* The relationship between voluntary and official activity in radio and television indicated here ought to be fairly correct. It corresponds to a list of religious programs from the Norwegian Broadcasting System published in the *Yearbook for the Church of Norway* (Årbok for Den Norske Kirke). *Channel 4:* Here, however, the relationship has been set up more on the basis of personal evaluation, since data on the voluntary sector are completely lacking. *Channel 5:* Religious activity among children and young persons is mostly in the hands of the voluntary organizations, but there also exist many Sunday schools and youth clubs connected to the official organs. *Channel 6:* Practically all social work is carried on by the voluntary organizations. *Channel 7:* Most publishing and periodical activity is carried on by the voluntary organizations, with the exception of the many parish newsletters.

Naturally, there also exists voluntary religious work above and beyond that which can clearly be placed within the framework of the Church of Norway (see for example Klausen 1960 and Paine 1965). Any future discussion of voluntary religious activity in Norway will have to treat these variants as well.

3.3. Official/voluntary religious conflict

There is a basic, deep-rooted conflict between official and voluntary religious activity. Its various components may be schematically presented as follows:

a) Ideological conflict
1) *Theological questions.* The conflict (already mentioned in 3.1..) between a conservative and a liberal wing is also present in the relationship between voluntary and official organs.

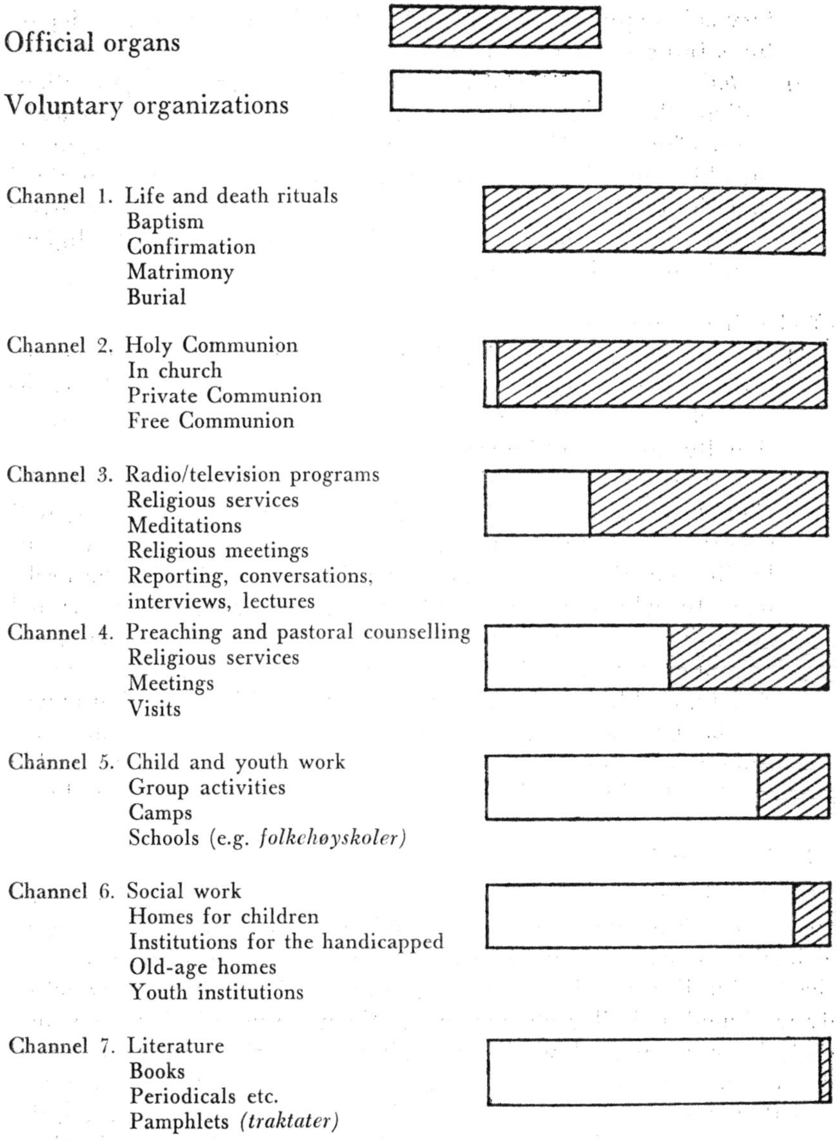

Official organs

Voluntary organizations

Channel 1. Life and death rituals
      Baptism
      Confirmation
      Matrimony
      Burial

Channel 2. Holy Communion
      In church
      Private Communion
      Free Communion

Channel 3. Radio/television programs
      Religious services
      Meditations
      Religious meetings
      Reporting, conversations,
      interviews, lectures

Channel 4. Preaching and pastoral counselling
      Religious services
      Meetings
      Visits

Channel 5. Child and youth work
      Group activities
      Camps
      Schools (e.g. *folkehøyskoler*)

Channel 6. Social work
      Homes for children
      Institutions for the handicapped
      Old-age homes
      Youth institutions

Channel 7. Literature
      Books
      Periodicals etc.
      Pamphlets *(traktater)*

Fig. 1. Channels for religious impulses. An approximate survey of official and voluntary organizations.

2) *Use of sanctions.* The voluntary organizations maintain that the official organs do not make use of sanctions, especially in the following situations: when clergy and preachers depart from accepted doctrine and when moral norms are broken. The volun-

tary side maintains that the Church of Norway tolerates departures from moral rules without reacting.
3) *Appointment to leading positions.* The voluntary organizations
criticize the fact that the criteria for appointment to offices within the Church of Norway are not charismatic. Here we again see
the old dispute between layman and clergy. It is also maintained
that the bodies which appoint and judge applicants for office
(parish councils, the government) do not possess the right religious
qualifications themselves.

b) Conflict of interest
  1) *Division of work: church/voluntary organizations.* The voluntary
  organizations have expressed disapproval that official organs
  (e.g. clergy, parish council) have been taking up work traditionally carried out by them.
  2) *Use of limited resources.* Such a well-ramified system as the
  Church of Norway, with its official and voluntary organs, will
  necessarily require considerable personnel to fill the various
  leading positions. The conflict can be exemplified by the problem: In which sectors would the scarce qualified personnel
  make their contribution? Since religious activity, like other forms
  of group activity, follows the general development tendencies of
  society, problems also arise in connection with population movements, urbanization, and new residential areas: What form
  should religious activity take in such situations, when suitable
  meeting facilities and qualified personnel are in short supply?

3.4. *Some conclusions*

We opened our discussion of religious contributors by pointing to the
apparent lack of pluralism to be found in Norway. In the section on
official religious activity we saw that there exist deep-rooted tendencies to pluralism within that sector; in the section on voluntary activity we found a similar phenomenon. When we now include the conflicts between official work and voluntary work, we discover that
the contributor side is deeply divided into various conflicting factions.

Although there naturally exist tendencies towards co-operation, the
conflicts mentioned here – especially that between official and voluntary activity in the Church – are considerable enough for us to ask:
How can this structure possibly be held together? Perhaps the fact
that it is a state church is a structural condition hindering a complete
split. Perhaps this creates the necessary minimum of the community
feeling in the various parties. If this is true, we have here a
fact of great importance in any discussion of a possible separation of
State and Church: such a separation might well have the consequence

that the various factions would no longer be able to co-exist within
the same Church.

4. RECEIVERS OF RELIGION

The Norwegian people as a whole form the most inclusive category of
'receivers' of impulses from the contributors. This does not mean that
all these receivers are equally receptive to impulses from the contributors. It is probable that some receivers more actively seek impulses
than do others, and that they more often pass on these impulses to
others, but we have no data on persons or 'roles' which might form
such a step by step dissemination of impulses.

In the following section, we shall first consider some characteristics
of the distribution of the population according to religion. Then we
shall examine some public opinion surveys which indicate something
about people's attitudes towards religion and their religious activity;
and, finally, we shall venture a few remarks on what we feel is the
main form of religious attitude in Norway.

4.1. *Distribution of the population by religion*

The vast majority of Norwegians are members of the Church of
Norway. This is true in both rural and urban areas, of both men and

Table IX. *Resident population belonging to religous groups other than the Church
of Norway, by sex, urban/rural area, 1950 (percentage)*

	Men		Women	
	Rural	Urban	Rural	Urban
Roman Catholic	2.5	5.9	1.7	6.5
Methodist	4.9	14.0	5.7	15.6
Baptist	7.3	5.4	8.6	6.9
Seventh Day Adventist	3.6	3.8	4.5	5.7
Free Lutheran	15.6	13.3	14.3	12.4
Assembly of God	2.3	0.2	2.1	0.2
Mission Society	2.5	2.6	2.4	2.8
Pentecostal	27.1	14.0	32.9	18.4
Other groups with adult baptism	1.9	1.0	2.0	1.1
Jehovah's Witness	1.7	2.1	1.4	2.0
Jewish	0.1	1.5	0.2	1.3
No religion*	19.8	25.9	13.4	14.9
Others	10.7	10.3	10.8	12.2
Total	100.0	100.0	100.0	100.0
	(33,797)	(22,668)	(37,272)	(29,577)

Source: NOS XI 153, pp. 34-35.

* In absolute figures: 6,689; 5,873; 5,006; 4,417.

women, and of all age groups. As late as 1960, only 3.7 per cent of the resident population were not members of the Church of Norway; of these, more were living in urban areas – 4.9 per cent – than in rural areas – 3.2 per cent.

Table IX shows the distribution of those of the resident population who are not members of the Church of Norway, by religious groups. The material, from 1950, is distributed by rural and urban areas and by sex. (Completely comparable information is not available from the 1960 census.) The Table indicates that Pentecostal groups, the Evangelical Lutheran Free Church, and the Methodist Church account for the largest number. Taken together, these three groups account for the majority of those who are not members of the Church of Norway, but who do belong to a religious group; other religious groups account for only a small percentage. In addition, we notice some differences between urban areas and rural areas as to religious groups other than the Church of Norway. The Methodist Church is clearly more important in urban than in rural areas, while the reverse is true of Pentecostal groups; this is true of both men and women.

That the vast majority of Norwegians belong to one or another religious group need not, of course, mean that Norwegians are an exceptionally religious people. On the contrary, it is often maintained that membership in a religious group – especially a state church – is largely connected with a generally passive, non-religious attitude. We shall return to this question later.

Table X shows the distribution of non-members of the Church of Norway by religious groups and position (1960). Particularly interesting would be any differentiating characteristics to be found in those persons who belong to no religious group at all: but the Table indicates that this group differs little from all the others who are not members of the Church of Norway. An exception to this is that in the former group we find more persons in technical, scientific, literary, and artistic works; somewhat more in administration, etc., but fewer housewives. Roman Catholics are found more in technical and scientific work than in agriculture, forestry, and fishing or as housewives (in other words, a concentration of Roman Catholics in urban areas and in 'intellectual' professions – a tendency perhaps peculiar to Scandinavia). For Methodists, somewhat more members among workers in urban areas, and somewhat fewer in agriculture, etc. Seventh Day Adventists: there are somewhat fewer members in administration, etc., and somewhat more members who are housewives.

A comparison of those who belong to no religious group with members of the Church of Norway in terms of occupation shows few marked differences (comparison based on figures from 1950, people 15 years old or more, urban and rural areas independent of each

246

Table X. Non-members of the Church of Norway, distributed by religious groups and position (percentage)

	Technical, scientific, artistic, humanistic	Administrative white-collar independent tradesman, other sales	Agriculture, forestry, fishing	Independent craftsman, transportation, small businessman	Worker other than agriculture and forestry	Housewife, etc.	Pensioner, etc.	Other	Number	Total
1. Total non-members of Church of Norway	5.3	9.0	4.7	2.0	23.6	21.5	5.9	28.0	(134,551)	100.0
2. Roman Catholic......	12.4	8.3	1.2	1.2	22.3	16.1	7.6	30.9	(7,875)	100.0
3. Methodist	5.5	11.6	1.0	1.9	27.7	23.9	4.9	23.5	(11,196)	100.0
4. Baptist	3.5	7.8	6.3	1.8	25.5	25.2	6.1	23.8	(9,315)	100.0
5. Adventist	5.9	4.7	3.8	2.8	25.7	26.1	5.5	25.8	(5,272)	100.0
6. Free Lutheran	3.7	9.5	6.6	2.1	21.8	20.7	4.5	31.1	(16,773)	100.0
7. Pentecostal	3.2	7.0	5.5	1.8	23.3	24.0	6.4	28.8	(34,122)	100.0
8. Other	4.8	9.0	4.5	2.1	23.6	22.4	6.2	27.4	(27,653)	100.0
9. No religious group	8.4	12.4	5.0	2.4	23.7	15.0	5.7	27.4	(22,345)	100.0

Source: NOS XII 140, Table 4, pp. 30–31.

247

other). A few tendencies, however, are interesting. The number of independent businessmen and administrative personnel is a little larger among those who adhere to no religion. This does not mean that leaving the Church of Norway shows any tendency of being an 'upper-class' phenomenon, however, since there are also more workers in crafts and industry among those who do not belong to any religion (especially in rural areas). The most marked difference is the smaller number of housewives among the non-affiliated. We shall shortly return to women's stronger bond to religious life.

4.2. Religiosity and religious activity

Is it true, as is often assumed, that a high rate of membership in a religious group (especially a state church) is connected with a generally passive, non-religious attitude? Or, more pointedly, is it in fact not *religion* we are dealing with in analysing the Norwegian population's relationship to the Church of Norway? From the Norwegian Gallup Institute we have available material which may help to measure religiosity in a presumably representative cross-section of the Norwegian population. The material deals partly with *religiosity* and religious beliefs, partly with *religious activity*.

We must remember the various methodological weaknesses which material of this type always presents. Especially difficult is the lack of representativeness and reliability. Furthermore, the problem of validity arises when questions in an opinion poll are taken to represent internalized attitudes – probably a particularly vital problem in connection with questions concerning religion.

To begin with, let us note that in 1960, 26 per cent of a nation-wide sample of adult Norwegians answered 'Yes' and 21 per cent 'Maybe' to the question 'Do you consider yourself a personal Christian?' (The approximate English equivalent would be 'to have made a decision for Christ' – translator's note). Forty-nine per cent answered a straight 'No', and 2 per cent 'Don't know' (Galtung 1961, Table and Diagram A.2.10). The proportion of those who considered themselves personal Christians seems to have remained fairly constant: in 1965, 28 per cent answered 'Yes' to the same question. There are more personal Christians among older than younger persons (46 per cent aged 60 years or more, 28 per cent 30–59 years, 14 per cent 20–29 years), among persons in rural areas than among those in urban areas (34, 23 per cent), among persons in the low income group than in the high income group (32, 23 per cent), and more in Trøndelag and northern Norway than elsewhere (36 per cent in Trøndelag and northern Norway, 26 per cent in southern and western Norway, 25 per cent in eastern Norway). This latter finding is somewhat unusual, as other

248

Table XI. *Belief in a life after death, in Norway and an average of seven countries (percentage)*

	Norway	Average of seven countries
Believe in life after death	71	59
Do not believe in life after death	15	25
Don't know	14	16
Total	100	100

Source: Gallup, undated.

Table XII. *Belief in a life after death, in different countries (percentage)*

	All asked	Women	Men
USA	74	78	68
Norway	71	79	64
The Netherlands	63	67	59
Great Britain	56	62	49
Switzerland	55	61	48
India	54	not given	not given
West Germany	38	45	31

Source: Gallup, undated.

material would indicate a concentration of religious activity in southern and western Norway.

In a joint investigation in seven countries (Norway one of them) questions on religious items were posed to a presumably representative sample of the population (dates not given). The six other countries were India, the Netherlands, Great Britain, Switzerland, the USA, and West Germany. One of the questions was 'Do you believe, or do you not believe, in a life after death?' In Table XI, the Norwegian answers are compared with the average of the seven countries. More people in Norway believe in a life after death than in other countries. The material in Table XII is distributed by country and by sex. Of the percentages of those asked who do believe in an afterlife, Norway ranks second after the USA and considerably higher than the Netherlands, which is third. Norway's high rating is in good agreement with the other available data: in a 1948 investigation, which in part dealt with other countries, Norway ranked first, with the USA somewhat lower. As Table XII indicates, for all countries from which information is available, women more often than men believe in life after death.

Several problems become apparent if we attempt to interpret these data. First, we are dealing with countries which have different religions. Second, the question, and therefore the answer, can have different meanings in different cultural contexts. Third, methodological problems can vary from country to country; for example, they can be much greater in a country like India – something which may account for India's low rank on belief as measured by this question. However, we believe it reasonable to conclude that Norway ranks rather high in relation to other countries on the question of belief in a life after death. This is also valid when we consider men and women individually.

Gallup has also conducted a survey on belief in God (1948). The question 'Do you believe in God?' was asked in eight countries, among them Norway. As we see from Table XIII, the results are not in complete agreement with the results from the questions about a life after death. First, the variation in the material as a whole is not so great, nor is this in itself unreasonable. It takes rather a lot for anyone to answer 'No, I don't believe in God'. If this reasoning is correct, the small percentage differences are probably of little sociological meaning in this Table. But then – and more important for us – we see that Norway is a bit lower than both the USA and Australia in the question of belief. The most important division is between Australia and Norway, while the differences between Norway and all the other countries are not so great.

Even though Norway's position on a belief in God is a little different from its belief in a life after death, it still ranks higher than many other countries on the former question. All things considered, Norwegians seem to rank relatively high as to the acceptance of some key religious beliefs.

Table XIII. *Belief in God in eight countries (percentage)*

	Believe	Do not believe	Not sure Don't know	Total
USA	94	3	3	100
Australia	93	5	2	100
Norway	84*	7	9	100
England	84	—	16	100
Finland	83	5	12	100
Denmark	80	9	11	100
Sweden	80	8	12	100
Czechoslovakia	77	15	8	100

Source: Gallup 1948.

* Ninety-two per cent of women and 76 per cent of men say that they believe in God. We do not have access to similar information from the other countries.

These religious beliefs are adhered to in varying degrees by different categories of the Norwegian population. With one exception, we find the same tendencies as for the question of whether one is a personal Christian: the exception is for *regional differences*. On belief in a life after death, southern and western Norway distinguish themselves.

Sex is also an important factor in determining the acceptance of beliefs. Women consistently show a higher degree of acceptance than do men, a difference probably rooted in the differences in role structure. Because of their position in society's social structure, women consistently have fewer contacts which could have a secularizing influence (work, science, technology, etc.). The material indicates that such a difference exists not only in Norway but in other countries as well (cf. Table XII). However, we must bear in mind that these data are limited to Western culture; in many non-Western societies men play a more central part in religious life than do women.

On the basis of the data on religiosity presented above, we might expect Norway to rank high in comparison with other countries as to church attendance. Information available, however, does not support this hypothesis. Concerning church attendance, the Gallup investigation shows that Norway ranks *lowest* of the seven countries polled, and that the difference between Norway and the country next above it was very marked. The data are presented in Tables XIV and XV (dates not given). The question was: 'Aside from a wedding, baptism, funeral, or other such occasion, when were you last in church?' In a 1948 Gallup poll, conducted in part in other countries, the question was: 'Have you attended divine service during the last two weeks?' The results were similar. To the second question, the percentage answering 'Yes' in the seven countries was as follows: Norway 17 per cent, Denmark 20 per cent, Sweden 20 per cent, Finland 25 per cent, England 30 per cent, Australia 35 per cent, Czechoslovakia 35 per cent. (The question was not asked in the USA.) It was further shown (1948) that in Norway women attended divine services more often than men.

While church attendance is a very important form of collective manifestation of religiosity, there are of course many other forms. Activity in a religious organization is an important example. A Gallup poll limited to Norway indicates that the degree of such activity is also relatively low in this respect (1956); in any case low when loosely compared with impressions from, for example, the USA. To the question: 'About how often do you attend Christian meetings?' the answers were as follows: every other week or more often 14 per cent, from once a month to five or six times a year 5 per cent, three or four times a year 5 per cent, once or twice a year 5 per cent, seldom, very seldom, only on special occasions 19 per cent, never 46 per cent

251

(the remainder answered 'Don't know' or 'as often as I can'). To the question 'Would you like to attend Christian meetings more often?' 76 per cent answered 'No'.

But even though the degree of activity as expressed in terms of church attendance and participation in religious organizations is relatively low in Norway on the whole, we must bear in mind that there are regional and social variations. This is very clearly indicated by Rokkan and Valen (1964). Concerning church attendance, Rokkan and Valen demonstrate, first, that such activity is significantly more frequent in peripheral country districts than in urbanized areas and cities, although there are more churches and more church services in the towns than in the remote country areas. Second, these authors show that church attendance is significantly more frequent in southern Norway than in other regions of the country. Rokkan and Valen also find certain differences in membership in religious organizations.

Church attendance and participation in religious meetings are the most collective forms of religious activity on which we have data. Religious activity stimulated by such mass media as radio and television falls somewhere between public and private religious activity – one participates, to a certain extent, with an unknown number of others, but without face-to-face contact. Data are lacking here, and as far as we know there are no international comparisons available. But some Gallup data on radio listening in Norway indicate that the number of radio listeners is greater than the number of church-goers; but even this does not represent a really large and concentrated participation. To the question 'About how often do you listen to divine service on the radio on Sundays?' (1953), more answered 'every Sunday' than anything else; 38 per cent said that they listened to divine service on the radio every Sunday, every other Sunday 14 per cent, once in a while 29 per cent, never 18 per cent, don't know 3 per cent. More women than men listen to divine service every Sunday, 47 per cent as against 30 per cent.[1] All things considered, we get the impression that this 'semi-collective' form of religious activity is frequent

Table XIV. *Church attendance in Norway and an average of seven countries (percentage)*

Were last in church:	Norway	Average of seven countries
Last Sunday	8	31
Sunday before last	4	8
Within the last 12 months	51	32
Not within the last 12 months	37	29
Total	100	100

Source: Gallup, undated.

Table XV. *Church attendance in seven countries (percentage)*

	Last Sunday	Sunday before last	Last 12 months	Not last 12 months	Total
USA	48	8	26	18	100
The Netherlands	47	3	11	39	100
Switzerland	37	11	31	21	100
West Germany	33	7	34	26	100
India	24	9	37	30	100
Great Britain	23	6	34	17	100
Norway	8	4	51	37	100*

Source: Gallup, undated.

*Error in original source.

in comparison to the completely collective form. But we must add that on Sunday morning the radio can simply be turned on, without anyone's particularly noticing what is being said. Much indicates that this is the case in many families. Of those who said that they listened to divine service on the radio, 45 per cent stated that they only listened to 'part of it', and 64 per cent stated that they were doing other 'little' things at the same time. However, in addition to Sunday morning services, many persons will regularly listen to other religious radio programs such as weekday morning meditations, for example.

No information is available on purely private religious practice, such as prayer, meditation on religious problems. But it is very possible that many Norwegians manifest such individualistic religious practices.

According to Norwegian Gallup polls, there are many more people who believe in central religious ideas than there are who participate in collective religious activity (church attendance). If we may assume that religious belief will express itself in one form of practice or another, then it is reasonable to believe that Norwegians express their belief primarily in private. In other words, Norwegians are perhaps first and foremost 'privately' religious.

Let us place this general characterization – the suitability of which will naturally vary for different groups of the population – in a somewhat more comprehensive typology of religious beliefs and practices. From Gallup data, Americans and Australians would seem to be to a greater extent 'publicly' religious, either in place of or in addition to being privately religious. The discrepancy between the number of believers and the numbers of those who show their faith publicly (collectively) is significantly smaller than in Norway. Such a characteristic is not inconsistent with the accepted, possibly stereotyped image of the difference between American and Norwegian national

253

character. As opposed to Norwegians, Americans are considered to be out-going, sociable, contact-seeking types. However, the large percentage differences between countries can be explained without reference to such a problematic concept as national character: we can simply state that church attendance is more of a social norm in the USA and Australia than in Norway.

Again, we must emphasize that the conclusions reached here are based on certain assumptions. This is not least because it has been impossible to cross-tabulate the information available on belief and practice, while at the same time the conclusions reached really do presuppose such cross-tabulation, and not just comparisons of rank order. In an opinion poll conducted in Norway, France, and Poland, information on belief was cross-tabulated with information on (collective) religious activity. In Norway, 29 per cent of those asked stated that they were 'believing, not active', while the corresponding figures for France and Poland were 42 and 24 per cent. Apparently, these results do not completely support the view that Norwegians are particularly privately religious – for that, the Norwegian figure for 'believing, not active', is too low. However, the differences between the countries may be the result of difference in the form of the question asked. In Norway, people were asked if they considered themselves to be personal Christians, while the questions on belief asked in France and Poland were much broader. (The figures were supplied by the International Peace Research Institute, Oslo.)

What can the Gallup material indicate about the main problem under discussion here, which is: To what degree is the high rate of membership in churches – especially in the Church of Norway – connected with a passive, non-religious attitude? Let us concentrate on membership in the Church of Norway, which accounts for the great majority of those who are members of any church group.

The material indicates that membership in the Church of Norway is not connected with a completely passive attitude to religious questions. While it is certainly reasonable to assume that Norwegian society has gone through a significant period of secularization in recent times, this secularization has scarcely been complete, in that there are too many Norwegians who accept central religious ideas.

This general conclusion, however, cannot be passed by without further comment. Even though many Norwegians have a certain religious bent – if in no other way, of a cognitive kind – this bent is relatively seldom activated and channelled by the concrete attempts on the part of the Church of Norway. Some of the activity of the Church of Norway does come under the heading of what above was called 'semi-collective' (radio programs, etc.), but even though participation is somewhat greater in this area, it is still far from convincingly high.

Nevertheless, a clear majority of the Norwegian people do support the Church of Norway and its activity. Of a presumably representative cross-section, 85 per cent were of the opinion that the Church of Norway 'has a mission in our society' (1961); 65 per cent thought that the Church ought rightly to be organized as a state church (1956); 89 per cent thought it right to baptize infants; 95 per cent thought it right that children should receive religious instruction in school (1956); and 84 per cent of those with children said that they had taught their children to say their prayers before going to bed, or that they were going to do so (1965). But, among other things, in the light of a rather exceptional lack of concentrated contact between the Church's workers and its congregations, it is reasonable to interpret this support as an expression of a purely traditional attitude. A great many Norwegians presumably like the fact that the Church of Norway exists as a symbol of the stability of values and respectability, and they like to have contact with the Church of Norway on such formal occasions as baptism, confirmation, weddings, and funerals – but nothing more than that.

4.3. Popular religiosity

This conclusion, however, raises several further questions. Especially pressing is the following problem: If it is true that a considerable portion of the Norwegian population has a religious bent that the Church of Norway does not manage to activate or channel – what happens? How does this bent find expression? We have indicated that it may get a kind of private expression – that Norwegians are largely privately religious. However, this view does not quite hold. On the basis of Danish and Swedish investigations we may propose a more adequate hypothesis: that this religious bent mainly expresses itself in a simple, quite unchurchly, 'folk religion', a clinging to childhood beliefs that are kept private – an attitude rather different from the personal Christian's, who has made his 'decision for Christ' (see e.g. Rod 1961, Gustafsson 1965, pp. 46–50, Salomonsen 1966, pp. 63–70, Åhman 1966, pp. 100–105). Let us look a bit more deeply into this folk religion, this clinging to childhood beliefs, to see what it may contain.

Jacob Rod, in his investigation of this phenomenon in Denmark, divides it into three basic articles of belief : belief in God, in a virtuous life, and in immortality. This treble division may well be relevant for Norway as well. Salomonsen has summarized Rod's three-point catechism as follows (Salomonsen 1966, pp. 65–66):

> *God:* Folk religion conceives only of one God, one Power, not a dualism of an evil power and a good one. God is almost a kind of God of Fate, or control. What happens is willed by this Fate: 'It was fated to hap-

255

pen that way'. We find a decisive difference between folk religion and Christianity with respect to the figure of Jesus Christ. Only Christ's teachings and His example are of any importance to the former, as there is no place for a saviour in a naive fatalistic religion.

Virtue: Also here the battle between good and evil has been somewhat muted. The evil is no longer absolutely evil: it is unfortunate, unlucky, undesirable. Nor is the good absolutely good: it is fortunate, lucky, desirable. It is in this relative meaning that one believes in a good, virtuous life.

Immortality: The belief in the immortality of the soul has continued from pre-Christian times, and is a belief shared by both the 'folk religions' and the church-attending person as well.

It therefore would appear, from the last point, that it is the combination of belief in immortality, relative morality, and a God of Fate which gives this popular folk religion its special catechism. And it is not unreasonable to assume that it is such a set of beliefs that underlies the extremely high percentage of persons we have found answering 'Yes' to a belief in God and in life after death. Nor is it unreasonable to suppose that it is first and foremost such persons who would consider the church's ritual actions more as social than actually religious functions. Such believers would possess a very low degree of group-consciousness; *the content of their religious beliefs would to a considerable degree be the result of the uncomplicated religious instruction presented in the first years of elementary school,* and their cultic actions would mostly consist of very simple, perhaps even superstitious actions and rules of conduct. On all these points, adherents of such a folk religion would differ from the personal Christians in Norway. These Christians – who clearly constitute only a minority – probably have a more complicated set of beliefs more in line with the church's own; they probably possess a higher degree of group consciousness; the content of their religious beliefs is hardly a reflection of basic religious instruction learned long ago; and they most probably experience the church's fundamental rites of passage, as well as regular divine service, as being actions of definite religious importance.

5. CONCLUDING REMARKS

By considering the information available on the clergy as contributors and the information available on the Norwegian populace as receivers, we have seen an interesting picture develop of the relationship between the two parties. On the one hand are the most important representatives of organized religion, which has a variety of contributions to make, and not a few internal disputes and divisions. On the

256

other hand are the receivers, a population with a varying level of activity and group consciousness, but showing a definite lack of contact with the representatives on the contributor side. There exists a certain religious bent or interest, but it seems to find expression in a simple, folk religiosity.

What about the future? Will this religious bent, this general interest in religion, continue – whether taking its form in folk religion or otherwise – or will Norwegian society become more and more secularized, ending in general atheism? Naturally, all we can do is to speculate.

Let us then ask: Is it possible, or probable, that non-religious systems of ideas will eventually take over the most important functions of religion – and of the not-so-clear folk religion? Let us consider the functions most often connected with religion and speculate as to what may happen with them.

The function of religion as an *integrating factor* in society or in parts of society – sociologists have maintained this – can probably be taken over by another ideology in Norway. National and political ideologies here are the obvious alternatives. Integration is said to be one of the special functions of ideology and is very well developed. Furthermore, the increased pluralization of society will gradually make the integrating function of religion more difficult, if not impossible.

The official limiting and control of deviants was, previously, to a great extent a task for religion. Today, this function has largely been taken over by non-religious ideologies, and the clergyman's relationship with the 'sinner' has in many cases given way to the physician's relationship with the 'sick' and the lawyer's relationship with the 'criminal'. The assumption of control by medicine and the law may become even more complete, although it can scarcely be thought that they will be able to take over all the controlling functions of state religion. But the forms of deviation which can be called neither illnesses nor crimes can probably be defined and controlled by people's ordinary morality as well as by religious ideas.

It is also necessary to examine the *psychological* functions of religion, which to a certain extent can be, and indeed already have been, taken over by non-religious systems. Most important in this connection is the fact that man's uncertain and often frustrating relationships to the physical and social conditions of life are now frequently relieved by science and technology, rather than religion. It is quite possible that this development will continue.

Of course, this does not mean that all forms of insecurity and frustration are lessened in modern society. It is often maintained that some problems are more serious, that modern society creates neuroses. Tor

257

Aukrust (1958) is one contemporary writer to deal with this at length, emphasizing that modern man's very feeling of helplessness when faced with our technological culture has helped bring about a 'religious renaissance'. Indeed, because of the existence of *individual* psychological difficulties in our society it seems reasonable to assume it impossible to find completely sufficient functional alternatives to religion. It is difficult to find worthwhile alternate ideologies for two of religion's psychological functions: 1) an explanation of what happens in our physical and social environment, and 2) a solution to the threat of death.

The sciences are probably religion's strongest competitors as to the explanatory function. Natural science can now solve many problems and explain many phenomena of our physical environment which were previously incomprehensible. It is not unimaginable that in the future the social sciences will be able to explain the problems of our social environment. But even the effect of scientific explanations on people is limited. In the first place, the sciences are all too willing to admit that there are problems which at the moment are insoluble. In the second place, and perhaps more important, scientific explanations are often so complicated that they are far from satisfactory to the majority of laymen. We shall therefore assume that religion in one form or another cannot yet be fully replaced as an explanation of significant events in nature and in society.

Religion's emotional solution to the problem of death may possibly be taken over by a non-religious way of thought, and to a certain extent such a shift is taking place. At present, certain attitudes based on medical research and practice are giving religion the most competition in this area. Medical research is continually lengthening life expectancy, while through the various mass media, through the school system, and through the patient-physician relationship, more and more health information is being made available to enable people to live a longer and healthier life. These prescriptions for a better life are frequently presented in an attractive form, and people's interest in them is remarkable. People are interested and engaged in acquiring more rules and in following the rules they already have. The point here is not first and foremost the effect of such medical advice on life expectancy, but rather their probable psychological significance. One of the main reasons for people's interest in them is probably an increased feeling of security in the face of the unpredictability of death. In this case, these medical rules probably have the same psychological effect as non-scientific ways of life do; they give the individual a feeling of living in a well-ordered system. In addition, they also probably give people a reassuring feeling of behaving rationally, which is a central value in our society.

But even though rules based on medical research and practice may be forming a non-religious way of thinking in our society which can take over most of religion's psychological functions, we do not believe that such a system can completely solve the problem. In the first place, these medical precepts also give rise to an element of insecurity in people. Because of medicine's scientific nature – which is just what people want – old rules are confusingly often replaced by new ones, and new and dangerous causes of death are discovered and publicized. Even though the element of insecurity scarcely outweighs the assuring and calming function of the scientific health precepts, insecurity is present as a limiting factor, in solving the problem of the threat which death poses. Secondly, the majority of people realize that death cannot be put off indefinitely, and the fear of death and the insecurity arising from it cannot be completely controlled. If the time of death were predictable, the fear of death would in another way become more acute. These simple, straightforward facts make it necessary to have an interpretation of death in addition to the one medicine gives. Religion – in any case, the Christian religion – has a great psychological advantage over medicine in that it defines death not as a threatening end to life but rather as the beginning of a new and better existence.

In summation: we do not believe that the Norwegian population will become totally unreligious. Forms of belief and activity may well change – but will scarcely cease to exist.

NOTES

[1] In addition, the material shows the following differences between different categories; the elderly listen more often than the young; low-income people listen more often than high-income people; rural people listen more often urban people; workers listen more often than white-collar workers. The fact that people in the lower social classes listen to the radio more often than others is connected with the fact that they are in general more active listeners - nearly without regard to what program is being braodcast. See Aubert's chapter on social stratification in Norway, and Mathiesen (1965), p. 89.

VIII. The Health System

By Yngvar Løchen

1. INTRODUCTION

One-third of all those who during a five-year period consulted a doctor in a small fishing community in Finnmark suffered from some kind of chronic illness (Bremer 1951). In the course of a four-year period, over 80 per cent of the population of a rural community in eastern Norway had had occasion to consult a general practitioner (Bentsen 1966). It has been estimated that on any given workday, about 3 per cent of the adult working population are ill enough not to be at work. And of elderly persons, 70 years and upwards, 80 per cent complain of poor health (Strøm 1956).

Now, no one knows how high the figures are for actual illness. Many persons become ill without this being statistically registered in any way. Furthermore, illness and health are not unambiguous concepts; their use varies from time to time, and from place to place. As to mortality, however, the facts are more certain. We know that yearly some 35,000 persons die in Norway. While not all die from illnesses, this is definitely the most important single cause of death. Thus our first subject in this chapter will be mortality conditions.

Illness occurs often, and can strike anyone; health, however, means well-being, and is also a pre-condition for a person's achieving certain other aims. Popular views on illness and health have not always been the same, and they vary from culture to culture. As our second topic in this chapter we shall deal with Norwegian attitudes on this subject.

Illness is a threat to society and its functioning;[1] health is a necessity. Thus, most societies organize some kind of health system: some societies emphasize magic, while in more advanced ones medicine plays the more important role.

Our third subject will be the organized health services, which form an important part of the welfare state. This ideological principle is connected with a certain organizational form, and the principle, which often meets severe criticism from capitalist and socialist countries alike, is practised by many countries other than Norway.

The health system involves a wide spectrum of persons with ill-nesses and other difficulties. Norwegian hospitals and other medical institutions alone treat more than 450,000 hospitalization cases an-nually. But recruitment to the status of client/patient is affected by factors other than illness alone, some of which we shall touch on later.

Our fourth topic will be a presentation of various data on those persons who as clients/patients receive services from the health system.

And, finally, we conclude with a discussion of a few sociologically relevant tension points within the Norwegian health service.

2. MORTALITY IN NORWAY

2.1. Mortality in Norway compared with that in various other countries

We do not know exactly how mortality is affected by social structure. It is a fact that social structure can control – indeed put a stop to – certain causes of death, while enhancing others. That is why it is of great sociological interest to compare mortality in different countries.[2]

Differences in mortality statistics can often be more apparent than real. Frequently it is difficult to diagnose cause of death, and many errors creep in. And, in comparing various countries, we must recall that differences in registration can severely skew the general picture. Also, some illnesses are highly typically age-specific, so that the age composition of a population will also influence figures. However, it

Table I. *Deaths per 100,000 of population, from various causes, in selected countries, 1960*

Country	Infectious dis-eases (including tuberculosis)	Tubercu-losis	Cardio-vascular diseases	Malig-nant tumours	Acci-dents	Sui-cide
Norway	11.9	6.3	439.6	163.6	43.8	6.4
Sweden	11.2	8.0	522.9	185.7	46.2	17.4
Denmark	8.7	4.2	463.9	209.5	45.0	20.3
West Germany*	21.7	16.4	450.8	208.4	56.3	18.7
Great Britain**	12.5	7.5	605.5	215.6	38.7	11.2
Italy*	30.4	18.2	427.7	150.3	38.8	6.4
USA	11.6	5.9	513.2	148.7	51.8	10.8
Japan	45.6	34.2	256.1	100.4	41.7	21.3
Ceylon	65.2	16.4	73.4	22.2	30.0	9.9

Sources: WHO 1963; NOS XII 107, p. 36.

* 1959 figures.
** Excluding Northern Ireland.

would be going too far to ignore the real differences over and above these considerations.

From Table I we see that infectious diseases as a cause of death are about equally infrequent in Norway, Sweden, Great Britain, and the USA, while West Germany still rates surprisingly high. In general, such diseases have been brought under control in countries with a high general standard of living. Italy, Japan, and Ceylon show that infectious diseases even today can pose a serious threat to human life.

Cardio-vascular ailments (including those of the central nervous system) are less frequent in Norway than in Denmark, Sweden, Great Britain, or the USA. Norway has about the same level here as West Germany and Italy, but one much higher than that in Japan or Ceylon.

Among cardio-vascular illnesses, heart attacks and coronaries dominate the picture. These are often presented as the price we must pay for civilization's benefits. Changed dietary habits, inactive life, tobacco-smoking habits have all been included as causes. Stress is often mentioned as well.

Now, if such diseases actually are an expression of life forms in a modern society, Norway should soon stabilize herself at the same high level as other Western countries. Indeed, there are indications that an increase, especially with respect to heart attacks, is more pronounced in Norway than elsewhere.

Malignant tumours are responsible for fewer deaths in Norway than in Sweden, Denmark, West Germany, or Great Britain. The USA, however, ranks lower than Norway in this respect. Cancer takes more lives among elderly persons than younger ones, and so we must take age composition into consideration. Some of the variations among countries may also be due to such factors as tobacco consumption and air pollution.

The relative number of deaths due to accidental causes does not vary greatly from country to country, and there are no important differences among the Scandinavian countries in this respect.

Suicide, however, would seem to vary considerably among the Scandinavian countries. But some of these differences may be ascribed to different rules concerning registration of such deaths, and especially with respect to Norway there seems reason to believe statistics to be less than fully developed. Registration is better in Denmark and Sweden: in Norway there are many suicidal deaths, due to poisoning, for instance, that are registered as accidents. However, we cannot ignore the possibility of real differences in suicide rates.

The American psychiatrist Herbert Hendin has attempted to explain this phenomenon (Hendin 1965). Starting with the theory that the varying social structure in the Scandinavian countries each creates its personality type, he concludes that suicide fits in better with the

Swedish and Danish national personality type than with the Norwegian. Hendin presents the hypothesis – highly flattering to Norwegians – that their low suicide rate is due to their independent character, their better self-control with respect to poor personal performance and loss of loved ones. Suicide in Norway, when it does occur, is a moral act. 'It stems,' says Hendin, 'from aggressive antisocial behaviour and strong guilt feelings aroused from such behaviour, with the entire constellation cast in a puritanical setting' (p. 147).

The *most important* cause of death in Norway is cardio-vascular diseases: in 1964, 51 per cent of all deaths – nearly 18,000 – were due to such disorders (NOS XII 196, p. 21). As mentioned, heart attacks and coronary illnesses formed the main subgroup. The second most important case is malignant tumours, accounting for approximately 18 per cent (6,225 of all deaths in the same year). Even though cancer is thus not the main cause of death in Norway, it is still the disease more feared than any other. (In a Gallup poll – 22 April 1950 – 54 per cent responded that they feared cancer most; 17 per cent indicated tuberculosis, 3 per cent polio, and 2 per cent insanity.) This fear of cancer can be so strong that some persons answered that should cancer be detected in them, they would prefer not to know the truth about their own condition. These are, however, few: four of five would rather know the truth, according to a Gallup poll of 4 June 1949.

This relative order of causes of death also holds true for Sweden, Denmark, England, Italy, and the USA, as well as some other countries not included here. Thus it seems reasonable to conclude that, in general, the same types of diseases dominate and threaten human lives within our modern type of society.

2.2. *Variations in mortality in Norway*

Infectious diseases, earlier a main cause of death, have gradually been conquered in Norway. Especially in the course of the past decades, much control has been won here. A good example is tuberculosis. In 1900 6,400 persons in a population of two million died from this disease. Today annual deaths from tuberculosis are around the 200 mark, in a population of about 3.7 million.

Other diseases have taken the place formerly occupied by the infectious ones. The increase in cardio-vascular complaints is especially noteworthy. During World War II the situation improved, a fact often mentioned in discussions on the importance of dietary habits. All cardio-vascular diseases taken together have increased for the male population, from 394 deaths per 100,000 of the population in 1936–1940, to 545 per 100,000 in 1964. The corresponding figures for women show an increase from 260 to 405 (NOS XII, p. 39). Men 40 and older

Table II. *Most important causes of death in Norway at selected times*

Cause of death	1878*	1936-1940	1941-1945	1951-1955	1960
			Death per 100,000 inhabitants yearly		
Cardio-vascular diseases	23	170	146	235	289
Malignant tumours	38	133	131	159	164
Old-age weakness syndrome	45	101	73	68	63
Diseases of the central nervous system	20	98	90	126	150
Violent death	3	62	115	53	51
Pneumonia, bronchitis	117	107	97	47	55
Tuberculosis	127	91	72	18	6
Other infectious diseases	149	31	48	10	6

Source: Axel Strøm 1963, p. 96.

* In 1878 cause of death was known for only one-half of all deaths. Classification rules have also changed several times.

seem particularly susceptible, and heart attacks are occurring earlier and earlier. With increasing age the different risks for men and women gradually even out, until they are about equal for the 70–80 year group.

Table II shows an increase in malignant tumours, a category which includes all forms of cancers. This picture is a composite one: stomach cancer has become less frequent, while lung cancer has increased to more than make up for this. There seems to be a certain decrease in cancer among women, but a marked increase among men. The especially pronounced increase in male lung cancer may be due to tobacco smoking, which spread rapidly after World War I.

As a total category, violent deaths have not increased. But while drownings, which until recently formed the main group under this heading, have decreased dramatically, traffic fatalities have increased greatly. In 1939, only 116 persons were killed in traffic accidents: in 1965 the figure was 423. An additional 3,420 persons were seriously injured and 4,765 sustained minor injuries (NOS A 79, Table I; NOS XII 218, p. 169). Traffic accidents account for a considerable portion of invalids and disabled persons in today's society.

Men are more accident prone. This has a variety of explanations, not least the occupational risks. Some authors have also related this difference to men's and boys' need of demonstrating their masculinity by exposing themselves to danger (Brun-Gulbrandsen and Ås 1960, Ås 1962).

In 1964, 11 per cent of all deaths occurred when the victims were 1–50 years of age; 28 per cent 50–70 years; and 61 per cent above the

age of 60. In the age groups 1–44 years, accidents, suicide, and h[
icide comprise the most important causes of death; later cardio-[
cular diseases dominate the picture.

Mortality varies somewhat with geographical location, the variations
seeming to affect men most strongly. Men have a considerably higher
mortality when they live in urban or densely populated areas, with
respect especially to cardio-vascular diseases, but also to malignant
tumours. Violent deaths are more frequent in rural areas (NOS XII
180, p. 53).

Since the counties of Norway vary in their degrees of urbanization,
we should also expect to find variations in mortality among counties.
Indeed, Oslo and Bergen counties do have high mortality rates; the
predominantly rural county of Sogn og Fjordane has the lowest. But
highest of all is the extreme northern county of Finnmark, with respect to fatal respiratory infections. Tuberculosis was long a major
problem in northern Norway (NOS A 132 Table 1).

There are few data on mortality in relation to other social variables.
Mortality statistics for Norway are not grouped by occupation, and the
stratification aspect must remain mostly unstudied for the present. One
study, however, has approached the problem by the causes of death
among various status groups, defined according to where in Oslo individuals lived. One conclusion was:

> In the 50-year period 1890—1939 there was a considerable over-mortality
> due to tuberculosis, 'other infectious diseases', and respiratory ailments in
> Oslo's 'East Side' area, as compared with its 'West Side'. This over-mor-
> tality mainly affected children and young persons, and provides a good
> example of the effect socio-economic status has on illness and death
> (Gjestland and Mork 1962).

A few investigations have also been made of mortality within
specific occupational groups. Mortality is higher for sailors and seamen than in other occupations, for example: here it seems that accidents play an important role (Arner and Tenfjord 1964).

3. HEALTH AS A VALUE

A common Norwegian saying has it that 'As long as your health is
good, nothing else matters' – meaning that in the long run no other
value is as important as good health. This health ideal manifests itself
variously in Norwegian society. Of those asked in a 10 November
1951 Gallup study, one in four wished to lose weight. (Another Gallup
survey, March 1952, indicated that the average Norwegian ate 3.6
meals a day, incidentally.) Since it was first and foremost women
who wished to lose weight, we may be dealing with beauty ideals as

265

well. Further, it is especially city-dwellers and white-collar workers who wish to lose weight: either because they are actually fatter, or because this ideal is most prevalent among the middle class, or both.

Many people take strengthening tonics during the winter: 39 per cent regularly took cod-liver oil, vitamin preparations, yeast, and so on. This was more typical of women than of men, of city-dwellers than of rural persons. Few doubted the positive effects of this practice (Gallup, 17 January 1953). In addition, much is spent annually on sun-tan oils and creams, etc., and advertisements for 'sun-vacations' in southern Europe frequently employ health arguments.[3]

This need for realizing the health ideal (which may not be any stronger in Norway than elsewhere) has some interesting consequences. Probably one of these is an increase in medical consultations. In addition, quite a large proportion of the population enters into a semi-medical consumer role, in that they, without being in contact with a physician or other medical personnel, consume medicines. This role pattern is reminiscent more of the relationship between producer and consumer than that between physician and patient.

In Chapter X of this book we find the conclusion that Norwegians spend much of their leisure time in contact with the out-of-doors: one source indicates hiking as the third most popular leisure activity. Outdoor activities are considered a defence against the collectivism threatening us all, and this may be true. But the outdoor life is also connected with a health ideal and norms of how to maintain one's health.

We also connect sports with health, from which the concept 'health sports' has originated. All in all, it is emphasized that physical activity is good for one's health.

While we have no exact figures on those who participate in sports to maintain health, Chapter X gives general information on sports. At any rate, on an average autumn Sunday, two-thirds of the Norwegian population take some kind of physical exercise, according to a Gallup poll, 6 October 1956. Indeed, 56 per cent hiked one kilometre or more. People also feel that today's youth are in better physical condition than were their parents at the same age. The most important reasons are improved general habits and living conditions and sports (Gallup, 30 June 1956). We do not know whether Norway really is more athletic and interested in exercise than other countries, or whether this attitude is more typical of any particular social group. But that there do exist norms to the effect that one should do something to keep in shape is indisputable. Health is a value to be prized, not only in order to avoid illness and its unpleasantness, but also because health is considered a value in its own right.

Even though this health ideal affects habits and behaviour, there are also indicators of another, nearly opposite ideal as well. It can be desirable to have certain health problems, especially if these can be attributed to honourable over-exertion and over-work. The Gallup data (26 March 1949) do not exclude the possibility that people often try to give an impression of being more tired and worn out than they actually are: one-third of those asked said they had the impression that others seemed tired and worn-out, while only one-fifth said they themselves felt that way. Health can be one component in the total battery of impressions we present to others.

Exactly where health stands on the value scale is difficult to judge. Despite strong warnings, many expose themselves to health risks when other 'more important' values enter the picture. For example, one out of every five young persons goes bare-headed despite their own belief that this is indeed bad for one's health (Gallup, 29 March 1958). It may be more important to seem tough than to be healthy. According to general opinion, the most dangerous things for one's health are alcohol, tobacco, little sleep, too many late parties, and excessive eating (Gallup, 9 October 1954): 22 per cent considered fatty foods, special fats and oils and fatty acids, as being the most important causes of heart ailments; 10 per cent thought the cause to be overweight, while 14 per cent indicated stress, over-exertion, and difficult working conditions. Also, 47 per cent believed that smoking, nicotine, and tobacco were most responsible for lung cancer, while 22 per cent blamed cigarettes and cigarette paper (Gallup, 31 August 1966).

Overwhelming statistical material is now available to show the connection between smoking – especially cigarette smoking – and lung cancer (Lundar 1965, for example). All the same, we continue to smoke a lot. A Gallup poll, 7 February 1949, found that 36 per cent of the surveyed adult population were regular smokers; in 1954 (Gallup, 6 February 1954), 35 per cent replied that they smoked cigarettes. In 1957 (Gallup, 26 October 1957) the figure for cigarette smokers was 42 per cent; while in 1964 (Gallup, 6 June 1964) 46 per cent said that they smoked.

One out of every three 19-year-olds completing secondary education is a habitual smoker (Nilsen 1964); the corresponding figure for young men meeting for preliminary examination in Østfold county in the same year was 38 per cent (Larsen 1965). Of a random sample of urban youth aged 18–19, 41 per cent say they smoke regularly (Christie and Hauge 1962, Kreyberg 1954).

We are exposed to a whole series of irritants and annoyances that appear to be part and parcel of modern life. For example, one out of every five Norwegians feels bothered by excessive noise, and of these, one-third say that this has impaired their health and general well-being (Gallup, 6 December 1958). Let us note that in Norway there exist organizations whose aim is to get the noise level lowered, and that actions have been carried against, for example, expansion of the centrally located airport at Fornebu. The same category of modern problems would also include traffic accidents (affecting mainly children).

Now, if only a person knew definitely that he would get rheumatic head pains from not wearing some kind of head covering in cold weather, that lung cancer would follow a period of intense smoking, that a nervous breakdown would come from a hard career battle – then perhaps more people would change their behaviour and re-adjust their values. But in fact the dangers are so far removed in time that one takes the chance. The consequences always hit others, never oneself.

Health measures can collide with other values. For example, it may be objected that certain measures should be left to nature alone. One highly controversial matter is fluoridation of drinking water, hotly debated some years ago in Norway. The director of health believes that there are few preventive measures today so well based in scientific research, and that by this means there would be good chances of controlling Norway's greatest health problem, dental caries. Viewed against this background, the stormy opposition raised seems all the more surprising, and the health director has understandably termed it 'completely irrational, . . . and emotional' (Evang 1961, p. 101). As a result, the matter has been more or less abandoned for the time being. A survey, however, indicated that many persons had hardly paid much attention to the issues: 77 per cent had not formed any personal opinion; of the 23 per cent that had done so, 42 per cent were against, 49 per cent for fluoridation. Opposition was shown to be strongest in lower income brackets and in rural areas (Gallup, 7 July 1962).

Also in the relationship between the health authorities and certain religious groups, tensions can occur. Members of some sects are against medical treatment in all or some of its forms, partly because such treatment goes against their religious beliefs and codes, and partly because they have no trust in medical expertise. For example, one couple refused to permit a completely necessary blood transfusion for their dying child. Great was the relief probably felt by all when it was discovered that the health authorities could by law transcend the guardianship of the parents and thereby assure that the child received proper treatment. One question that has been discussed several times concerns the effects of pentecostal-evangelical revival meetings. Many expert psychiatrists have maintained that certain sects give their revival meetings a form such as to endanger the members' health. But 35 per cent of the population asked was not willing

to give health authorities extended powers of control and interfer
in such meetings. The figures were far higher among those who
answered that they voted Christian People's Party (Gallup, 23 Octo..
1954). Of those who opposed giving health authorities extended
powers, 17 per cent did not think that revival meetings could contribute
to nervous breakdowns, while 41 per cent gave as the reason for their
reservations that the matter of revival meetings was a private concern
where the individual should be free to do as he wished.

Health does not always appear, then, as the supreme value. This
raises the question of the restrictions on medicine, to which we shall
return later.

4. THE HEALTH SERVICE

A sociologist might perhaps say that the health service as an institution attempts to realize health values. It implements the transition from
being sick to being well, while preventing the reverse. A doctor might
say the health service has preventive and curative functions and activities, rehabilitation and care of those not able to care for themselves.
These different functions have not always been considered equally important. With the advances made by bacteriology in the past century,
it became clear that preventive efforts could control or entirely stop
outbreaks of illness, and much work was done. Gradually, major advances in treatment were made, and today it is this aspect of medicine
most physicians concentrate on.

Recently, however, the pendulum has swung in the other direction,
such that preventive medicine on the one hand, and rehabilitation of
the previously ill or functionally disabled on the other, are winning
territory. We can also note that long-term care of chronically ill or
weak persons is increasing in importance.

In the course of several years' study of a psychiatric hospital, I was
able to witness how this re-evaluation of the goals of medicine took
place within an institution. Internal conditions reflected general
changes in medical thinking. Rehabilitation became more important in
the ideology, and much was done to improve conditions within the hospital for the patients who would be remaining there. This does not
mean that less emphasis was put on treatment, however (see Løchen
1965).

In a small country like Norway, where the members of the population are so mutually dependent, the individual's sickness and need will
be strongly felt by the collectivity. Furthermore, in Norway the basic
idealistic view of things is that the individual's sickness and need is
not only an individual, but also a social problem. The individual is
able to count on receiving aid from others, should he be hit by sickness.

269

Organizationally, it has been fairly easy to support and continue this basic view in Norway. It has always been expected that the state and public sector should help solve the country's problems. Because Norway has always been sparsely populated and rather poor, it has been necessary to gather the country's limited resources under state-controlled measures and activities. This general aspect of the political-administrative structure has of course created some problems (which are discussed in more detail in Chapter VI), but has also made it easier to create the health service which today has become a vital part of the public apparatus.

The health service is based on a high degree of state and public engagement. Even if there has also existed a fairly clear division between preventive and curative aspects within this service, we still do not have separate health services, each limited to serving different groups in society. In principle at any rate, the health service is for all groups, independent of the social or cultural differences which otherwise characterize society. With respect to the health system, Norway is in principle liberated from the norms that otherwise define the individual's place in the social structure.

Norway is a welfare state. But the concept of the welfare state is not applied in the same way in all countries where it exists. Nor was Norway the first to practise it. In Norway the state does not have total responsibility for planning and solving health and welfare problems, because other authorities and private organizations also enter the picture. The system which has developed in Norway up till now is more a compromise between varying traditions and social forces active in the country.

A great majority of the population (85 per cent) would characterize Norway as a welfare state (Gallup, 25 January 1967). They emphasize the fact that Norway and her inhabitants are well-off compared with other countries, that there is a high standard of living and economic prosperity, that social security and social goods are well developed. The 15 per cent who did not consider Norway as a welfare state mentioned bad wage conditions, too little aid for the poor, too much injustice, and still too many unsolved problems. These questions are further discussed in Chapter III, Stratification.

4.1. *Financing*

The main financing source for the health service is social security. This first appeared in 1911, while the present law was passed in 1956. Today the entire population is covered – in 1920 only about one-fifth was. No one can avoid membership in the social security system.

Rikstrygdeverket (National Insurance System) is responsible for the central administration of the social security system; the local social security offices have local responsibility. For sailors on overseas duty and for officials on duty abroad there exists a special division.

The social security system in Norway covers, in part or totally, a great many of the health service's activities and services. Of these, the assistance given for medical aid (physicians) and hospital room fees is perhaps especially important. The financial support comes from the participants: social security members pay premiums based on income level, and their employers pay an additional sum. In addition come contributions from the municipality and the state. The 1966 social security budget amounted to nearly N. kr. 1500 million; state and municipal contributions amounted to 45 per cent.

However, not everything is covered by the social security system. If a person consults a physician, he must pay some of the fee himself. Hospitals have great expenses. The (National) Ministry of Prices and Wages decides what proportion the hospitals are to receive from social security funds, taking into consideration the state of the national economy. If this rate is set so low that the actual expenses are not covered, the remaining amount must be supplied by the hospital management and owners.

It is planned to include the social security system in the new people's security system that became operative in late 1966. The system of aid to occupationally disabled and the unemployed is also to be incorporated within the new system. This latter will distribute aid to the aged, disabled, and those without a bread-winner, thus incorporating the present systems of old-age pensions, rehabilitation aid, and aid to the disabled, as well as aid to widows, mothers, and those without a bread-winner in the family. The National Insurance System has been allotted responsibility for central administration, while local social security offices and county agencies will have local responsibility.

This new people's social security (folketrygden) has been an important political issue. Some have felt it arrived too early, that not enough time has been allotted for planning. But the political situation made it difficult to postpone a decision, and the new measure was voted through.

The state must also allot funds directly to the health service. In 1962, such appropriations amounted to about N.kr. 90 million – in 1965, more than N. kr. 120 million. These sums went to public health, the National Hospital (Rikshospitalet), which is owned by the state, as well as to other purposes. For care of the mentally ill, and general psychiatric care, about N. kr. 130 million were allotted in 1965 (NOS XII 170, pp. 101 ff.) .

Hospitals and institutions for tuberculosis patients, the mentally ill, epileptics, and the feeble-minded also receive money by means of

271

special laws operating directly through the national budget. The National Clinic for Drug Addicts in Hov i Land also receives funds directly from the national budget.

4.2. Administration

Norway has never had a separate ministry of health. The Health Directorate is both a division within the Ministry of Social Affairs and a separate agency. The present Directorate was organized in 1945.

It has a broad scope of working activities and tasks. Here all the cases are dealt with where the state has economic control and responsibility and formulates problems and takes the initiative. Here we find budget planning as well. Furthermore, the Directorate has, in agreement with the Norwegian Medical Association (legeforeningen), assumed responsibility in the selection of physicians for filling available positions – a good proof of the general trust and approval accorded to public authorities. The Directorate interprets laws and sees to it that practice is in accordance with legislated norms, as well as assisting in formulating new proposals. The district physician (distriktslegen) plays an important role in local health administration. He works within a circumscribed geographical area, where his responsibilities and tasks are many. Having both public functions and a private practice, he is paid by the state for the former and by social security together with his patients for the latter.

The 1860 'Law Concerning Health Commissions etc.' sets forth that there shall be a health commission in every municipality. These commissions (the present-day helseråd) see to it that the health legislation is followed in practice. Their members are chosen by, and from the ranks of the municipal governing councils. The commission chairman is a physician, usually the district physician; he represents the central health authorities while at the same time keeping watch over local conditions.

The county medical officer (fylkeslegen) supervises county health services, and must prepare reports on health conditions in his county. He forms the link between the central and local administration. He is adviser to the county council chairman on health matters; he prepares the local health budgets and later participates in the county council's discussions on these. He is of course vital in planning new county hospitals. The county medical officer is paid half by the national government and half by the county.

In recent years, one of his most important jobs has been to act as chairman in the agencies making decisions concerning aid to be given in accordance with legislation on rehabilitation and aid to the disabled, both now incorporated in the new people's social security discussed above (see Løchen and Martinsen 1962, Løchen 1966). This work brings him in closer contact with treatment and rehabilitation aspects of medicine. Among other things, an expansion has taken place in the county medical officers' offices.

4.3. Physical facilities, personnel

In 1964, Norway had about 370 hospitals. This figure includes general hospitals, clinics, smaller clinics, various specialized hospitals and psychiatric hospitals, tuberculosis sanatoriums, maternity clinics, maternity homes, and long-term treatment centres (NOS XII 196, Tables 3 and 4). If we further include the treatment homes for psychiatric and mentally retarded patients, the figure approaches 570 (NOS XII 189, Table 1). The 30-odd treatment centres for alcoholics would bring us to 600. The total number of beds is more than 42,000 (NOS XII 170, Table 55).

By far the majority of hospitals are managed and owned by the counties and municipalities. Somewhere around 20 per cent of all available patient beds are located in hospitals belonging to private health organizations (e.g. the Red Cross) or religious groups.

Private activity is strongest in the specialized sectors: one-third of the beds in specialized hospitals and one-half of those in maternity clinics and maternity homes are in private hands. Private organizations account for a large share of the smaller hospitals and clinics, especially in North Norway. Midwives in private practice actually run the majority of maternity homes. But more than half of all the beds in private hands are located in general hospitals, clinics, and smaller clinics. Without this private enterprise, the situation might well be worse today.

In Norway – in contrast to the usual practice in English-speaking countries – the admitting physician's medical responsibility for his individual patient stops when the latter enters a non-private hospital. From then on, the hospital takes over. There are, however, private clinics where the personal physician does attend his patient in the hospital. All hospitals owned by the public sector employ physicians and other personnel on a full-time basis with regular salary. State-owned hospitals pay physicians' salaries determined by agreement between the Norwegian Medical Association and the Ministry of Prices and Salaries; other hospitals regulate salaries on the basis of agreements between the hospital owners and the Medical Association. Physicians occupying higher positions may also have a certain amount of private practice as well.

As to *personnel*, physicians form one of the oldest professions in Norway. But it took a long time before this group became sufficiently

273

standardized and unified so that its members could rightly be considered as forming a 'profession'. One reason for this is that education and training were so varied.

Many of those practising in Norway were born abroad, and there existed both academic and ethnic differences within the group. Its close connections with such occupations as that of barber, plus the notable proportion of foreign-born persons of unknown origin – i.e. all the low-status groups – all played their role in giving the medical profession a highly marginal status, even as late as the past century.

In the period 1817–1849, the Royal Norwegian University *(Det Kongelige Frederiks Universitet)* granted 325 medical degrees. The number of theology degrees granted was more than twice this; of law degrees, triple. Clearly, medicine was not the profession most young academic persons chose.

Today, however, we see a different situation: a Gallup poll (30 March 1963) revealed that if the average person were to give advice to a young talented person as to what profession to choose, one out of every five would advise medicine.

The number of physicians (medical graduates) has risen gradually. In 1855 there were 300; by 1885 the figure had doubled and by the turn of the century there was nearly a four-fold increase. At the end of 1964, the number of physicians was a little under 4,800, including Norwegian-educated physicians living abroad. If we exclude these latter, we reach a figure of 811 inhabitants per physician – a favourable ratio in comparison with other countries (NOS XII 196, p. 10).

Physicians work within various fields in the health service, and many, sometimes quite drastic changes have occurred as to how physicians are distributed. In 1815, more than 50 per cent of all physicians were employed by the state, while in 1950 the figure was 13.9 per cent (Aubert et al. 1960).

From 1810 and until quite recently there has been a tendency for doctors to establish themselves in private practice. One out of every ten male medical graduates in the period 1810–1849 ended up in private practice; in the period 1910–1939, more than one out of every three.

The number of hospital physicians has also increased, although not as greatly as has that of private practitioners. Earlier it was the increase in private practitioners that was most pronounced; the increase in hospital physicians is more typical of recent years (Lindbekk 1967, p. 80).

The increase in these two groups has taken place at the expense of military physicians and publicly employed physicians. Or to state it differently: a distancing has occurred from the state apparatus, or an increasing privatization of the medical profession. In this respect

274

there is a similarity to other professions, whose members have likewise tended to distance themselves more and more from state engagement and instead establish themselves in more independent, private activity. However, this relationship is complicated with respect to the medical profession.

The tendency to choose private practice is now decreasing. While 46 per cent of all medical graduates in 1910–1939 ended in private practice, only 36 per cent of those graduating between 1940–1949 were in private practice 15 years after receiving their degrees. And for those graduating 1950–1954, the corresponding figure 10 years after graduation was only 17 per cent (Lindbekk 1967, pp. 266–268). Now, these figures may approach each other over time because a physician's position 10 to 15 years after graduation need not be the position he remains in for the rest of his life. Other data, however, do indicate that the situation of private practice would appear to be threatened.

The medical profession today is characterized first and foremost by increased institutionalization and specialization. Recruitment to hospital positions is greater than to other positions, and hospital physicians in 1966 comprised 44 per cent of all the country's physicians. At the same time there exists a tendency towards specialization that would seem to cut across the division between private practice and hospital work. In 1966, 41 per cent of all physicians were accredited specialists. During 1954–1964 the Norwegian Medical Association accredited nearly 100 new specialists annually. The greatest increase was within psychiatry. Today the four largest specialities are internal medicine, surgery, tuberculosis and lung ailments, and psychiatry (Den Norske Lægeforening, Årbøker 1954–1964).

Table III. *Physicians in 1956 and 1966. Field, and proportion of specialists (percentage)*

Field	Total physicians 1956	Total physicians 1966	Specialists 1956	Specialists 1966
Hospital	38.1	44.1	37.7	51.3
Higher public health administration and health service administration	2.4	4.8	54.2	66.9
Public health physicians	13.2	12.4	19.5	13.7
State-employed physicians	13.2	12.4	19.5	13.7
Armed services physicians	1.5	2.8	3.8	8.9
Private practitioners	41.7	32.1	33.9	38.7
Doctors in industry, etc.	0.7	1.1	36.9	43.8
Teaching, research	2.4	3.7	29.8	29.3
Total	100.0	100.0	33.1	41.1
Number of physicians	3,546	4,470	1,175	1,839

Source: Innstilling om legetjenesten og tannlegetjenesten 1967, p. 211.

In Table III we see that the percentage of private practitioners diminished drastically from 1956 to 1966, with a decrease in absolute numbers. This is due to the decrease in general practitioners, where the number sank from 976 to 877. Within the medical profession there is agreement that this figure is too low in relation to the need, and health authorities are seriously worried (Bjørnson 1965). The category 'public health doctors' has increased somewhat in number, and by far the majority of these physicians also have private practices in addition to their official duties.

A skewed geographical distribution of the country's physicians has remained fairly constant during the present century. The increase in number of physicians has not led to any relative evening out between the various districts and areas of the country. Even though there are today far more physicians in Finnmark than earlier, the county is relatively no better off than before. There is a clear concentration of physicians in the Oslo area. Eastern Norway as a whole, which has less than 50 per cent of the country's population, has more than 60 per cent of its physicians; North Norway, with 12.3 per cent of the population, has 7.7 per cent of its physicians. Especially with respect to specialists, the geographical distribution is uneven.

A survey of physicians practising in peripheral areas from 10 to 20 years after graduating shows an under-representation of women, of graduates receiving especially high grades, and of graduates coming from an academic family background. The same survey also indicates an over-representation of medical graduates from farmer and (elementary) teacher families, as well as of those who themselves were born in peripheral districts. This last factor was closely connected with localization in peripheral areas 20 years after graduation. Thus, whether or not a physician practises in a non-central area seems to depend on a whole series of factors not easy to control (Lindbekk 1962).

Medical graduates frequently come from the 'better classes'. One-third of those graduating in recent years have fathers who have an academic background or who are businessmen; one-fifth have fathers who are farmers, workers, and artisans (Lindbekk 1962).

The proportion of those from lower-class backgrounds has long been increasing; however, quite recently this trend seems to have stopped. This may be because such newer professions as engineering absorb a good many from the lower classes.

Within the medical profession we find a whole series of dividing and unifying forces. Among the most important of the latter are fairly homogeneous social background, standardized academic training, common experiences in the profession, and high social status.

Medical graduates know each other's working field. There exists much movement between the various sectors in the profession. Perhaps this is one reason why the Norwegian Medical Association, founded in 1886, is now able to represent the profession as a whole, as well as exert a certain normative influence. In contrast to the situation in several other professions, university teachers in medicine also remain 'within the profession': that university professors have so frequently been elected to responsible positions in the medical association shows this (see Lindbekk 1967a, p. 151, Table 32).

There are about 20,000 *registered nurses* in Norway. Half of these are active; due to this rapid turnover, as well as to difficulties in recruitment, the nursing shortage is great. Furthermore nurses are not evenly distributed by county. Almost one of three works in Oslo, with only about 8 per cent working in the three northernmost counties. About 2,000 of the active, trained nurses work outside hospitals and institutions.

Nursing education is organized differently from medical education. For one thing, it is far less standardized. There exist some 30 nursing colleges in Norway, one-third managed by the public authorities, the rest by private health organizations and religious groups.

Dentists, even more than physicians, tend to collect in urban areas. At the beginning of the 1960s, one-third of the population lived in urban, two-thirds in rural areas; however, two-thirds of all the dentists lived in cities, while one-third lived in the country. In 1963, there were 1,385 inhabitants per dentist – but in the rural county of Hordaland the figure was 3,140 per dentist; in northern Finnmark, 3,067. The figure for Oslo was 1,042, but this was not the lowest – Bergen had 729 inhabitants per dentist.

According to the law concerning primary schools, all children have the right to dental treatment if the municipality has allotted funds for school dental services or has seen to it that expenses are covered in some way. The 'People's dental service' provision is more far-reaching: all persons between the ages of 6 and 18 are to receive free dental care. This service may provide similar possibilities for other age groups. While medical help is to a large extent in the hands of private practitioners, and is largely paid through the social security system, public dental care is carried out by dentists in tenure positions and is not financed by social security.

There has been a certain tendency for dentists to leave private practice for public positions (Ås 1962). This may parallel the trend within the medical profession: both physicians and dentists are driven away from private practice – dentists to public jobs, physicians to hospitals. And it is precisely in the public dental service that the dentist can find a work situation similar to that of the physician in the hospitals. The public dentist works in a fully equipped clinic, frequently with regular working hours and close contact with his colleagues.

277

However, there is no reason to believe that dentists ideologically prefer public service. Rather, the exodus from private practice seems more connected with the fact that the earlier combination 'private practice plus school dental service' is being replaced, due to changes in school legislation. The number of dentists going into private practice in itself does not appear to have changed.

Within the category 'health personnel' there are a series of marginal groups, the most marginal being the quacks. Indeed, whether they should at all be included in a description of this category is debatable. The health authorities try to fight them. From a sociological point of view, however, it is interesting to note that not a few persons are willing to receive treatment not based on formalized science, and that there does exist a market for such. It seems reasonable to assume that quackery is connected with traditional lay elements within the general field of medical treatment.

When the law concerning quackery was to undergo revision in 1936, the various county medical officers sent in reports on the existing quacks within their county. Some 150 persons were mentioned, persons who without formal medical training supported themselves, partly or in full, by treatment of the ill. However, the law is so formulated that it also includes chiropractors, osteopaths, and psychoanalysts (without medico-psychiatric training) – and these groups can hardly be counted as 'quacks'.

The total personnel to be found within the Norwegian health services amounted in the sixties to more than 35,000 persons – or about 2.6 per cent of the total working population. All the same, the shortage can at times be so acute that it is difficult, if not impossible, to start new projects for which financial support does exist. In addition, there are problems in keeping certain hospital wards going. Lack of personnel and personnel training comprises the greatest problem of the Norwegian health services today.

4.4. A commentary on the health service

In Norway, the following parties are all more or less directly involved in attempts to realize health values: the government and parliament, members of the medical profession, of course, and other occupational groups, the various political parties, and the voters. Things are so arranged that we have both state and private organs, obligatory and voluntary participation, national and municipal administration. Health personnel are both dependent on and independent of the public sector. True, the public sector dominates, but not so completely as to deprive private instances of all influence.

The four big voluntary organizations – *Nasjonalforeningen for folkehelsen* (The National Association for Public Health), *Norges Røde Kors* (Norwegian Red Cross), *Norsk Folkehjelp,* and *Norske Kvinners Sanitetsforening* (Norwegian Women's Health Association) – had by the early 1960s some 1.5 million members, or a number equal to about a half of the total population 15 years of age or older. Obviously it would be quite misleading to state that the Norwegian health system is totally dominated by the public sector.

Earlier, the National Association for Public Health was named the National Association against Tuberculosis – an indicator of how tuberculosis no longer is the main problem today, and of how the association has broadened its field of interest in accordance with today's broader spectrum of illnesses. Indeed, the organizational consequences of such changes in goals would be a good theme for research.

The present system can well be considered a compromise and an expression of Norway's traditions. Many have a little to say, no one has the final word. We discern a certain ambivalence in relations vis-à-vis the public sector. The system contains various tendencies, which make it rich and vital but also prevent any one part from dominating completely.

Aid is also given to those who are not ill in the traditional sense. It is impossible to state where the health service stops and social work takes over. In some projects we find regular health personnel, in others not. The degree and type of administrative control, as well as the public sector's share, can vary considerably. However, state responsibility in the welfare state is far more embracing than the health service as such. A whole series of projects receive appropriations through the national budget under the rubric 'social expenses', and all fall within the concept of the welfare state: health service, aid to the occupationally injured and disabled, unemployment, aid to the elderly and to invalids, rehabilitation, family aid, general social aid, assistance to war pensions, and tax relief measures for families with children, among others.

5. THE RECIPIENTS

The health system offers various forms of medical services. Between the personnel who are to administer such services and those who are to receive them, a social relationship is created. The content of this relationship will change according to the aim; the role of the helper varies, as does that of the receiver.

In connection with the health system's attempts to prevent illnesses, the population comes in brief contact with representatives from the

279

health authorities, without in advance having to be ill. Vaccination is an example. Smallpox vacccination takes place on a large scale. From the reports compiled by the public physicians we find that in 1964 some 52,000 initial vaccinations and about 44,000 re-vaccinations were carried out. Almost 80 per cent of the former group were children under the age of one year, which is quite natural, since the law requires that all children be vaccinated against smallpox within the first year of life (NOS XII 196, p. 18).

After the well-known Salk vaccine against polio had been introduced in the USA, and some of those vaccinated contracted the disease itself, sometimes with fatal outcome, the Norwegian Gallup Institute asked whether all Norwegian children ought to receive this vaccination (Gallup, 6 August 1955). The question was repeated one year later (Gallup, 15 September 1956). There was a significant shift: in 1955, 46 per cent were for, 28 per cent against vaccination (26 per cent undecided); by 1956, 67 per cent were for and 22 per cent against (with 11 per cent undecided). An interesting supplement came in the following year (Gallup, 21 September 1957). After the vaccine had been released to the public, so that anyone under the age of 40 could be vaccinated by his physician, 19 per cent had in fact done so; and 45 per cent of those with pre-school children had had them vaccinated.

In the period 1950–1959, 286,000 received BCG vaccinations. The decrease in tuberculosis has been greatest among the vaccinated groups, while increased welfare standards have also been important (Bjartveit and Waaler 1965).

There are still some 15,000–20,000 persons under observation for active or cured tubercular diseases, an indication that tuberculosis no longer represents a death sentence. It has been estimated that 38 per cent of the population is spontaneously positive, 29 per cent positive BCG vaccination, and 33 per cent tuberculin-negative. The infection risk is still present. Even if no new cases appeared, tuberculosis in Norway would not be wiped out until after the year 2000, as not until then will the infectious portion of the population have died out (Galtung-Hansen 1965).

As it is, about 1,000 new cases are detected annually, primarily by means of chest X-rays. In 1947 the Ministry of Social Affairs was by law given power to require chest X-rays for the entire population, or parts of it. By the end of 1957, a total of 4,142,498 examinations had been carried out by the State Chest X-ray Commission (Galtung-Hansen and Riddervold 1959).

Figures for those reporting for chest X-rays in the period 1949–1957 varied from 72 to 84 per cent of the male and 80 to 91 per cent of the female population. In 1957, 13 per cent of the men and 10 per cent of the women failed to report, despite the fact that they were required to do so. In general, acceptance of any health measure is connected with social factors. In the 1962 Oslo investigation of tuberculosis, 92,000 persons failed to report: the groups where tuberculosis is still most prevalent are precisely the ones where fewest persons report for X-rays.

Treatment requires totally different social forms. The receiver of the services has an illness, a disease, and he is treated primarily in his own interest – there is a transition from being sick, to becoming a patient or client. Such a status can be attained within the various types of treatment arrangements: hospital, general physician, rehabilitation measures, etc. As to exactly how recruitment to this status takes place, we know little systematically.

Since the entire Norwegian population must belong to the social security system, its statistics ought to present a reliable picture of the number of patients. However, in reality many cases are excluded because the statistics cover only those instances where sick pay or hospital expenses are paid via the system.

Illness insurance *(syketrygden)* had about 2,000,000 direct members; 1,200,000 have the right to receive sick pay. In addition come 1,775,000 members of families. Among those entitled to sick pay in 1964, there were 40 cases per 100 members where illness lasted three days or more, the minimum duration required (Rikstrygdeverket 1966, p. 10).

However, these figures are not an accurate expression of morbidity among direct members, as several incidences of illness within the same year can pertain to the same person.

Statistics from the Oslo Social Security Office show that illness in the limbs, respiratory organs, and cardio-vascular problems resulted in the greatest number of days of sick leave among members (i.e. those entitled to sick pay or to paid hospital expenses). Injuries are also common. Mental illness occurs more frequently than does illness in the digestive system or infectious diseases.

Public health physicians are required to report cases of infectious and epidemic diseases, which, however, comprise only a portion of the total illness panorama, and reports on them provide no reliable point of departure for computing the total number of patients. More than 400,000 consult a physician because of acute respiratory infections, angina, and pneumonia in the course of a year. All in all, more than half a million cases of infectious and epidemic diseases are registered annually. Of these, the socially-discriminating venereal diseases account for a fraction – some 3,500–4,000 cases annually. This figure is increasing, but is certainly still small in comparison with the actual incidence.

The general hospitals, clinics, and smaller clinics admitted 440,000 patients in 1965, a figure which is increasing each year. The number of cases treated is larger by about 16,000. In the same year, about 16,000 persons died in hospitals (NOS 193, p. 14).

By adding up the number of patients in the various specialized wards, we can get an idea of the distribution of diagnoses. However, for many reasons, this method is not always reliable. For one thing, the patients in a ward may not always correspond to its function. For example, practice has revealed that two out of every three internal medicine patients are elderly persons with diseases that are, from the point of view of the specialist, fairly simple, even trivial. Thus, an internal medicine ward easily turns into a geriatric one (Molne and Hjort 1965). Some time ago, in fact, geriatrics was separated from internal medicine so as to relieve the latter of the 'trivial' problems typical of elderly patients, to provide better opportunity to investigate research problems. The question now is whether this was in fact realistic, or whether we see today an example of medicine orienting itself away from the patient.

Almost one out of every three patients in internal medicine wards appears to need psychiatric assistance; 29 per cent may be diagnosed as psychically ill as against 71 per cent somatically (Horn 1952). Of a group of psychiatric clinic patients, 47 per cent had previously been patients in somatic wards under other diagnoses (Anchersen 1953). Such facts may well make us doubt whether recruitment to final patient status corresponds with the individual's actual problem.

As to tuberculosis, in 1963 the various tuberculosis treatment centres and sanatoriums admitted 4,000 persons. In this year, treatment was given to 5,500; 200 died.

The number of persons undergoing treatment or care for severe mental disorders is about 17,000. About one-half of these are in hospitals, the rest in treatment homes or private care.

In 1964, there were more than 6,500 patients admitted directly to psychiatric hospitals. About 2,900 were admitted for the first time – about 1,500 women and 1,400 men. In other words, first-time patients comprised less than 44 per cent of all admissions. One out of every four of those admitted was diagnosed as reactive psychosis, one out of eight as schizophrenic. Reactive psychosis was more frequent among women, schizophrenia among men. Further 70 per cent were admitted because of psychoses and 20 per cent because of neuroses (NOS XII 189, Table 1).

Widows, widowers, and divorced persons take on the status of psychiatric patient more frequently than do married or single persons. The rate for divorced persons is incidentally three times that for widows or widowers (Ødegaard 1953). Also, divorced men and widows are admitted more frequently to psychiatric clinics (Sundby and Nyhus

282

1963). We find the highest admission frequencies among members of occupations which have the lowest social prestige (Ødegaard 1956).

Fairly exhaustive investigations have been made of the work of the general practitioner. The most important of these showed that a population of 6,000 in a rural eastern Norwegian district had 40,000 contacts with physicians in the course of a four-year period, 1952–1955. There were about 20,000 instances of illness leading to such contacts (Bentsen 1965, 1966).

Because of Norway's system of compensation, income ought not to be the decisive factor for whether or not people contact a physician, an impression also supported by the survey. All the same, there were certain things which indicated that recruitment to the status of patient might be connected with income: there were more women with very low incomes who did not contact a physician than there were women with high incomes. But, in general, persons with low income had more contact with physicians, probably because they fall ill more frequently.

One out of every five consultations was due to respiratory diseases; less than one-tenth concerned mental illness. However, more than one-fifth of the population was registered by the survey as having psychic problems. The group also seemed to have many different diagnoses, so that it was responsible for nearly 45 per cent of all instances of contact with a physician.

There are varying opinions concerning the incidence of psychiatric problems in general medical practice. One report from the northern county of Nordland indicates very low figures, but it classifies headaches, tiredness, insomnia, dizziness, etc. as somatic disturbances (Iversen 1959). Figures from a rural district in western Norway correspond closely to those from the eastern area just mentioned (Kringlen 1965).

In the course of the period 1939–1944 it was found that 25 per cent of the men and 30 per cent of the women who consulted a doctor in a small fishing community complained of some chronic ailment. Five per cent of all the men who consulted a doctor had a chronic psychic problem; the figure for the women was nearly 15 per cent. Here, psychic ailments occurring together with somatic ones are not included, nor are psycho-somatic problems (Bremer 1951). 'Purely psychiatric' ailments accounted for 20 per cent of a series of medical visits arranged through the intermediary agency of the Oslo Physicians' Service (Oslo Legevakt); if we include the mixed cases, the figure is some 30 per cent (Albrechtsen and Kringlen 1965). Furthermore, including the more drastic cases handled directly through the Oslo Health Agency's Psychiatric Division, we reach a total of 35 per cent (Hirsch 1964).

The health system is also concerned with family problems, although the extent of such aid is not great. In the northerly towns of Steinkjer and Bodø, family counselling offices have existed on an experimental basis since about 1960. In their first three years of operation, these offices handled about 500 new cases apiece; first and foremost, unwanted pregnancies,[4] then diverse family problems (finances, housing, work) and problems in child-rearing and in adjustment difficulties (Report to the Storting no. 77, 1964–1965).

Another concern of the health service is with persons who can no longer be treated. Many are cared for in various types of institutions. Invalids no longer able to work receive disability pensions when their working capacity is reduced by 50 per cent or more. By the end of 1968 there were 100,000 persons receiving such pensions – about 4–5 per cent of the population aged 18–70.

Some 30 per cent of all such cases are diagnosed as mainly psychiatric. In this, age is important, as is place of residence. Notable variations exist among the different counties: in Finnmark over 5 per cent of the population aged 18–70 receive pensions, while Vestfold has only 2.8 per cent (Rikstrygdeverket 1966). This is also connected with varying local employment possibilities.

It is not possible to say how many of the actual cases of disability are caught up by the pension system, but since reporting them as such carries financial advantages, it seems reasonable to assume that a fair proportion of the existing cases are known. On the basis of a population survey in Skåne in southern Sweden, it was estimated that 8 per cent of the women and 5.8 per cent of the men were unable to work. The Danish Institute for Social Research has indicated physical handicaps in about 6 per cent of the population aged 15–61.

Three important factors are mental illness, age and place of residence. Also, various occupations are differently represented: there are few white-collar workers but many manual labourers.

Many persons consult non-professional 'healers'. A 1951–1952 survey of patients in one hospital revealed that one-third (of 247 patients) had at one time or another consulted such 'healers'. The most frequently mentioned were homeopaths and chiropractors, followed by eye-diagnosticians and 'wise old' women and men. The patients had consulted them most frequently about pains, chronic arthritis, and eczema – cases in which doctors had not been able to help them. Thirty-five were of the opinion that the healer had helped them; 12 were in doubt; and 32 felt that the treatment had not helped.

Almost one-half (43 per cent) of the adult Norwegian population felt that persons usually termed 'quacks' may in some cases help where a doctor cannot (Gallup, 26 November 1949). Fourteen per cent of the population had applied to such healers for help. This was more common among persons in Trøndelag and North Norway than among persons in southern, western, or eastern Norway.

In 1950 Norway was visited by the American preachers Freeman and Branham, a visit that created some uproar. A Gallup poll immediately afterwards (24 June 1950) revealed amazing results: 38 per cent believed in the efficacy of healing by prayer and the laying on of hands. The women were more 'believing' than men (44 per cent, 32 per cent); older persons more so than younger; persons from rural areas more than those from towns and cities; more from southern and western Norway than from Trøndelag, North Norway or eastern Norway – which seems to contradict our findings about visits to healers.

More surprising was that one out of every four Norwegians felt that all illness can be cured by means of prayer and laying on of hands. In 1954 (Gallup, 6 November 1954) one out of four surveyed replied that he or she knew of cases where a sick person was cured by means of prayer. There were great differences between men and women: only 18 per cent of the men knew of such cases, as against 38 per cent of the women.

These results apparently contradict the impression that the Norwegian population has an uncompromisingly secular attitude towards illness. Further research will be necessary to clarify this question. Altogether, our data indicate that 'quackery' and non-professional healing have a fairly well-established position in Norway. Strict legislation on this point would scarcely help, as many persons would consider it an unjustified intervention in their private and religious freedom.

6. CONCLUDING REMARKS

The Norwegian health system has many tasks. Among them are preventive activities, treatment, and rehabilitation. Persons unable to help themselves are cared for. Each one of these tasks creates special social problems and roles, and between the various roles tensions can appear. Up to now, treatment has received most attention and most funds, but as new functions are taken on, new problems and new tensions will also turn up. This process is already under way.

Preventive medicine implies a special responsibility between health personnel and persons not necessarily sick. These are supposed to co-operate, not only because some time in the future they may conceivably become sick, but also because in that way the risk of others' becoming sick can be lessened. Preventive medicine places greater collective responsibility on the 'users' than is the case elsewhere in medicine: nor is this collective viewpoint particularly characteristic of society otherwise. It can indeed be difficult to assure full and active popular co-operation.

It can be medically necessary to change people's habits – an uncommon activity for the physician who in other situations would tend to avoid sitting in judgement on another's way of life. Many persons have difficulty associating their own habits with health risks, so it is necessary to explain and inform the population about the connection, in an easily understandable way. Here 'pop-medicine' similar to the 'pop' tendencies found in other areas would be one solution. It can be difficult to maintain intact the respectability of medicine if it is at the same time to be 'pop'. Nor are medical truths eternal, and the general faith in medicine may be impaired if the public is encouraged to practise certain habits or take certain medicines, only to see these experts' ideas change after a while.

For the health system, it can at times be difficult to work in preventive and curative medicine simultaneously. Curative medicine is directed against an already present illness, and thus is more individually than collectively oriented: it takes place under hidden, sheltered, anonymous conditions where the healer usually avoids making reference to his opinions on the patient's habits or way of life. Treatment is voluntary, whereas preventive measures frequently require the public to cooperate with health authorities.

Other combinations of medical responsibilities may also create dilemmas. Pension possibilities may interfere with rehabilitation work. Attempts to make institutions more home-like and enjoyable can interfere with treatment.

It is reasonable to expect of the health service that it be universal in practice, benefiting everyone. After all, everyone helps pay for it. In Norway we also find similar demands in other fields, for example the North Norwegian demand for extension of railroads and television broadcasting. The actual distribution of health personnel and institutions does not meet these ideal expectations, a skewness frequently commented upon in public debate. Various solutions have been offered. Clearly, the population wishes legislation that would make it possible to order younger doctors to practise in districts with a severe lack of physicians (Gallup, 2 February 1953: two out of three persons surveyed were in favour of such legislation). Such legislation does exist for dentists, a law that many dentists regard as unfair. With respect to physicians, attempts have concentrated on stimulating interest in such district service.

One main point is the relation between medicine's supply of treatment and society's actual illness and problem panorama. Even though a large share of the Norwegian population does in fact come in contact with health personnel in the course of a year, it is still beyond doubt that there exists more illness in society than that reported for help. The number of actual patients is far from a satisfactory expression of the real amount of illness. Such figures are far too low, especially those for psychological and social-medical problems in the population.

Medicine is developing and changing, if not one-sidedly, at least to some degree in the direction of a technical, specialized, natural science orientation. As we all know, this has produced spectacular results. However, even such a positive development can have its negative aspects: the technical, specialized treatment becomes first and foremost concentrated on the patient's somatic disorders, while psychic and social problems are more or less ignored. Many persons who suffer primarily from psychic or inter-personal difficulties will not even enter the client status. Thus, medical activity does not cover the entire illness panorama, as problems in the areas of psychiatry and social difficulties receive insufficient attention.

The skewness is further emphasized by the tendency to concentrate treatment in hospitals, where the heavy work burdens and the need for patient beds may adversely affect the chance of personal treatment (Braatøy 1952). Recruitment for general medical practice – where the physician may meet his patients in precisely this personal way – is rapidly decreasing; the individual physician is made to feel that the best way of 'succeeding' in the profession lies via hospital practice, where there are also better chances for research. The all-round physician – who, true enough, has been idealized far out of proportion, but still, who did take responsibility for many persons in many differing situations – is becoming rarer and rarer.

Professional interests within medicine may be difficult to combine with patient-oriented interests: medicine can thus become more occupied with its problems than with its patients.

But medicine does react. We have many proofs of this. Interest in psychiatry is increasing; social medicine has arrived; medical education is a topic of public debate. New occupational groups enter the picture: for example, social workers have been growing stronger, with respect to both traditional and unorthodox treatment methods (Holter 1960, Løchen and Martinsen 1962).

Within society's panorama of illness and problems we also find a series of cases bordering on 'normal' difficulties. I am here thinking of the various diffuse, psychological, social-medical problems and behavioural disorders often found especially in socially deprived low-status groups. And indeed, if we recall the average status and background conditions of members of the medical profession today, there seems reason to wonder whether physicians are favourably situated to understand precisely the former group of problems. There is, at any rate, an

287

increasing awareness that such conditions are in fact illness, and the general concept of illness is expanding.

Some of these groups make great demands on physicians' time, and their needs are hard to satisfy. Annually, some 30 million sleeping pills are prescribed and sold in Norway, and it seems reasonable to connect these with precisely this client group. A large majority of the general population (86 per cent) say that they never take any kind of sleeping pills (Gallup, 3 November 1962), indicating that this high consumption applies to a small group.

It is as yet impossible to predict what standpoint society is going to take vis-à-vis these groups, and whether they will receive the same rights and obligations as other sick persons. An alcoholic or narcotics addict can, at present, not receive disability pension if these problems are his chief diagnosis: instead, the less 'noble' municipal welfare enters the picture. Today there are, in both society and in treatment circles, diverging opinions, also as to who is the more competent to offer assistance.

Another problem in the Norwegian system is that it is frequently necessary to create strong opinion before the authorities can do much. Thus, many worthy tasks have as yet received little attention. An example of this has been aid to the handicapped, which, thanks to recent efforts, may now be entering an active period.

The health service is expensive to maintain. It is hard enough to obtain sufficient funds for already started projects and measures, but the greatest problems appear when new projects are to be established and funded. There are limits as to how far the public sector can go; expenses in the health sector have to compete with other items on the budget. At the same time, however, the general public has come to expect more in the way of an effective health service: and here one superficial solution is simply to give the impression that a lot is being done, when in reality little is happening.

Tensions are also apparent on the individual level. Some persons feel that social security premiums are high enough already. A 1958 Gallup poll (23 August 1958) on taxes, state expenses, and social measures revealed that 38 per cent would rather live in a society where the state helped only those who would otherwise live in distress, leaving the rest of the population to see to its own financial needs, rather than in a society where the state and society try as much as possible to see to the individual's well-being by social measures.

Some people fear that the position of health personnel may have become less free. There are those who feel that the anonymous 'treatment relation' in some cases can be invaded by social forces irrelevant to the treatment itself. This is a point worth studying. One aspect is, paradoxically, that it becomes more difficult to distinguish between

288

common morality and medical practice, since we are learning that certain illnesses may be due to a harmful way of life. Some illnesses may be caused by depraved habits, and these illnesses come close to the domain of sin. A second aspect is the relationship between health personnel and the government, through the social security system, and often by the fact of public ownership of the hospital which employs them. This may put them in an ambiguous position, exactly in the middle, where it becomes more difficult to devote themselves to the interests of the individual patient. How important this is I can hardly say, but it is not uncommon to hear this argument from those who criticize the Norwegian system, not least for ideological reasons. I feel, however, that a third aspect, which may be difficult to distinguish from the other two, is much more important. This stems from the fact that health personnel are used for tasks beyond those of traditional medicine. This occurs in institutions obliged to apply social control in addition to treatment – a problem of long standing. Health personnel are also forced to make decisions where administrative, legal, and medical considerations all enter, not least in applying the social security laws. In this process the specifically medical viewpoint may come under pressure from more technical-administrative or juridical approaches to the case. It is rewarding to see that the needs of a great part of the population are covered by social security; still, this demands standardized rules that simply and rapidly distinguish between who may and who may not receive aid. It is not unlikely, then, that the individualistic, medical point of view – the one of social medicine in particular – must yield. Ultimately, this is a conflict to be fought out between the medical authorities and the social security system, having to do with the principles of how to help human misery.

Finally, it may be that the medical profession and medical activities are undergoing a process of commercialization. Some persons have accused doctors of being as interested in making a profit as are the members of any other occupation; in fact, critics have also at times accused them of being more interested in profit than in the patient. For example, one not infrequently hears of North Norway that young doctors go there in order to be able to pay off rapidly their financial debts incurred at the university; even if this were true, it would hardly be correct to criticize them for this. Furthermore, as far as I can judge, this scarcely seems true, given the actual conditions there. Other similar points are the general protests of physicians against increasingly progressive taxation and young interns' demands for higher salaries. Such behaviour seems incongruent with the concept of the medical profession as a calling. But since we are dealing with impressions only, studies and research are needed to clarify this point.

Many of these tensions are international; others more specially Norwegian, connected with Norway's way of solving her problems. some are chronic, others acute. In order to distinguish among these and to help lead developments along the best path, we shall need further sociological analyses.

NOTES

[1] This is most dramatically illustrated by the Black Death, a form of boil-and-lung plague, still found in the Far East, accounting for 10 million human deaths in India and China in the last 100 years. In 1349 this plague arrived in Norway, after having devastated Europe, in the city of Bergen, via a British ship. The plague, striking Norway at a weak period economically, was definitely an accompanying factor in destroying her independent form of government and at last bringing her under Danish rule (Holmsen 1961).

[2] In Chapter 1, mortality in Norway is treated from a general point of view. In the present we concern ourselves solely with causes of death.

[3] There has also been considerable popular support for the idea of an inter-Nordic resort for rheumatism sufferers in the South (Gallup 27 June 1953). In the same survey, one of out every four persons replied that they suffered from rheumatism in some form. Finnmark county is also planning to construct a resort in the South for its health personnel.

[4] The abortion question has moral as well as medical and social aspects. The whole problem is connected with the recent changes in the role of women. In the report to the Penal Law Council concerning grounds for abortion, the number of 1954 abortions is estimated at 17,000 — or 27 per cent of all pregnancies. Of these, there were an estimated 37 per cent spontaneous abortions or miscarriages, 18 per cent legal, and a full 45 per cent estimate for illegal abortions. A study of 200 women who applied for abortion through the Oslo Mothers' Health Office in 1951 showed that the most frequent reason given was health, followed by inadequate living conditions. Norwegian public opinion unconditionally supports abortion in cases where there is danger of the baby's being born malformed; 71 per cent believed that abortion was justified (Gallup, 3 November 1962). A discussion of this complicated question is to be found in Strøm (1963, p. 257).

IX. The Mass Media of Communication

By Per Torsvik

1. INTRODUCTION

Because in the welfare society, the mass media are such an easily available good, we tend to be unaware of the fact that the vast production of mass-spread information is a feature exclusive to Europe, North America, and a few other areas in the world. Europe, Canada, and the USA consume some 80 per cent of the world's production of newsprint, and nearly three-fourths of the television stations and two-thirds of the radio stations serve these culturally distinct areas.

Within these areas, however, the development of national and international communications networks has been enormous. Today, newspapers magazines, and books are printed on a scale totally different from that of 30 years ago, but the greatest advances are based on new techniques: since the first tentative attempts in the early 1930s, television has experienced a success greater than anything then imagined. Radio, which saw a decline during the initial period of television growth, is now experiencing an equally successful renaissance, thanks to inexpensive transistor sets.

Like most of Western Europe, Norway has had a considerable increase in mass media consumption since 1945, as seen from Figure 1. Newspaper circulation in number of copies per 100 inhabitants has increased to nearly twice that previous to the war. The weekly magazines have had a similar success, although with a rather drastic decline in the 1950s.

Radio and television have provided the greatest net increase within the mass media family. Since the first television broadcasts in 1960, the number of television licenses has increased rapidly.[1] Norway, among the last countries in Europe to establish regular television broadcasting, is today approaching a coverage close to the European average. An increase in number of radio sets is more surprising. The number of radio sets per 100 inhabitants today is probably higher than the corresponding figures for newspapers.[2]

We have no systematic investigations on the composition of mass

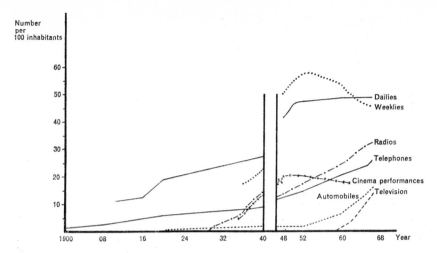

Figure 1. Mass media and communications media per 100 inhabitants in Norway, 1900-1968.

Source: *Statistisk Årbok for Norge, Norsk Aviskatalog, Norsk Ukepresses Opplagskatalog, Lisensarkivet, NRK.*

media content at various times. But some changes may be easily observed: there are drastic changes when we turn to the *type* of information produced and transmitted. As compared to radio programs and newspapers in the inter-war period, we find a broader scope and a more varied menu in today's media content.

For the consumer, this means more options to *alternative* information. It may be obtained from more places, in more ways, and in different situations. Newspapers are widespread, most magazines have a nationwide coverage, and in the late 1960s television extended to the northernmost regions. Cinema performances are admittedly concentrated in the cities, but mobile cinema units covered a considerable part of the countryside.

Still, there are great differences between the various districts. Most localities do not have their 'own' newspapers, and in even more districts the distribution is inferior. Up till 1968, television coverage was not nation wide, and, in some districts, radio and television reception can be poor. The selection and the distribution of movies vary, depending upon the initiative of the cinema-goers themselves. On the individual level, search for information may present problems. A newcomer in the neighbourhood or someone beginning a new job may find it difficult to obtain information, may not know where to turn, or the information he is looking for may not be available in the neighbourhood. Even the most trivial type of information-seeking may be looked upon as contextually dependent. Even if information-seeking and exposure seem consistently correlated with education, social position, sex, and age, local variations in Norwegian communities make it unrealistic to ignore ecological conditions. The following presentation considers some of these points: the spread of mass media and its content constitute the frame of reference within which individual behaviour is considered.

2. NEWSPAPERS

Relative to her population, Norway has many newspapers. Most of these are independent of each other, with few organizational ties except in the social democratic press – and these are more a result of technical convenience or made up with an eye to advertising revenue. Editorially most newspapers stand on their own. Even if the number

Table I. *Number of newspapers, by region and size, 1900-1966*

Year	Total number of newspapers	Eastern Norway Small	Medium	Large*	Southern Norway Small	Medium	Large
1900	172	58	25	9	13	3	—
1910	221	73	28	10	14	4	—
1920	244	54	37	21	13	7	1
1931	249	42	44	28	13	4	3
1941	201	35	21	36	11	—	6
1951	207	33	22	36	14	4	4
1960	190	26	19	45	9	3	6
1966	175	20	16	44	7	2	7

Year		Western Norway Small	Medium	Large	Trøndelag Small	Medium	Large	Northern Norway Small	Medium	Large
1900	172	24	4	3	16	1	2	14	—	—
1910	221	36	7	3	16	3	3	24	—	—
1920	244	26	9	12	20	8	3	30	2	1
1931	249	34	5	13	17	4	5	32	4	1
1941	201	26	8	9	12	3	5	24	22	3
1951	207	29	7	12	12	—	4	23	6	1
1960	190	28	3	15	9	1	2	12	3	9
1966	175	24	2	18	7	1	4	8	6	4

Source: Poststyret (Post Office): *Innenrikske Blad og Tidsskrifter, 1900-1966.*

* Small = total yearly weight less than 5,000 grams.
Medium = total yearly weight between 5,000 and 10,000 grams.
Large = total yearly weight over 10,000 grams.
Few and unreliable accounts of newspaper statistics are available up to 1937.
For further information, see Torsvik (1969).

of individual enterprises is large, and the average newspaper relatively small, the number of daily copies per household is more impressive: on a world basis, Norway ranks sixth in this respect (UNESCO 1964). Not all papers appear daily: out of 160 affiliated newspapers registered in the Norwegian Newspaper Directory (Norsk Aviskatalog), only 84 are dailies. These, however, account for most of the circulation: 1.4 million copies out of a total of 1.7 million.

It should be noted that Norway has no Sunday newspapers. Nor does there appear to be much popular demand for them: the Norwegian Gallup Institute, investigating attitudes to this question in 1954, reported that two-thirds of those asked were content with a six-day newspaper week. Among those opposing Sunday newspapers there were more women than men, more living in southern and western Norway; and as to political parties, practically all of those belonging to the Christian People's Party (Kristelig Folkeparti) were opposed (Gallup, 12 July 1954).

A small number of newspapers are responsible for much of the total circulation: the six largest alone issue more than half a million copies daily. Before the turn of the century no high-circulation newspapers existed at all, and the few larger ones established themselves early in the four main cities. From 1900, the number of large newspapers has increased steadily, more in eastern Norway than elsewhere; there is a tendency towards *geographic* concentration of newspapers and circulation in the largest, most densely populated areas. Table I shows the size of Norway's newspapers from the turn of the century to the present.

This concentration has affected the small, non-daily papers (see Høyer 1964, 1968). Between 1950 and 1965, 43 newspapers with circulation less than 5,000 folded, while the combined circulation of such small papers decreased by more than one-fourth (Gallup 29 September 1967). *Relative* position in the market is even more decisive for a newspaper's chances of survival. Frequently the second largest paper receives the small proportion of an increase in total circulation figures.

Possibilities of alternative newspaper choices vary from district to district. Nearly 90 per cent of all households have access to at least one newspaper published within the area, while more than two-thirds can choose between two or more such newspapers (Table II).

More and more varied newspapers are sold in the centrally located municipalities, while many of the peripheral ones lack a local press of their own (see Table III). In some municipalities, less than one newspaper is sold per every four households, while urban and more densely populated municipalities have from one and one half to three newspapers per household.

294

Table II. *Local trade areas with alternative newspaper choices, 1965*

Number of newspapers produced in district	Number of trade areas	Number of households in district	Total number of newspapers
0	33	141,295	—
1	33	200,663	33
2	37	376,552	74
3	8	142,073	24
4 or more	4	336,725	27
Total	115	1,197,308	158

Source: Based on *Norsk Aviskatalog* 1965-1966.

Circulation and coverage clearly limit the reader's choice, and differences in *content* set further restrictions. For the politically alert reader, this may have consequences which will be discussed later. Other differences are less clear. One, however, is of some significance: it is commonly referred to as the existence of a local, rural press versus the regional newspapers.

Local in this sense clearly has a geographical reference but more often seems to denote a degree of *parochialness* in outlook: some newspapers seem to have a predominantly local frame of reference in their selection of news.

Table IV shows that most Norwegians have fairly good access to national and local information via the press. Some 17 per cent of the households, however, are located in areas in which the press is predominantly local. Saturation of the mass media is considerably lower in these areas: the marginal districts have less than one daily copy per household.

A distribution is presented in Table V; here the 119 *trade areas* are stratified according to newspaper coverage. Within each level, newspapers are classified on the national/local dimension. The classification is based solely on content criteria, without reference to circulation or spread. These criteria are, however, highly correlated.

Table III. *Newspaper coverage in various types of municipalities, 1965 (percentage)*

Type	High coverage	Low coverage	Number of municipalities
Central municipality	61.2	38.8	147
More peripheral municipality	55.7	44.3	192
Peripheral municipality	52.0	48.0	127
All municipalities	56.4	43.6	466

Source: See Table V.

The most poorly covered areas are a communications periphery: we find fewer copies per household than elsewhere, and the resident newspapers are different with respect to content. At the lowest level we find only one paper which gives extensive, national news coverage, while in non-peripheral areas the relation between local and national press is far more balanced. Options for the reader in peripheral districts are less favourable: in order to get information beyond that limited to his own area, he must turn to papers edited and published outside his district or turn to other media entirely. He will then receive a paper somewhat outdated, and with unsatisfactory news coverage of his own area. In order to control the content classification in Table V, we have specified within each level how many newspapers subscribe to the national wire service *(Norsk Telegrambyrå)*. For most newspapers, this is the only link to national and international reporting. In the least covered areas, only three out of ten newspapers subscribe to NTB. The remaining papers are compelled to use material immediately available or a more or less incidental network of correspondents. On the other hand, these figures tell us much of the role of the local press in Norway. Relatively few of the local papers have been the victims of 'newspaper death', which has cut the number of newspaper units so drastically in the last 50 years. Indeed, even within the areas otherwise well covered by larger urban newspapers we find local papers, which, by means of their extremely local character, have maintained a reading public who find in their pages something different from what the larger papers will supply. In number of newspaper units (not copies) the local press is still the larger: there are more than one and a half times as many local newspapers as larger national ones.

2.1. *The press and politics*[3]

The Norwegian press is predominantly political, i.e. the papers responsible for the greatest bulk of the circulation announce themselves by a political label. Appeals to the voters may vary: some papers will present an almost continuous campaign while others have practically omitted the political vocabulary entirely and left the obligation to vote the only consistent political theme during an election campaign.

This provides a convenient cross-classification of two content variables. This also shows the most important dimension in the development of the Norwegian press: the development of the militant newspapers of the last century into established political organs.

The smaller, apolitical newspapers have really never moved out of the upper right-hand corner of this paradigm, while the growth of the militant newspaper of the last century roughly corresponds to that of

		Political commitments	
		Strong	Weak
Frame of reference	Local	Papers are: small, political alert crusading appealing to militant voters	Papers are: small, parochial without political content appealing to local citizenry
	National	Papers are: larger politically established informally tied to party appealing to party electorate	Papers are: larger politically diffuse sided, but with no party ties appealing to total electorate and consumers

the main political parties. This period of strong national commitments may, in the case of the largest newspapers at least, lead to a state of affairs in which community service is predominant, the political appeal is diffuse, and the consumer seems more important than the voter.

To this over-all picture, however, more details should be filled in. In most cases, party ties are quite informal. Only two Norwegian papers are directly owned by a political party – *Arbeiderbladet* (Labour) and *Friheten* (Communist), both Oslo papers. Otherwise, however, Norwegian papers seem to be more politically involved than their counterparts in most other countries. Only 23 per cent of the total circulation of Norwegian papers is non-affiliated in this sense. Many of the small local papers may be said to be non-political in an

Table IV. *Trade areas with 'national' and 'local' newspapers, number of newspapers and circulation, 1957*

Type of coverage	Number of areas	Number of households in area	'Local' papers: number/circulation	'National' papers number/circulation
Mainly local papers	8	171,711	48/168,000	3/29,000
Mainly national papers	17	845,023	48/622,000	62/574,000

Source: Rokkan and Torsvik 1960.

Table V. *Newspaper availablity in trade districts, by level of coverage*

Level of coverage in district	Number of districts*	Number of districts with 'own' newspaper	Number of national papers in district	Number of papers with news agency serv.	Total number of newspapers**
More than 1.50 copies per household	35	32	28	45	92
From 1.30 to 1.49 copies per household	28	26	28	41	63
From 1.00 to 1.29 copies per household	33	22	21	20	34
Less than 1.00 copy per household	21	10	1	3	13

Source: Archive on coverage statistics, Institute for Press Research, University of Oslo.

* Two trade districts have been omitted due to lack of data.
** The total number of newspapers in this Table differs from that given in Table IV. Table V is based on total number of newspapers regardless of circulation figures, whereas Table IV deals with only those papers which publish data on circulation.

Table VI. *Political areas in Norway*

Party	Number of papers*	Circulation	Percentage of total circulation
Høyre (Conservative)	36	528,816	32
Arbeiderpartiet (Labour)	39	402,544	24
Venstre (Liberal)	24	378,006	23
Kristelig Folkeparti (Christian People's)	2	34,478	2
Senterpartiet (Centre, formerly Agrarian)	5	51,620	3
Sosialistisk Folkeparti (Socialist People's)	1	4,326	—
Non-Socialist combinations	5	48,719	3
Non-affiliated	29	223,166	13
No information	19	—	—
Total	161	1,640,636	100

Source: *Norsk Aviskatalog 1965-66.*

* Only those publishing circulation figures.

298

Table VII. Circulation of party-political newspapers, and party strength,* by area, 1965 (percentage)

Area		Socialist people's	Labour	Liberal	Christian people's	Centre	Conservative	Non-Socialist combined	A-political	Total
Norway as a whole	Votes	6.0	43.0	9.7	7.4	9.6	20.9	1.9	—	1,952,853
	Circ.	0.4	24.5	23.7	1.1	2.9	31.4	2.0	14.0	1,532,975
East Central	Votes	6.7	42.2	7.2	4.9	4.9	30.7	2.1	—	689,257
	Circ.	0.4	22.0	13.1	0.9	1.2	45.6	0.3	16.5	560,140
East Inland	Votes	6.6	52.6	5.7	5.7	12.9	14.1	—	—	398,895
	Circ.	0.4	34.0	9.7	0.0	9.7	24.7	4.9	16.8	275,565
South	Votes	3.9	35.7	21.1	13.5	8.7	17.0	—	—	103,466
	Circ.	0.3	16.8	54.1	0.6	2.1	18.3	—	7.9	86,668
West	Votes	4.2	32.5	15.8	13.5	11.8	15.7	6.2	—	369,580
	Circ.	0.3	18.5	55.3	3.3	2.6	12.1	—	7.9	343,347
Middle	Votes	5.3	44.5	9.7	7.3	15.7	15.6	—	—	183,351
	Circ.	0.3	21.2	9.1	0.3	0.1	49.9	13.4	5.7	118,330
North	Votes	7.5	48.4	8.8	5.7	10.0	17.4	—	—	208,304
	Circ.	0.5	37.7	10.8	0.1	—	27.7	0.3	22.9	148,925

Source: Election survey 1965.
* Figures for Communist press not available.

Table VIII. *Newspaper subscription by area, 1960*

Area	Percentage subscribing regularly to at least one paper
East	85
South and West	88
Middle and North	77
Towns and cities	85
Rural areas	82
Norway as a whole	84

Source: Gallup survey, February 1960.

objective sense: very little party politics can be found in their columns.

Table VI presents a survey of the politics of the press. The Conservative side is by far the largest, with almost one-third of the total circulation and relatively many papers. The Liberal and Socialist presses are about equal in size, but part of the circulation figures in the category 'non-Socialist combinations' is actually represented by Liberal papers.

There seems little correspondence between the size of the political press and votes cast in the elections. This is most marked in the Labour case: the party receives about 50 per cent of election votes, but accounts for only one-fourth of the total newspaper circulation.

Table VII, however, seems to indicate a connection between voting patterns and spread of the political press. In distributing circulation figures and voting figures by commune, we find that the Labour press is frequently strongest in districts where the Labour Party receives 50 per cent or more of the election votes.

There is a marked difference in the districts in which the Labour press comes close to a majority and those in which their papers are in a minority position. For Labourites in the last situation, this dilemma of seeking information as loyal voters or as community members is regularly solved in favour of the party press. In districts where the party press is the dominating one, it is also likely to be the community service organ, and the dilemma does not exist. We find similar correlations between voting pattern and newspaper spread with respect to Liberals in rural areas and urbanizing rural areas, and with respect to Conservatives in the towns and cities. The Christian People's Party, Centre, and perhaps especially the Socialist People's Party are, throughout the country, under-represented as to newspapers.

2.2. *Readership*

The breakthrough of the newspaper as general reading came in the years between the turn of the century and World War I. At that time

300

Norway already possessed a well-developed press. As early as 1890 the Postal Service had registered 123 publications which could be termed newspapers; it was not until the turn of the century, however, that circulation increased to the point of making copies economically available to all.

Few households today are without a regular paper. Interview surveys between 1957 and 1969 show consistently that only 4 per cent of those asked came from households where no paper was regularly available[4] (election surveys 1957–1965–1969). Higher figures are, however, found by Gallup: In a 1960 survey 16 per cent replied that the household did not subscribe to any newspaper (Gallup 1960). The discrepancy is probably accounted for by a difference in subscribing to a newspaper and otherwise making a newspaper available, for instance by borrowing or buying one.

The figures in Table VIII are from the latter survey. We see that non-subscribers are distributed fairly evenly in all areas, with the exception of northern Norway. Here we find far fewer *regular subscribers;* and even though one third of those asked in this area replied that they regularly *purchased* at least one paper, this figure is not particularly higher than that we would find for the country otherwise. Purchasing habits are stable. The readers usually receive their papers by long-term subscription, and as a rule remain loyal to the paper. We may discern a slight difference between working-class households and others: while white-collar workers, self-employed, and retired persons average 13 per cent of the non-subscribing households, the corresponding figure for working-class households is 19 per cent; also fewer newspapers are purchased by members of working-class households (Gallup 1960).

Workers are more marginal newspaper consumers than are white-collar workers. They have less opportunity to read or obtain papers at work, which is one reason we find more white-collar workers who read more than one paper. Nor do the workers compensate by subscribing to the same extent as do white-collar workers. The availability of a daily paper is less, both at home and at work.

This represents a difference in educational level. A general picture is presented in Table IX. The Table distinguishes only between those who *regularly* and those who *seldom or never* read a newspaper: *extent* or *type* of newspaper reading is not included. A good third of the male population with only elementary school education are regular readers, and the percentage increases with higher education. Women are generally less frequent newspaper readers at all levels, but here also education plays a role: any formal schooling after elementary school increases the reading percentage: beyond the elementary level a significantly higher proportion of women regularly read a paper.

301

Table IX. *Newspaper reading, by education and sex (percentage)*

Newspaper reading	Elementary only		Folkehøyskole or equivalent		Realskole and above	
	M	W	M	W	M	W
Regularly	35	9	41	18	60	17
Seldom or never	64	89	58	80	39	82
No answer	1	2	1	2	1	1
Total	100	100	100	100	100	100
N =	284	368	219	156	135	145

Source: Election survey 1957.

In the material we have here, there are too few women with higher education for us to be able to get any reliable figures. The tendency seems clear: sex differences existing at the lower educational levels seem to lessen at the post-*gymnasium* level.

The *scope* of newspaper reading increases with higher education. Figures for 1963 from the Fakta Institute in Oslo show a considerable increase in those with higher education who read more than one paper, whereas the non-readers remain constant at all educational levels (Fakta 1964). The need for more, and above all more varied information increases with formal education, and the need for more variation is at least partly met by regularly reading more than one newspaper. Almost half of those with higher/highest levels of education regularly read more than one paper, as against about one-fourth of those with the lowest educational level.

We have no reliable data enabling us to study when and how in early life newspaper reading habits are established. Most routine investigations sample only those 15 years of age or older. We are likely to find regular readers in the early teenage group, although they may not be many. Survey data from 1965 and 1968 indicate a significantly smaller proportion of regular newspaper readers in the lower age groups (Augedal 1970). During the last decade, however, newspapers more frequently try to appeal to the younger and mid-teenage groups by including types of material earlier found only in magazines.

The high proportion of regular subscribers makes it a likely assumption that most reading takes place in the household. It would appear that the need for newspaper reading, whether as a search for information or as amusement, is tied to a settled position in society: marriage, home, and children are all commitments that seem to reduce the chances for mobility and make for a greater interest in the local community.

An analysis of the 1957 election survey shows that while women, no matter what their marriage status, are seldom regular newspaper readers; men most frequently are when they have settled down, started a home, and become fathers. About one-fourth of the childless young male population are regular newspaper readers, while 41 per cent of this age group with children and almost one-half of the older male population with children are regular readers. Furthermore, these reading habits remain even after the period when there are children living in the parents' home.

Considerations on *instrumental* reading may help explain the differences just mentioned between the male and female population. It may be predicted that the average housewife will be looking for information of a type most readily available from neighbours or other mass media: thus, a great many housewives are regular readers of weekly magazines.[5] These magazines have far more women readers than men readers and present a preponderance of information concerning house and home.

Only when we turn to readers in their more committed roles can we explain the differences. There have been few such studies in Norway, although there is the one undertaken by Rokkan and Torsvik (1960). Instead, the existing differences in individual choice of newspaper have inspired studies which take their point of departure in the apparent lack of correspondence between political preference as shown in elections and a 'loyal' newspaper choice for daily reading. Gallup (1960) has shown that more than one-fourth of those voting Conservative and nearly one-half of those voting Labour or Liberal are not 'loyal' to their party in this respect.

Those who vote Christian People's Party, Centre, Socialist People's Party, or Communist are even less favourably situated. Their party press does not have a large nation-wide network, so that they are largely forced to look for political information through other channels or by means of more politically neutral newspapers.[6]

Many voters will thus have a conflict between their personal political preference and their choice of daily paper: either they will have to choose a big, dominating paper able to give them a maximum of general information, or they will choose a paper that corresponds to their political views but that presents less general information. Only in those cases where their own political views are represented by the dominating newspaper locally available will they be able to get both in one and the same paper. For large portions of the Labour voters this will be a problem. However, not all readers will feel the situation as a conflict. They may, for example, seek other types of information primarily from their paper, choosing the largest local one precisely because it provides the most general information. Either this information is of such a type as not to conflict with their political views, or it is considered as neutral or apolitical.[7]

303

Table X. *Choice of newspaper, by political preference (percentage)*

Political preference	Only newspapers of own party	Newspapers of several parties	Only newspapers of other parties	Number
Socialist (Labour-Communist)	28.5*	39.0	28.5	637
Non-Socialist	81.0	15.0	1.3	621

Source: Election survey 1875.

* Totals of percentages are less than 100 because one category (those without newspapers) has been left out.

From Table X we see that more than 28 per cent of the Labour voters have only party-oriented newspapers in their households, and that an equally large portion has only non-socialist papers. Somewhat more than one-third have both socialist and either non-socialist or non-partisan papers. This is in great contrast to the non-socialist voters' situation: there are far more households with only non-socialist papers, and practically none with only socialist ones.

The large, dominating newspapers have more or less adjusted to this situation. Attracting readers from all political parties, they have de-emphasized their own political views. In his content analysis of editorials in Norwegian papers, Svennik Høyer found that the leading papers tend to employ milder, less harsh terms and to refer more frequently to broad, widely accepted symbols (Høyer 1960). Smaller papers, making their appeal to a public politically more homogeneous, more frequently hold extreme political views, both in choice of theme and in use of words and symbols. The more heterogeneous the group of readers, the less the paper's political background dominates. This seems to solve the conflict for many. They do not find the political references bothersome, and they thus adjust to the paper as the paper has adjusted itself to them.

The feeling of conflict is perhaps more closely related to the degree of political involvement and obligation the reader feels in his social and political roles. There are great differences in how much attention is paid to the political material offered by the papers. Labour voters with only non-Socialist papers in their households tend to ignore the papers' presentation of political matters, while those readers who are loyal to their party in choice of paper more often receive their political information by regular reading of political material in the paper.

Labour voters actively looking for information in the mass media tend to have a party paper available in the household, even though this paper may not be the community service organ: active political

Table XI. *Newspaper preference, political activity, and information-seeking, among Labour voters in areas with low accessibility of Labour press (percentage)*

	No. socialist papers in household	One or more socialist papers	No. newspapers in household	Total
Read political material in the paper(s):				
Regularly	35	63	2	46
Seldom	52	45	3	153
Index of information-seeking*:				
High	37	61	2	49
Medium	47	50	3	74
Low	55	41	4	80
Political activity:				
Active (member, attends meetings, participates in election work)	42	56	2	43
Only votes in elections	48	49	3	117
Does not vote, passive	53	42	4	43

Source: Rokkan and Torsvik 1960.

* Index based on newspaper reading and radio exposure.

involvement makes the choice of newspapers less haphazard. Table XI typically demonstrates this: in 'low accessibility areas' Labour voters are just as likely to have a newspaper opposing them politically if they by and large tend to overlook political information. The active information-seekers in a majority of cases keep their party paper even if it is not a local paper. In this group of 'party loyal' readers we also find those who are actively seeking information in more than one medium, i.e. those with a high score on the information-seeking index.

Within this group of active readers we are most likely to find the political opinion leaders. In the Norwegian case they seem to be of special significance to the largest party, whose press is in a minority position in most districts. With the stable electorate so characteristic of Norway since World War II and until very recently, the chances for obtaining marginal votes at the polls have been minimal. The purpose of mass appeals is no longer to win large groups of new converts to the various parties. Instead, it has become far more important to retain the already established voters, and to mobilize the active ones to renewed activity (see Rokkan 1964). This evens out the disparate points of departure for Norway's political press: the dominating non-socialist press, which draws its readers from outside the confines of the parties proper and which therefore de-emphasizes political information; and the socialist press – i.e. that of the Labour, Socialist

People's, and Communist Parties – which are most often in a minority, but are far more politically committed and more deliberately aimed at the political opinion elite.

2.3. *Newspaper content*

The last barriers to mass newspaper distribution were eliminated by the appearance of three features of modern life: general compulsory school attendance, the invention of the rotary press, and the availability of efficient means of distribution. A new type of newspaper was required: the new, large, and heterogeneous reading public made it necessary for the press to cover all fields of human activity, while improved communications increased manifold the possibilities of wide distribution. It is far from coincidental that the period immediately following the world wars has seen an explosive increase in the demand for newspapers.

The variety found in a large Norwegian paper today is probably greater than what the average person 'needs' or 'uses'. A twelve-page paper contains about 1800 column inches. Of these, about 60 per cent of the material will deal with trade and business, politics, and announcements, not including advertisements. This is a fairly typical pattern.

The manner in which political matters are presented varies with the paper and its political leanings. We have already seen that smaller papers which appeal to a politically more homogeneous public often accentuate their political viewpoints, and also tend to employ more pointed formulations than the large, regional papers. These also contain relatively *more* political material. The Labour press is usually this type of minority paper, and in Table XII we see that these papers are composed of more than one-fifth strictly political material. Of this, nearly one-fourth more than in other party newspapers is concerned

Table XII. *Proportion of political material in newspapers, by political party, 1964*

Party leanings (N)	Economic policy	Party politics	Social policy	Parlia- ment	Local politics	Politics in general	Total
Conservative (10)	2.5	3.8	1.5	3.1	2.9	3.3	17.4
Liberal (9)	2.1	2.3	3.5	1.8	4.0	3.0	16.7
Labour (10)	1.8	5.0	4.7	2.8	4.8	3.6	22.7
Christian People's (2)	6.5	0.8	8.8	1.4	1.4	5.1	18.1
Centre (3)	1.6	0.5	2.1	5.3	2.6	2.6	14.8
Independent	3.1	0.9	2.1	2.0	7.4	2.6	18.1

Source: Data are collected in a pre-survey of the total distribution of newspaper contents in a sample of 37 Norwegian papers, on one day in March 1964.

with party politics. Other papers average less column space devoted to politics, whether they are apolitical and independent, or connected to a political party. Indeed, we find as much political material in the independent as in the party political papers, although the former concern themselves less with *party* politics. This also applies to the newspapers connected with the Centre and Christian People's Parties.

The independent press put a fair degree of emphasis on *local* politics – that proceeding from municipal councils falls within this category. The majority of the independent papers included in this survey were smaller local papers providing extremely detailed reporting on precisely this subject.

The differences between newspapers consist in their varying selection of material, but it is difficult to find good tests of *how* this selection is in fact made (see Østgaard 1965). The material provided by the central news agency, NTB, comprises only a small portion of the total, but an analysis of this does yield some interesting variations.

A study of all Oslo papers for one day in March 1962 shows that out of 17.2 NTB telegrams sent to all these papers over a certain period of time, very different selections were made by the various papers. Only 10 per cent of the total number of telegrams appeared in as many as four or more papers, although some 40 per cent appeared in more than one. Among the former 10 per cent we find the papers' 'big headlines' of the day. The papers seem to select at random between the less important telegrams. Furthermore, of the reports appearing in three or more papers, 50 per cent have a political content, as against only 29 per cent of reports appearing in only one paper.

The selection of non-political material seems to be much more haphazard, while that of political material shows more conformity between the various papers: if a telegram report is political, its chances of being used by most papers are fairly good.

Some further approaches seem promising in the analysis of the flow of information in the press. The national/local dichotomy is crucial in the selection of news. We can study the proportion of domestic political information and foreign affairs to purely local information as options presented to the readers. This seems to be of particular interest in a period in which the introduction of a national television network has drawn the peripheral districts of Norway more close to the centre: increased communication is indeed the strongest 'nationalizing' factor in existence. People travel more, move more, and are increasingly being exposed to the same type of information wherever they live. The expansion of the regional press acts the same way, but we still find a large number of local papers with specialized local coverage. Clearly the press, more than any other mass medium, helps maintain local interest and and identification.

The analysis of news material with national and international reference focuses on the place of origin as the operative element. Studying the telegrams during a week in the Norwegian Telegram Bureau, M. Bakke indicates that the flow of news from Europe and North America coincides with the flow of merchandise: a disproportionately large number of telegrams originate in countries which constitute the largest trade partners (Bakke 1970).

Geographical distance and commerce explain only part of the variance; the degree of economic development, diplomatic relations, and language in the sender countries are modifying elements. This tells us a great deal about the importance of *cultural distance* in the selection of news stories: there seems to be a relation between preference of news stories and cultural closeness. This is not a linear correlation: there are a majority of telegrams from culturally proximate countries and relatively few from distant places, but some parts of the world, falling in a middle category of this dimension, are left in a news vacuum that is insufficiently explained by cultural distance.

2.4. Personnel

Even though there exist relatively many newspapers, the professional category of 'journalist' is not particularly large in Norway. The 1960 census shows 1,811 journalists and editors, where 27 per cent are editors. The figure includes journalist apprentices, freelancers, and others in the periphery of this profession. The membership list of the Norwegian Press Association included 1,452 names (in 1965), or a number about the same as that of bishops, ministers, and other church officials, and about twice the total number of university teachers in 1960.

More than two-thirds of these journalists are employed in the larger news bureaus or in newspapers with a circulation of over 10,000. The smallest papers have small staffs: papers whose circulation is below the 5,000 mark employ only 6 per cent of all Norway's journalists (Werner 1966, 1967). Many of these papers are small enterprises with a minimum of technical and editorial staff – frequently not more than four or five persons. Their job is only slightly specialized: they are the true all-round journalists. The main distinction is the one between the editor and the rest of the editorial-journalistic staff, although even here the lines may be imprecise. Beyond their own routine coverage, most journalists working on smaller papers rarely specialize. Two-thirds of all journalists are ordinary reporters: only 6 per cent are registered as special reporters, illustrators, or photographers. It is generally required of journalists that they be generally informed on most fields, and the occupational differentiation is no greater than that all

308

categories can be gathered under *Norsk Journalistlag* and *Arbeider-partiets Presseforening*, the two trade unions for journalists.

Recruitment to this profession has varied somewhat; while no formal education is required, the number of educated persons entering the field was quite large in the beginning of the 1930s: 17 per cent of those who started working as journalists between 1930 and 1965 had completed higher education. The minimum of education for young cub reporters today is in practice *examen artium* and/or special training in journalism, such as that offered by *Norsk Journalistskole* (the Norwegian School of Journalism). The larger papers compete for journalists with further education than *artium:* the larger the paper, the larger its proportion of journalists with higher education. This is not due solely to differences in salary, although such do exist. Frequently, the larger papers offer better working conditions and such compensations as travel, study grants, etc. A study of the distribution of grants and stipends among journalists indicates that the chances of securing a stipend are best provided you are male, 40–60 years of age, higher educated, and employed in a large newspaper.

Although journalism in Norway is more than 200 years old, only in the last 40 years has it actually become professionalized. Organizational problems dominated nearly all professional gatherings from 1920 up to World War II. Not until 1938 was a proposal for a *normal-kontrakt* for journalists generally accepted, and standard salary and wage agreements have existed only since the last war. Since 1945 rules of ethics have been codified, while at the same time efforts to secure journalists the right to maintain anonymity regarding their sources have found some legal acceptance.

Aside from the last ten years, when the professional unions combined with the state have taken some of the responsibility for preparing journalists for the profession, education has been based on the traditional method of on-the-job training.

There are no good descriptions of normal Norwegian journalistic practice, nor of the role of the journalist, although the amount of material actually gathered is impressive. Since the early 1920s, a committee formed by the trade unions has dealt with all cases of professional disagreements involving either newspapers or journalists. For each case the committee has prepared an opinion on to what degree the case conforms to the ethics of the profession, without, however, the rules having been codified.

The political cast so characteristic of the Norwegian press can in itself lead to conflicts of importance for the process of professionalization – as indeed it has. Conflicting views exist concerning the newspaper as a part of the political system or as an organization whose primary aim should be to carry news. The demands for professionalization have strongly emphasized the latter point, while maximal career possibilities have most frequently been tied to the former. Indeed, the study of the journalist's career within these two fundamentally differing systems may well be another fruitful way of investigating this important role in communications.

3. THE WEEKLY PRESS

The weekly press is generally associated less with information and more with diversion, day-dreaming, 'killing time'. Such an association is correct to the extent that the weekly press caters to a market of leisure and relaxation. Only in the course of the past generation has this market been exploited with any great numerical success, but it is not in itself new. The weekly press has taken over the role played by the wide-spread 'folk literature' or popular press of the nineteenth century. The Norwegian pioneer in social research, Eilert Sundt, in his studies of social life, in 1855 found relatively few books among a sample of families in the working-class district of Ruseløkkbakken in Oslo (Eilert Sundt 1858). Only in one single case of the many hundreds of families he visited did he find traces of the mass literature actually existing at the time. We have no systematic information on circulation figures. The great stream of cheap novels and magazines got underway only after Sundt had completed his investigations, but even as early as the 1820s and 1830s there was a steady increase in the number of titles, which hardly had much lasting interest but did achieve wide circulation. The 'flood' came in the second half of the century. One novel is said to have had a printing of 200,000 copies, and must have been circulated far beyond Christiania (Oslo proper) (Heiestad 1946). Many of the forerunners of the popular press were already started in the general spirit of presenting popular information, while other organs had clear political views. Common to them all was their short lifespan. The entertainment market was not primarily theirs, but belonged to the serials, the cheap novels, and the magazines. Although few could claim the same success, many appeared in printings of a size which would be considered high in Norway even today.[8]

By the turn of the century we have a well-established line of weekly magazines beginning to find their form of expression. The magazine *Allers Familie Journal,* started in the 1880s, set an example for the others, as far as content and editorial policy went. At any event, it must be considered the prototype of a family magazine, at least until 1940. Since the war there have been more specialization and diversity, and other types of magazines, as well as new forms of presentation and layout, etc., have appeared.

The total circulation for weekly magazines is around two million, corresponding to roughly one weekly copy per household. We have figures only on the number of purchasers – not on how many borrow or share copies with others. One study of leisure activities in Norway has indicated that about four million magazines are read each week; this yields a fairly high number of readers per copy, as not all adults are regular magazine readers (Nilsen 1958). This numerical success has mainly been achieved since 1945. In 1938, half a million copies were sold each week; in 1939, 650,000. By 1960, the figure had increased four-fold, an increase corresponding to the modern pattern of increased consumption and more leisure.

Between 1954 and 1958, total circulation increased from 1.4 to 1.5 million. A peak was reached in 1960, and total circulation has been decreasing slightly since then *(Ukepressekatalogen 1954–1968)*.

The decrease has been most marked in the whole of southern Norway, especially in the central eastern region (Oslo and surroundings), greatest in towns and cities, and least in the countryside. The rate of decrease has corresponded somewhat to the spread of television. Obviously, reading weekly magazines is a marginal activity which many people stop doing as soon as another competitor for their leisure time appears. After regular television broadcasting was initiated in 1960, magazine distribution in Oslo decreased from 1.9 magazines (copies) per household to 1.3 in 1966. Television is hardly the sole reason, but it has undoubtedly speeded up a tendency already underway. The Norwegian weekly magazine industry is confronted with a fair amount of tough competition: television and an increasing number of imported magazines.

In contrast to the newspapers, weekly magazines have a nationwide circulation: about 75 per cent of the latter are distributed via a central agency in Oslo which supplies more than 10,000 sales outlets, thus making the weeklies easily available practically anywhere in the country.

Weekly magazines are read most frequently in towns, cities, and urbanizing areas; but there are marginal readers, those who most easily give up magazine reading as soon as alternative media appear.

Most of those who read weeklies, read from one to three a week. The really enthusiastic readers do not account for the high reader figures: a 1957 survey showed that 19 per cent of those asked regularly have one, 22 per cent two, 18 per cent three weekly magazines in their households (election survey 1957). Four or more magazines were regularly available in 7 per cent, while another 7 per cent replied that they never had weeklies in the household. While these are total figures, covering all types of weeklies, they do not show that most readers stick to a fairly low number of titles.

Table XIII. *Magazine reading, by sex (percentage)*

Magazine*	Read regularly		Read occasionally	
	Women	Men	Women	Men
Norsk Ukeblad (G)	26	16	35	25
Allers (G)	23	14	29	20
Illustrert (G)	15	10	22	15
Alle Kvinners Blad (W)	14	3	23	6
Hjemmet (G)	11	7	17	12
Det Nye (R)	10	3	15	6
Kvinner og Klær (W)	9	1	17	3
Norsk Dameblad (W)	8	2	14	2
Alt for Damene (W)	5	1	10	2
Vi Menn (M)	4	14	7	25
Romantikk (R)	3	1	6	2
Aktuell (P)	2	6	8	16
Love (R)	2	1	5	2
Magasinet for Alle (G)	2	5	3	7
Nå (P)	2	3	5	9
Alle Menns Blad (M)	1	4	2	9

	Women	*Men*
Do not read any magazine regularly:	31	47
Never read magazines:	19	31

Source: FAKTA 1964.

* (W) = women's magazine, (G) = general family magazine, (M) = men's magazine, (N) = news magazine, (R) = romantic story magazine, (P) = political.

Men, more often than women, are non-readers: 51 per cent as against 38 per cent reply that they do not read weeklies. The difference between these figures and those above is probably due to the difference between *purchasing* and *reading* a magazine (Torsvik 1960). Table XIII presents reading habits for women and men as concerns the largest weeklies. Women are by far the most frequent readers, both as regular readers and occasional ones. An exception must be made for two political weeklies, *Nå* and *Aktuell*. However, it is difficult to say whether the difference is due to greater political interest among the male public, or to the fact that both these magazines carry a fair amount of typically 'masculine' material. The family magazines *Norsk Ukeblad, Allers, Hjemmet,* and *Illustrert Familieblad* attract readers of both sexes; we also find a small, regular group of female readers of men's magazines. The low figures for the teenage magazines *Romantikk* and *Love* represent a fairly small group of young girls who regularly buy these two.

Most women come in contact with the weekly press as either regular or occasional readers: only one of five women, as against every other man, replied that they never read weekly magazines.

The weekly press captures its public at an early age. While we have no reliable data on the reading public under 15 years of age, it seems clear that reading habits are generally established early. As we move upward through the age groups we find many who stop reading, at least who stop *regular* reading. Egil Nilsen found in 1958 that 67 per cent of the age group 15–19 years were readers, while only 41 per cent of those over 60 were. FAKTA's investigations have shown the same trend. The decline among women as regular readers is especially drastic. In general this decline affects the big family magazines, whereas the smaller, more specialized magazines seem to retain their readers.

Magazine reading varies little with income, as shown by Table XIV, but seems to be somewhat more typical in the middle-income categories than in the lowest and the highest. Egil Nilsen (1958) found more magazine readers among workers than among white-collar workers, most marked in rural areas. The difference was less in urban areas, but this may well have changed in the intervening years since this investigation was made: it is precisely in urban areas that the weekly press has lost most readers. Perhaps workers have been the last to 'change media' with the introduction of television.

3.1. *Content in the weekly magazines*

In the post-war years, the weekly press has had to change to suit a different market than that before World War II. Today it must compete with both the daily press and television, both of which cover considerable amounts of the weekly press's traditional spheres. Newspapers and weekly magazines are more similar today than 30 years ago. The weekly press today presents a far larger and more varied selection of material than before. Factual and informative material has increased, taking the place earlier occupied by fictional material, although short stories and romantic novelettes may still dominate. We now have more realistic subject matter, articles on automobiles, traffic, house and family – in general, a more comprehensive presentation of

Table XIV. *Percentage who read at least one magazine regularly, by income and sex*

Income	Men	Women
Low	56	46
Low middle	73	59
High middle	75	56
High	69	48

Source: FAKTA 1964.

Table XV. *Distribution of subject matter in magazines, by type of magazine, 1939 and 1964 (percentage)*

Content category*	Family** 1939	Family** 1964	Women's*** 1939	Women's*** 1964	Men's**** 1939	Men's**** 1964
Entertainment	47.6	48.1	21.7	35.3	66.3	27.1
Instruction	17.0	17.8	63.1	46.6	9.5	11.3
Information	9.2	9.5	4.1	1.2	3.7	36.7
Other	26.2	24.6	11.1	16.9	20.5	24.9
Total	100.0	100.0	100.0	100.0	100.0	100.0

Source: Torsvik 1965.

* Entertainment: Love, crime, subject matter for children and teenagers, personal portraits.
  Instruction: Fashions, handicrafts, home decoration, food, advice, automobiles, traffic.
  Information: Sports, tourism, culture and sciences, social questions, religion, war history.
  ** This category includes: *Norsk Ukeblad, Magasinet for Alle, Hjemmet, Allers, Illustrert* — for both 1939 and 1964.
  *** This category includes: *Norsk Dameblad, Alle Kvinners Blad, Kvinner og Klær* — for both 1939 and 1964 — and *Alt for Damene* — for 1964.
  **** This category includes: *Alle menn, Skib O'Hoi* — for both 1939 and 1964 — and *Ui Menn* — for 1964.

goods and values which have become more and more easily available to the average consumer, even though here the competition from the daily papers is also felt.

Roughly speaking, weekly magazines may be divided into three main groups: *general* magazines (the oldest, most traditional group); magazines aiming at *special* reader groups (women, men, children, teenagers), and the *pictorial* magazines (in which the text is quite irrelevant for understanding the material presented). This last group is probably less important in Norway than is generally assumed, with circulation figures far below that of most of the weekly press.

Entertainment material dominates in the family magazines. On the average, they contain about 50 per cent short stories, romantic novelettes, and other types of fiction (see Table XV). The more specialized magazines put less emphasis on entertainment, and, as far as the women's magazines are concerned, present a considerable amount of instructive material (practical advice, problem solution, etc.), while informative material is more frequently found in the predominantly male-oriented magazines.

The weekly magazines have become increasingly specialized. While the family magazines still compete for the same market, many new magazines especially aimed at children, young people, women, or men have appeared. The distribution of subject matter presented in the specifically women's magazines as opposed to the specifically men's magazines shows typical differences. The women's magazines emphasize matters connected with the family and home, such as fashions, handicrafts, home decoration, child raising, social subjects, religious subjects – although the latter to a lesser extent. As opposed to the *home-centricity* found in the women's magazines, men's magazines have concentrated on matters *external in relation to the home.*

The distribution of subject matter in these magazine types has expanded so as to emphasize further traditional views on sex roles in our society: the home-centred female role, and a male role tied to occupation and external activities. This tendency is far more pronounced today in all magazines studied than it was in 1939. More and more, the women's magazines have favoured subject matter thought to be 'more suitable' for women, while men's magazines have tended more toward subject matter expected to be preferred by an active, outgoing type of man.

3.2. Background and setting in magazine fiction

Even though informative subject matter has increased in the post-war years, fiction still dominates the weekly press. While generally avoiding literary analysis, the social sciences have been quite interested in studying the values, characters, and settings of these short stories and novelettes. It is frequently precisely the fictional content of the weekly magazines that is generally deprecated, yet in Norway there have been no systematic analyses in this field. The available material is indeed considerable, and from other countries we have many such cultural-anthropological studies, among the most original that of Martel and McCall (1964).

These analyses have often been oriented towards the values of characters presented in the story under study, while the general framework for the plot has been neglected. Usually we find fairly vague descriptions of the geographical setting (Johns, Heine and Gerth 1949). We can expect to find a tendency towards more diffuse occupational descriptions, so that fewer settings will be identifiable as specific occupations or professions. More specific descriptions of such backgrounds would require a degree of realism which, for various reasons, can hardly be expected in the fiction presented in weekly magazines. In one exploratory investigation (Torsvik 1965) no concrete hypotheses were formulated in this connection. The reasons for the rough assumption made, lie in the mutual expectations between reader and weekly press, concerning maximal possibilities for reader-identification, as well as the wish to offend as few groups as possible. Thus we find the

315

tendency to remove the action to anonymous urban settings and to concentrate on occupational backgrounds of a type found in any fairly industrialized society.

Also, there is an aspect on the production side: the weekly press in Norway is in fact dependent on regularly available syndicated material, written for translation and distributed on an international basis. For this material to be easily translatable and comprehended on a wide basis, background and setting must necessarily be as diffuse as possible, with respect both to locale and to occupational descriptions.

Investigation shows that most fictional material has an urban setting. The completely exotic background, with sheiks or Indian princes, has nearly disappeared. The need for 'foreign' and 'strange' but at the same time sufficiently realistic settings is met by using the post-war international bureaucracy as a framework.

The presentation of family and occupational settings shows large differences, both from magazine to magazine, and over time. The tendency in the women's magazines is the same as that in choice of theme: centricity about the home and family. Aside from men's magazines, which must be considered only very slightly family oriented in subject matter, the fiction in women's and family magazines has shown a drastic trend towards favouring family settings. In 1939, family and occupational settings were about equally represented in women's magazine fiction, while 66 per cent of the subject matter could not be defined along this dimension. In 1964 the share of family settings was double that of occupational settings, and the same trend applies to the family magazines.

Of course, it is possible that setting is not so important in post-war magazine fiction as it was in the fiction of the inter-war years. Then there were greater chances that an exotic setting would in itself be a sufficient framework for an otherwise banal story. Today it is difficult to find a setting sufficiently exotic while at the same time complying with a minimum degree of realism; the world has become much smaller indeed.

Roughly measured, the differences between magazines before and after World War II are so great that they cannot be ignored. Both the framework for fictional contributions and the presentation of values have approached a more representative popular average. The weekly magazines represent a type of popular culture far more universal today than 30 years ago, and the readership cuts across many otherwise important status lines in society. It is reasonable to look for an explanation here.

4. RADIO AND TELEVISION

People apparently accustom themselves to television with amazing rapidity. Despite all prognoses, in the course of six years television managed to reach the same proportion of the population which it took radio some 15 to 20 years to reach (see Figure 1). By the end of 1970, nine out of 10 Norwegian households had television. Radio did not achieve this coverage until about 1950, some 30 years after its introduction in Norway.

Most people were mentally prepared for the advent of television. In May 1953 more than one-half the population were planning to get a television set as soon as possible, while about one-fifth declared themselves in opposition (Gallup 1953). Thus, more than three-fourths of the population had already made up their minds about the desirability of television, despite the fact that at the time only 4 per cent actually had seen a telecast themselves. In the course of 1967 the introductory phase was completed: more than 60 per cent of Norway's households watched television more or less regularly. In 1961 and 1962 the sales of television sets were limited only by the expansion tempo and perhaps also the number of broadcast hours: with a total of only 20 broadcast hours weekly, each hour was rather expensive for the consumer. All the same, the number of licenses doubled yearly, with the most dramatic increase in northern Norway. In 1965 – the first year television broadcasts were available in these areas – television coverage increased from 0.8 to 10 per cent of all households in the districts; in 1966 the increase continued at the same rate. By the end of that year, more than one-fifth of all households in the northernmost districts had television, a level which eastern and central Norway took four years to reach.

Table XVI. *Television available, by population density in various types of commune (percentage)*

| Television avail-ability | Low density | | | Medium density | | | High density | | |
	Cities	Indus-trial	Agric., forestry	Agric., forestry, industr.	Fishing	Indus-trial	Agric., forestry	Fishing
Have in household	69	62	65	44	19	47	29	13
Can watch in others' home	20	28	24	31	22	31	29	28
Not available	11	9	10	24	60	21	38	54
Total	100	100	100	100	100	100	100	100
N =	302	170	299	258	124	178	191	100

Source: Torsvik 1966, Table 1.

Table XVII. *Television owners, by income, 1965 (percentage)*

Time of purchase	Less than 6.5	6.5-12.5	12.5-18.5	18.5-24.5	24.5-30.5	More than 30.5
			Income (in 1,000 N.kr.)			
Early (after the introduction of television)	11	15	22	35	41	46
Late	8	11	15	22	23	30
Non-owner	78	72	61	41	35	23
Total	100	100	100	100	100	100
N =	166	225	297	376	272	215

Source: Torsvik 1966, Table 2.

The spread of television was mainly a question tied to the expansion tempo on the technical side. First to be covered were the more densely populated areas in eastern Norway, as well as those of western and southern Norway; then followed the central and the northern areas. Within the individual areas, however, the spread has followed a definite pattern: last to be reached by television were the groups which in other respects are marginal: economically, politically, socially. As late as five to six years after the first inauguration program, television was still decidedly an urban phenomenon. Rural areas were far less saturated than cities and towns, as Table XVI (from 1960) shows.

In communes with low or medium population density the proportion of families with television was least in areas with a predominantly fishing population, *higher* where the typical occupation was agriculture or forestry, and *highest* in areas with some industry. The proportion increases with urbanization. In the largest towns and cities only 10 per cent of the population had *no access* to television, while between 50 and 60 per cent of the adult population in the most peripheral fishing districts were in this situation (see Torsvik 1966, 1967a).

Not only the geographically most distant sectors of the population are late in being reached by television; the same applies to those on the social and economic periphery. Income was decisive for whether or not an individual bought a television set at an early stage. Table XVII shows the distribution of early and late buyers of television sets, by income group. Nearly half the members of the highest income groups were among the first to purchase sets, as against only some 10 per cent of the lowest income groups. The proportion increases with increasing income, both for early and later purchasers.

This same holds true within all status and occupational categories: the proportion of early purchasers increases with higher income. This is, however, least true of the lower white-collar workers, who appear to be less 'income-sensitive' than other groups in their relations with television. They comprise the highest percentage of early purchasers in the lowest income groups – indeed, their share here is double that of any other members in this income category (see Torsvik 1967a, Table 3). It seems reasonable to assume that, in this group, factors other than income alone have been important in the decision of if and when to buy a television set, or that motivation has been so strong that low income has not presented much of a barrier.

Also, families with children have been subject to heavier pressure to buy a set than have childless families. Families with the greatest number of children were among the most eager purchasers. The dividing line here goes between families with 2-4 children and families with *more* or *fewer* children. Young couples with children under six years of age comprise the largest proportion of early purchasers here, while the smallest proportion was made up of elderly persons living alone, without children in the household: only 17 per cent of this latter group were early purchasers.

People watch television quite a lot. Of those who either owned television sets or had regular access to television in 1965, one-half watched at least one program daily; a further one-fifth watched television several times a week; the final one-third reported that they seldom or never watched television. The distribution was about the same for all status groups, although with a slight tendency for higher-status white-collar workers and independent businessmen to comprise the largest proportion of the occasional viewers – perhaps a result of having less time at home – while the more regular working hours of most white-collar workers would give the latter more opportunities of regularly watching television at home.

Few analyses have been made of program preferences. The Norwegian National Broadcasting System (NRK) undertakes one radio/television study regularly, and from viewing habits it appears that program preference for television follows the same, well-known pattern exhibited for radio. Most attention is concentrated on a few central program types, while children's programs, theatre performances, and religious programs are highly marginal. However, more than radio, television has a large audience for informative and political programs. The factor of *visualization* appears to be important in this connection, as the corresponding programs on the radio consistently have a smaller, more special audience. Measured in number of television programs viewed, the frequency increased with age, with teenagers being the most moderate group (see Table XVIII).

Both its adoption tempo and the exposure frequency indicate that television holds a greater attraction than does any other medium. It

Table XVIII. *Television viewing, by age*

Age	Average number of television programs per week
15-24	6.17
25-44	8.19
45-64	9.12
65 and above	10.90

Source: Norwegian Central Bureau of Statistics, 1967.

also seems to be able to retain its audience. With such a point of departure, it is naturally tempting to inquire into the social effects television might have. Our possibilities for answering this question, however, are limited, because, for one thing, television is a child of our own generation, and we do not yet know how this and future generations will utilize it.

In politics, however, television has already proved a success. During the 1965 election, in which the first full-fledged television campaign took place, the campaign reached many more voters than in any other preceding campaign we were able to study. Almost half the voters in 1957 had no contact whatever with the radio election campaign programs, while in 1965 radio/television reached 85 per cent of the voting public (see Table XIX). Much of this was due to television: more television viewers followed a larger number of programs, for a longer period of time, and stayed up later at night to watch election programs, than did radio listeners (see Torsvik 1967c, Valen and Torsvik 1967).

Thus, the political programs shown on television brought far more voters into direct contact with politics than previously. The television

Table XIX. *Following election programs in radio and TV,
1957 and 1965 (percentage)*

No. of programs listened to/watched	Radio 1957	Radio/TV 1965
Most election programs*	18.4	60.0
Few**	32.7	25.0
None	46.8	14.1
No answer	2.1	0.9
Total	100.0	100.0

Source: Valen and Torsvik 1967, Table 1.

* 1957: '3 or more programs'; 1965: 'one-half' or 'most of the programs'.
** 1957: '1-2 programs'; 1965: 'few programs'.

audience during the 1965 election campaign also included a great many of the more passive voters, who normally would not be especially interested in political programs. Thus, television has been perhaps one of the most important mobilization factors in elections since 1960. Since this was more obvious during the 1963 elections than during the 1967 general elections, perhaps the mobilization effect is greater in its introductory phase, as well as stronger in peripheral areas than in central ones. Information from the 1963 and 1965 elections indicates that this effect diminishes once television is well established in the locality (see Valen and Torsvik 1967).

Experiences from most other countries where television has become generally accepted show that radio has changed in character. Since both radio and television in Norway are, by law, under the direction of a state monopoly organization, it would be reasonable to expect a certain give-and-take policy between the two. The main debate about radio/television did not get started until years after the introduction of a full television network; and it is this recent debate that has brought out certain viewpoints on the relation between the two media. To quite an extent we find an adaptation policy as to programs, but more striking are the changes in listening/viewing habits. The Norwegian Gallup Institute found evidence of this in 1961: when asked about the use of portable radios in public places – on the beach, etc. – nearly half the sample replied that they found music and radio generally pleasant and acceptable in such situations, while only 25 per cent found it annoying. In addition to the obvious conclusion, these results also indicate a new type of radio listening, based on the new, inexpensive transistor radios easily transported anywhere. Today there are probably more than a half a million portable radios in Norway, a considerable number of them owned in addition to non-portable sets. People listen outdoors, on the highways, on the way to work. Today radio reaches more people than earlier, in more places, and at different hours of the day. This has probably changed listening preferences greatly: earlier, radio had its real audience in the evenings, at the 'top' broadcasting times, as well as early in the morning. The middle of the day was a dull time. Now, however, broadcasting hours are spread out over most of the day, and the public listens much more frequently than before.

Large groups of listeners wish to hear music: the demand for music programs seems insatiable. Back in 1948, when radio in Norway had not yet reached the heights of popularity attained in the 1950s, Danish and Swedish radio stations found large audiences in Norway. In the course of one week, three-fourths of the Norwegian radio audience tuned in on Swedish or Danish stations, more than 80 per cent of them to music programs (Gallup 1948). For those who consider radio's prime purpose to be didactic, we have even more frustrating figures: in 1950, only 14 per cent of a sample of the adult Norwegian population wished to have more lecture, historical, or generally informative programs (Gallup 1950).

Radio reached its peak of popularity in the 1950s. That was the era of the big entertainment programs, the Saturday shows that emptied the streets and the cinemas. These shows were replaced by television after 1960, and radio has only partly re-found its own form.

Radio and television will become the dominant media in the average family's time in the years to come. This family will certainly enjoy both radio and television. In view of developments in other countries, it may be tempting to concentrate on presenting more light music programs, which are undemanding. However, there exists an equally manifest need for news interest and reporting programs. In the beginning of the 1950s, listener figures for such programs were as high as 80 to 90 per cent, nor have they dropped appreciably in the competition with television. These are the programs that draw the big radio audiences, although not for great periods at a time. Other programs attract a varying audience, depending on program type and hour of transmission.

The enormous expansion in radio/television will necessarily make great demands on the program service and programs offered. And this alone makes it as yet impossible to state that these media have found their 'form'. The most drastic changes are yet to come: when the national radio monopolies are once seriously threatened, when satellite transmissions cut across all national boundaries, and the video-cassette has invaded the home. Then the question will be whether the national monopolies can continue to be exclusive and whether they can afford it. Such developments will change all existing arguments for or against advertising, for or against program types.

And yet, perhaps the greatest change lies in that radio, television, and the daily press are now on the way to becoming only partly non-private and state controlled: the radio and television monopolies of today are threatened by private stations with commercial backing, while the press is trying to maintain its individuality and wide scope by becoming more dependent on state support.

NOTES

[1] In Norway, as elsewhere in Scandinavia, the right to broadcast is a state monopoly. Set owners are charged an annual fee for the right to keep sets.

[2] According to survey data (1969), 64 per cent of families have one radio only, 26 per cent have two, and 8 per cent have three or more radios.

[3] For a discussion of this problem, see Rokkan and Torsvik (1960) and Rokkan (1970, Chapters 13, 14).

[4] To the question: 'How many newspapers are regularly available in your household', 4 per cent answered 'no papers', 47 per cent said 'one paper' and 43 per cent gave answers to the affect that two or more newspapers were regularly brought home. No answer was obtained from 7 per cent.

[5] Family and women's magazines in Norway appear once a week.

[6] In a survey from 1965, left-wing radicals scored significantly higher exposure rates to the election campaign in television and radio: every second voter to Socialist People's Party (SF) watched 'most of the program' (Torsvik, 1967b).

[7] For further discussion, see Rokkan 1970, Chapter 13, Westerståhl and Jansson 1958.

[8] Norwegian magazines run between 100,000 and 300,000 in circulation.

X. Leisure and Recreation

By Odd Ramsøy

1. INTRODUCTION

Sociological descriptions, such as this volume, traditionally deal with ultimate and serious matters, with the very structure of society. But Norway in a social sense does not consist of only purposeful or instrumental institutions. Play, fun, relaxation, and recreation are also vital elements in everyday life – at least they should be, according to central Norwegian values. In our spare time we express what we are; we and our children get much real identity from leisure – perhaps even mainly through informal contact and company with our fellow beings.

Let us take the following quotation from Huizinga's *Homo Ludens* as our point of departure:

> A certain play factor has been extremely active throughout the cultural process and is the basis of many fundamental aspects of social life. Playful competition as a social impulse is older than culture itself and is imbued in all life as a kind of fermenting agent. Rites grew from sacred play; poetry was born in play and grew through play. We must conclude, therefore, that civilization is played in its earliest phases. Civilization does not *come from* play, like a baby liberated from the womb of its mother; civilization rises by and as play, and the two never separate. How far then does this play factor go into subsequent cultural epochs? We must ask how much of the playful attitude is still present in our day and our world (Huizinga 1955, p. 173).

Huizinga arrived at the depressing conclusion that the play factor unfortunately has become steadily weaker in our civilization since the eighteenth century. (The book was written shortly before the outbreak of World War II.) Even if Huizinga was right in his conclusion, we have little reason to share his regret; we have to face the realities in the present world rather than be depressed by the fact that the play element, the play idea, reached a zenith with the Rococo. How far does the play element go in our society?

We reflect Huizinga's notions when we see the complex of activities and norms around play, relaxation, leisure, and recreation as an important theme within the Norwegian social structure. Why do we play, and what are the results of play? When and how do we play? Who plays what?

We can discuss only some of the points here. First, we will give meaning to the play element by placing it in its relation to other institutions and in relation to a concept of leisure. Next we shall see how much leisure we have and what we use it for. Finally, we shall consider two areas where play and leisure coincide, namely sports and art.

2. LEISURE AND RECREATION AS AN INSTITUTION

We will presume that society's inner structure is differentiated according to problem areas. To high but varying degrees these problem areas are matters of public concern. Who shall have power, and how is the exercise of power to be regulated? What is to be produced, and how is distribution to be organized? How are new citizens to be related to past generations, and how are they to be trained to constitute a society in the future?

Some problem areas in society constitute a private sphere, excluding official society. These problem areas vary from society to society, with time, and, within a society, according to person and position. It is relative to such limits that the free, impulsive, and seeking individual must establish himself in his environment. Family life to some extent falls within such limits; in a sense, this is true for religion as well. But the leisure institution is the specialized structure for the private sphere.

This leisure institution consists of the standardized arrangements that provide people with leisure and alternatives for its use. The fact that questions connected with 'the leisure problem' and 'the leisure society' have become recurrent subjects for public debate is in itself sufficient reason for discussing leisure. From our point of view, this gives an empirical basis for considering leisure as a relatively central issue in a sociological survey. We have also indicated a theoretical basis: the leisure institution is the part of human life where the individual is in principle left to himself, to make his own decisions spontaneously with no further purpose than immediate or short-term satisfaction. Leisure is society's vacation from society – and society must provide this vacation.

This is an idealized concept of leisure. Its actual use may be so different as to belie the concept. This, however, will be an empirical rather than a theoretical problem: the main value with regard to the use of leisure in Norwegian society is that it is ultimately to be used according to the desires of the individual and in spontaneous and creative activities. If reality is different, we shall have to add a new entry to the list of discrepancies between the ideal and the real.

In principle, we have equated leisure with the spontaneous and impulsive, with the irresponsible. In reality, spontaneity and leisure may fall into almost completely separate categories. For details we can only refer to further empirical investigations. To what extent can we be directly and spontaneously engaged in work? And, to what extent are Norwegians in different social positions involuntarily restricted in using their leisure? The first question is vital in discussions about alienation, but we shall not go into it here. Some indications about commitment to work are presented later, however. The second question, which concerns actual and subjectively experienced choices in the use of leisure, deserves further research. The problem concerns the borderline between leisure and work. Work-related obligations invade leisure at many levels (social relations between colleagues is one example); but work relations may also enrich leisure (social intercourse with work companions after working hours is an example, or a re-formulation of the example above). It should also be mentioned that work may be used as a pretext or refuge from leisure and private life.

Leisure is, more than other institutional settings, a private sphere. Yet, as we shall see, it is true that Norwegian society is officially and actively involved in the use of leisure.

The extent of leisure is not standardized. On the one hand, an important pattern in our society is that employees average a forty-hour week, have a number of public holidays, and four weeks' annual vacation. If we think ahead with more or less utopian ideas, we may anticipate that leisure problems will increase dramatically when the work day is even further reduced to, say, only two or three hours. But on the other hand, we must remember that a sharp distinction between work and leisure can apply only to a minority of the population. A sharp distinction in this respect is applicable to employees, but not to children and old people, or to housewives, fishermen, farmers, and others engaged in independent activity, nor to intellectuals or to artists or persons with two jobs. Some have only leisure; others work almost all of their waking hours; for still others any distinction between work and leisure is meaningless.

Nevertheless, we shall examine leisure in relation to work, presuming that work is profitable and for this reason necessary from the point of view of the individual. In this context, leisure can have many meanings. We shall mention five:

1) For those who are constantly or at times engaged in fully consuming activity, leisure means brief periods that allow just enough relaxation before one is again fully absorbed in work. This is the heroic cultural ideal, represented by the productive artist.

2) For those who want to enjoy a free life, work consists of those brief periods when one is forced to subject oneself to a job in order to provide the necessary subsistence; leisure is the main content in life, long and non-obligating. This is the hedonistic cultural ideal, represented by the vagrant.[1]

3) An idealized standard solution to the work/leisure complex in an affluent society is a short and undemanding work day, with corresponding leisure time and a standardized long vacation – leisure to be spent on worthy activities, possibly organized by public agencies or voluntary organizations as cultural activity in company with others. This is the ideal of the welfare state.

4) The preceding type of leisure and work can be interpreted as long and empty leisure in combination with an undemanding work day; neither work nor leisure has any attraction; this is a travesty of the welfare state.

5) 'Forced leisure' is not uncommon even in the affluent society. Smaller or larger numbers are underemployed or unemployed. Leisure can give meaning to a life without meaningful work; to a person who is unemployed or under-employed, the leisure problem is one of finding more work.

The ideology of the welfare state would assume that society's norm system tends to move as many as possible of its members from groups 5 and 4 into group 3, and that 'positive' and 'negative' deviants, of whom there will be few, belong to groups 1 and 2 respectively.

Does this classification correspond to common-sense concepts of work and leisure? How many belong to the various categories? At the present time these questions cannot be answered.

3. LEISURE: EXTENT AND USE

3.1. *Unemployment*

Enforced leisure in the form of unemployment is uncommon in central parts of Norwegian society. The contrast to conditions in the 1930s is sharp, and important in the present society. While in 1938 unemployment among organized labour was up to some 22 per cent, in the 1960s it averaged some 3 per cent, with seasonal variations from some 2 to 5 per cent (NOS XII 195, p. 50).

In proportion to total employment, the number of completely unemployed registered at employment offices was 3 per cent at the end of 1962 (NOS9 XII 195, pp. 47, 50). Official statistics indicate that Norway is in a favourable position in this respect when compared with other nations.

3.2. Variations in the extent of leisure

With a few important exceptions, the average work day for the *employed* in Norway is eight hours with four weeks' annual vacation and a fixed number of public holidays. It is common belief in Norway that the country has a larger number of public holidays with no work than any other country. Information provided by ILO, however, proves this belief to be wrong. With 10 public holidays per year in addition to the standard vacation, Norway has a larger number of holidays than Great Britain, the Netherlands, and Switzerland, but a few less than Sweden, Denmark, Finland, France, and Austria. In total sum, however, Norwegian industrial workers in 1962 had a shorter annual work period than workers in any other country in Western Europe apart from Sweden. Cf. *Innstilling om gjennomføringen av 4 ukers ferien m. v. fra Ferielovutvalget av 1963* (Report from the National Vacation Committee of 1963 on the implementation of the 4 weeks vacation etc., Oslo, 1964, p. 4). This leaves a daily leisure of approximately eight hours. But there are some who must spend up to three hours every day on travel to and from their job. Much of the remaining leisure time is spent in various kinds of job qualifications, on activities that may border on or move into the area of hobby activities, general education or courses of an entertainment type. There is also reason to believe that among young white-collar workers, particularly among those living in larger cities, career-oriented use of leisure is a pressure element and a dominant feature of life. Furthermore, many people hold more than one job.

Let us begin, however, with information on working hours in agriculture. Data from 1915 and 1956 indicate an average work day in agriculture of ten hours in the summer and eight and a half hours in the winter with rest periods subtracted; there is no indication of a reduced work day in this forty-year period (NOS XI 330, p. 42).

In 1965 white-collar workers in private industry had a work week of about 37–40 hours. Some 74 per cent of stock-room foremen and sales staff had an average work week of 45 hours. In retailing, the work week in 1966 varied from 45 down to 35 hours. In banks and insurance companies the figure was under 40 hours. Of workers in industry, 87 per cent averaged a normal work week of 45 hours (see *Foreløpig innstilling fra arbeidstidskomitéen av 1964*, pp. 10–12).

Figures for workers in industry and mining for 1965 show a normal work week of 45 hours. However, in reality the actual figures for a full week – i.e. one without vacation or moveable holidays – came to 42.4 hours for men and 37.8 hours for women; for a calendar week (i.e. an average week where vacation and public holidays are taken into account) the figures were 38.1 for men and 33.9 for women (NOS

328

XII 218, p. 47). By law, the normal work week was reduced from 45 to 42.5 hours in 1968.

The pervading feature of these figures, and in Norwegian society in general, is the distinction between blue- and white-collar workers. Workers generally have longer working hours and proportionally less leisure; it is also possible that they have longer travel time to and from work. It appears reasonable to view the longer, fixed working hours as a heritage from the old society, where white-collar workers had a series of privileges (salary, uniform or work attire, prestige, power).

Overtime does not seriously cut into leisure except for a few categories, such as secretaries in government service. According to a Gallup poll, 35 per cent (presumably of all employed persons) have the opportunity to work overtime and three-fourths of them make use of this opportunity. It is more usual for workers (82 per cent) to take overtime than for white-collar workers (52 per cent). Of those who did not take advantage of their opportunity to work overtime, 57 per cent of the women and 38 per cent of the men indicated that time pressure of various kinds prevented them from taking on extra work; 19 per cent of the women and 24 per cent of the men mentioned the heavy tax burden on extra income (Gallup 18 April 1959).

It would be interesting to know how much of official working time is spent at actual work, and how the remaining part of this time is spent. Time off during working hours spans from idling due to the nature of the job and its integration in a joint task (for example, the role of the kettle drummer in a symphony orchestra), through higher or more pressing obligations (illness, summons for service as a jury member), to protest or withdrawal (sit-down strike, go-slow-tactics, shirking responsibilities, feigned illness). It is probably true that the different categories of employees have varying amounts of leisure time within their working hours; as already stated, the distribution of actual work activities within normal working hours is in need of sociological inquiry.

The main conclusion from the above data is that in Norway there is a regulated work week of approximately 40 hours and that working time has been noticeably reduced within recent memory. We can subscribe to a British comment: while a hundred years ago the average life span was 40 years and the work week was around 70 hours, today the average life span is 70 years and the work week around 40 hours (Cohen 1963).

Gallup data indicate that present working hours constitute an accepted compromise between the desire for leisure and the wish for higher income through longer working hours. Gallup poll, 9 September 1950: 64 per cent prefer a small salary increase within existing

329

working hours while 21 per cent prefer proportional reduction of the working hours. Of these 21 per cent, 30 per cent would prefer reduced working hours even with a reduction in salary. Gallup poll, 27 October 1962: 57 per cent prefer higher salary while 29 per cent prefer reduced working hours in a choice between higher salary and a cut in working time.

Gallup polls also give some indication of general but varying satisfaction with work. 'Do you get satisfaction from the work that is now your source of income?' was answered in the affirmative by 86 per cent; 77 per cent also replied that they would not prefer another job. Job satisfaction, as measured by replies to the second question compared to replies to the first question, shows a falling tendency for four categories: housewives (15 per cent would prefer different work), independents (19 per cent), white-collar workers (25 per cent), and workers (36 per cent) (Gallup 1955).

We should not overestimate the extent to which the leisure society has in fact arrived. Only 12 per cent of farm wives had as much as one week of summer vacation in 1957 (NOS XII 107, p. 82). Various Gallup polls in the 1949–1962 period give us reason to conclude that approximately a third of the population have a summer vacation in the sense that they go away from their homes. Some details from 1952: 42 per cent do not take any summer vacation (23 per cent in towns, 55 per cent in rural areas). Of those who do take a vacation, 66 per cent were going away from their place of residence. Half of those on vacation were only relaxing; 11 per cent worked with their hobbies; the remainder either performed their normal work or other work that had been neglected.

3.3. Use of leisure

Sufficient material is not available to give a reasonably comprehensive and accurate picture of the use of leisure and of extra work interests in Norway. An initial rough survey was made by Egil Nilsen in his *Interesser hos voksne* (1958). Another beginning was made with Jan Brøgger's *Om gjengstruktur i et ungdomsmiljø (1963)*, which gives meaningful insight into a leisure milieu unknown to most of us.

Nilsen's work represents an effort to map leisure time interests among adults, particularly with regard to interests relevant to educational activity. Nilsen himself points out that his survey, which was based on mailed questionnaires, suffers from methodological weaknesses, such as a low percentage of returned forms. Nevertheless, it indicates the approximate role of various leisure time interests. A general overview is given in Table I, which also includes data collected in a Gallup poll.

Uses of leisure time	1958* Nilsen	1956** Gallup
Reading (column 2: reading books)		
Listening to the radio	66	
Hiking	54	
Company with friends	41	
Going to the movies	36	29
Going to church	25	
Going to the theatre	25	6
Hearing lectures	23	
Watching sports events	21	26
Religious meetings	19	
Hobby activities	18	38
Dancing	18	
Clubs, societies, associations	16	27
Concerts	14	4
Participating in sports	14	8
Bridge, chess, etc.	13	
Taking courses	10	
Participating in study groups	5	
No answer	3	
Visiting others		78
Having guests		52
Religious services and meetings		23
	2642	ca. 2100

* Nilsen 1958: 'How do you prefer to spend your leisure? Alternative answers were checked by persons filling in the form on their own.

** Gallup poll 19 October 1965: 'Do you participate in the following activities or events outside your working hours as often as 12 times a year, that is, as often as once each month?' Alternative choices of answers were provided. (Some of the answers are not included above.)

The two columns are probably equally correct in their answers. Differences both in the selection of the sample itself and in the circumstances of the data collection were so great that a high degree of correspondence in the distribution of answers could not be expected. Nilsen's questions generally concerned ideals or preferences, while the Gallup poll, at least in form, put strict demands on actual participation in the various forms of activity. This is probably the reason why such 'elevated' activities as going to the theatre, and listening to lectures and concerts show higher figures in the Nilsen data. As Nilsen points out on the basis of his data, Norwegians appear to be great readers and radio listeners. If we include the third activity mentioned by more than half of the interviewed persons (hiking), we have a trio of the most frequently mentioned types of leisure time activities, all of which allow complete withdrawal by the individual from contact with others. The Gallup poll, on the other hand, shows high figures for gregarious activity (social intercourse). Apart from these facts, I can see no unique features in the results of the polls apart from the facts that about a quarter of the subjects indicate religious interests and that clearly obligating and purposeful activities such as taking courses and participating in study groups are less frequent than all other activities. Obviously, however, even these low percentages involve a sizeable number of people.

Gallup also has data from Sweden – showing the same general distribution. Gallup finds these differences in degree of participation: men are more active than women, town people more active than rural residents, high income groups more active than low income groups, and young people more active than the elderly. And in all four comparisons the less active group is more active than its counterpart in one respect: religious matters. Women, furthermore, participate more than men in gregarious activities.

Nilsen found that 88 per cent read newspapers regularly; 56 per cent read weekly magazines (illustrated weeklies), and 17 per cent read one or more books. With regard to the reading of books, Nilsen's survey showed similar results to those found in Einar Ness's survey of reading habits in a small town (Ness 1953). Nilsen has estimated that 40 per cent of those who read books 'within the year' had read at least ten books in six months.

The data coincide in general with the results from a Gallup survey taken earlier the same year: 37 per cent stated that they had not read any book within the year and approximately a third of those who read books had read at least ten books (Gallup 1958). Within the year, however, is probably a somewhat indefinite period for those interviewed.

Nilsen found that 56 per cent are members of one or more associations; 28 per cent are not members of any clubs or associations; 17 per cent did not answer the question. For the whole adult population Nilsen estimates that 1.15 million members hold more than 2.3 million memberships; on the average, each member is a member of two associations. The distribution among some of the most frequently mentioned associations is as follows: trade unions and professional associations 15 per cent, sports clubs 14 per cent, religious groups 10 per cent, music and choral societies 5 per cent, and political associations 4 per cent.

Further data on the use of leisure are provided by Gallup. Approximately one-third of the population (38 per cent) state that they have been to the movies within the last month (16 December 1950); 21 per cent are very fond of music (43 per cent 'a little'); 27 per cent say that they play an instrument, 10 per cent that they participate in a choir or orchestra (7 October, 1950). The availability of and interest in con-

Table II. *Availability of concerts and theatre performances (percentage)*

	Concerts	Theatre performances
Regularly at the place of residence or close enough	35	34
Reasonably regular attendance (where available)	22	38
Where not available: Would attend with reasonable regularity if available at place of residence or close enough to be easily available	56	60

Source: Gallup poll 18 December 1948.

certs and theatre performances are indicated by the somewhat out-dated information in Table II.

According to this information, approximately one-third of the population (in 1948) had reasonable access (in geographical terms) to concerts and theatre performances. This situation has been changed considerably through the introduction of *Riksteateret* (National Touring Theatre), and television has come in addition. Of those who have access, some 20 per cent attend concerts and some 40 per cent say that they attend theatre performances. It is remarkable that the percentage of those who would attend if they had the opportunity is so much higher, almost 60 per cent in both cases. Prestige considerations certainly affect these figures. We should also remember that resistance on the basis of religious considerations applies to those who do not attend such performances and who would not attend if they had the opportunity.

With respect to theatre interest among students, Arvid Brastad has found that almost one third of the students at the University of Bergen did not see a theatre performance during a three-year period; one-third saw only one play per semester (*Dagbladet,* 18 October 1965). Women attend theatre performances twice as frequently as men do. Reasons for not going to the theatre usually included the cumbersome preparations in connection with seeing a play, and, in part, the high cost. Reasons for going to the theatre concentrate on the entertainment aspect, relaxation, and pleasant entertainment, while students give more grandiloquent views on the mission and purpose of the legitimate stage. Whereas they themselves go to find entertainment (the few times they do go), they feel the theatre should enlighten, instruct, and develop the audience.

Some of our leisure is occupied for specific purposes. Sociologically, Christmas is dedicated to the family; the Easter holidays to skiing in the mountains,[2] 17 May (Constitution Day) to society – each with varying degrees of religious attachment.

Our leisure is expanding. More important, our leisure habits are

Table III. *Registered automobiles (private) and television licences at the end of the year (in thousands)*

	1961	1962	1963	1964	1965
Automobiles	269	315	357	408	458
Television licences	107	204	292	407	490

Source: NOS XII 195, pp. 164, 177.

being gradually changed by technology and increasing prosperity. Overall, the change will be slow, yet we may be justified in talking about a 'leisure revolution', consisting in part of the new meaning of leisure to the common man, and in part of the new economic and social meanings of consumption patterns. These new patterns can be summed up as a tremendous private investment in permanent consumer goods for leisure use. This investment is indicated in Table III.

The list of such investment objects is long and includes motor boats camping trailers, camping areas, cabins and summer homes, phonograph records, hobby equipment (power tools, fishing tackle, swimming equipment). Leisure equipment in the traditional luxury class hardly shows a similar growth tendency. We can probably say that in economic terms the leisure explosion has been marked by the following trends: 1) an explosive growth in new types of equipment (television, camping trailers), 2) differentiation in traditional equipment and a high degree of specialization (special ski types for cross-country skiing, 'television soccer balls', and other specialized sports equipment; outboard motors, speedboats and sailing dinghies; art reproductions; pocket books), and relatively little change with respect to traditional luxury items (original paintings, larger sailing boats).

A large proportion of what is consumed by leisure activities is marked by escape and dream. In this category we may include alcoholic beverages, tobacco, cosmetics, sleeping pills and other medicines, and legalized gambling. Some figures indicate high consumption levels. Legalized gambling includes *Det Norske Pengelotteri* (a state lottery), with 1967 sales at N. kr. 149 million, *Norsk Tipping A/S* (higher sales and more widespread), and totalizator betting at horse races at kr. 100 million in 1967. Consumption of purchased alcoholic beverages was more than kr. 1,400 million in 1966 (NOS XII 218, p. 271). In addition, illegally distilled liquor is consumed and sometimes sold. Sverre Brun-Gulbrandsen has conservatively estimated that in 1962 some 15 per cent of the total liquor consumed was illegally distilled and that there has been a considerable increase in illegal liquor since 1956 (Brun-Gulbrandsen 1967, p. 99). Tobacco and alcohol consumption was around kr. 2,500 million in 1966. Combined alcohol and tobacco consumption and gambling add up to a total public sale of more than N.kr. 3,000 million, or approximately 10 per cent of total private consumption. Other leisure-oriented consumption in 1966 came to about 6 or 7 per cent of total private consumption (NOS XII 218, p. 54).

The above features of the use of leisure in Norway give only some indications. The predominant use of leisure in all societies is for sleep (cf. Aubert and White 1959). However, even though we have emphasized the large portion of leisure activity which may give rise to isolation, leisure may also be the framework in institutions that bind us together – suffice it to mention a vital spectrum from flirting, through game and play structures, to voluntary organizations.

Voluntary organizations apparently occupy the leisure of many by providing recreation-oriented activities. *Norges Idrettsforbund* (Norwegian Sports Union) is one of our major organizations. Other voluntary organizations are more strongly oriented towards a specific purpose, the purpose, however, marking members in varying degrees. Large organizations of this type are the political parties, Red Cross, *Norske Kvinners Sanitetsforening* (Norwegian Women's Health Association), and *Norges Kooperative Landsforening* (The Norwegian Co-operative Society). These and other organizations are engaged in idealistic, religious, and political activities of sometimes decisive importance for Norwegian society; even though such organizations have professional staffs, they also involve considerable leisure activity. Often, of course, established purposes may serve as camouflage for gregarious functions. Although religious interests may be strong in the coastal areas in southern and western Norway, it is difficult to understand that the established religious and missionary purposes require the existence of some 12,000 missionary societies in these areas (cf. Øidne 1957).

In addition to purposeful and gregarious functions, voluntary organizations also serve to unite persons who would otherwise be distant, and to unite a few who already are and want to stay distant from others. Typically, sports clubs unite persons from many professions and span a wide range of the social structure. We may say that voluntary organizations typically serve to integrate across class lines, but segregate by sex. This integrating mechanism, however, should not be overemphasized. Both sports and sports clubs are to some extent class oriented; the professional status of wrestlers, cyclists, and ice skaters is markedly lower than that of mountain climbers, tennis players, golfers, and equestrians. Generally speaking, we may expect common sports (thus we exclude wrestling, golf, and swimming and include such sports as cross-country orientation, hand-ball, and marksmanship) and the few, regionally unattached clubs to have a particularly democratic composition and atmosphere.

We have also mentioned that some clubs may isolate a few who are distant from others. To mention golf again, at least its physical and economic basis must necessarily reflect a class distinction. (The cost of playing golf for one season in Oslo is approximately N.kr. 1,000.) Even more evident is the open (or unconscious) desire for isolation in some idealistic societies. Extremist religious sects are one example, antivivisectionists' and taxpayers' societies possibly others.

Some mention should also be made of international tourism. Norwegians consider their country to be an outstanding tourist attraction. However, not until 1962 was the cost of Norwegians' travelling abroad outweighed by the income from foreign tourists in Norway. In an international perspective, Norway's role as a tourist country is negligible. In 1966 only Turkey of sixteen European countries had a lower income from tourism than Norway (*Landslaget for reiselivet i Norge 1967*, p. 6).

Finally, there are some local surveys on the use of leisure. As a curiosity we may mention that the classical French sociologist Frederic Le Play visited the cobalt dye works at Modum in 1845 and wrote a description of a worker's family in his major work on labour conditions in Europe (Le Play 1877). In this first sociological field study in Norway, main emphasis was put on the description of a single family, particularly its economic conditions, but we also learn that the main recreation for workers was small game hunting and salmon fishing. These activities were 'completely free to all and provide welcome variation from ordinary work and provide an important addition to the food supply' (p. 61). Recreation for women and children consisted of picking berries. Furthermore Home Guard practice provided opportunity for well-planned recreation. After the ordinary military exercises the personnel indulged in marksmanship contests. Le Play concludes: 'In general, activities among worthy Norwegians are on a higher level than among average persons elsewhere in Europe. However, if one can judge from isolated instances it is probable that enjoyment of alcohol, particularly distilled liquor, is a favourite distraction for many workers and even for independent farmers' (p. 62).

Fredrik Barth found that the use of leisure in a mountain valley in the 1940s and 1950s was a non-specialized part of an integrated pattern of life (Barth 1952). There were four women's societies. A sports club faded out, apparently because group sports did not fit into the social pattern. Informal groups were composed through friendship patterns that were constantly changing and seldom included more than two persons or two couples. The basis was joint conflict with others. But these activities were quite unimportant. The single, isolated farm, with its man–wife and parents–children pattern, was the central grouping. The only specialized leisure institution was a biweekly dance in the assembly hall; this was generally the only social recreation for the men. Drinking was heavy and the dance went on throughout the night. Fighting was not common because those who had quarrels with others stayed away.

Jan Brøgger's survey of gang structure in a juvenile milieu gives a more dramatic picture (Brøgger 1963). Here, a specialized clientele is involved – big city, east end, 15- to 17-year-old boys with taboos against girls, and in one gang, crimes, drinking, and fighting. In part, one gets the impression that a gang marked by violence and crime is distinguished by a relatively independent inner structure and culture. Thus it was the opinion of the boys that 'the gang came into existence because of an instinct'; one of the members felt that he was driven to the meeting place by 'an invisible force' (p. 159). A compensating culture in a socially poor milieu is probably involved. A remarkable feature of this article is that it emphasizes so strongly the challenge involved in attempting to understand processes barely noticeable in informal company. In this milieu there has developed 'a certain social atmosphere, a way of addressing each other and of behaviour that is very hard to perceive and describe. This social atmosphere was not only reflected in the manner of speaking; but also in the subject chosen and, above all, in physical posture and expression. It is hard to say how these phenomena can best be described and analysed. But frequently it was quite obvious that something was communicated between gang members even when not a word was spoken. In such situations the atmosphere could be quite distinct – sometimes completely relaxed and sometimes tense and irritable' (pp. 156–157).

4. PUBLIC INVOLVEMENT IN LEISURE ACTIVITIES

Only in a limited sense can leisure involve the single individual, who may be regarded as being alternately engaged in work and relaxation or creative leisure activities. As we have seen, much leisure may be spent on reading, listening to the radio, watching television, hiking, hunting, fishing, and various other forms of individual activity. Reading, for instance, in itself implies complete, yet only partial withdrawal from others. But even in such activities, the individual is not alone. In a sense, the culture of which the individual is a part does provide him with a framework for leisure activities. To go hiking is not only an accidental or deliberate choice that may prove to the individual that he stands alone; hiking is also a solid, though vague and ambiguous symbol element in Norwegian culture.

In other leisure activities the individual will be more directly involved with others. In most forms of play, game, and sports, the individual is directly dependent upon others. This is why we have team sports. In a modern society, providing ample opportunities for leisure activity is a social matter and of public concern. Generally speaking, this must be so; neither the citizens in a society nor its leaders can regard the dissemination, growth, and development of that society's culture as a private matter. Schools, museums, and churches are elements of society that we regard as an obviously collective responsibility. Public commitment to the support of leisure, however, is not limited to these traditional areas. A main feature of this public role appears to consist in the quite meagre subsidizing of producers and organizations in high culture (opera, theatre, music). Furthermore, the state honours individuals by giving stipends (artists salaries, grants). Another feature can be seen in the encouragement of constructive leisure activities (in balance between the mental and the physical: study groups, courses, hobby activities, sports, and recreation through support of voluntary organizations). Subsistence is provided to high culture and leisure activities and offered through voluntary organizations. This public role in general is not controversial; it will increase because requirements will increase, because our resources will grow, and, possibly, because our value norms governing the allocation of resources may be altered in the direction of a more active and expansive policy in these matters. The public role in this area is more frequently and more significantly criticized for being too passive and thrifty than for being too active and extravagant. The Norwegian Culture Fund *(Norsk Kulturfond)* is a pioneer in this field, distributing N. kr. 15 million annually.

The following overview indicates the broad public role in leisure activities in Norwegian society. It is largely based on Scholer (1960).

The Ministry of Church and Education has in its Cultural Section an Office for Science (dealing with scientific museums and collections), a National Library Inspection (for school, public, and travelling libraries), and an Office for Art and Cultural Activities, which in co-operation with the Joint Committee on Amateur Theatres, and the National Committee of the Association of People's Academies, works on study groups, lectures, evening courses, and gives financial support to theatres, films, music, and other art purposes, i.e. *Riksteateret* (the National Travelling Theatre), *Statens Filmsentral* (The National Film Archive), *Norsk Film A/S* (a film producing company) and *Norsk Bygdekino* A/S (a travelling film theatre), and finally, a National Youth and Sports Office, which in co-operation with the National Sports Council, the National Youth Council, and the National Outdoors Council, works with sports arenas, community centres, school sports, municipal sports, and youth committees, and with the organization Youth Work Activities.

338

In the period 1950–1958 a total of N.kr. 8.5 million were spent in support of the construction of 178 community centres. In 1958 alone 800 applications for support to community centres were dealt with. Community centre projects, however, may be opposed by religious groups: thus, by 1 January, 1959, the two counties of Rogaland and East Agder had only two community centres each, and the county of West Agder had none (as compared with 178 community centres in all of the country's 20 counties).

As an indication of the variety in public subsidy of leisure activities, one might mention activities and organizations receiving financial support for youth activities through the Youth Secion of the National Youth and Sports Office and the National Youth Council in 1951–1959. More than N. kr. 1 million were distributed for some 60 activities, ranging from temperance work through song and folk dance groups, competitions organized by the Youth Groups of the Norwegian Horticultural Association, to hatcheries of the Hunters' and Sports Fishermen's organizations. A variety of religious and political organizations were also given financial support (Scholer p. 265).

In addition to the role played by the Ministry of Church and Education, the Ministry of Municipal Affairs is concerned with leisure activities through the National Outdoors Council and the National Vacations Fund. In 1958 the National Vacations Fund distributed more than N.kr. 1.7 million to tourist and ski associations for construction and maintenance of cabins and lodges, to youth hostels and vacation homes, to vacations for the old and disabled, for other purposes (involving some 130 organizations), and finally to vacations for housewives (Scholer, pp. 295–303). More specialized and leisure-oriented services are performed by the Ministry of Family and Consumer Affairs through the Committee on Housewives' Vacations, to a very considerable extent by the Ministry of Defence through the Armed Forces Welfare Service, and, finally, by the Ministry of Commerce and Shipping through the Government Welfare Service for Merchant Seamen – the world's largest rental service for 16 mm films which also arranges the world's largest soccer series (Scholer p. 215).

This survey shows that the government's role in leisure activities and in cultural dissemination is comprehensive and important (even though the survey does not include municipal services such as the Oslo Municipal Youth Committee, which is primarily directed towards unorganized youth), and that government subsidy to leisure activities is probably vital to the great number of voluntary organizations actively supported through their own efforts. Public support presupposes considerable voluntary efforts on the part of the organizations. The government leans heavily on representative councils in the organization of leisure and cultural services, such as the Joint Committee on Study Groups, the National Youth Council, the National Council of Artists, the Welfare Council for Merchant Seamen. (A survey of the relationship between public and voluntary efforts in leisure-oriented cultural services is available in *Innstilling om organisering av og støtte til det frivillige opplysnings- og kulturarbeid* (Report on the organization and support of voluntary information and cultural services), Ministry of Church and Education, 1960.)

Even if the public role, as indicated above, in what may be generally labelled leisure activities is primarily one of providing public funds for worthy purposes, we may also at times observe a more dramatic role of a new kind. In part these new developments consist in establishing new patterns for economic support (for example *Norsk Tipping A/S*, the soccer betting pool, whose net earnings are distributed to scientific research and to athletics, and the Norwegian Culture Fund, providing financial support to a variety of legitimate cultural purposes), and in part they consist in preserving the possibilities for future leisure activities by restricting the general expansion of society (e.g. the Sea Shore Act, which restricts new construction along the sea shore.

5. SPECIAL SUBJECTS

Two special subjects, sports and arts, have been only cursorily dealt with above and are in need of more detailed discussion.

Further discussion of sports is necessary because this is a common and important activity that, both to the active participator and to the spectator, is generally a leisure time activity. Art and interest in art should be further discussed because they are considered among the noblest activities in society and because art and interest in art play a central theoretical role. It is trivial that producer and consumer differ in their relationship to the work/leisure division.

5.1. *Sports*

The central question with regard to the role of sports in our society is whether sports are a means of escape, an opiate for the masses, possibly as a last refuge offering some excitement to the apathetic, or whether sports in our society provide recreation for the mind and for the body. It is difficult to offer any other answer to this question than to say that sports play both roles. Our attitudes to the question have a tendency to become polarized. Many of us take an active interest in sports; some see only the seamy side of sports; and it is not easy to take a general and balanced point of view or to avoid taking a position. Because sports and interests in sports are so common, a lack of interest easily becomes a condemnation of society and, hence, reflects a reaction that is not determined by the properties of sports only, but that has deeper roots. Because sports are, in a sense, irrational, sports fans need a defence that easily becomes irrational.

The number of genuine performers in sports is small. Gallup polls indicate that 6 per cent are active in sports and that 19 per cent have formerly been active (Gallup 1951). With a vaguer formulation of the question the percentage of active may be put at 41 per cent. However, this high figure will include an unknown number of persons who ski only for exercise (20 per cent give skiing as their sport, while only 5 per cent name other sports) (Gallup 1948). More complete information on the subject is available in the other Scandinavian countries. (For Denmark, see Andersen et al. 1957; for Sweden, see Euler 1953.)

Christie's data on 19-year-old men born in 1933 indicate that city boys are as active as boys from rural districts. In Oslo, 48.8 per cent consider themselves to be diligent skiers and 12.5 per cent were prize winners, while 5.8 per cent left the question unanswered (30.4 per cent had done little skiing and 2.6 per cent had no training at all). In other cities, the figures were comparable to those from Oslo, while in rural districts there were 37.6 per cent diligent skiers and 12.5 per cent prize winners; 13.4 per cent left the question unanswered; 30 per cent had done little skiing and 7 per cent had no training (Christie 1960).

Sports interest, as we know, is even more common. Gallup data reveal the following: 52 per cent gave an affirmative reply to the question whether they take an interest in skiing (1958). A similar question with regard to soccer received 25 per cent affirmative answers (1959). The question 'Which sport do you enjoy watching most?', points to three major sports: skiing (26 per cent), soccer (26 per cent), and speed skating (17 per cent) (1948). Other sports were below the 5 per cent limit. Only 14 per cent dismissed the question by not identifying any sport. In a peak year for sports interest, 11 per cent answered 'don't know' and 24 per cent answered that they were not interested in whether or not Norwegians would win any victories in the Winter Olympics (1952). A maximum figure for interest in sports was indicated in the spring of 1964 when 90 per cent declared that they had 'heard' radio transmissions from the Winter Olympics. It is difficult, of course, to interpret the meaning of this kind of listening, yet there can be no doubt that on such occasions Norwegians are easily engaged both in sports events and in nationalism or patriotism. In sum, we may estimate that between a tenth and a third of the Norwegian people have but little interest in sports. Somewhat more than a third are highly interested in sports.

Also in terms of organizations, sports have a strong position in Norwegian society. *Norges Idrettsforbund* (the Norwegian Sports Association), with 2,700 clubs and some 330,000 members is, together with

341

the labour movement and the temperance movement, one of the three mass organizations in Norwegian society.

To the question of why sports have such a strong position, the answers are only tentative, although there are many of them.

First of all, it is probably true that sports interest may easily qualify one for participation in conversation. It is, for instance, quite easy for a 12-year-old to master relevant information on speed skating results and to know more than his father on a subject of wide general interest. And one does not need to know much to enjoy a good soccer match.

Secondly, sports and sport interests may be regarded in a symbolic context, although it is not easy to determine if hypotheses on the meaning of symbols are valid. Active participation in sports perhaps represents an effort to gain victory or suffer defeat in a wider sense than in sports alone. The person with a passive interest in sports, who 'wears out the bleachers', may be regarded in a similar manner under a hypothesis of identification with the performers. More precise hypotheses may be offered. Thus a soccer match may possibly be interpreted in Freudian terms: after all, the purpose is to put an object into a cage by the use of force and skill. Personally, I prefer a more general type of symbolism: a soccer game may serve as a truly elegant symbol for the fact that it is possible, through co-operation with others, to reach a goal in spite of the difficulties presented by opponents and by the rules of the game.

Nor should we disregard the very simple explanation: just like art, sports are for many people something that is pleasant and spontaneously enjoyable; it is an activity that has meaning only in itself and is not part of the means/ends complex surrounding us and pressing on us in our daily lives.

One minor effect may be observed in regard to language. It is surprising how many terms and expressions there are in our everyday language that are taken from sports jargon or have their concrete meaning in sports. Here we are not interested in the origin of these expressions but rather in pointing out that parts of our everyday language are rooted in meanings from the world of sports. Norwegian has daily expressions equivalent to: take-off, win, cut ahead, in the long run, support player, slow start, bull's eye, home stretch, be on thin ice, false step, finish, a draw or tie, have an easy game, stay in the ring. The potential for further contributions to language from sports is far from exhausted, and new expressions and new meanings for old expressions are developed through sports jargon.

5.2. *Art*

We shall have to limit ourselves to some suggestions on the role of art from a sociological point of view.

Without support in exact data, we have said that art and interest in it are among the noblest activities in society. To some exent such a statement will probably reflect the personal values of the author, or values that are highly regarded in a limited social environment. It is my belief, however, that the dominant values in our society contain a general, though possibly latent, highly positive evaluation of the personal creativity and social response connected with artistic activity. However, I can support this viewpoint with a hypothesis only: there would be a solid majority in all social groups with the view that, even with a high probability of success in any profession, a person of excellent artistic talent should choose a career in the arts rather than in such highly regarded careers as those of a judge, a medical doctor, or politician. (Quite possibly this is a rather heroic attitude, based on the exceptional cases in arts, such as the case of Edvard Munch, rather than upon the more frequent case of the restaurant musician – but this possibility does not weaken the argument in the present context.)

The lofty position of art reflects the fact that art is an ultimate source of 'meaning' – a reservoir for the possible mooring of the individual in a social and physical environment. As a structure for communication of symbols and meaning, art is distinguished from religion by being far more abstract and sophisticated and by not having the great problems of intellectual foundations as those attached to religion. Art, furthermore, is distinguished from science by its emotional rather than cognitive specialization. Art, again, is specialized. Music offers patterns that are both esoteric and physical, removed from concrete human content, but rich in qualities of beauty, harmony and disharmony, variations and constancy that may generate emotional responses. Pictorial art, on the other hand, offers concrete patterns where likeness and beauty may be elements, but where the real content may be that we are confronted by a humanly produced and tangible reality, with potential meaningful contents that the individual can find or create through emotional and cognitive engagement. Finally, literary art (including theatre, but with poetic specialization in other directions) is, in a human sense, a concrete art: in a physical sense literature may be less concrete than music, but literature specializes in problems of human relations and identity. This is probably true also of the theatre of the absurd, less true of some of the modern trends in poetry.

The lofty position of art may result from its role and tasks but also derives from the fact that in working with those tasks one must have both emotional and technical resources of a very special kind. With his proficiency and his creative abilities, the artist is the last respectable mystical element in society.

The artist is a charismatic person whose product we often approach

343

with feelings close to the religious: 'For some people, art is something very holy, something that may be approached only with humility' (Ole Henrik Moe in *Aftenposten*, 28 May 1964).

Trygve Braatøy, in his analysis of the writings of Knut Hamsun, made an effort to discredit this religious parallel in our attitude to art and artists (Braatøy 1929). To Fartein Valen, the composer, religion and art were intimately interwoven; he experienced God aiding his work through dreams (Gurvin 1962).

Edvard Munch may provide the best example of the general mystical element in art: having worked intensely with a picture, he could wake up the next morning with no idea about how the painting had been created. Rolf Stenersen draws a portrait of this bizarre, unhappy, and charismatic person, who through his combination of vulnerability and creative powers, became such a unique element in our culture (Stenersen 1964). The following passage should be quoted: 'Painting to me is an illness and an ecstasy. An illness I do not want to be cured from. An intoxication I must have. Sometimes in the morning I will find a picture that I painted during the night. Many of my best pictures I painted almost without knowing. I do not fear photography as long as it cannot be used in heaven or hell. I shall paint human beings who breathe and feel, who love and suffer. People shall understand the holy in this and take their hats off, as if in church' (pp. 26–27). The charismatic element in the artist is probably often overemphasized by the artist himself, as well as by his contemporaries and by posterity. Note Stenersen's observation that Munch apparently did not realize that there is any other moon than a full moon (p. 28).

The above is probably a philosophical approach to the sociology of art. I have tried to see the general, the real content in art (possibly with a romantic slant). It is not always easy to distinguish between statements that seek to describe attitudes towards art in Norwegian society and statements that express a more spontaneous understanding of the essence of art; the emphasis above is on the latter. There is a need for a more empirical sociology of art. Who become artists, and how? How do artists support themselves? How many artists are there in Norway? How many make a living from art only? Does painting have an unusually strong position in Norway, and, if so, why? The 1960 census indicates that slightly more than 250 people are authors and men of letters in literary pursuits, whereas there are almost 1,300 painters and sculptors. However, there are fewer than 300 'accredited artists' under the Board of the Association of Pictorial Arts (NOS XII 129, p. 222). If it is true that the position of the artist is a particularly lofty one, how can the artist arrange his relationship with his surroundings – with ordinary people? One solution is prevalent among American jazz musicians: contempt and withdrawal (Becker 1951). A similar tendency may be seen in the fact that in the jargon of Norwegian musicians, for example, the word 'prune' is used about pieces of music that in the musician's opinion are out-dated or below standard, but are still admired by the audience; the prune category apparently also includes works by Beethoven that are standard fare in symphony concerts.

Similar questions may be asked on the consumer side of art, but as with the producer side, we are not able to go into detail. It should be noted, however, that because art requires training, challenges conventions, and is highly regarded, much interest in art is a search for prestige rather than an interest in art for art's sake.

Because of the close interplay between art and politics in the period around the turn of the century, Norwegian society is peculiarly indebted to its artists. There is reason to believe that the golden age of literature in Norway in the second half of the nineteenth century, with Henrik Ibsen, Bjørnstjerne Bjørnson, Alexander Kielland, and Jonas Lie, served to convince international opinion, and particularly British politicians, about the viability of Norwegian culture, thus engendering sufficient international support for Norway in the dissolution of the union with Sweden in 1905 (cf. Holmsen and Jensen 1949).

6. CONCLUDING REMARKS

Norway is probably a very highly nationalistic society. Perhaps as a result of the nation's young age (although we Norwegians tend to regard the country as being extremely old) and a fear that we are culturally and physically poor, and as a result of a small and thinly spread population, defensive and pride-inspired attitudes to our society are common and run deep. (In his tale of the Norwegian trolls, H. C. Andersen gives a delightful description of these attitudes.)

What we may term the leisure sector has been peculiarly marked in two ways by these attitudes. First of all, sports in Norway are strongly affected by nationalism. (Yet possibly no more so than sports in other countries. Are Norwegian sports, and Norwegian society, perhaps nationalistic only when regarded from certain points of view within Norwegian society itself?) Second, our leisure is intimately tied to nature, which we regard as being the real Norway. Norwegian culture pushes or coaxes us out into nature – in the main, away from society. Yet at the same time this kind of activity strengthens our ties to society. The fact of our isolation from others becomes at the same time a mark of distinction we bear in common with other Norwegians. The very strong position of outdoor life may possibly derive from Norway's being such a collectivist and homogeneous society: joint and common affairs are broadly defined and engage us all. At times we may rightfully escape this pressure.

Another principal feature of our leisure activities is concerned with the future. Norway, like other countries, is in the midst of a technical revolution that, in industrially advanced countries, gives rise to the question of a future leisure culture. David Riesman sees a well-developed leisure culture as the salvation of our civilization (Riesman 1952). This is becoming a common issue: with the revolution caused by automation in production processes, the demand for labour will decrease to the extent that long before the year 2000 we will have a work week of less than thirty hours (Cohen 1963). How are we to fill the increased leisure time with meaningful activities? (A fine contrast between the bleak and the hopeful aspects of this perspective is given in a series of articles, 'Leisure and the Arts in 1984', in *New Scientist*, No. 394, 1964. Notice in particular Sir Herbert Read, 'Atrophied Muscles and Empty Art', and Joan Littlewood, 'A Laboratory of Fun'.)

We have become used to such formulations of the leisure society of the future, but they should, nevertheless, be regarded with scepticism. First of all, they are relevant only with respect to highly developed countries and are based on concepts of an international system of privileged and underprivileged societies that is already breaking down.

Second, the formulation of such problems is based on too simple concepts of the relationship between productive capacity, demand, and hours of work. Other significant factors may interfere in an equation that predicts a rapid decrease in work time on the premise of a more or less constant volume of demand, combined with a revolution in methods of production. Some of the changes in work hours will be neutralized by increased demand for goods and services. Some of the increase in leisure will be compensated by an increase in extra work or outside work, by double jobs, and by independent work. A simple equation, where work time and leisure are regarded as a single variable function dependent on a revolution of productive processes, cannot be easily combined with the realistic point of view that work time is also defined normatively: strong forces will work towards maintaining a work period just long enough to allow for adequate and satisfactory leisure time. It is not a question of an automatic process; political and organizational conditions will indeed play a role in deciding the future amount of leisure.

In the third place, it is tempting to state that real leisure problems cannot develop until the last book has been written and read, the last picture painted, until humanitarian and political activities have been completed, and until the possibilities of research in the laboratory and

346

into, for example, the secrets of the sea and of space have been exhausted. Yet to point to the enormous possibilities for personal engagement in meaningful leisure activity is also to bypass the fact that leisure problems do exist even today, mostly in some groups within major urban areas. Even with vastly expanding leisure, the 'leisure problem' will be primarily a question of motivation, rather than one of lacking opportunities. Fundamental questions of motivation cannot be solved through leisure; perhaps, therefore, the problems of leisure in the society of the future depend most on the nature of its work.

NOTES

[1] On the social position of vagrants, see Nils Christie, *Tvangsarbeid og alkoholbruk* (Forced labour and alcohol consumption) Oslo, 1960. To state that vagrants represent a cultural ideal may be to beg misunderstanding. We must emphasize that few Norwegians, even amongst the vagrants, actually have a desire to fill that role. Yet it is hardly unreasonable to maintain that there is something in the role of the vagrant that attracts most of us, possibly because that role appeals, if unrealistically, to a longing for freedom. Most of us react positively to the squatters in Cannery Row. In effect, both the artist and the vagrant are regarded with ambivalence, the artist with remarkable idealization and admiration, the vagrant with remarkable condemnation.

[2] Here, as in other instances where we lack exact data, we easily fall prey to romantic interpretations. That Easter is dedicated in an ideal-typical or even normative manner to skiing in the mountains may be true enough. But it remains an open question whether the tremendous exodus from Oslo at Easter is not in large measure due to the trivial fact that more than half of the Oslo population was born in other parts of the country. Much of the heavy Easter traffic may just indicate that many Oslo residents are not at home in the city.

XI. The Administration of Justice and its Clients

By Nils Christie

1. INTRODUCTION

One of the main tasks of the judicial system is the prevention and resolution of conflicts. A second task is control of society's official use of power. The need to fulfil these tasks has a pervasive influence upon the organization of the judicial system as well as upon the selection and education of the personnel concerned.

Table I gives information on the main types of judicial decisions in Norway. Over 125,000 contested cases were decided in Norway in 1965. Half of these, however, were concerned with minor offences, rather trifling infringements of the law that mostly incur a fine.

Tables II and III show us which judicial bodies have dealt with these cases. We see from Table II that the main burden of the civil cases has fallen on the so-called conciliation councils *(forliksrådene)*, elected bodies found in every municipality. The rural and urban courts *(herredsrettene, byrettene)* have also had a large share of the burden of civil cases, while the courts of appeal and the Supreme Court are concerned with only a very limited number of cases.

Table III shows that major crimes are generally dealt with (summarily on a plea of guilty) in the magistrate's courts *(forhørsrettene)*, if indeed recourse to the courts is not avoided altogether by suspen-

Table I. *Judicial decisions in Norway 1965**

Number of civil cases	55,639
Number of convictions for major crimes	7,112
Number of convictions for minor offences	62,276
Total	125,027

Sources: NOS A 163 and A 175.

* The criminal statistics deal simply with the number of persons tried, and since more than one person can be tried in a single case, the number of cases will be somewhat fewer than the figures given.

Table II. *Judicial decisions in civil cases in Norway in 1965*

Supreme Court	239
Courts of appeal	1,171
Rural and urban district courts	10,791
Conciliation councils	43,438
Total	55,639

Source: NOS A 163; 595 bankruptcies, settlements, and forced sales are excluded.

sion of the prosecution (*påtaleunnlatelse*). The latter procedure implies that the prosecuting authority is satisfied of the accused's guilt, but considers it unnecessary to proceed to court for the infliction of a penalty. Preponderant, however, in Table III are the figures for fines accepted. These refer to cases in which, as in the procedure just mentioned, the guilt of the accused is clear; by agreeing to pay a fine he avoids attending court and the case is disposed of swiftly and simply.

What types of contested cases do the courts deal with? For the conciliation councils, no satisfactory case statistics are available. But as regards the rural and urban municipal courts, some of the main types of disputes are set out in Table IV. Of the more than 10,000 cases decided, nearly one-third are concerned with family matters: separations, divorces, cases on questions of descent, and paternity and child maintenance cases. These cases are mostly of a type in which the law – i.e. society – requires the intervention of a court in order to achieve a solution, as the parties are not permitted to settle matters between themselves. Another main source of disputes is the renting of houses. Liability cases, on the other hand, account for less than 10 per cent of the total. The businessman, with his numerous contractual obligations,

Table III. *Persons convicted, fined, or dealt with by suspension of the prosecution, in criminal cases in Norway in 1965*

	Major crimes	Minor offences	Total
Supreme Court	117	40	157
Courts of appeal	184	21	205
Rural and urban district courts	1,373	2,314	3,687
Magistrates' courts	2,793	2,878	5,671
Fines accepted (on the authority of the police)	516	57,023	57,539
Suspension of the prosecution (on the authority of the public prosecutor)	2,129	—	2,129
Total	7,112	62,276	69,388

Source: NOS A 175 II, Tables IV and V.

Table IV. *Main types of civil disputes decided by rural and urban district courts in 1965*

	Number	Percentage
Allodial cases	52	
Cases of annulment and property titles	313	3.3
Presumption of death	16	0.1
Separations	1,359	
Divorces	710	
Other matrimonial cases	337	33.1
Descent	35	
Paternity and child maintenance	825	
Guardianship	311	
Labour disputes	13	0.1
Bills of exhange	1,312	12.2
Renting of house property	1,423	13.2
Inheritance	44	0.4
Liability cases	891	8.3
Real property	451	4.2
Mortgages and trademarks	31	0.3
Labour and service conditions	120	1.1
Maritime law	57	0.5
Taxation	88	0.8
Administrative cases	30	0.3
Other cases	2,373	22.0
Total number of cases decided	10,791	100.0

is involved in a net of business connections with his counterparties or their friends. Even if he should actually win a contested case, it would not pay him in the long run to go to court. Private arbitration will often be a more satisfactory solution when disagreement has gone too far. Mostly it is only an outsider – or a cantankerous individual – who will go so far as a forensic clash.

Table V. *Main types of crimes committed by persons convicted, fined, or dealt with by suspension of the prosecution in 1965*

Taking motor vehicle without owner's consent	859
Serious thefts	1,980
Minor thefts and pilfering	2,147
Embezzlement and fraud	381
Crimes of violence	602
Sexual offences	288
Other major crimes	598
Minor offences connected with illegal distribution of liquor	1,786
Motoring and traffic offences	33,456

Source: NOS A 175, II, Tables 1 and 2, p. 6.

We get an impression of the main types of criminal cases from Table V. The largest numbers stem from minor offences having to do with drink and with driving. On the other hand, when it comes to major crimes the picture is dominated by theft, with nearly 5,000 convictions, as against some 600 convictions for crimes of violence and some 280 convictions for sexual offences. The legal transgressions that set the machinery of justice in motion in Norway are first and foremost the result of our coveting our neighbour's goods. On the other hand, attacks on life and limb provide comparatively few cases for the courts in Norway – in strong contrast to conditions prevailing in many other countries.

2. FOUNDATION OF THE LAW

Two main features of the legal system are closely linked to its tasks of preventing and resolving conflicts and of controlling power.

The first of these is that the judicial decisions should be well founded in law, and the second is the special nature of the personnel and organization of the courts.

Many conflicts are prevented or resolved without recourse to the courts, because there are clear directives in the form of laws issued by bodies that combine power and authority. In Norway the official source is *Norges Lover 1682–1964* (Laws of Norway 1682–1964), published by the legal faculty of the University of Oslo, with a new edition every second year. This work does not contain all the laws, but nevertheless it runs to nearly 3,000 closely printed pages.

Table VI gives a survey of when Norway received some of these laws and the extent to which legislative activity in Norway has increased in the last part of the period considered. A survey of the annual number of new laws from 1865 to 1964 is also included. The survey shows that a modern industrial community is increasingly dependent on legislative regulation. Three main features are outstanding in this material:

1. A very great increase in legislative activity took place in Norway from 1865 up to 1915, both as regards number of laws and number of pages devoted to them.
2. After that there was only a gentle rise continuing to the 1950s – and later on a steady level – in the total number of laws, and almost a decrease in the number of pages.
3. There has been a clear tendency throughout the whole period for amendments of the laws to take up a steadily increasing percentage of the total legislative output.

351

Altogether this means that the total legislative output must be far greater today than at the beginning of the period considered. Presumably this means that laymen have become more than ever dependent on their legal advisers for finding their way through the jungle of laws that has grown up.

Any further interpretation of these statistics comes up against a number of difficulties. First, there is the question of whether the laws made within the different periods covered by the statistics are of equal importance. It may, for instance, be that laws made at the turn of the century are of more fundamental importance – are concerned with more important values and/or are more frequently in use – than later laws. A second possible source of error is provided by the periodical substitution of departmental regulations for laws. In some periods

Table VI. *Amount of legislation in Norway 1865-1964, annual average over five-year periods**

Year**	New laws	Amend- ments***	Total legis- lation	Number of pages	Amendments as a percentage
1865-1869	13.3	10.0	23.2	28.6	43
1870-1874	6.8	7.4	14.2	14.2	52
1875-1879	8.2	9.8	18.0	17.4	54
1880-1884	10.6	5.4	16.0	17.8	34
1885-1889	6.6	9.2	15.8	30.4	58
1890-1894	15.2	18.4	33.6	46.0	55
1895-1899	14.4	12.6	27.0	59.2	47
1899-1904	10.0	13.2	23.2	83.4	57
1904-1909	12.4	17.4	29.8	74.8	58
1910-1914	13.2	20.8	34.0	64.8	61
1915-1919	32.0	37.4	69.4	181.2	54
1920-1924	21.2	43.0	64.2	101.2	67
1925-1929	20.6	40.6	61.2	103.6	66
1930-1934	21.2	44.6	65.8	122.4	68
1935-1939	28.2	46.6	74.8	105.0	62
1940-1944†	2.0	1.8	3.8	10.0	47
1945-1949	44.8	63.2	108.0	111.6	59
1950-1954	24.2	65.6	89.8	103.0	73
1955-1959	22.8	70.0	92.8	108.4	75
1959-1964	19.4	70.0	89.4	107.2	78

* The figures are taken from the Parliamentary Records of the Lower House, with the exception that the figures for 1865-1869 are taken from separate publications of each year's legislation, the numbers of pages in this case being converted to accord with the numbering during the period 1871-1964.

** Changes in the Constitution are not included.

*** The heading covers changes in the law, and extensions of, and additions to, earlier laws.

† From 9 April 1940 to 14 June 1945 the Storting was not in session.

the Storting has kept full control in its own hands and has consequently been obliged to legislate fully. In other periods the Storting has been willing to delegate comprehensive powers to the administration – and then the number of laws made decreases while the number of administrative decrees issued increases.

In dealing with this problem we find ourselves approaching political sociology. Knut Dahl Jacobsen has treated this problem in his discussion of periods of delegation and retraction of legislative powers (1964, pp. 199–200).

Naturally enough, the laws will not be fashioned to cover all potential and actual conflicts. For one thing, new situations arise before they are taken up by the slow and laborious process of legislation. Furthermore, powerful forces often obstruct legislation, or prevent the law from coming down decisively in favour of any one party involved.

Figure 1 illustrates some of these problems by setting out the various levels of condemnation in separate concentric zones. In the centre are types of conduct arousing highest consensus in favour of suppression: homicide, breaking and entering, rape, the classic examples. In dealing with these, legislators will not be reticent; there is complete accordance and the legislation will face few risks. But even here some difficulties arise: euthanasia is one example, breaking and entering in order to obtain evidence against a master spy is another, while rape may often enough be accompanied by mitigating circumstances that make the legislator's task more complicated. In the next circle further complications ensue; as regards the activities included here, we no longer find absolute consensus; agreement continues to decrease as distance from the centre grows. Other eventualities also attend upon an increasing distance from the centre. Penalties imposed will generally be milder; the legislators will lean over backwards before they venture into the area. *If* they venture in, they will often be reluctant to inflict penalties in the event of breaches of the law. Such law is often more the result of endeavours to create concord between contending parties than to protect any one party.

Aubert, Eckhoff, and Sveri (1952) found an example of this in the law regulating the working conditions of domestic servants. This law, say the authors, 'clearly represents a compromise by which domestic servants have obtained their material rights, while housewives are protected against drastic sacrifices thanks to ineffective enforcement'. The price control and wage regulation legislation after World War II was pervaded with the same sort of thing. The law imposed formal restriction – to the delight of the labour movement – but lacked effective means of enforcement – to the delight of the business community. The end-product was a sort of peace-keeping activity (Aubert 1950).

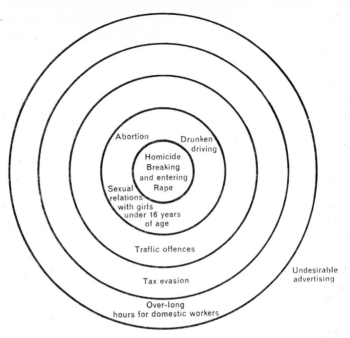

Figure 1. Zones showing degree of condemnation

Another, but related, legislative tendency in situations of conflict is to obscure the issue. As Max Gluckman has pointed out, imprecise legal and political concepts will sometimes serve as oil in the social machinery (but sometimes as sand) (Gluckman 1956). The looseness permits combinations of objectives that under logical analysis would appear impossible, thus veiling conflicts that would make social life awkward.

This whole field teems with research problems. One of the most striking questions is why a certain type of conduct is placed more centrally or less centrally in the diagram showing what the community condemns. Andenæs touches on some of the relevant factors when he asserts that a country's criminal law gives a better picture of the existing social conditions and moral concepts than do most other types of law. This is particularly true of our society in earlier times, states Andenæs, when one considers that the laws of Norway right up to 1842 provided for penal servitude for life for those who 'curse their parents' and the death penalty for those who struck them, but contained no penal provisions against parents who neglected or ill-used their children (Andenæs 1956, p. 4). A second important problem is caused by a general sluggishness in the legal system. Some of the values that are today considered to be worthy of major protection

354

should, perhaps, be replaced with others that from an objective point of view are far more important. Cars kill and maim far more children in Norway in the course of a single year than sexual offenders can lay hands on in the course of a generation. Seen from an international point of view political crimes are, of course, of more importance for us all than traditional misdemeanours. But it is difficult to effect a revision because the experiences of law-makers will generally be those of a previous generation. Furthermore, the present era has created problems different in principle from those of all earlier eras – in that we have all become entirely dependent on persons with whom we have not had, or will not have any close personal relationship.

3. ORGANIZATION OF THE LAW COURTS

Obscuring the issue, ambiguity, and the failure of the law to keep pace with present problems will result in many conflicts remaining unsolved. The legal system sends these on to the law courts.

Figure 2 gives summarized information about the Norwegian courts. In the first place, in every single type of law court, an organization has been constructed that somehow contrives to keep a balance between the contending parties, but that at the same time enables a solution of the conflict. The conciliation council has three members, not two or four, and all the other types of law courts follow this rule of having an uneven number of judges. The parties are similarly represented in civil cases; in criminal cases they are either alone with the judge and the court supervisor (*rettsvitne*) or attend with their counsels in cases in which a prosecutor appears.

A second characteristic is that the cases generally begin in the lowest courts. It is there that one is confronted with large numbers of cases. Then the numbers gradually diminish from the conciliation council to the rural or urban district courts, on to the court of appeals, and so finally to the Supreme Court, which deals with a comparatively small number of cases. The system is built up like a pyramid – a single pyramid, not two or more. This is essential to the purpose of *internal* control. A case may be appealed, *but the factual truth of the matter is established once and for all.* This arrangement strengthens both the opportunity for and the confidence in the internal control in the system, and also leads to its uniformity. The object is to make the law the same – if not for all cases at least for all similar cases.

A third main feature apparent from Figure 2 is the anti-specialist tendency within these various types of law courts. This shows itself in two principal ways. The lay element is overwhelmingly strong throughout. In the conciliation council *(forliksråd)* only laymen or

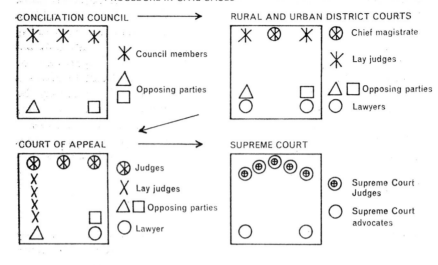

PROCEDURE IN CIVIL CASES

CONCILIATION COUNCIL ⟶ RURAL AND URBAN DISTRICT COURTS

✳ Council members
△ □ Opposing parties

⊗ Chief magistrate
✳ Lay judges
△ □ Opposing parties
○ Lawyers

COURT OF APPEAL ⟶ SUPREME COURT

⊗ Judges
✗ Lay judges
△ □ Opposing parties
○ Lawyer

⊕ Supreme Court Judges
○ Supreme Court advocates

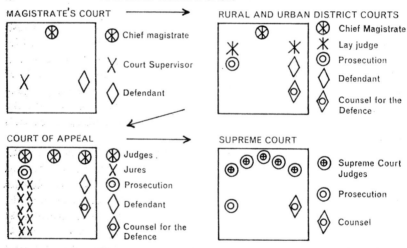

PROCEDURE IN CRIMINAL CASES

MAGISTRATE'S COURT ⟶ RURAL AND URBAN DISTRICT COURTS

⊗ Chief magistrate
✗ Court Supervisor
◇ Defendant

⊗ Chief Magistrate
✳ Lay judge
◎ Prosecution
◇ Defendant
◈ Counsel for the Defence

COURT OF APPEAL ⟶ SUPREME COURT

⊗ Judges
✗ Jures
◎ Prosecution
◇ Defendant
◈ Counsel for the Defence

⊕ Supreme Court Judges
◎ Prosecution
◈ Counsel

Figure 2. Main elements in the organization of the law courts.

Source: Andenæs, Aukrust and Hauge (1951, p. 59).

popularly elected members are found, not lawyers. In the rural or urban district courts, laymen are in the majority, and from time to time they avail themselves of their majority to overrule the professional judge. They can acquit or convict against his opinion. Aubert has examined the outcome of criminal cases in six rural district courts in the region of eastern Norway in 1950–1961 (Aubert 1963). He finds that the professional judge has been in the minority in a little more than 6 per cent of the total number of criminal cases. In the high court for criminal and civil appeals, and for serious criminal cases *(lagmannsrett)*, the lay influence is even more clearly apparent, most dramatically so in the criminal cases, where the lay members in private decide the absolutely vital question of guilt. Only in the Supreme Court do legal experts have the field to themselves, but it is worth noting that the Supreme Court is not entrusted with the task of evaluating the evidence relating to the question of guilt in the case. An acquittal in the high court cannot be appealed to the Supreme Court.

The second manifestation of the anti-specialist tendency is that there are very few special courts; furthermore, lawyers specialize only moderately in the types of cases they handle.

The distinctive character of the law courts is clearly seen if we compare lawyers' qualifications with those of doctors in a hospital. Both types of institutions are served, partly at least, by persons with an extremely long academic education. But it is typical of the personnel of the law courts that they all have the same qualifications. Their knowledge and abilities are similar; they are all experts in legal solutions, but each does not make some further contribution of specialized knowledge to the common fund. In the hospital system, the position is quite different. In addition to a common basic medical qualification, the most qualified personnel in a hospital will be distinguished by the fact that each has his own speciality. Lawyers in the law courts generally share the same knowledge and can play each other's parts at any time – as they often do when a defending or prosecuting counsel is raised to the bench. In the hospital system, on the other hand, the whole point is that the specialist has access to knowledge that the others do not share. Altogether, therefore, a team of doctors in a hospital would have access to a far greater accumulation of knowledge than the lawyers in a law court. On the other hand – and this is what is essential in the present context – *the lawyers would accordingly be able to exercise a far more careful control of each other than the doctors would be able to do.* For the doctors this is not so important, since all of them normally have the same objective, to get the patient well again. But in the system of the law courts, where the objective is to solve a conflict, non-specialization and mutual control are of great importance. The courtroom cannot contain so great a store of knowledge as the operating theatre, but the wounds to be healed by courts demand, perhaps, other techniques of social organization. Opportunities for internal control are further strengthened by a series of mechanisms that promote *open communication* within the system. All that is said or put forward in a courtroom shall be available to all. If, for example, the victim of rape cannot bring herself to give evidence in the accused's presence (or vice versa), the judge may well grant that the accused retire for a short time. But it is then strongly emphasized that the defending counsel or the judge himself must give the party concerned a careful account of what has been said in his or her absence. That proceedings in a law court are, as a rule, open to the public, works in the same direction.

Altogether these conditions help improve the opportunities for solving conflicts within the framework of the judicial system. This system is nearly always faced with situations in which granting justice to one person leads to the discontent of another. Much depends on whether the loser can be made to accept the result peacefully. The constitution of the law courts can be said to offer the greatest possibilities for such an outcome to a case. The balance maintained between the contending forces makes each party feel that he has an opportunity of making himself heard, and that the necessary conditions for dispensing justice are present. The strong lay element helps to prevent experts, with their esoteric values, from being excessively technical in their decisions. Furthermore, the fact that the few specialists involved can all control one another gives the loser a further guarantee that his loss was not wholly unjustified. All these elements also protect the dispensers of justice against reprisals from the loser or losers.

The complete contrast to this type of judicial system is found in the type of trial popularly called inquisition. Under that system the accused could be punished if he did not answer questions. The hearing took place behind closed doors and without the presence of a counsel for the defence. The accused had no right to examine the evidence against him at the preinquiry stage. In the past, full acquittal was in some instances accorded only if undoubted innocence was established, and, above all, the judge combined in his role all the activities that are today spread among the judge, the prosecutor, and defending counsel. Corresponding principles applied in civil cases.

It is scarcely fortuitous that the inquisitorial process has lost ground during a period marked by an evening out of social rank. Given an extreme difference of rank between the judge and the accused, a complicated system comprising a number of different and mutually controlling roles becomes out of the question. The delinquent or the parties in a civil suit stand so low in relation to the judge that it becomes irrelevant what he or they may think of what occurs. The loser has little opportunity to strike back and is regarded as a person of little interest. Besides, it is quite possible that the extreme difference in rank will actually make it easier to accept a decision no matter what the form of judgement – the decree comes from so great a height that the form it takes can scarcely be discerned or, at any rate, understood.

Opposite circumstances will have considerable significance for one who is judged by his peers of whose conduct he can form an estimate. I think I have found an example of such an effect in the working of the temperance boards, whose process is rather inquisitorial. The members of these boards are by law accorded considerable powers to take steps against persons suspected of misusing alcohol. In practice, however, they show themselves to be very reluctant to do so. Less than 2 per cent of the boards' contact with alcoholics has been established through their own initiative, while nearly 80 per cent of those brought to the attention of the boards are brought by the police – the very body that the boards are supposed to prevent their cases from coming in contact with! This reluctance on the part of the boards to show initiative is, presumably, largely due to the members' feelings of being in jeopardy. The members are neighbours, and accordingly the social equals of those who may be brought before them. Consequently the boards lack the protective mechanism that the courts normally enjoy.

4. THE SOCIAL BACKGROUNDS OF MEMBERS OF THE LEGAL PROFESSION

In line with the foregoing we should find that the specialists in the legal system have a relatively high rank. Those who resolve conflicts – and in this context, especially the judges – presumably find their task somewhat lighter if their social standing is above the average.

This is confirmed by the relevant evidence. We give below a list ranked by position in the offical procession at the opening and dissolution of Parliament. Rarely do we get so clear a picture of the composition of the highest ranks of the social strata in the Norwegian community. Here they come in rows and in files arranged according to increasing rank, from curates and resident curates to rural deans and

Table VII. *Position in the official procession at the opening and dissolution of the Storting*

In front of the procession: 2 police superintendents.

	Salaries in N.kr.*
Group VII	
Curates	19,250
Resident curates	22,200
Vicars	25,600
Chief excise officer	32,100
University secretary	35,800
University bursar	35,800

Group VI
Administrator of deceased estates	42,400
State auctioneer	42,400
Heads of bureaus and offices	33,900
Heads of technical departments'	42,400
Rectors	25,600 — 35,800
Rural deans	27,100 — 37,700
Deans of cathedrals	42,400 — (44,500)
City judges	42,400
Judges' clerks in the Supreme Court	32,100
Chief magistrates	42,400
Lay assessors	44,500

Group V
Head of C.I.D. in Oslo	40,400
Head librarian of University Library	46,600
Councillors	46,600
Professors	46,600

Group IV
Chief of Police in Oslo	50,600
Directors	46,600
Justice of appeal	50,600

Group III
Heads of departments	46,600
Chief of Protocol in the Foreign Office	48,600
Mayor of Oslo	58,000
Attorney-General	60,700
Director of Public Prosecutions	54,600
Head of the National Archives	46,600
Rector of the University	46,600
Managing Director, Norwegian Hydroelectric Board	50,600
Director of the Bank of Norway	62,800
Bishops	48,600
County prefects	48,600

Group II
Permanent Secretaries	52,600
Under-Secretaries of State	48,600
Permanent Secretary of State	52,600

Group I
Ombudsman	71,800
Supreme Court Judges	48,600

Group Ia
Chief Justice of the Supreme Court	62,800
His Majesty the King, with his court and the appointed deputation from the Storting	
Cabinet Ministers	58,000
Regular officers of the Armed Services	

---

*The salaries given here relate to the period 1 May 1964 – 31 March 1965.

various minor judges, and on up to the Supreme Court judges and finally to the Chief Justice of the Supreme Court, who immediately precedes His Majesty the King and his court. Also, the size of an official's salary is in close accordance with his ranking in the procession.

Naturally enough there is considerable correspondence between achieved status and status at birth. Ulf Torgersen asserts, on the basis of research into the family backgrounds of the Supreme Court judges, 'that there is a marked recruitment from and intermarriage with the professional middle classes, and to a certain extent the upper class' (Torgersen 1960).

Aubert and his co-workers have published figures concerning the father's occupations of law school graduates for the period 1800–1950, and also for new students up to 1959 (Aubert et al. 1960). If we count as lawyer fathers all judges, senior civil servants in central and local government, and finally advocates and attorneys, the percentages with lawyer fathers are as given in Table VIII. No less than 33 per cent of those taking law degrees had lawyer fathers at the beginning of the period. Later, the percentages decreased somewhat, but a sort of self-perpetuation in recruitment to the legal profession remains. Aubert has also, in another connection, shown that the children of lawyer fathers will attain more senior legal appointments than the children of fathers from other professions (Aubert 1959).

5. SOCIALIZATION TO THE PROFESSION

As far as lawyers and, especially, judges are concerned, there are more factors than similar social origins that give rise to their homogeneity. For lawyers as for all other professional groups with a long

Table VIII. *Percentages of lawyer fathers among law graduates and students 1814-1959*

1814	33.6
1815-1829	18.2
1830-1849	23.1
1850-1869	20.3
1870-1889	19.6
1890-1909	15.9
1910-1929	18.9
1930-1940	15.5
1941-1955, high school before 1945	10.7
1950-1959, high school after 1946	12.9
New law students 1958 and 1959	19.6

Source: Vilhelm Aubert et al., 1960.

education, various important things clearly occur in the course of and just after the actual study period. Legal studies represent a long process of socialization to the legal profession, in the same way that medical studies are a socialization to the medical profession. A comparison between these two studies will perhaps lead to a more complete understanding of the relative nature of the two professions. In both subjects there is an analogy to be drawn between university studies and later professional life.

Two main differences between the two subjects are striking. The first concerns the content and organization of the studies, the other the matter of controlling the eventual practising of the profession.

5.1. Content and organization of the studies

Both as regards content and organization, legal studies are marked by *a very high degree of homogeneity*. This is reflected in, among other things, *the course of studies*. The student is permitted to choose only one special subject, which constitutes only one-thirteenth of the total marks in the examination. Moreover – in contrast to medical studies – there is no further instruction clearly designed for *the training of lawyers as specialists*. The few special courses arranged now and then by authorities who are outside the university, moreover, are nothing compared with the complicated apparatus provided – and also made use of – by the medical profession. The homogeneous character of legal studies is also reflected in other ways. All professorships in the legal faculty are announced as vacant professorships in jurisprudence: it is taken for granted that the evaluation committee is capable of striking a balance between applicants whose main work has been in such different fields as maritime law, territorial limits, price controls, or the problems of contractors. When the faculty has any doubt about choosing between two applicants, all the faculty members sit down and read the applicants' main work. It is also characteristic that the successful applicant rarely knows beforehand which will be the main field in which he will teach. It is the faculty that decides the field he is to cover. A new recruit whose doctorate and scientific output have been entirely concerned with criminal law may well be required to lecture about copyrights, patents, and trademarks if the former field is occupied and the latter temporarily vacant. From an opposite point of view, it is considered tactless if someone later on intrudes upon another's allotted sphere of instruction, for example by publishing textbooks relating to it. It is generally considered that every person competent to be a professor in jurisprudence has a certain degree of competence in every sphere of jurisprudence. Of course, the system creaks now and then. The greater the interval that has elapsed since taking their degree, the more will professors feel themselves amateurs in another's sphere of instruction. Some parts of jurisprudence will also be more specialized than others, especially as one may need to be acquainted with working practices in the sphere the rules apply to. Nevertheless, in its main essentials the assumption of general competence in jurisprudence will hold good – because the technique required to solve legal problems is essentially the same whether the actual or potential conflict concerns copyright, criminal punishment, married women's property, or foreign territories. The contrast with the medical faculty is clear. There it is specialization per se that predominates, and, indeed, in accordance with our earlier reasoning, ought to predominate. The doctor is not, like the lawyer, concerned with the balancing of a conflict, and specialization becomes possible (Christie 1961).

Another distinctive feature of legal, as compared with medical, education is illustrated by the part the potential client plays in each. Just as it is natural that the patient himself in all his complexity dominates the picture in the instruction of the medical student, so it is natural that the potential client only as an exception makes his presence felt in the instruction of the law student. The potential client has no place there except to demonstrate another approach to the problem. In the legal world one is concerned with *cases*, abstractions that satisfy important needs of the community. The lawyer knows beforehand the main features relevant in a case. The legal system is to a far greater degree than the medical a closed system in which it is decided in advance which factors are relevant. The introduction of the client at the instructional stage will therefore have mainly a distracting effect. In the medical system, on the other hand, the patient in all his complexity can scarcely be avoided, partly because this is an empirical science whose essential limits are difficult to define and can never be regarded as finally settled, and partly because medical activity has the patient's welfare as its aim. This brings us to our next main point.

5.2. Control of the student's mastery of the subject

Legal activity is mainly concerned with the prevention and resolution of conflicts. Legal studies are therefore designed as training in such activity – training in the clarification, evaluation, and balancing of often directly conflicting issues. But here several difficulties intrude. The conflicting values can appear – to the expert as to the layman – to be equally balanced. Both parties may, from one point of view or another, have a claim to an indivisible property, but the judge can only award it to one of them. Sometimes he solves the problem by stretching the system and alluding to the possibility of creating a precedent[1] to a greater degree than usual, but often this is not possible. The consequences are not foreseeable, or mutually conflicting, or it may be against the law or usage to take them into account. One is struck by the contrast with medical activity.

Of course, the physician is also often faced with conflicting considerations. But, in the first place, these considerations are normally confined to one and the same patient. The kidney requires an operation, but the heart perhaps will not stand the operation. And the result, whether the decision was right or not, is at any rate *to some degree measurable*. The doctor's activity requires a short-range view of the consequences. At all stages in his activity there is *opportunity to observe whether the consequences are occurring, whether the goals are being attained*. Medical studies also give, perhaps, training in the overcoming of doubt. A physician must often act – and the student is trained to act – nearly in the dark. Compared with the lawyer's activity, there are nevertheless a long series of built-in 'answers' in medical activity – wounds which do not heal, legs in splints that grow crooked, after-effects that should not have appeared, failure to recover.[2]

Even if the main emphasis in medical instruction should be put upon mastery of doubt, the authoritative word is based on experience where treatement, no matter how uncertain the physician was, produced a desirable result. For the lawyer, on the other hand, there are no built-in answers in the system *except such as stem from the estimations of other lawyers*. There is a need for other objective criteria – the equivalents of patients who die at the wrong times. And these criteria are provided in Norway by a university examination system, which in both its organization and lasting effects has not its like in any other subject.

The examination results themselves are given an importance very difficult for the uninitiated to grasp. Each student knows the examination results of every other student to the second decimal place, and this result follows a person to the end of his days. A lawyer with a mark of 2.23 can go happily and safely throughout his existence; one with a mark of 2.95 is forever condemned to a place among the lowly in the profession. He can never become a Supreme Court judge, a high court judge, or a public prosecutor; nor can he be an advocate in the Supreme Court. But one with a mark of 2.50 can also have a difficult time of it. He is nearly good enough to enter the legal department of the Ministry of Justice – but not quite. He must content himself with what is out of the reach of the 2.95 man. Right from the first meeting between previously unacquainted lawyers it is not abnormal that the participants look up each other's examination results in a reference book that – typically – is easily available.

364

Completely in line with the importance of these magical figures, there has been constructed for the lawyers what is presumably the most complicated examination system that can be found at the university. The studies are arranged in two sections, both of which conclude with six days of written examinations followed by an oral examination.

For each paper set two examiners are appointed to read all the answers. They put all the answers to this paper into rank order. They each cover the relative ranking of the answers to this one paper. They cover the answer paper with comments and criticism – it is characteristic that law students are enjoined to leave a vertical half of the sheet clear for comments[3] – and they proceed to award marks to all the answers.

They usually agree on a mark for each answer, but they can also formally dissent. Since there are six papers, 12 persons in each department will be employed with this part of the examination, and thus for both sections of the examination 24 persons. But additionally there are set up a number of boards of three examiners each, who go through all six papers for a small number of candidates. On the basis of information from the teams of two examiners, the three-man boards will know how the selected candidates stand in relation to the average for that semester, and so on the basis of all six papers will arrive at a final mark for the whole examination.

This three-man board also holds the oral examination. When large numbers are involved, there can be five or six such teams of three active in each section. Most of the members of these teams will also have the task of examining one of the papers, but the number of examiners in both sections can easily amount to 30–35 persons. In the spring semester 1965, there were 30 examiners for 257 candidates; in the autumn semester 1965, there were 21 examiners for 157 candidates.

And in accordance with the main pattern, these examiners are not just anybody. The leading examiners in each section are always two university professors. Additionally, several of the permanent lecturers take part on a rotating basis, and the rest are chosen from a panel of leading lawyers selected by the legal faculty. To be put on the panel is a burden, but also an honour. The list is scrutinized at faculty meetings and is published in the official calendar. There is no such list in any other subject that reaches such heights. A-level results and degree marks are published at the end of each semester in the Norwegian Law Times – standard reading for all Norwegian lawyers. When each individual took his degree may be discovered from the official calendar, which lists all civil servants and all attorneys practising. It is perhaps difficult to know what constitutes a good law but not what constitutes a good lawyer.

A grading system of the type that has been developed for the legal faculty, being so strongly adhesive that the mark sticks to the candidate for the rest of his life, is an effective enough alternative to the daily test to which a doctor is subjected. But other alternatives can, of course, be thought of. In Sweden, for example, far less weight is given to control by examination and to the examination results. On the other hand a more centralized organization of the courts has been built up, with its own courses of instruction – and thereby control of and assessment of personnel.

5.3. *Some consequences for Norwegian society*

The curricular organization and expecially the examination system for lawyers is uncommonly well suited to integrating the profession with the society. The system described has *perhaps* been created as a result of other needs, but whatever its history it must be assumed to have integration as its consequence.

Every society has a series of obscurities and inconsistencies in its accepted standards. The lawyers are the professional group who have specialized in solving many of the problems this creates. Lawyers give priority to value. Further, they are trained to differentiate more and more subtly on the basis of given premises. By this means they manage to solve conflicts. But even the most elaborate dogmatic system will, of course, fail to cover every single new situation – or combination of old situations. It is when the limits of the system have been reached that the lawyers will presumably find their task made lighter by the fact that *they have by their examination system created an internal hierarchy of professional value arbiters.* In this manner, they do not give equal weight to all opinions, but at a very early stage weigh opinions according to two criteria: examination grades in the case of all, and the rank of the court in the case of judges.[4]

In this way it can be said that there arises an interesting analogy between the system of internal control and the ranking system in the legal structure *before* and *after* studies. In both cases, top lawyers have a great degree of control over the situation. There are few at the top both in and outside the university. We have only one Supreme Court, and only one professor in jurisprudence at work daily in any one field. As mentioned, a field once allotted is jealously guarded. The causes are, among other things, economic, but the consequences are well suited to avoiding conflicts on values. Outwardly there is only one real university expert in each field. No doubt it is difficult to say precisely what constitutes a good lawyer. But practising lawyers *who are considered good by others* have, both within the university and in the field of law as a whole, maximum possibilities for influencing both the students and the practitioners who attempt to copy them, and also for making certain that those who follow them in their legal activity will be richly rewarded. The chosen will, by their control of both the examinations and the courts, most swiftly advance to the highest controlling bodies both in- and outside the university; and Norwegian society is thus assured of a homogeneous group of value arbiters.

6. RECRUITMENT TO THE JUDICIARY

The judiciary enjoys a central place in every discussion of legal institutions. It is therefore of special interest to examine somewhat more closely the paths which lead to the bench. Some societies arrange things on a political basis, thereby allowing the voters to wield considerable influence over the chief resolvers of conflicts. Others go to the other extreme and let the judiciary itself decide who the new judges shall be; the voters' influence then is of course correspondingly reduced. Some societies obtain their judges from the ranks of outstanding attorneys and thereby get brilliant and uncompromising personalities, often with a very conservative political outlook. In Norway, they are largely obtained from the ministries and from the ranks of senior civil servants and government officials. Eivind Hanssen has done research on all applicants for judicial office during the periods 1937–1939 and 1950–1952. Only a small portion of the applicants came from the ranks of the Supreme Court advocates and from counsel; and this portion decreased in the latter period. When these non-public servants seek judicial office, they aim low on the ladder. The top judicial positions are sought by *other judges* (Hanssen 1954).

And their prayers are granted. Torgersen has undertaken research into all the judicial appointments in the period from 1945 to 1952. The ministries and the central administration produce decidedly the largest group of successful applicants (Torgersen 1954).

Torgersen also has figures showing the high examination grades among judges. He also shows that a diminishing number of appointments go to persons under 40 years of age.

Altogether this method of recruiting judges probably contributes further to assuring the Norwegian community of a very homogeneous group of value arbiters. We lack the necessary material for pronouncing to what extent this leads to a judicial class that shows an unreasonably strong loyalty to the state and the administration when they are embroiled in legal conflicts. But there is scarcely any doubt that the judicial type created satisfies demands that the upholders of the law themselves find very important.

As has been said by one of Norway's foremost legal experts, one not commonly associated with the path of caution:

> The extremely independent personality who goes his own way without paying regard to any quarter, or who breaks radically with traditional points of view, or launches bold new theories or evaluations, is not suited to being a judge (Eckhoff 1965, p. 30).

7. THE PARTIES TO LEGAL CASES

We do not know a great deal about the parties to civil suits. On the other hand we know more about those who come in contact with criminal law than we do about civil litigants and the entire personnel of the legal system put together. There is a sociological moral in this. The delinquent presents the community with a problem. His conduct requires explanation, while he himself can scarcely object to any investigation that may be undertaken or to any findings that may be made. The personnel of the legal system are a more legitimate part of Norwegian society and a part that will, as experience shows, loudly voice its objections to the account sociologists give of it.

As for civil litigants, they include us all. Or do they? We do not really know, for lack of relevant data. Our only statistical information is about the main types of disputes that come before the rural and urban districts courts (Tables IV and V). We must therefore limit ourselves almost exclusively to those parties who are unwilling subjects of the administration of justice as a consequence of their own breaches of the law. But let us make it clear at the outset that we by no means *wish* to limit ourselves in this way, and that we are well aware of the considerable tasks of research on civil litigants that demand attention in the future.

Any description of those who come in contact with the criminal law will present two main problems. First, not all breaches of the law become known, nor are all lawbreakers apprehended. What selective process is at work here? Second, only some of those who are apprehended are punished for their misdeeds. Who are the ones so singled out?

It has gradually become clear that the officially registered lawbreakers constitute only a fraction – and an unrepresentative fraction – of all who break the law. Various selective mechanisms are at work. The nature of the crime itself has some effect. More attention is given to whether a death is a case of homicide than whether a lost wallet is a case of theft. Much depends too on who commits the crime. It is a less formidable task, besides being technically simpler, to arrest a tramp than a wholesale dealer, just as it is easier to avoid full resource

368

Table IX. *Male recruits from Oslo, by actual criminal offences*

Point score*	Percentage of recruits
0	5.0
1-2	9.1
3-5	18.7
6-10	30.8
11-15	19.2
16-20	8.1
21-25	4.6
26-35	3.4
36-55	1.1
Total	100.0
N =	1,820

Source: Christie, Andenæs and Skirbekk 1965.

* Calculated by awarding 3 points for the most extreme offences, 2 for criminal offences of average severity, and 1 for the mildest offences.

to the courts when the transgressor is very young than when he is at what is considered a more responsible age. Very few of those who break the law find their way so far through the selctive processes that they are officially proclaimed lawbreakers by the judgment of a court.

On the other hand, we do know that breaches of the law actually take place to a very considerable extent in Norway. Table IX is taken from a study of young men assembled for pre-military classification (Christie, Andenæs, and Skirbekk 1965). The persons concerned had their anonymity guaranteed, and they replied to a series of questions about breaches of the law which they might possibly have committed. The replies to each questionnaire were then summed up. The most serious offences committed rated 3 points, the least serious 1 point. Persons who replied that they had committed all the offences in the questionnaire could reach a total of 55 points, while those who replied negatively to all the questions would receive a total of zero. And it can be seen that entirely negative returns were very uncommon. Only 5 per cent of the subjects in Oslo asserted they were not guilty of any of the forms of lawbreaking activity in the questionnaire. But it is also quite clear that these young men have not chosen a criminal way of life. The majority of the answers were concentrated at the less serious end of the distribution curve. Nearly all commit breaches of the law, but only a few and only seldom. Criminality, while not unknown, is very far from being the average citizen's way of life.

Figure 3 gives us an impression of the type of criminal activity that occurs. Again, we confine ourselves to Oslo, and we find here that

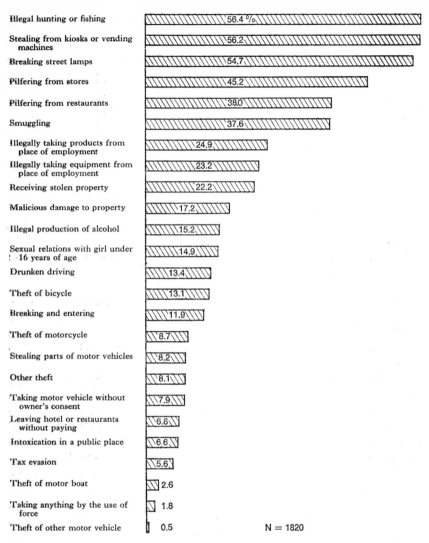

Illegal hunting or fishing	56.4 %
Stealing from kiosks or vending machines	56.2
Breaking street lamps	54.7
Pilfering from stores	45.2
Pilfering from restaurants	38.0
Smuggling	37.6
Illegally taking products from place of employment	24.9
Illegally taking equipment from place of employment	23.2
Receiving stolen property	22.2
Malicious damage to property	17.2
Illegal production of alcohol	15.2
Sexual relations with girl under 16 years of age	14.9
Drunken driving	13.4
Theft of bicycle	13.1
Breaking and entering	11.9
Theft of motorcycle	8.7
Stealing parts of motor vehicles	8.2
Other theft	8.1
Taking motor vehicle without owner's consent	7.9
Leaving hotel or restaurants without paying	6.8
Intoxication in a public place	6.6
Tax evasion	5.6
Theft of motor boat	2.6
Taking anything by the use of force	1.8
Theft of other motor vehicle	0,5 N = 1820

Figure 3. Type of criminal activity in Oslo.

Source: Christie, Andenæs and Skirbekk 1965.

illegal hunting and fishing are the most commonly admitted breaches of the law. But these are closely followed by stealing from kiosks or vending machines, followed again by breaking street lamps, closely followed by pilfering from stores. This may not amount to very serious lawbreaking, but it is quite sufficient to incur the sanctions of the criminal law.

Considering that we are here conccerned with rather young men, it

370

is, for example, striking that no less than 13.5 per cent admit that they have driven while under the influence of drink, an offence for which the normal penalty is an unconditional prison sentence. The percentage becomes even higher if we confine ouselves to those who have the opportunity to drive under the influence of drink. Of those who state that they drove a car nearly every day in the year the inquiry took place, we arrive at fully 25 per cent who admit that they have driven a car under the influence of drink.

But even if we are all lawbreakers, we do not all come in contact with the criminal law. Christie has carried out an inquiry into how many young men born in 1933 have been officially registered for breaches of the law (Christie 1960). Up to an age of 24–25 years a total of 5 per cent in this age cohort had been registered in the official criminal register. If we also include persons punished under military law or who had been to corrective schools, the percentage rises to nearly 6 per cent. The percentage will continue to rise as this age cohort approaches three score years and ten, but not to such a very great extent. The cohort group has already passed through the period of highest criminal activity and will scarcely reach a percentage higher than 7–8 with respect to number of registrations. Younger cohorts have, however, shown a far higher number of registrations and will presumably reach percentages of 12–14 per cent for the country as a whole (Røstad 1967). Figures for Oslo will be even higher.

Nevertheless there is a great difference between the figures for the number of actual lawbreakers and the number of those registered. Much of the explanation for this lies in the fact that many of the actual offences admitted are so trifling that the offenders would not have been entered in the Criminal Register even if they had been reported and brought to book. Table X shows the importance of this factor. We can see straightaway that the largest categories are those represented by the uncharted spaces on the crime map. These are the cases in which no definite person was suspected or were shelved for lack of evidence. Next comes a large category in which the charges were withdrawn. At the bottom we find the small category, 17.4 per cent, in which the cases resulted in a charge being brought against somebody. In addition about 6 per cent of the cases conclude with the offender accepting a fine or with suspension of the prosecution. Generally we can reckon that one-third of all the reported breaches of the law are cleared up. Crimes for gain, which are certainly the most numerous, have the fewest cases cleared up; on the other hand, sexual offences and crimes of violence have well up to 50 or 60 per cent of the cases cleared up.

Against this whole background we hope to have shown why the question we are concerned with is who are those who come in contact with the criminal law, *not* who are those who transgress the law. The two categories are not the same.

Who, then, are those who come in contact with the criminal law, or more precisely with criminal punishment? They are first and foremost men. Women are practically never registered for breaches of the law in Norway, and when they are it is usually for rather trifling matters. Among the accused in 1965, according to the police statistics, only 8 per cent were women, and among those convicted, fined, or having their prosecution suspended, some 9 per cent were women. The only type of offence which women commit to nearly the same extent as men is slander. Of this they are guilty in 42 per cent of all the reported cases. Receiving stolen property is another offence in the commission of which women play a relatively large part.

Women's fight for equal rights does not seem to have led to equality when it comes to the more negative forms of behaviour. On the contrary, the trend has been the opposite of what we would expect in keeping with the increase in women's rights generally. In 1960 women comprised 22.2 per cent of all those punished in Norway; in 1960 only 4.7 per cent. Both the absolute numbers and the percentages of women in relation to all those punished have decreased steadily. This decrease is due to two circumstances in particular. First and foremost, throughout the whole period there has been a steady reduction in both absolute and relative number of women committing crimes for gain. In addition, there has also occurred a very marked decrease in the number of women convicted of sexual offences. This latter decrease is due to the fact that a whole series of sexual prohibitions that mainly fell upon women either have been rescinded or at any rate are not enforced any longer. Brun-Gulbrandsen (1958) has undertaken an inquiry in this field. He questions the usual assertion that there has been a closer rapprochement between the two sexes.

The ideal woman in films, weeklies, and best sellers seems in many ways to be more 'womanly' than most housewives could dream of being, and the heroes of the films and detective stories seem to be more masculine than is necessary for most of the practical tasks a man is normally called upon to perform.

And it is also in this difference between the man's role and the woman's, between what is expected of a man and what is expected of a woman in modern society, that Brun-Gulbrandsen has found the true explanation of the differences between the sexes as regards registered crime. What is expected of boys and men is such that it increases the probability that they will break the law. For neither of the sexes is lawbreaking considered a prescribed mode of conduct, but is is less bad if boys do it than if girls do. At the same time boys are less strictly controlled by their social environment.

372

Table X. *Cases investigated in 1965, by final decision or recommendation of police*

	Number of cases	Percentage
No definite person suspected	23,869	50.2
Shelved for lack of evidence	6,360	13.4
Charges withdrawn	3,669	7.7
Minor under 24 years of age	1,08	3.8
No charges brought, for other reasons	474	1.0
Fine instead of sentence	660	1.4
Suspension of the prosecution	2,444	5.1
Charges brought	8,229	17.4
Total	47,654	100.0

Source: NOS A 171, Part 1, pp. 10, 18.

Another main attribute of the registered offenders is their very young age. Figure 4 shows accused persons in 1962 by their age and sex. The curve for men is especially clear. From a cautious start at five years of age, giving 0.10 registered per 1,000 very young gentlemen, the curve climbs steeply to the 14-year level, where no less than

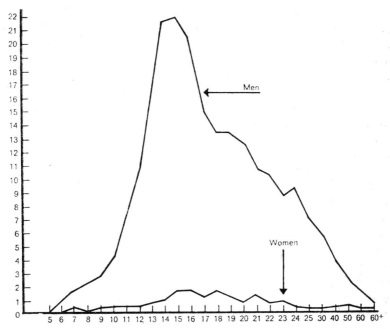

Figure 4. Accused persons per 1,000 inhabitants by age and sex, 1965.
Source: NOS A 171, XIV, p. 31.

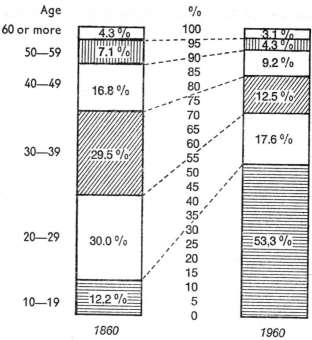

Figure 5. Age distribution of lawbreakers, 1860 and 1960.
Source: For 1860, *Criminal Statistics for Norway, 1860*, B, No. 1, pp. 8–9; for 1960, NOS A 40, p. 20.

21.98 are registered per 1,000. After that the curve slopes slowly down until it ebbs out in old age. For women the figures are much lower throughout, and they lack the same marked swing. With them the peak is not reached before 15 years of age. Offences having to do with malicious damage, breach of the peace, and pilfering are most frequent among the youngest. Taking a motor vehicle without the owner's consent is also a youthful offence, even if the under-14 category is naturally enough scarcely involved in this. More than half of all accused of this offence are under 18 years of age, i.e. they have not yet reached the age when they are eligible for a driving licence. At present, however, a steady increase in the number of older people committing this offence can be found. This is the outcome of the modern use of the motor vehicle when committing crimes for gain; progress has made it steadily more difficult to be an old-fashioned burglar with bicycle and gym shoes.

A comparison of the distributions according to age in 1860 and in 1960 is given in Figure 5. Far more are included in the younger age groups today than there were a hundred years ago. Lawbreakers are now children and youth instead of grown men, a shift which can be interpreted in several ways. The usual way is to interpret it as a sign of a decline in morals: lawlessness has invaded the hearts of children. But the development can also be interpreted in another way. The relative number of registered lawbreakers has remained very stable in Norway during the last hundred years. Since the number of 14-year-olds indicted has increased, it follows that the number of 50-year-olds has at the same time decreased, which must be quite reassuring for those who would be more anxious if they came up against adult rather than juvenile criminals.

The most youthful offenders have a clear tendency to act in groups. Table XI shows that of those aged 5 to 9 years, only 15 per cent acted alone, 39 per cent had one accomplice, 22 per cent had two, and not less than 25 per cent had three or more accomplices. Among 10- to 13-year-olds the circumstances are about the same. But then in the next age class the number of those who act alone increases, and in the age class 18 to 20 years, about half assert that they have been alone in committing the offence. For the oldest offenders a full 88 per cent acted alone.

We know very little about the nature of Norwegian group offenders – very little about the structure and backgrounds of the groups. The only inquiry to pay special attention to whether any definitely organized groups can actually be found is Brøgger's study of a rather strongly criminal environment where he carried out participant observation. He tends to the conclusion that there is a lack of any definite group structure. In this youthful environment very little is to be found in the way of clearly defined roles. Such demarcations are normally an expression of a system embracing reciprocal rights and duties, and their absence consequently indicates a rather loose structure. There were few signs of solidarity and organization in these groups, e.g. no distinctive uniform. Moreover, only to a very limited degree was there any recognition of mutual obligation, there being at the same time very little

Table XI. *Accused persons in 1965, by age and number of accomplices (percentage)*

Accomplices	5-9 years	10-13	14-17	18-20	21-24	25-39	40-56	60 and over	Total
0	15	16	30	49	60	72	79	88	46
1	38	31	36	30	25	19	13	8	27
2	22	23	17	13	10	6	5	3	14
3 or more	25	30	17	8	5	3	3	1	13
Total	100	100	100	100	100	100	100	100	100

Source: NOS A 171, Vol. 1, p. 13.

in the way of clear leadership. Brøgger found most leadership, and on the whole the most definite structure, among the gang that from a criminal point of view was the most active in this environment. The leadership was stronger here than elsewhere, because the leader had a monopoly of something that nobody else in the group had, namely contact with other individuals and other groups. He had this monopoly because the other members in this group had an exceptionally limited ability to make contacts.

Ragnar Hauge (1963, 1964) has put forward a hypothesis that the more peripheral members of the loosely-knit youth groups will presumably be those most deeply engaged in criminal activity. He here combines a knowledge of group structure with the phenomenon of fictitious social pressure – the well-known phenomenon that everyone believes that everyone else either is or thinks something quite different from what he really is or thinks. The more peripheral members in the youth groups will have poorer contact with what is really happening in the gang, and will thereby more easily be led astray by the others' talk – which *is* only talk. The central members will know that no one really lives up to all the idealized descriptions of heavy drinking, active sex life with the local 13-year-olds, and nightly burglaries. The peripheral members, however, will not have the same opportunities for checking the information, and often have, besides, a special need for distinguishing themselves in order to advance themselves in the gang. As a result, they live up to what the others know is only a manner of speaking. For the time being we do not know how far this hypothesis holds good.

Norway's registered offenders are generally young men who generally come from or dwell in towns. A little more than two-thirds of all reported major crimes occur in such districts. There are 6.5 reported major crimes per 1,000 inhabitants in the rural districts, compared with 21.9 per 1,000 in the towns in 1965. As regards figures for those accused of major crimes – cases in which the perpetrator is known to the police – the towns continue to dominate the picture. But the relation between town and country becomes a little more even, probably because the risk of discovery is less in the towns.

To be registered as an offender is to experience an *important social reverse*. But it is not only in relation to the law that offenders are losers. With regard to both occupation and education they rank lower than non-offenders.

Of all 19-year-olds in 1952, more than two-thirds of the registered offenders had only a primary education, while less than half of the non-offenders had to content themselves with so poor an education (Christie 1960, p. 159). In Oslo the differences were even more marked. The lawbreakers on the whole had to content themselves with an education worse than that of their fathers – and this in an age when children commonly obtain more education than their parents.

Some of these offenders probably had to leave school because of their offences. But this cannot be the whole story. We know from several studies among those expelled from school that there is usually a long process leading to such expulsion. A series of failures at school often leads to their being held in less esteem by their companions.. As a result, they gradually go over to new groups, especially to those in which school results are of no importance in evaluating one another. It is rather the other way around – good school results rank low with the new companions. The educationally handicapped often go over into the group that represents a *reaction movement* against the normal community.

In line with this educational background, registered offenders later in life must content themselves with very modest occupations. Thoroughly conspicuous is the disproportionately large number of registered offenders found within the occupational category of seamen. Christie (1960) found that of the 19-years-olds in 1952 not less than 22 per cent of the registered offenders gave this as their occupational background, compared with only 9 per cent of the rest of the age cohort. Møglestue (1962) reports to have found similar differences in a sample of prisoners. This greatly disproportionate representation is presumably due both to the fact that seamen's work is sought by delinquents of various types, and to the fact that it is an extra burden for persons with special problems. Brun-Gulbrandsen and Irgens-Jensen (1964) have demonstrated that the alcoholic problems of youths on their maiden voyage worsen as the number of months at sea increases, even if the number of handicaps they originally had to face remains constant.

To sum up, we can say that clientele of the criminal courts differ to a considerable degree from the average population. A more thorough analysis would show that the differences become greater the more serious the offence. The whole body of first-time offenders is differentiated mainly by being male, young, urban, worse-educated than average. But if we focus on persons who after a long series of offences are lodged in long-term prisons or in the corrective schools for young lawbreakers, we subsequently encounter persons who are stamped with the mark of physical, psychological, and social handicaps in all of their life's spheres. This category – which many of us take to be the typical criminal – is rather small. It is in many respects as atypical of all registered offenders as they are of all lawbreakers. But we must not forget that this small and atypical category deserves the highest degree of attention, because of the often very serious problems they create for the surrounding community and for themselves.

Norwegian criminal activity has a generally 'benign' character –

it is especially striking how little violence it contains compared with, for example, its American counterpart. But it is not free from violence, nor is it free from problems – either for the victim, the perpetrator, or the community as a whole. Let us now proceed to see how attempts are made to combat it.

8. LEGAL SANCTIONS

Norwegian law distinguishes between major crimes and minor offences, misdemeanours. Table XII gives the number of persons punished for major crimes according to age and the penalty meted out to them. The largest proportion of them cannot be considered punished at all, in that prosecution has been suspended or conditional sentence granted in about 30 per cent of the cases.

Suspension of the prosecution *(påtaleunnlatelse)* does not mean that the slate is wiped clean. In the case of juvenile offenders it means as a rule that the case is passed on to the child welfare council for further measures. Suspension of the prosecution can mean the first step towards detention for several years at a special institution. But this is not usual. Most often the child welfare council will not do anything further in the case.

Table XII shows the sanctions used against the most serious breaches of the laws – the major crimes. But we thereby omit an important category of minor, but hard-hit offenders: the minor offences connected with drunkenness and the illegal distillation and distribu-

Table XII. *Persons punished for major crimes distributed according to age and type of penalty (percentage)*

Type of penalty	Age					
	14-17 years	18-20 years	21-24 years	25- years	Over-all percent-age	Total N
Suspension of prosecution	76.2	15.0	3.5	2.4	29.9	2,129
Fine	2.1	10.0	11.1	14.1	8.9	634
No penalty imposed	0.0	0.0	0.0	0.0	0.0	1
Suspended sentence	6.7	9.7	3.6	3.4	5.7	406
Conditional prison sentence	11.8	39.6	42.3	36.5	29.3	2,087
Unconditional prison sentence	2.6	24.8	39.5	43.3	25.7	1,824
Corrective school	0.6	0.9	0.0	0.0	0.4	2
Security measures only	0.0	0.0	0.0	0.2	0.1	4
Total	100.0	100.0	100.0	100.0	100.0	7,112

Source: NOS A 175 II, Table 5, p. 10.

378

Table XIII. *Persons confined in prison institutions in 1965 by type of offence*

	N	Percentage
All major crimes	1,897	37.5
Minor offences against traffic laws (drunken driving)	2,492	49.3
Minor offences concerned with drunkenness and vagrancy	632	12.5
Minor offences against liquor laws	5	0.1
Minor offences against the military code	9	0.2
Other minor offences	22	0.4
Total	5,057	100.0

Source: NOS A 177, III. Table 3, p. 5.

tion of spirits, and also with motor vehicles. In both categories, fines are the usual sanction. But imprisonment is not uncommon; and because the numbers involved are so large, the result is that the major criminals altogether do not constitute more than one-third of all those who in the course of a year are confined in prison institutions. Table XIII throws light on the situation. More persons are imprisoned for the misdemeanour of drunken driving than for all major crimes put together, and likewise minor offences having to do with drunkenness and vagrancy account for 15 per cent of all confinements. These statistics omit an important category: those serving a sentence in lieu of paying a fine. The infliction of a fine is always accompanied by the imposition of a term of imprisonment in lieu of payment. Persons addicted to alcohol are usually so hard up for cash that the alternative of the term of imprisonment must often be served in the cases of offences connected with drunkenness. Midbøe (1960) found that between five and six thousand imprisonments a year after World War II were due to such cases.

9. LEGAL SANCTIONS IN HISTORICAL PERSPECTIVE

In 1966, there was a daily average of 1,780 persons in Norwegian prisons. Or, expressed another way: 47 of every 100,000 inhabitants were at any given time in prison – a low number in comparison with that of other countries. Norway's rate is somewhat lower than Denmark's or Sweden's, and considerably lower than that of Finland (170 per 100,000) or the USA (about 200 per 100,000).

Figure 6 shows trends in the number of prisoners in Norway from 1815 to the 1960s. In the early 1800s the relative number in-

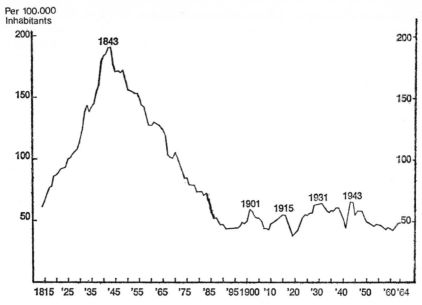

Figure 6. Average number of prisoners per 100,000 inhabitants in Norway, 1814—1964.

creased sharply – probably because earlier punishments (e.g. loss of life or limb) were replaced by prison sentences. From the 1850s onwards, however, the use of prison sentences declined as well, until the relative number of prisoners had at the turn of the century stabilized itself at about today's level. One possible explanation for the decline in the second half of the past century may be that the penal value of days in prison increased, so that less time was needed to atone for the same type of offence. This development has probably also continued into the present century, but has been somewhat neutralized by prison sentences being used for such other purposes as corrective education or treatment (Christie 1966).

10. PRISON LIFE

Much research has been done into what goes on inside prison walls. Organizational sociologists have been interested in what happens within this unique form of total institution – where people sleep, work, eat, play, or vegetate within a limited area and under common supervision. In many ways, prisons represent an extreme case of total institutions, because they are literally so difficult to escape from and because the caste distinction between prisoners and prison employees is far more

380

rigid than that found in hospitals, monasteries, or ships. In addition, prisons are unique in that one's stay there is meant as punishment, an evil meant to be an evil. This does not imply that the prison personnel attempt to make the prisoner's stay as unpleasant as possible – on the contrary, both international conventions and national regulations emphasize that loss of liberty is in itself a great enough evil, without anything else to add to the burden. But this loss of liberty is and remains a loss willed by someone else. Because it represents a moral rejection, it will also remain a constant threat to the prisoner's opinion of himself. All the concrete details of prison existence – being searched on arrival, letter censorship, group marching through long corridors, being locked in, the rattle of keys – all this becomes at the same time a symbol of free society's rejection. True, Norwegian sailors, hunters, military personnel, and soldiers are also acquainted with a relatively high degree of discipline, a hard life, long separation from the opposite sex. But in prison none of this is the result of free choice, being instead the consequence of one's own mistakes and others' censure.

The suffering involved in a prison sentence makes it necessary for the prisoner to create some kind of protection. This suffering becomes in a way the guiding force behind much of what happens, representing a stress transformed into behaviour and actions. The stress becomes so violent because the system itself is so airtight. Not all react outwardly; some withdraw into a dream world, sometimes so effectively that there is no wish to leave the cell. But others do react; some become preoccupied with their own cases, others with what goes on in prison.

Galtung (1959) maintains that during a prisoner's entire stay, a ceaseless mental reworking of his individual case goes on. Gradually, realities are changed into an image more acceptable to oneself and to others, while the feeling of guilt decreases correspondingly. The prisoner's offence becomes not 'wrong', but at most 'stupid – and thus easier to bear. Different prisoners employ different techniques. Some maintain that the law is wrong: it ought not apply to cases like their own. Others accept the law, but insist they have committed offences lying ouside the framework actually covered by the law. A third possibility is that the law is acceptable, but so is the crime as well. There has been a conflict of norms in which the individual had to break the law – mercy killing being the typical example. More frequent is probably the view that the law is right and the offence wrong, but 'I couldn't help it' because of personal circumstances. Here enter arguments from criminology, and the lawbreaker defends his offence on a deterministic basis. There is also the possibility of comparing oneself and one's fate with that of others – the prisoner can, for example, compare himself with all those who were not caught, or with all those convicted of the same offence but who seem to have been punished less severely. Day in and day out, for months, the prisoner reworks these possibilities – well aided by his fellow prisoners – in order to lighten the stress.

The second type of defence has to do with what happens during the prison stay itself. Thomas Mathiesen (1965) has made this a main theme of research. His investigation of Ila security prison showed that a considerable number of prisoners waged an energetic battle against the authorities: not by fighting for other norms, nor referring to criminal values or emphasizing differences, but on the contrary by applying norms and values they had *in common* with the authorities. According to Mathiesen, the Ila prisoner's main defence is to prove that even his superiors do not completely follow the accepted norms of society. No society has fully consistent norms, something most of us realize – and apply to our advantage. 'Thou shalt not lie' – no, but neither need you rush in with the truth in any and every situation. The penal security system, and thus the Ila prison as well, are built on partly inconsistent values, and with different groups of personnel to watch over these values. Treatment considerations will easily lead to situations where benefits are distributed according to highly individual criteria. Less dangerous prisoners will receive more leave and shorter sentences than will dangerous prisoners; those in need of treatment will be sent for talks with the chief physician instead of being sent to a prison cell. But at the same time there will be a counter-press from those who maintain that the benefits ought to be distributed on the basis of a few, obvious criteria: and here the prisoner will utilize that type of defence best suited to his situation and the type of personnel he is confronting.

The same type of strategy appears if we compare various prisons. Prisoners in institutions emphasizing *surveillance* will complain that this breaks with basic, generally accepted values – values to the effect that the idea behind a prison sentence is to help change and even 'cure' the prisoner. On the other hand, those in *treatment*-centred institutions will maintain that this individualization creates a whole set of unjust conditions, and thus breaks with other equally basic values

Perhaps we have here arrived at a fundamental dilemma in society's reactions and sanctions against the lawbreaker: the choice between treatment and punishment. In its fight against lawbreakers, society employs those concepts and strategies presumed to give maximal possibilities for control. Christie has shown how forced labour sentences imposed on vagrants – in practice, this becomes long sentences at the rigorous institution Opstad – became possible because this sanction was defined as something other than 'punishment' (Christie 1960). Thus, it was not necessary to try to achieve a normal balance between the severity of the offence and the size of the sanction. Similar strategies are also used by the prisoners in their defences against the authorities. In his study of 13 Scandinavian prisons, Wheeler (1962) observed conditions 'from the inside'. Prisoners were asked whether they considered the sentence just, whether they thought treatment in prison just, as well as whether they felt their stay there would help them. Some of the most interesting results came from a comparison of answers from two treatment-oriented institutions, Ila and Herted-vester, with answers from two more traditional penal institutions, Bots-fengslet and Vridsløselille.

The main results appear fairly clear: persons in penal institutions find both their sentence and indeed their treatment *more just* than do those in treatment-oriented institutions. But the former consider themselves *less helped* by their stay. Furthermore, the feeling of being helped, of gaining something from one's stay, increases over time for those in treatement-oriented institutions, but decreases over time for those in traditional prisons. Maybe it is simply impossible to have one's cake and eat it too, in this area of life as in others.

11. THE EFFECTS OF LEGAL SANCTIONS

The study of the effects of what society does with her lawbreakers is a field in real expansion, but with few clear answers as yet. First of all it is important here to distinguish between the effects on society as a whole, and the effects on the individual lawbreaker. The former can lead over into questions on the social functions of punishment (Aubert 1954), or to the somewhat more limited area of the effects of 'general preventative considerations' (Andenæs 1966). Although we have little certain knowledge concerning this latter aspect, we do know that no modern industrial nation seems to be able to exist without the control represented by the law and its various personnel.

As to the effect penal sanctions have on the individual lawbreaker, the question immediately presents itself: what type of effect are we looking for – short or long term, mental or physical, effects concerning general social capacity or effects concerning the possibility of re-peating such an offence? Naturally enough, especially the last mentioned is frequently discussed. Knowledge and experience we have gathered from prison life are scarcely conducive to the view that institutions are useful in rehabilitating prisoners. The suspicion that a prison acts as a school for criminals is an old one, recently verified by Bondeson's study (1968). Generally speaking, however, we may say that there is no proof that any one type of institution or length of prison sentence is likely to give more or fewer relapses than any other. The difficulty is, of course, getting permission to arrange controlled experiments in this field. Relapse statistics are of little use, and the *ex post facto* studies which have been made can scarcely be said to present the final answer. There also exist several studies of 'institution' versus 'non-institution'; Bengt Børjeson has conducted the best *ex post facto* investigation here (1966). A controlled experiment is also under way in California (Dept. of Youth Authority 1967). The major question is whether such experiments have managed to control the 'Hawthorne effect' – the effect of one or more of the parties knowing that they are taking part in an experiment. The relapse rate seems to be somewhat lower for 'non-institution', but the final results are not yet available in the form of hard data.

NOTES

[1] Frede Castberg writes, 'In Norway as elsewhere it is generally realized that one is mistaken if one thinks that a positive legal system is "closed" in the sense that every question can be solved by a sure deduction from general rules and concepts' (Castberg 1964, p. 125).

[2] The Health services are contending in a characteristically effective way against the lack of supervision in modern industrial society by checking the quality of both the individual doctor's work and that of the hospital. This is done by putting the patient's history through an electronic computer that can show whether what has been done corresponds with what ought to have been done in the case, and whether the outcome accords with normal standards. A similar technique has been proposed for making checks in psychiatric wards.

[3] A practice that continues in later work in the government Ministries and the law faculty.

[4] This can sometimes give some judges double authority (the Supreme Court judge with the highest marks) and sometimes block nearly every expression of opinion on legal priority (the 3.10 man in private practice), but sometimes it can lead to a conflict, as when the textbook author takes the Supreme Court to task, or vice versa.

XII. Norway in the World Community

By Johan Galtung

1. INTRODUCTION

We shall deal with Norway's relation to the world community of nations in two ways here: first, by comparing Norway with other nations, finding out whether Norway ranks high or low on several variables; and second, by viewing Norway as a part of the world community, as one nation among many, in constant interaction with others in her efforts to realize central values.

In the following, therefore, we shall first attempt to draw a complete picture of Norway's place in the world community, how she is situated in relation to other countries: the *comparative* aspect of Norway's relation to the world community (sections 2–6). From this we may draw some conclusions that will form the basis for various viewpoints as to how we might expect such a country to act in relation to other countries (section 7): the *relational* aspect (sections 8–15). We shall view the relational as a function of the comparative – and here we hasten to add that such a picture may easily become one-sided. True, a country's position may to a great degree have a decisive influence on its politics, but the converse may also apply: through various forms of interaction a country may attempt to establish a certain position in the world; and this we shall keep in mind during our presentation here.

2. WITH WHOM DOES NORWAY COMPARE HERSELF?

Norway is a member of a world community consisting, at the present, of about 135 nations (of which 122 are members of the United Nations); in addition there are some 80–90 areas with about 50 million inhabitants without national status. Altogether, this is a large group indeed, and it is only in the last few decades that communications have brought most parts of the world in close contact with each other. Therefore we can hardly expect a small country to attempt to compare itself or interact with the entire world community. Such ambitions are still the province of the great powers.

With whom, then, does Norway choose to compare herself in the world community? One way of finding this out is by exploring who Norway's 'models' are. The expression 'the countries it is natural to compare ourselves with' plays an important role in motivating proposals in Norway, both official and private. In a small, young, and somewhat hesitant country, proposals for change will be met with scepticism – unless it can be shown that larger, older, and seemingly more assured countries – or at least countries of the same kind – have already carried out similar proposals. This is so, not because this necessarily provides experiences for study, but because the initiator does not run the risk of standing alone – or, even worse, standing *above* the reference group, endangering group solidarity by pretending to 'be something'. Any initiator has a stronger position if he can show that his proposal is not just a product of his or his group's special value orientation, but an expression of a general tendency in 'our part' of the world community.

To get an idea of which nations 'it is natural for us to compare ourselves with' we reviewed 36 government reports to the Storting from the period 1962–1968 and noted the frequency of references to other countries. The average frequency was then computed: the results are presented in Table I.

Thirteen of the 14 countries on the list – the exception is Italy, which has not infrequently been used as a negative comparison – ('Anyhow, we must be better than Italy') are among the 19 richest in the world, as measured in GNP per capita. Obviously, Norway's base for comparison is in the world upper class. Norway's reference group in the world community has these qualities: rich, completely Western, and North Atlantic. At the top are the Scandinavian countries, together with the three Western great (economic) powers. And at the very top are Norway's two former overlords (Denmark and Sweden), together with the greatest of the Western great powers. The Latin countries all rank rather low on this scale, while the socialist and the developing countries do not appear at all. Judging from this list alone, we would say that *Norway compares herself with that which is near, rich, Western, and, first and foremost, Germanic; next come the Latin and the more distant countries.* It is thus characteristic that Germany ranks far above France, and the Netherlands far above Belgium as reference countries. The rest of the world, especially the Socialist and the developing countries, would seem to serve to some extent as a 'negative reference group'.

These are the countries it is 'unnatural' for Norway to compare herself with, which in turn would mean that these are countries Nor-

Table I. *'Countries it is natural for us to compare ourselves with'**

Rank	Country	Relative frequency
1	Sweden	27.2
2	Great Britain	13.4
3	USA	12.7
4	Denmark	9.2
5	Germany (West)	7.9
6	Finland	7.0
7	Italy	4.7
8	France	3.8
9	Netherlands	3.4
10	Canada	1.9
11	Austria	1.5
12	Switzerland	1.5
13	Belgium	1.1
14	Luxembourg	0.3

* Other countries had frequencies too low to be included.

way would rather not see ranked above herself in important international statistics.

We might say it is not bad for so small a country as Norway to have such great models as Great Britain and the USA, numbers 2 and 3 on the list. But, on the other hand, Sweden ranks much higher than either of these, and much higher than Denmark. Sweden's position is probably due not only to her geographical proximity, but also to her comparable economic structure.

A survey of the largest firms in Scandinavia reveals that Sweden ranks far above the others, thereby serving as a model for other countries also interested in industrialization; Denmark, on the other hand, ranks much lower, and thus would be a more natural model if Norway were more interested in trade and agriculture (see Table II).

Denmark's largest industrial concerns are number 35 (Danish Sugar Refineries) and number 42 (Burmeister & Wain), while the largest Norwegian concerns are number 12 (Borregaard) and number 30 (Norsk Hydro). A certain asymmetry in relation to Sweden and Denmark is thus a recurrent phenomenon in comparisons with Norway's closest neighbours in Scandinavia.

The reference group holds true for the upper strata in Norway: *official Norway,* government departments and committees referring to other countries in their reports to the Storting and its commmittees. Let us now compare this picture with countries the *average Norwegian* seems to rank highest – for example, which countries he could think of settling down in (see Table III).

Finland, which occupied fifth place in Table I, has now disappeared

387

Table II. *Largest concerns in Scandinavia, by country*

Country	Number of the 233 concerns with turnover higher than 100 million Sw. kr.	Rank among the largest in industry	Rank among the largest in trade
Denmark	18	35, 42	1
Finland	46	9, 18	2
Norway	21	12, 30	—
Sweden	148	1-8, 10-11, 13-17, 19-29	—

Source: *Ekonomen* 1965.

from the picture. This illustrates the contrast between the political concept of 'Nordic countries' and that existing in the popular consciousness. Otherwise, however, there is fairly good consistency in the picture. But we have a distinct climatic factor in Table III: Australia, Spain, and Argentina–Brazil owe their position on this list, to some extent at least, to the fact that climate was the second most important reason for the 33 per cent who would think of settling abroad.

Let us draw another variable which also illustrates our choice of reference group: Which nationalities can Norwegians conceive of having as *sons-in-law?* (Week's Gallup, *Aftenposten*). Five countries were listed, and opposition to the countries *in* the reference group was, as expected, very low: only 6 per cent were against having a son-in-law from Sweden, 8 per cent against one from the USA. Opposition to our marginal countries and countries *outside* the reference group

Table III. *Which countries can Norwegians think of settling down in?*

Rank	Country	Percentage
1	USA	24
2	Sweden	17
3	Italy	7
4	Denmark	7
5	Australia	7
6	Canada	5
7	Spain	5
8	Great Britain	4
9	Switzerland	4
10	West Germany	3
11	France	3
12	Argentina-Brazil	2

Source: The Week's Gallup, *Aftenposten*, 27 June 1966.

Table IV. *Norway's, Sweden's, and Great Britain's distribution on deciles*

I, X	12	24	27
II, IX	14	12	16
III, VIII	13	13	12
IV, VII	16	9	10
V, VI	16	13	8
Total distribution	71	71	73

was, on the other hand, *high:* 28 per cent against a son-in-law from the USSR, 29 per cent against an Italian, and 45 per cent against a Negro. Therefore, we regard Table I, especially the upper part, as a fairly good expression of what we are interested in understanding.

An important consequence of the arrangement in Table I is that it is only a small part of the world with which Norway in practice compares herself. In other words, while there is nothing to prevent our presenting statistics placing Norway in the *total* world picture, it is improbable that this placement would have much influence on how political leaders or Norwegians in general evaluate Norway's position in the total picture. Norway's position is, for the most part, evaluated relative to the quite small number of countries indicated in Table I; and, *Norway's position is, on the whole, at the bottom of this part of the world community*. Norwegians appear to have selected a basis for comparison which makes Norway the smallest among the great, instead of the greatest among the small. If the basis for comparison had been more modest, Norway would have ranked otherwise; but as it stands, Norway has more than enough to look up to, look forward to, and be motivated by.

But the world does not consist solely of these countries. The reference group was perhaps fairly valid as a world picture in the period of colonialism prior to World War II, but not today. The total placement is important, because it indicates to what degree Norway has placed herself in relation to the older world picture without developing a position in the new one, and without capturing phenomena typical of the rest of the world. And since every passing day brings the entire world closer and closer together, such a limited reference group may increasingly lead to new consequences. We must therefore evaluate a country like Norway both in the total picture and in relation to its own comparison countries – and then have a look at how these comparisons work out in relation to each other.

3. NORWAY'S POSITION IN THE WORLD COMMUNITY: A BIRD'S-EYE VIEW

Here we shall study Norway's position in the world community on the basis of data in *World Handbook of Political and Social Indicators* (Russett et al. 1964). Even though many variables have been excluded, the choice is comprehensive enough to give a good total picture of a nation. (For some of the variables, however, the data are a bit old.) Altogether, there are 75 variables for a highly varying number of nations (ranging from 12 for degree of equality in income after taxes, to 133 for area and population), depending on how complete and reliable the available information. Only four variables were lacking for Norway, a good indicator of the extent and efficiency of its national socio-economic book-keeping system, and ability to report to international organizations.

To place is to compare, to find out how Norway stands in relation to others. That is to say, rank, more than absolute values, is of interest here: whether Norway is among the upper 10 per cent, next 10 per cent, etc., down to the bottom 10 per cent. Such a 10 per cent group, or *decile* of the distribution, will therefore be our measure of Norway's position.

We are immediately struck by how Norway changes decile from one distribution to another: *Norway shows an extremely uneven profile*, probably one of the most uneven in the entire world community. To get a more exact impression of this, we have compared Norway's position with that of the two uppermost countries in the reference group, Sweden and Great Britain (see Table IV).

There is a marked difference. While Sweden and Great Britain have a clear tendency towards the extreme deciles, Norway shows an even distribution. Norway is to be found everywhere possible in the distribution: in other words, Norway occupies highly different positions in the world community, and is thus in marked rank disequilibrium. (It should be remembered that high rank is sometimes found in the top decile, sometimes in the bottom decile.)

In concrete terms, this means that, as far as some variables are concerned, Norway ranks as an average country, a very ordinary country, in a world perspective. This is true, for, for instance, the three most important variables concerning national size: Norway is number 55 (of 133) on area, number 93 (also of 133) on population, and number 34 (of 124) on GNP. If everything else about Norway were in accordance with this middle position, there would indeed be little to make Norway distinctive in a world perspective.

But the distribution in Table IV shows that Norway is extreme in a number of cases, and this forms a part of Norway's profile in relation to other countries. These cases may be divided into the seven areas that follow.

3.1. *Norway is a developed country*

Norway belongs to the world upper class; she lies at the bottom of the first decile as number 11 (of 122) on the criterion most frequently employed to show level of development: GNP per capita. Like other developed countries, Norway has, to a large extent, created an economic system not based on agriculture: her rank is number 79 (of 98) on 'fraction of working population in agriculture'; number 62 (of 75) on 'fraction of total production value derived from agriculture', and number 15 (of 78) on 'percentage of population employed in secondary sector'. However, Norway's tertiary sector is not very highly developed; more highly developed countries have already come much further in conversion of secondary to tertiary employment (e.g. conversion of industrial workers to office workers). We ought to mention that one main reason for the weak position of agriculture in Norway is geographical: Norway is one of the countries with most inhabitants (number 18 of 155 countries) per 1,000 hectares *cultivated* land (1 hectare = 2.47 acres).

3.2. *Norway has a high standard of health*

Norway is clearly one of the developed countries with respect to birth rate and mortality: both these are very low (respectively, 76 of 86, and 44 of 56 countries). The average life expectancy for women is the world's second highest (after Sweden): 75 years, according to these data. (This may well fall with increase in automobile traffic: 14 countries were above Norway in traffic deaths, of which 13 were in the reference group.) Norway is equally low on infant mortality (number 47 of 50 countries), number of inhabitants per physician (number 101 of 126), and number of inhabitants per hospital bed (number 115 of 129). Norway's standard of health is clearly high on a world scale.

3.3. *Norway has a high standard of general education*

Norway is one of the countries with least illiteracy and has a very high enrollment in elementary and secondary schools: number 17 of 125 countries. *But this picture is much weakened* when we view education at university and technical college levels: here Norway is only number 44 of 105 countries, far below the other Scandinavian countries (which are numbers 12, 17, and 25), and with a number of developing countries ahead of her. In amount of funds spent on research (in percentage of GNP), Norway is, generally speaking, at the bottom of the reference group (data from *Forskningsnytt* 1967, pp. 66–69).

3.4. Norway has a high level of equalization of social benefits

While international statistics are somewhat incomplete on this point, they still give some bases for our purposes. Let us take size of farms in the agricultural sector: Norway is number 11 (of 50) on degree of *equality*. This is also reflected in the tendency for the greater part of farms to be privately owned: Norway is number 44 (of 55) in agriculture on a tenant basis. Income distribution also exhibits strongly egalitarian features on a world scale: on income before taxes Norway is only number six of 20 with respect to equality; but on income *after* taxes Norway is number 2 (true enough, only of 12 countries; here more data are needed!), *after Australia*. Income distribution is discussed more thoroughly in Chapter III of this volume.

3.5. Norway has a high standard of internal communications

Norway is number 7 (of 125 countries) on number of printed copies of newspapers per day per inhabitant (and undoubtedly number I on number of newspapers per inhabitant). On radios Norway is number 12 (of 118 countries), but is far behind with respect to television sets (although growth rates are high). It might be objected that newspapers and radios are, first and foremost, media the *elite* employ to communicate with the population; but people in Norway also communicate a lot with each other: Norway is number 12 (of 76 countries) on internal mail per inhabitant. However, on mail to foreign countries per inhabitant Norway is lower, number 23 of 74 countries. This is probably connected with Norway's *relatively* high degree of urbanization – number 32 of 120 – but this degree is low in relation to other developed countries. And the statistics on mail probably ought to be viewed in light of the high standard of general education. Norway ranks below the other Scandinavian countries on number of telephones and television sets per inhabitant, and below Denmark and Sweden on number of automobiles per inhabitant.

3.6. Norway is a highly homogeneous country

In homogeneity Norway ranks not only among the highest, but in part as the very highest: as number 1 (of 66) with respect to percentage of population speaking the country's dominant language ('Norwegian' – although many Norwegians would undoubtedly place more emphasis on the differences between various 'Norwegian languages' than would international statistics), and as one of the lowest countries on the list with respect to percentage of Roman Catholics and Moslems. This homogeneity manifests itself in various ways: where there are no marked group dividing lines on the basis of racial or ethnic criteria, there will, as a rule, be little organized violence between groups: Norway ranks lowest of 74 countries. Also, at the present, Norway has very low immigration and emigration rates: practically everyone in Norway is Norwegian, and most Norwegians are in Norway (although not all those of Norwegian descent). Thus, immigrants will have few of their own countrymen to turn to, and emigrants will seldom find large Norwegian colonies abroad. This is probably also an important factor behind the relatively low rate of mail exchange with foreign countries.

3.7. *Norway is a highly static country*

We have seen that Norway has a high standard of development: but this reflects, to a great extent, a development *which has taken place already*. Norway's population is increasing very slowly (Norway is here number 97 of 111 countries). She has a very high growth rate with respect to capital formation, but GNP per capita changes only slowly – here Norway is number 34 of 68 countries, with a number of socialist and developing countries ahead of her. This may of course be seen as expressing the fact that the higher a country has come, the harder it is to develop further – while the lower a country is, the more it has to catch up.

We find the same saturation phenomenon in other growth rates as well. Percentage engaged in agriculture is decreasing, but not particularly rapidly: Norway is number 25 (of 49) in rate of decrease. Furthermore, a criterion such as number of inhabitants per hospital bed, which ought to decrease in a developed country, is indeed decreasing – but here Norway is only number 49 (of 90 countries) in rate of decrease.

Another indicator pointing to Norway as a relatively stable country (i.e. great changes should not be expected in the future) is David McClelland's index of 'achievement-orientation' (also reproduced in Russett 1964, Table 56). This is compiled on the basis of the content of school children's books, to what degree these books depict men who through work and toil and ambition attained great results. The theory is that such tales will give children attitudes which will be transformed into creative activity when they grow up. The opposite is books emphasizing luck or moral qualities. Here the Norwegian folktale figure Espen Askeladd as a *motif* would certainly seem to indicate the second type – Askeladd is cunning, all right, but he is first and foremost good, and considerate for others. Indeed, Norway is number 26 of 41 countries, while *above* Norway we find a great many developing countries, socialist countries, and European countries Norway usually does not compare herself with (e.g. number 1: Turkey). Great Britain and Sweden follow directly after Norway. And Denmark – which in many respects should be considered a highly-cultivated, developing country with intensive agriculture, by geographical chance placed in Scandinavia – comes almost at the bottom (number 38). Incidentally, all the top countries on this list are republics.

We do not wish to put too much emphasis on this discovery, although it does indeed fit in in several connections: such data can be somewhat coincidental. But if this can be said to be a valid discovery, it is compatible with the many low growth rates Norway has, and it reinforces the image that rapid development in the world community is now taking place in many countries outside Norway. This is of course connected with the fact that Norway is, to some extent, *arrivé*, judged by current criteria. Norway has attained a form which makes possible continued rapid economic growth; but in the social structure itself, in institutional expansion, the data do not indicate that Norway today represents a high degree of dynamism.

McClelland, however, has an interesting side perspective on this. According to him, various factors promote achievement-orientation, one of them being the father's absence from the home setting, such that the father cannot dominate his children to any great extent. Two conditions favour such long-term absence: frequent warfare, and a large merchant navy. And Norway, although not ranking high on the first, certainly ranks all the higher on the second factor. In building up her merchant navy in the last century, Norway thus – according to McClelland – got more than she originally bargained for: the merchant navy brought in revenue, while the absence of authoritarian fathers created a fund of achievement orientation which in turn could be converted into entrepreneurial activity in industry and elsewhere later on in the century and indeed on into the twentieth century as well. This development generating factor, however, is weakened: with increasingly higher standard of living, fewer persons (and especially those who have already started a family) will want to be, or have to be, separated from their children for long periods of time, so that the merchant fleet is increasingly manned by foreigners; Norwegians stay at home with their families – and achievement orientation is weakened. We only present this reasoning for what it is worth – an interesting side perspective worthy of more investigation.

These then are the seven characteristic features presented by this particular source. However, we ought to mention some other data on Norway's position in the world community, because they differ from what many believe.

Norway ranks very high in percentage of election votes for socialist parties – number 5 (of 58 countries; Communist parties are here not classified as socialist). This is connected with the total picture of Norway drawn above, but there are two conclusions we ought *not* to draw

394

from the fact that Norway was for a long time under a Labour Government (*Arbeiderpartiet*):

First, Norway is right in the middle on indicators of size of public sector in the total, over-all picture: neither very high nor very low, whether on state expenditures, state revenue, or labour force employed by the state. Second, Norway is not particularly high on amount of national product utilized for welfare expenditure. Ten other countries are ahead of Norway here: among them five members of the EEC (all except Luxembourg) and the three other Scandinavian countries. (Iceland is generally not included in statistical surveys (*UN Statistical Yearbook* 1958).) At the top is Germany, among other factors thanks to Bismarck's policies, having a standard of welfare almost three times that of Norway (as measured by this indicator); Austria ranks as number 2.

But all this does not mean that Norway is not marked by 'state-ism'; that is, the state is not a fundamental factor on the national scene. We shall now take a closer look at this special feature of our picture.

4. NORWAY AS AN EXTREMELY ANTI-PLURALISTIC COUNTRY

An important factor in evaluating a country's social and political structure is the degree of pluralism in that country. By degree of pluralism we mean whether all the country's inhabitants are subjected to the same type of influence from institutions, or whether the population is divided into groups, each with its own institutions. In short: Is the population cut from the same pattern, or has the society various patterns to offer? Does the population express its wishes and feelings in the same institutions, or in various different institutions?

Our immediate impression is that Norway must be an extremely anti-pluralistic country. It is dominated by one school system, one set of institutions for higher education, one church denomination, one national broadcasting system for radio and television; and all four of these are, in addition, state controlled. Such a first impression is not at all weakened by confrontation with such indicators of pluralism as percentage of population born abroad, organization of the school system, organization of religious life and organization of radio/television. For all these indicators we have compared Norway with several other countries, both far and near – a sufficient number to shed light on the general picture of Norway's extreme position.

4.1. *Percentage of population born abroad*

This is an important factor in this connection, as pluralism is strengthened if a large pergentage of the population has been born and brought up abroad.

Table V presents a survey of percentage of population born abroad for several countries, in decreasing order. (Unfortunately, we have no data on how long the stay abroad was, and thereby how much these persons could have been influenced by the foreign country before leaving for Norway.)

Table V. *Percentage of population in selected countries born abroad, 1950-1966*

Rank	Country	Percentage
1	Australia	16.9
2	Canada	14.7
3	France	7.4
4	Switzerland	4.4
5	Sweden	4.0
6	Turkey	3.4
7	Great Britain	2.9
8	Brazil	2.3
9	Thailand	1.9
10	Norway	1.7
11	Finland	0.7
12	USA*	0.5

Sources: Statistical Yearbooks and Census Reports for the respective countries, 1950-1966.

* USA has, however, 19 per cent of the population registered as of 'foreign stock'.

At the top we have two typical immigration countries. We see furthermore that many of the countries in the reference group rank higher than Norway: Norway's position is low, as mentioned earlier, but not extremely so.

4.2. *Percentage of pupils attending private schools*

Most of the school system is, in the majority of countries, a state concern, so that any pluralism in this area will generally take the form of private schools. Of course, we must recall that this is not an unproblematic indicator: within the public school system itself there can in reality be great variations (from district to district, between types of schools, between various courses and subject divisions); and there can be built into the system a form of decentralization and freedom of choice for the individual teacher, both of which tend to increase

Table VI. *Pupils in private schools in selected countries, 1950-1966 (percentage)*

Rank	Country	Primary School	Secondary School	Remarks
1	Chile	25.9	34.1	
2	Ecuador	19.3	31.7	
3	France	15.1	22.8	
4	USA	15.0	11.2	
5	England	8.3	29.5	
6	Denmark	7.4	16.4	
7	Canada	(4.3)	(4.3)	Primary and secondary combined
8	Austria	2.2	7.9	Percentage of *classes*
9	West Germany	0.83	32.7	Percentage of schools
10	Japan	0.50	3.21	
11	Norway	0.36	3.1	

Source: See Table V.

pluralism. Likewise, private schools may be rather similar to each other – indeed, rather similar to those in the public system as well. All the same, we feel this is a valid indicator worthy of notice. In Table VI, the countries are arranged in descending order for the primary schools – primary schools because we felt these to be most important in any socialization process.

Table VII. *Religious denominations in selected countries, 1950-1966*

Number*	Country	Percentage in the largest religious denominations	Percentage in the two largest religious denominations	No. of religious denominations with 1 per cent or more of population
1	USA	25.7	45.4	8
2	Korea	27.0	49.7	5
3	Australia	34.9	88.8	8
4	Netherlands	40.4	86.7	3
5	Canada	43.3	63.8	9
6	Japan	50.0	96.2	2
7	Switzerland	52.7	98.1	2
8	Austria	89.0	100.0	2
9	Finland	92.4	97.9	2
10	Brazil	92.5	96.9	3
11	Thailand	93.6	97.5	2
12	Norway	96.3	97.2	1
13	Turkey	99.0	99.4	1

Sources: See Table V.

* Order of increasing percentage for highest denomination.

397

There are in the world many countries ranking higher or lower than Norway on this list; but in this connection Norway is found to be lowest on both dimensions, with quite a few of the countries from the reference group above her. Also above Norway, however, are several countries Norway would not ordinarily compare herself with, except negatively, such as Chile and Ecuador – both of them countries marked by a strong but small upper class which desires and gets its own school system. Thus, we might perhaps say that Norway, in rejecting this class-dominated form of pluralism, not based on free choice, has also rejected the more elective forms of pluralism found in some of the countries in Table VI.

4.3. *Distribution of population as to religious denomination*

A nation's capacity for maintaining peaceful co-existence between two or more religious denominations is probably also a fairly good expression of pluralism – although it may instead simply indicate indifference. In the countries presented in Table VII, however, there is no special reason to prefer the latter interpretation. Countries are arranged in order of increasing percentage for the largest denomination.

Here we see Norway in a rather different perspective than the usual one: Norway is found together with countries strongly dominated by *one* denomination, although not necessarily Christian. The Evangelical Lutheran Church is thus even more strongly dominant in Norway than the Roman Catholic in Brazil or the Buddhist in Thailand, although it is not so strong as the Moslem faith in Turkey.

4.4. *Television and radio*

The socialist countries excepted, ownership and actual control of newspapers is pluralistic in most countries – at any rate, more so than institutionalization of religion, for example. But television and radio are considered by many as at least equally important, if not more so, as influential factors. Ownership of these media is therefore absolutely fundamental.

Table VIII presents data on 17 countries, arranged at random, as the data give no basis for clear ranking in most cases. We find Norway at the bottom with respect to pluralism, but joined there by several other countries in the reference group.

To sum up then, Norway is, to begin with, an unusually homogeneous country with respect to race and ethnic conditions (especially language). Only a small percentage of the population were born abroad and are thus potential culture carriers. True, we find a great many tourists (although most of them may be found to be Swedish auto-

Table VIII. *Television and radio corporations in selected countries, 1964—1965*

Country	Number of television corporations	Remarks on control, etc.	Number of radio corporations	Remarks	Number of languages
Denmark	1	State, US Military television on Greenland	1	State	3
Finland	1	State, sends commercial programs	1	State	2
France	1	State	1	State	2
Norway	1	State	1	State	1
Great Britain	2	State – ITA commercially controlled and financed	1	State	1
Greece	none		1	State	1
Iceland	none	US Military television	1	State	1
Italy	1	State	1	State	1
Netherlands	5	Private	1	Private	1
Portugal	1	State	23	State/Private	1
Spain	1	State	12	State/Private	1
Switzerland	1	State, some commercial broadcasting	1	State	4
Egypt	1	State	2	State/Private	6
Ethiopia	none		2	State/Private	3
USA	several	Private, commercial, educational broadcasting	9	Private	1
Nigeria	several	Commercial, educational broadcasting	1	State/Local government	17
Japan	70	State/private, one non-commercial, television several commercial, US military	59	State/Private	1

Sources: *The Europe Yearbook* 1965, and *The Middle East and North Africa* 1965.

mobile tourists), but their cultural message is more fleeting, not a lasting source of pluralism. This homogeneous population passes, for the most part, through the same school system, much more so than in other countries, and belongs, to a great extent, to the same religious denomination, also here much more so than elsewhere. To the extent that the population is exposed to radio and television, it is the same corporation which carries the message of a homogeneous Norway to them – a state corporation, which, moreover, works in close contact with both the state school system and the state church. In other words, the country itself, the state school system, state church, and state radio/television system have no sizable competitors within the national boundaries. Even though all four do possess a large degree of tolerance and scope, we must conclude that Norway is a highly protected country where sources of pluralism have dried up – if indeed there ever have been any there in modern times.

A glance at the Tables gives the impression that Norway must hold something like a world's record in anti-pluralism, at any rate in the non-socialist part of the world. This at once raises the question: Why has the country turned out like this? We shall only indicate some possible answers and interpretations.

First, a 'monolithic', 'unitary' system might simply be a logical consequence of a small, poor country's difficulties in making its scanty resources sufficient for competition with other countries. But such a view presupposes 1) that this is the result of logical thinking, and 2) that the logic holds. It cannot, however, be proved that a pluralistic system necessarily wastes resources or functions as less productive of resources than does a monolithic system.

A second, more attractive interpretation is connected with the concept of justice and universalism: everyone shall be treated equally, from Kirkenes in the extreme north to Lindesnes in the south; and this is best achieved by having all benefits extended by the same institutional framework. But, we might ask, where does this idea come from – and a possible answer might be found in the great degree of equality which seems always to have prevailed in Norway as compared with other countries: Norway never had a truly feudal upper class; the peasants and farmers to a large extent owned their land themselves.

It is the third interpretation, however, which we shall concentrate on. A social pattern does not appear from nowhere; it can be the result of an intense struggle, but it may also be an expression of continuity, simply an uninterrupted continuation of earlier patterns. And the anti-pluralistic pattern in Norway, marked by a high degree of state domination, is not a new Norwegian phenomenon. Instead, it is a natural successor to the system prevailing during Norway's period as a colonial land: several hundred years before 1814, perhaps up until 1905 – for that matter, also during the 1940–1945 German occupation. Most colonies are administered through a strong, local state administration controlling central organs (e.g. precisely such features as we have noted: immigration, school system, religion, mass media); this administration has its centre of gravity outside the colony's borders (in Copenhagen, Stockholm, Berlin), and the local population (the 'natives') are accustomed to regard the state as a source of authority, as the legal ruler in a multitude of connections. To contest its legitimacy is not to deny its significance, on the contrary. Thus, in practice Norway has a socio-political system in many ways reminiscent of developing countries, not because Norway is poor, but because developing countries also are young as nations and are marked by administrative patterns from colonial times. In this respect, then, we may view Norway as an old developing country, rather than a young, developed one.

Another perspective of the same theme is presented in Harry Eckstein's *Division and Cohesion in Democracy, A Study of Norway.* Eckstein's point is that Norway's stability is *not* due to the country's homogeneity, or that she again and again has one institution where many other countries have a more pluralistic solution. For Eckstein, *congruence* is a main point: an administration is stable to the extent that its way of exercising authority is reflected in other parts of the society: in organizations, economic life, school, the family. Eckstein distinguishes between countries where all such relationships to authority are *similar* (e.g. all democratic, or all authoritarian) and countries where they are *dissimilar;* and, according to his theory, a regime is most stable in the first case. Intuitively this seems reasonable indeed. The individual receives a kind of pattern for decision-making and social interaction in general; this pattern is then reinforced in other connections, eventually building a foundation for general attitudes to authority – a foundation which will stand the administrative authorities in good stead if they exercise power in the same way.

Eckstein views congruence as typical for Norway – and this explains Norway's stability. Much of his data help confirm this, especially data from Norwegian organizations. But it is difficult to see that the Norwegian family, school, or economic life is particularly democratically organized. There is a movement towards more democratization in these areas today, but Norwegian stability has been a long-lasting phenomenon. On the other hand, it might be maintained that most decisions made in Norway are semi-democratic: the people in control (whether parents, teachers, industry leaders, foremen and members of the board, or the Storting and cabinet) receive a kind of mandate from their subordinates which may be withdrawn to some extent; that those in control listen to their subjects without actually putting the issues to a vote among them; that they are semi-authoritarian, but in a friendly and consensus-oriented manner.

However the case may be, there is something about Eckstein's analysis that corresponds to our impression of Norway as a country with minimal internal variation. Congruence simply means similarity on a slightly more abstract plane: similarity in structure, in power relations and forms of social intercourse in general. But to find out whether Norway really stands out among many other countries in being exceptionally low on structural pluralism, we need comparative investigations not yet carried out. In general, however, we believe it justifiable to view this minimal internal variation as one of Norway's main characteristics, especially because she stands out among other countries in the reference group in this respect. This seems to hold true for rates and averages (homogeneity) as well as for more structural characteristics (monism and congruence), if we accept the somewhat scanty data presented here.

5. NORWAY AS AN EXCEPTIONALLY PEACEFUL COUNTRY

Another area where Norway holds an extreme position is absence of internal violence, although Norway shares this low level with 15 of the total 74 countries Russett covers. Therefore we need more refined data to distinguish Norway's position from the other countries, especially from the positions of the other 15 in the same class.

An investigation carried out by Jonathan Wilkenfeld (1968), based on data collected by Rudolph Rummel (1963), is useful here. Wilkenfeld makes a distinction between two main forms of conflict behaviour, domestic and foreign (i.e. inter- and intranational conflict behaviour).

Table IX. *The ten 'most peaceful' of 75 countries, 1955-1957*

Rank	Country	Index of peacefulness
1	Norway	—.924
2	Ireland	—.919
3	West Germany	—.918
4	Sweden	—.918
5	Australia	—.917
6	Netherlands	—.914
7	Denmark	—.907
8	New Zealand	—.906
9	Finland	—.901
10	Switzerland	—.870

Table X. *Working days lost because of conflict: Norway and Sweden*

Year	Percentage working days lost	Working days lost	Total number of working days
Norway:			
1930	41,877,300	204,797	0.5000
1951-1955	787,709,400	204,007	0.0300
1956-1960	813,829,200	862,878	0.1000
Sweden:			
1930	166,036,800	979,586	0.5800
1951-1955	2,022,605,100	1,081,282	0.0530
1956-1960	2,168,068,500	56,433	0.0028

Domestic conflict behaviour is then divided into three main groups, 'turmoil', 'revolutionary', and 'subversive'. Foreign conflict behaviour is also divided into three main groups, 'warlike', 'aggressive diplomatic', and 'belligerent'. 'Belligerency' defines an actively hostile mood, including such behaviour as severance of diplomatic relations, negative sanctions, and anti-foreign demonstrations. Wilkenfeld's study includes, then, six forms of conflict behaviour in all.

The study shows that *Norway is lowest on all six*. This study includes 75 countries; Table IX shows the ten countries who head the list in absence (therefore the minus sign) of these forms of conflict behaviour.

We see that 'countries it is natural to compare ourselves with' are well represented here. We ought to add that such investigations are necessarily ridden with some weaknesses, both in data collection and in data presentation. But the results are in accordance with other data: nine of the countries in Table IX are, for example, included in the group of 16 mentioned above.

Another measure of peacefulness within a country is the number of working days lost in conflict – although the interpretation can be extreme suppression (either physical or psychological) just as well as extreme ability to solve conflicts by arbitration. Unfortunately, it is difficult to obtain good data on this point, as number of working days lost is alone not sufficient as an indicator: the number must be viewed in relation to the total number of working days. We have, therefore, in Table X, carried out such a comparison only between Norway and the country highest in the reference group, Sweden. While both countries are very low in number of working days lost, Norway is the lower of the two, therefore leading in this form of peacefulness.

It might be objected that we have here dealt only with 'peace at the macro-level' – between countries, and between the large groupings

Table XI. *Frequency of divorce and suicide in Scandinavia, 1960*

Country	Divorces per 1,000 inhabitants	Suicides per 100,000 inhabitants
Denmark	1.46	20.3
Finland	0.82	20.4
Sweden	1.20	17.4
Iceland	0.71	8.0
Norway	0.66	6.4

Sources: Divorce: *UN Demographic Yearbook* 1962, Table 24. Suicide: NOS XII 107, Table 381, p. 320.

within the country. What about 'peace at the micro-level' – within the family, within the individual human being? Here we could draw in many forms of social disorganization and many countries, but the problem of statistical comparisons would become overwhelming. Therefore we shall confine ourselves to placing Norway in relation to the other Scandinavian countries on two forms of 'peace at the micro-level' (see Table XI).

Table XI further reinforces our impression of Norway's extreme position. The main thing, however, is to combine this picture with that we get from Table IX and the data underlying it: this gives a total impression of a country where violent forms of aggression are unusually well controlled. But aggression is often connected with performance orientation, so let us now turn to an indicator of performance.

6. NORWAY AS A PRODUCER OF SCIENCE AND SCHOLARSHIP

Since Norway ranks low in higher education, we might expect that research in general would have a modest scope. In a world where at least 90 per cent of all researchers and scholars who ever lived, live today – where their number is doubled every 15 years – in such a world, the mass effect of science and scholarship is important. There exist critical minimums in many branches of science, both with respect to quality and quantity of researchers, and with respect to equipment. To exceed these minimums requires a scientific and scholarly structure which is *a priori* difficult for a small country to build up, especially when college and university enrollment is so low.

To get an impression of Norway's position in the world-wide scientific picture, we have employed the statistics on the Nobel Prize's distribution by country and scientific field since its beginning in 1901.

A usual criticism of using the Nobel Prize as an indicator of what a country achieves is that the Prize is Western, more precisely, North-Western dominated. By this is meant not so much that it is awarded in 'our' part of the world (Stockholm and Oslo) by persons who, like everyone else, are most easily attracted by that which is nearest to themselves. Rather, and more important, it is especially those performances which our part of the world values highly that are rewarded. Another criticism is that the Nobel Prize rewards only performances in certain fields, and not, e.g. in social sciences, in music, in architecture. But, once these limitations are taken into consideration, the Nobel Prize is clearly of great value as a general direction indicator of which societies perform the 'best' within the framework of the Prize's five fields.

Norway's position here is extreme in a double sense. Five Nobel Prizes have been awarded to Norwegians, three in literature, and two Peace Prizes. Only the USA, Great Britain, Germany, France, and Sweden rank higher in total number of Nobel Prizes in these two fields; and, if this were calculated per inhabitant, Norway would *rank highest on the two fields put together* (Norway's Prizes, however, were all awarded quite some time ago). But now Norway's imbalance enters the picture. In physics, chemistry, physiology, and medicine – in science as such – *no Norwegian has achieved a performance deemed worthy of a Nobel Prize*. In 1969, however, Norwegians shared the prizes in chemistry and economics. Interestingly, the nine countries highest in Nobel Prizes for science are also among the 12 uppermost 'countries it is natural to compare ourselves with'; this would seem to indicate a dilemma for Norway in the world community.

7. NORWAY IN THE WORLD COMMUNITY – SOME THEORETICAL CONSIDERATIONS

Let us now sum up some of these impressions from comparisons between Norway and other countries. Norway generally compares herself with those countries which perform *most* in those directions which large parts of the world today have selected as important; furthermore, she ranks very high in those fields which do not require a highly-developed scientific infra-structure, fields which first and foremost deal with inner, human qualities or with the efforts of individual persons. But, in scientific fields where distribution of general abilities and intelligence plus high general education are indeed necessary but hardly sufficient in themselves, Norway falls behind.

However, we also feel it reasonable to view this in relation to Norway's homogeneity, egalitarianism, moralism, and anti-pluralism.

405

Norway is an extremely egalitarian country; and to maintain this egalitarianism, the main emphasis must lie on something which all can attain, regardless of social class, whether the country has certain aristocratic or certain meritocratic tendencies besides the egalitarian ones. This 'something' cannot be intellectual development, as this would tend to divide and separate, rather than to unite. In more heterogeneous and more pluralistic societies such a division would be more natural, as it would be one division among many; but in a homogeneous and anti-pluralistic society it would stand out. It therefore seems reasonable to believe that the country would emphasize morality rather than intellect, *emphasize being 'good' rather than being 'bright'* – and, to a certain extent, emphasize religion rather than science. The good man who has just found redemption is no threat to equality in the same way that a bright, creative man is. Indeed, he can function as compensation in a society, which, because despite everything else it is highly developed, to some extent must be built upon abilities of the 'bright'. The bright person is regarded as 'somebody who thinks he is something'; his attempts to find new approaches, new forms, will often appear disturbing, and it becomes important to put him in his place through informal social pressure. Elite schools for exceptionally gifted children – indeed, even strong university sectors that emphasize esoteric research and studies – these are viewed as 'un-Norwegian' institutions that either are rejected or come into being only with difficulty.

Anti-pluralism enters this picture in that the initiator, the creative person, rejected in one place, will often be rejected elsewhere, because elsewhere the same norms are also followed. Thus, experiments with new ideas seldom succeed: the initiator does not have the pluralistic society's 'second chance'. *Congruence* enters the picture in that the initiator is in practice often confronted with a network of institutions built up in the very way he is attempting to alter. Thus, an experimenter trying to alter, at *one* point may appear as if he were out to alter Norway herself. Clearly, the limited social experiment is *not* Norway's form.

But this does not mean that change cannot take place, only that such change will often occur on a national scale, legitimized by outside references to 'abroad' rather than to successful experiments within the country. It is in this perspective that we must view the entire *concept of reference group* introduced earlier. And the present low achievement orientation, if we are to stress McClelland's work, subdues tendencies which might break down the egalitarianism in society and strengthen the meritocracy too much. This in turn is directly connected with the low suicide rate: Hendin has indicated that when Norway ranks so much lower than Sweden, this is connected with the fact that Norway also ranks lower on ambition-oriented education and upbringing.

Norway can thus be described as a country that has achieved extreme peacefulness and equality by the help of homogeneity, antipluralism, and congruence. What Norwegians experience as contrasts (for instance on questions of language, religious views, sex/alcohol, all according to where one comes from in Norway) are very weak dissensions compared with what other countries have. In the effort to build up its system, Norway has developed considerably, but the system has now attained a degree of stability which may actually inhibit further development. At the same time, one of the prerequisites for rapid change based on own resources is lacking, namely, extensive investment in the scientific sector. In order to 'keep up', Norway must therefore become highly dependent on other countries, become an imitator rather than an initiator, thereby becoming extremely sensitive to other countries' evaluation. This introduces the entire question of the relational and not merely comparative position of Norway. Of the many distinctive features we have discussed in connection with Norway's position relative to other countries, one appears especially decisive for what the country is attempting to achieve on an *international* scale: characteristic of Norway is not that the country is developed, but the *extreme imbalance* in her total profile. Most of the indicators related to development are, as we have seen, very high (especially Norway's merchant navy fleet), whereas indicators of *size* are completely ordinary (this is true of military potential as well); on the other variables Norway ranks very low, even on a global scale. In general, Norway is an 'over-achiever' on a global scale, in relation to her resources. This has both its causes and its consequences.

The *causes* of imbalance probably lie in one factor: the country has, to an almost extreme degree, managed to turn its many disadvantages into advantages – for only recently did Norway rank very low in almost all respects, in relation to its neighbours. For example:

Norway lacked a true upper class of feudal extent. (In part, this was also true of the cultural upper class.) But on this basis the country built up a highly egalitarian society which encouraged mobilization of talent from the entire population, and not just from a small upper class.

Norway is geographically placed on the fringes of the world, with a disadvantageous climate. For that reason, she was mostly left in peace by her stronger neighbours, at the same time as these neighbours were sufficiently near enough to form a reference group which stimulated her longing for development. The population was not threatened by immigration, so that the density was and remains low.

Norway lay on the periphery with respect to communications, and her coast faces the open and often fierce sea. Thus the country converted to seamanship. Far-ranging ships sailed undisturbed in the peripheral waters of Northern Europe——a thing impossible in the Mediterranean. (Had Norway been placed there, she would have been kept in check by her neighbours, and would hardly have developed.) What was a *peripheral* position, with respect to communications, Norway managed to convert to a *central* one through navigation and the shipping industry. While other countries, in getting high rank, thereby attracted communications, *Norway made herself a central position in the communications system, thereby obtaining high rank.* Norway converted central position into rank, and not the usual reverse.

Norway was exceptionally poor in resources which could form the basis for industry and agriculture (except for water power). Instead, the population concentrated on fishing, shipping, and commerce, which then formed a basis for expansion and strong bonds with other countries, which the country in turn became completely dependent on.

As to the *consequences* of imbalance, we would in general expect a high degree of aggression from a nation which has made more out of its resources and possibilities than would be expected. We would not expect either the natural superiority – and status quo – orientation of the more balanced nation on the top of the world society, or the more servile attitude of the balanced nation at the bottom of world society. Instead, we would expect a general attitude of 'there must be something about us Norwegians, since we've managed to get so much out of so little'. Such a feeling will easily turn into self-righteousness, into an injured attitude if others attempt to question its validity, and into a feeling that Norwegians have something to offer that others need. In other words: that Norwegians would be a blessing for others, and that Norwegian ways of being and of doing things ought to benefit others.

This basic principle may combine both Norway's and Norwegians' *attitudes* and *actions* on the international plane. But how is a country that ranks so low as Norway on such pure power variables as GNP, population, and size – all of them factors necessary for military power – how is she to be aggressive? Aggression need not mean use of power in the sense of 'violence': aggression here is used to mean the attempt to change others, and it may be directed both inwards (as in suicide or apathy) or outwards (as in murder, other crimes, or creative behaviour). A nation or individual which has managed to make *more* out of its resources than one might expect, will on the whole direct its aggression outwards, while a nation or individual which has got less out of its resources, will direct it inwards.

Thus we believe that if Norway had not 3.7 million but 37 million inhabitants, and a GNP ten times greater than what she has, but the same location, the same area, and the same neighbours – then the way would be paved for strong aggression on the part of Norway. Self-righteousness, the feeling of being unjustly treated in being so low on certain variables, the feeling of being entitled to change this: all these would be present. Inner homogeneity and stability, institutional anti-pluralism, tendency towards congruence, equality within the country – all these would make it comparatively easy to mobilize the population under the banner of a national ideology and a central leadership, and under the promise of immediate rewards.

But Norway is not this fictive country, but only one tenth of it, and therefore no real threat to her neighbours. Thus she must find quite other ways and means for any use of power on an international plane. Norway's neighbours are more powerful and rich than herself; she cannot do as Israel (a country which, incidentally, Norway somewhat resembles and with which she also identifies rather strongly). The solution must lie on another plane than direct attempts at controlling other nations. And the international system of today does indeed offer several other possibilities for influence than classical territory-oriented warfare.

For one thing, the desire for influence can find fulfilment through active participation in international organizations both IGOs (inter-national governmental organizations) and INGOs (international non-governmental organizations). Norwegians can again do what they did with their merchant navy fleet: not only man the international community's moving company, but be its managing personnel as well. By maximum Norwegian participation in a maximum number of IGOs and INGOs, both in permanent secretariats and in delegations and conferences, as consultants and experts, Norway will be able to assert herself, let her voice be heard, and influence decisions favourable to the country's interests. Just as we speak of 'imperialism' when one country advances on another (military, politically, economically, cul-turally), we can also speak of a kind of 'infiltration' in international organs.

We would therefore expect certain attitude patterns among Nor-wegians and certain action patterns for Norway with respect to the international community. To this we now turn. But 'aggression', as defined above, is of course not the only basis for Norway's interaction patterns. It is a pattern we can expect in addition to the obvious one: namely, that Norway, as a hesitant, outward-oriented nation, will have a strong tendency to act like the majority of countries in the reference group, in order to further and insure what the country de-fines as her interests. It is, for example, rather clear that Norway will attempt to join international organizations where the reference group is represented poorly or not at all.

8. NORWEGIAN OPINION ON NORWAY AND THE WORLD COMMUNITY

There are three investigations of Norwegian opinion on international relations as shown by the many surveys conducted by the Norwegian Gallup polls.

The first is from Ingrid Eide's examination of these in *Norway and the Norwegians* (in Alstad 1969). In one survey, the inhabitants of various countries, among them the Scandinavian, were asked personally to rank countries in respect to scenic beauty, quality of food, national patriotism, female beauty, etc. All the countries showed a tendency for the majority to emphasize their own country's superiority. Norwegians, however, did so to a much greater degree than any others. And, indeed more important, only Norwegians ranked *Norway* highest on the list, while other countries received varying degrees of support from abroad in their self-glorification. It must be mentioned that Swedes considered Norwegians as ranking very high with respect to patriotism!

The second one is from Galtung's investigation of surveys on international co-operation (in Alstad 1969). The conclusion from many such surveys is this:

> The level of knowledge is low, sometimes very much so—and it appears to rise only through conflict and debate, and over time. Compared with other countries, however, the level of knowledge is not so very bad.
>
> Attitudes to other peoples, especially other races (and gipsies) show marked negative tendencies, at the same time as there appear certain tendencies to self-glorification. This, however, does not hinder a generally very high degree of acceptance concerning international co-operation — it is the personal contact that seems to create difficulties.
>
> Attitude towards co-operation appears to become more positive, the more extensive the cooperation is: There is greater interest for UN than for European co-operation, and greater interest for European co-operation than for Nordic.

In other words, we seem to see an expansive nation, in the sense that Norway opens up in relation to the world, but more from interest to go out to the world than to allow the world to approach her very closely. Thus Norway was, together with the Netherlands, the Western country under German occupation – aside from the Slavic countries – with the lowest percentage of surviving Jews. This was in part due to particular policies of the German administration in Norway – but it was probably also due to the low integration of Norwegian Jews into the population, which again can be traced to homogeneity and lack of training in true (not merely verbal) tolerance.

These features are also evident from Galtung's investigation of Gallup surveys on war, peace, and defence (in Alstad 1969):

There is no doubt that the general orientation is Western. The West is preferred to the East, the USA to the USSR, NATO to the Warsaw Pact, etc.

There are, however, nuances in the picture:

A general scepticism towards great powers causes many critical attitudes to the USA. In several situations, evaluation of the USA and USSR is almost symmetric, and Norway ranks very high in the reference group on this symmetric attitude.

There are also many positive features in the Norwegian attitude to the USSR: the USSR is the winner, the powerful, clever, mighty one.

There is no unqualified acceptance of all Western countries: great scepticism is found towards Germany, France, and, to a certain extent, Spain.

Generally, Norwegians are positive in respect to military defence: any critical attitudes are directed towards its individual national aspects. This, combined with the Western orientation, leads to a positive attitude to Nordic defence co-operation and to European defence co-operation (but in both cases there are many DK/NA).

The long-range perspective is generally optimistic, the short-range more pessimistic, but this depends on external events and crises. With lessened external pressure, worries about international events and relations disappear. Interest level is therefore low in periods when peace-building tactics can most easily be put into effect, and high in periods when a more threatening peace policy (military policy) may be easily launched. A strongly moral attitude lies behind many opinions. War is wrong; the aggressor shall be punished; he is not to be trusted. And if one's faith in a nation is violated, one ought to condemn that nation and turn against it.

In one comparative investigation of foreign policy opinion with Norway among the participants (the so-called Tri-nation survey of France, Norway, and Poland carried out in 1964), some of the findings place typically Norwegian attitudes in an international perspective.

Norway ranked above the other two countries in positive attitude to the UN: 48 per cent wished to base a world order after disarmament on the UN, as against 25 per cent in France and 29 per cent in Poland.

In Norway, 64 per cent wished to spend less on military defence, as against 40 per cent in France, and 32 per cent in Poland.

Norway was the highest of the three (45 per cent as against 33 per cent and 24 per cent) in agreeing to place a part of the country's military defence under UN leadership.

411

Norway was the highest of the three countries in giving the UN an important role as a peace-keeping factor.

Norway was the highest of the three in interest in disarmament proposals and international news in general.

Norway was the highest of the three in level of knowledge on international affairs — e.g., there were more people in Norway than in France who knew that France was a member of NATO *(The UNESCO Courier* 1967).

In general, then, we get the impression of a country whose people are internationally 'committed' and feel that it makes a difference that they are committed. The people have an image of how the world ought to be – *and that image requires first and foremost that the world be a larger edition of Norway.* This identification becomes even easier because the UN is in many ways congruent with the Norwegian authority structure.

We get an even better impression of this if we turn to another investigation which attempts to clarify Norwegian 'peace philosophy', i.e. how people believe peace may be achieved (taken from the *Images of the World in the Year 2000* study). The five most important factors, according to a sample of 500 persons, are shown in Table XII.

We see no references to balance of power, alliance politics, or power at all. Instead, we find the concept of 'realizing Norwegian conditions all over the world', in that relationships between nations in the world community shall become like relationships between people in the Norwegian community. In these five peace philosophies we thus find moralism, the idea of active support to international interaction – all of these supported by the idea that these will serve the cause of peace.

Table XII. *UN voting agreement. Norway and other countries, 1964—1966*

Level of acceptance*	Peace philosophy: 'in order to achieve peace . . .'
0.92	hunger and poverty must be abolished throughout the world
0.84	we must increase trade, exchange, and co-operation, also between countries who do not have friendly relations with each other
0.82	we must improve the UN, so that it will become more effective than today
0.80	it must be possible for people all over the world to choose their governments freely
0.75	the gap between rich and poor countries must disappear.

Source: International Peace Research Institute, Oslo: Norwegian Peace Philosophy (unpublished tables) 1967.

* Level of acceptance is an average based on a three-point scale. It may vary between + 1 and — 1.

412

9. NORWAY IN THE UN

Norway's general position in the world community is also reflected in the form of action in the UN. Since this organization is universal, the country is confronted with not only the entire reference group, but practically the entire world. What then does Norway try to achieve in the UN, what are her aims?

We shall attempt to approach the problem by seeing who it is that Norway votes *most* and *least* with in the UN. The UN is more a sort of market for voting on ideas in the international community than a forum making real decisions of a fundamental nature, which then are put into action. 'Tell me whom you vote with, and I'll tell you who you are', therefore, seems to be a good clue to understanding a country's behaviour in this organization.

Kurt Jacobsen has analysed voting in the UN over a 20-year period, and some of the results of his investigation are shown here. Who Nor-

Table XIII. *UN voting agreement, Norway and other countries, 1964-1966*

Rank	Most agreement	USA/ Great Britain* percentage	Least agreement	USA/ Great Britain* percentage
1	Denmark	90 L	Mongolia	26 L
2	Sweden	86 L	Byelorussia	31 L
3	Iceland	83 L	USSR	32 L
4	Ireland	81 L	Ukraine	32 L
5	Canada	76 H	Poland	32 L
6	Austria	76 L	Czechoslovakia	32 L
7	USA	74 H	Albania	33 L
8	New Zealand	74 H	Romania	33 L
9	Trinidad/Tobago	73 L	Hungary	33 L
10	Japan	72 H	Bulgaria	34 L
11	Italy	72 H	Mali	36 L
12	Netherlands	71 H	Algeria	37 L
13	Jamaica	71 H	Guinea	38 L
14	Turkey	70 H	Jordan	39 L
15	Finland	69 L	Saudi Arabia	40 L
16	Nicaragua	69 H	Afghanistan	41 L
17	Great Britain	69 H	Libya	41 L
18	Luxembourg	68 H	Morocco	41 L
19	Australia	67 H	Yemen	41 L
20	Brazil/Chile/ Panama/Peru	67 H	Egypt/Syria	43 L

Source: Kurt Jacobsen, *Voting Patterns in the UN*, International Peace Research Institute, Oslo.

* USA's and Great Britain's percentage of voting agreement with each country has also been calculated. 'L' indicates that their voting agreement with the country is lower than Norway's, 'H' indicates that it is higher.

way identifies herself most and least with can be seen from Table XIII.

Norway votes least with the Comecon countries and the most radical African and Arab countries. In other words, Norway does *not* associate herself with the countries in the world which today are most fundamentally change oriented, and this is what we would expect of a country which is both stable and highly developed.

Who it is Norway votes *most* with can be summed up briefly. First of all, the *Scandinavian countries,* with Finland far behind the others as we would expect due to Finland's special relationship to the USSR; and with Denmark ahead of Sweden, as we would expect, since Sweden is outside NATO. After these, however, do *not* come all the other NATO countries: of the 12 remaining NATO countries, only seven are among the top 20. Especially we notice that France and Belgium are not high (with 61 per cent and 63 per cent respectively), which would mean that Norway has a qualified solidarity with the EEC countries. As usual, the borderline is drawn between the Germanic and Latin countries.

But stronger than the NATO elements are those from several smaller countries, *of which six are members of the British Commonwealth and belong to its moderate, more Western-oriented wing.* These elements are so strong that if we had only this Table and were to guess the basis of it, we would have guessed that Norway belonged to the British Commonwealth (average agreement: 73) rather than to NATO (average agreement: 70).

The fourth element in this picture is the Latin American countries. If we go as far down in voting agreement as to 66 per cent we get 10 of them, i.e. one half (with Cuba as the lowest of the remaining, 51 per cent). In one respect this is Norway's way of approaching developing countries – through the old, 'white' developing countries in Latin America, who generally vote in agreement with the USA. Of the *new* developing countries which are not members of the British Commonwealth, Norway has highest voting agreement with Rwanda and Laos, 50 per cent. But with such an important spokesman for the Afro-Asian bloc as India, voting agreement is only 50 per cent. And with Uganda, the other country (in addition to India) to which Norway has sent considerable technical aid, Norway shows likewise only 50 per cent voting agreement.

Again, Norway appears as a North-Western nation, but not extreme in that direction. As we see from the Table, Norway rejects the Eastern Bloc and the South-Eastern countries, but not so much as do the USA and Great Britain. And Norway's agreement with the Scandinavian countries, neutral Austria and Ireland, and the more radical Commonwealth countries Jamaica and Trinidad–Tobago is

414

higher than that of the USA and Great Britain. In return, Norway's voting agreement with the more conservative Commonwealth countries, European countries, and Latin American countries is lower than that of the USA and Great Britain. In other words, Norway seems to have placed herself in a bridge-builder position between East and West and between South and North.

The list of 'countries we co-operate with in the UN' is not identical with the list of 'countries it is natural for us to compare ourselves with'. True, we do find most of the same countries: aside from Germany and Switzerland, not members of the UN, only the Latin countries Belgium and France are missing. But there are great differences in the order of countries within the lists. Probably the reason is that in the UN, geographical and cultural proximity are much less important, so that ideology, working companionship, and even purely personal factors enter the picture. *It may be that in the UN, Norway ventures forth more in the world community, and as a bridge to the 'new' world Norway uses the system of nations that England has built up.* Here Norway's one-sided concentration on English as a second language and her traditionally pro-British sentiments are of course important. In the UN, we see that Norway partly separates herself from her close contact with the USA and Great Britain, instead identifying herself with other countries which are also small, but also fairly rich. On a purely political-technical basis Norway concentrates on co-operation with the other Nordic countries (this co-operation was for a long time co-ordinated from Oslo) and on Ireland and Canada – who also have played very active roles in the UN.

How far this policy will take Norway is another matter. We might note that it takes her into the right-wing branch of the 'world community's Labour Party', to coin a phrase – but nowhere near into the 'world community's Socialist People's Party' (i.e. the party to the left of the Labour Party. Translator's note). In other words, Norway's UN policy is a true copy of her domestic policy, aside from the fact that she, through her UNCTAD policy, seems to have a more negative attitude to the less-privileged countries than she has to her own less-privileged citizens.

10. NORWAY AS A CONTRIBUTOR TO THE WORLD COMMUNITY

Because Norway attempts to become attached to international organizations, especially to those that are universal and where her reference group is best represented, we would expect Norway's contributions to *development aid* to favour strongly the multi-lateral organs, because

415

Norway could thereby help strengthen her own position within these organs. There is, naturally, also a negative reason: Norway, as opposed to many other countries in the reference group, has not had colonies in recent times and has therefore not established a set of interaction channels through which bilateral aid can flow naturally and easily (see Table XIV).

Norway ranks lowest (together with Denmark and Japan) on total contributions to developing countries, and it is not lack of private transactions that pulls Norway down. But on contributions to the most important multi-lateral organs in this field, Norway rises sharply again, with her typical imbalance. A measure of imbalance has been calculated in the far right-hand column (although the time references do vary somewhat), and the countries ordered accordingly. This shows how Norway, together with Denmark and closely with Sweden and Canada, leads in policy favouring the UN in development aid (but with Sweden clearly above on all dimensions, as usual). As a contrast we see France, who follows diametrically opposed politics with a clear predominance of bilateral forms of aid, both private and state.

Table XIV. *Ranking of 14 countries, according to per capita contributions in US dollars to developing countries*

Country (rank order)	a Private transactions 1956-1962	b Total transactions 1956-1962	c UN Development Program contribution 1966	d International Development Agency contributions 1966	Difference*
Norway	11.5	13.0	3	5	9.0
Denmark	11.5	13.0	2	6	9.0
Sweden	8.0	9.0	1	1	8.0
Canada	11.5	10.5	5	3	6.5
Netherlands	6.5	5.5	4	4	1.5
Japan	11.5	13.0	14	13	— 0.5
Austria	9.0	10.5	11	11	— 0.5
Belgium	14.0	7.5	9	10	— 2.0
Great Britain	5.0	4.0	8	2	— 3.0
Switzerland	1.0	2.0	6	—	— 4.0
West Germany	6.5	5.3	10	9	— 4.0
USA	3.5	3.0	7	7	— 4.0
Italy	3.5	7.5	13	12	— 5.0
France	2.0	1.0	12	8	— 9.0

Sources: For *a* and *b*, OECD 1964; for *c* and *d*, Norwegian State Department *(Utenriksdepartementet* 1967, p. 107.

* Column 2 minus columns 3 and 4 added together and divided by two.

Table XV. *Contributions to and via UN High Commision for Refugees, 1959-1963*

Country	Dollars per inhabitant
Norway	0.54
Netherlands	0.40
New Zealand	0.36
Denmark	0.26
Sweden	0.22
Iceland	0.20
Belgium	0.12

Source: Unpublished information from UN High Commission for Refugees, 1967.

We ought to mention in this connection that Norway was nation number 2, after the USA, in launching a government peace corps whose aim was to send low-paid volunteers to work in developing countries. Like other Norwegian bilateral aid projects, this has been marked by strong geographical concentration as to host countries.

We have mentioned morality, and the great emphasis placed on international organizations, like the UN, as basic characteristics of Norwegian orientation in the world community. We would therefore expect Norway's contributions to the world community via the UN's *refugee aid* programs to be especially high, because both characteristics are in a way united here. And this is indeed the case, as we see from Table XV.

Norway ranks at the top of a group of 'small, good countries', a milieu which also corresponds with most of our reference group.

Finally, let us take a look at Norway's contribution to the world community through Christian *missions*. This form of contribution ought to suit Norway especially well: here practically all the good reasons to go outside the national borders are united. Contributions may be made from individual to individual, instead of being ab-

Table XVI. *Missionaries sent and contributions collected for missions*

Country	Missionaries sent per 100,000 inhabitants	Total contributions, per inhabitant
Norway, 1965	27.4	9.3 N.kr.*
Norway, 1963	25.0	5.7 N.kr.
Sweden, 1963	19.0	3.7 Sw.kr.
Denmark, 1962	6.4	1.4 D.kr.

Sources: Mission statistics from the respective countries.

* Norway is much higher in 1965 than in 1963 because the 1963 statistics exclude various administrative expenditures included in 1965.

stracted to a relationship between nations; that is to say, contributions may be made in a way more in keeping with the Christian ethic dominant in Norway. The contributions may be combined with a fundamental value in Norway: Christianity. This message may be joined to concrete actions and a concrete way of life – the missionary's – which is also a way of carrying to others the Norwegian social structure.

To get a closer view of this we have employed two measures of degree of missionary activity *from* a country: number of missionaries per 100,000 inhabitants, and voluntary donations to missions, per inhabitant (see Table XVI).

Among the countries closest to Norway, it is clearly Norway who has the leading position in missionary activity. This is also true if we extend the framework of comparison.

11. NORWAY IN OTHER INTERNATIONAL ORGANIZATIONS

The world community has other international organizations than the UN: about 600 IGOs and 1,600 INGOs. Norway belongs to a great number of them, thereby increasing her possibilities for influence, indeed, far more than would be expected from Norway's tiny size. Thus, Norway is a member of the UN's special organizations, of GATT, OECD, EFTA, Council of Europe, and NATO. In general Norway has the same pattern of membership regarding these important organizations, as have most of the upper countries in the reference group – with important exceptions. Norway differs from Sweden in belonging to NATO, from the Common Market countries in belonging to EFTA, and from Great Britain in that the latter has

Table XVII. *Norway and the international organizations, non-governmental (INGOs) and governmental (IGOs) (1964, last columns 1954)*

INGO/capita	IGO/capita	International officials/capita
1. Israel	1. Panama	1. Switzerland
2. Norway	2. Costa Rica	2. Belgium
3. Switzerland	3. Nicaragua	3. Netherlands
4. Denmark	4. Mauritania	4. Denmark
5. Finland	5. Liberia	5. Sweden
6. New Zealand	6. Paraguay	6. France
7. Panama	7. Central African Rebublic	7. Norway
8. Ireland	8. Israel	8. Great Britain
9. Uruguay	9. Norway	9. Italy
10. Austria	10. Honduras	10. North America

a 'bridge to the continent' via membership in the Western European Union, to which the Common Market countries also belong. Otherwise, the reference group is clearly the same membership group, and the few points of difference are also some of the most explosive debate topics in Norway. And this leads us to modify our reasoning a bit: while it is doubtless true that Norway most often follows the countries in the reference group on questions of membership, it is also true that being together with other countries in an important international organization gives a basis for comparison which may lead to expanding the group.

The extent of Norwegian penetration into (and by) the system of international organizations can to some extent be judged from Table XVII.

The first two columns will naturally favour the small countries since there are many international organizations today of which most if not all nations almost have to be members. Thus Norway is number 14 in the world when it comes to number of IGOs, but number 9 when it comes to number of IGOs per capita, as can be seen from the Table. Together with Norway are many of the reference countries, except in the second column, where more or less compulsory membership gives high position to a number of small countries in other parts of the world.

In short, the non-territorial sphere, the field of international organizations, is an area where Norway may be said to compensate for what she lacks in territorial status. Of course, the crowning achievement in this little-noticed race came when the first position as a UN Secretary General was accorded to a Norwegian.

12. NORWAY IN BILATERAL DIPLOMACY

Norway has had her own foreign service only since 1905 and is thus a young country in this form of international interaction. The number employed in foreign services has, however, grown quite rapidly, from 55 in 1910, to 100 in 1939, and 201 in 1960. An increasingly larger part of the activity has been centred in the Ministry of Foreign Affairs, in Oslo: in 1910, 23 per cent of those employed in foreign service were stationed there, as against 35 per cent in 1960. And some of them are at all times available for delegations, etc. But about two-thirds are still permanently abroad, in the diplomatic or consular service.

Table XVIII presents well-known features in twentieth-century world politics: we see the central European great powers' relative decline, the USA's progress, the anti-Soviet front accentuated by the Cold War, the emergence of Afro-Asian countries, Latin America's

Table XVIII. *Location of personnel in Norwegian diplomatic and consular services (percentage)*

Location	1910	1920	1930	1939	1951	1960
Scandinavia	10	8	12	12	9	9
European Great Powers	40	31	28	23	20	18
Other European states	12	17	12	15	17	20
USA	12	17	16	19	20	19
USSR	12	5	9	6	3	3
Asia, Australia	10	6	12	12	11	13
Africa	0	3	2	4	3	2
Latin America	5	14	9	9	10	7
Delegations to international organizations	0	0	0	0	8	9
Total	101	101	100	100	100	100

Source: Galtung and Holmboe Ruge 1965, Table 6, p. 114.

Table XIX. *Countries with greatest number of diplomatic relations, 1909-1940**

Country	1909	1920	1930	1940
USA	1	3	3	1
France	3	2	1	2
Great Britain	2	5	2	3
Belgium	10	6	7	4
Italy	4	4	5	5
Netherlands	7	7	8	6
Argentina	11	8	11	8
Germany	5	20	4	8
Sweden	15	10	13	9
Brazil	13	15	15	10
Switzerland	19	9	9	11
Norway	20	14	16	12
Denmark	23	11	17	13
Cuba	—	—	—	14
Portugal	14	13	19	15
Mexico	12	19	28	16
Chile	18	16	27	17
Uruguay	16	21	22	81
Spain	6	1	6	19
Hungary		50	12	20

Source: Singer and Small 1966.

* A weighted average was used to calculate the number of diplomats from each country. For details, see source.

Table XX. *Norway's bilateral agreements, 1962*

Sweden	65	Finland	29
USA	55	USSR	28
Great Britain	49	West Germany	23
Denmark	42	Austria	22
France	41	Portugal	22

Source: *Utenrikskalenderen.*

steady decline in relative prestige, and, finally, international organizations as actors on the world stage. *Norway has kept up with these fluctuations,* has reacted to them adequately but slowly. A fairly constant factor is the approximately 600 Norwegian consulates abroad which naturally play an important part in connection with shipping and help diffuse a certain amount of Norwegian influence over the entire world community.

Bilateral diplomacy is in general symmetric: if Norway has diplomatic relations with a country, that country also has diplomatic relations with Norway. This then connects Norway to a number of countries, and an important question is this: How many such contacts has Norway, in relation to the net of contacts other countries have built up? Singer's investigation (Singer and Small 1966) of the international diplomatic network shows the position of Norway and other nations according to number of diplomatic relations up to 1940 (see Table XIX).

Norway's position in diplomacy corresponds more or less to her general position in standard of living and level of development. Most of the reference group were above her in 1940, with Denmark under. If the list were extended to cover the next decade, there would be several changes in the picture, but hardly in Norway's position: it is the new countries' and the socialist countries' rise, and the Latin American countries' decline that are the marked new features.

In this connection it is interesting to note one form of diplomatic relations Norway does *not* have: with the Vatican State. One might say that this is due to the low number of Roman Catholics in Norway, but of the 59 countries accredited the Vatican State, 12 have less than 2 per cent Roman Catholics (one of these is Finland). This lacuna should rather be seen in light of many of the factors mentioned earlier, such as homogeneity, missions and their message, etc. It is also quite possible that Norway loses more by not having this communication channel than does the Vatican.

Table XVIII presenting data on where Norwegian foreign service personnel are stationed, shows clearly that most activity is concentrated around the North Atlantic area. But the Table is not particularly detailed; to clarify this feature further, it may be useful to supplement Table XVIII with data on one of the classical expressions of bilateral diplomacy: the bilateral agreement (see Table XX).

In the order Table XX presents, then, we recognize the reference group – but we also see how Norway's largest neighbour, the Soviet Union, enters into Norway's international dealings even though the country is not included in the reference group. However, we should also remember that an agreement does not necessarily express a positive tie; it may just as easily express the necessity of regulating a conflict.

13. NORWAY'S TRADE PARTNERS

After viewing Norway's position in bilateral diplomacy it is natural for us to turn to Norway's choice of trade partners. The most important ones, measured in percentage of Norway's total export and import, are shown in Table XXI. We have data from two different years, as this item is among the most important in determining Norway's international position.

We see that Norway's most important trade partners are practically all the 'countries it is natural for us to compare ourselves with', and in practically the same order (rank correlation 0.87 for 1963, 0.88 for 1966). This seems to indicate that these concepts are closely adjusted

Table XXI. *Norway's main trade partners, percentage of import and export, 1963 and 1966*

| | 1963 | | | 1966 | |
Country	Export	Import	Country	Export	Import
Great Britain	18.7	17.8	Great Britain	18.8	13.7
Germany (West)	14.8	17.9	Sweden	15.3	18.8
Sweden	14.1	17.6	Germany (West)	13.3	16.1
USA	9.4	9.6	USA	8.9	17.5
Denmark	8.8	5.1	Denmark	7.1	5.8
France	3.7	3.8	Italy	3.1	3.2
Italy	3.2	2.0	France	3.0	3.1
Netherlands	3.1	3.8	Netherlands	2.8	4.4
Finland	1.8	0.9	Finland	2.1	1.1
Belgium/Luxembourg	1.9	2.7	Greece	1.9	0.1
Canada	1.7	4.1	Belgium/Luxembourg	1.9	2.2
Switzerland	1.2	2.3	Liberia	1.3	

Sources: 1963: NOS XII 107, Table 165, pp. 146-148. 1966: NOS XII 218, Table 175, pp. 136-139.

to fit each other: that Norway's reference group in the world community is primarily adjusted according to her trade relations.

But the most important factor in the trade picture is not shown in this Table: the degree of dependency between the country's economy and trade. The value of Norway's export and import in percentage of GNP is high: Norway is number 19 of 81 countries, with a rate of 51 per cent. More important, however, is that of the 18 countries ahead of Norway in dependency, only three are at Norway's level of development – Belgium, Luxembourg, and Denmark. Directly after Norway come four developing countries. In addition comes the fact that Norway, like so many developing countries, is highly dependent on one commodity, shipping, and that other Norwegian products show relatively little processing before sale. *We may therefore say that Norway's economic structure has many features in common with that of developing countries, in that the country is not self-sufficient, but dependent on international trade.* Norway, however, is not alone in this, but shares her situation with five small, Western European countries, who seem eager to participate in the Common Market – of which three (Benelux) are already members. The logic on this point in Norwegian foreign policy is thus shared very much by other countries in the same position.

14. NORWAY AND INTERNATIONAL TOURISM

Do foreign visitors come from 'countries it is natural for us to compare ourselves with' or from other countries? What is the relationship between the two images which Norwegians form of the world community in this respect?

The number of foreign visitors to Norway (not all are tourists) is, first of all, very high; second, it shows an enormous rate of increase. In 1930 there were 80,000 visitors; by 1939 this had risen to 239,295. In 1946 this had sunk to 195,201, but even the next year, 1947, surpassed the pre-war level, with 303,326 visitors. The million mark was passed ten years later – in 1957 there were 1,019,614 – and in 1963, 3,970,000. This last figure is well over the total Norwegian population, in itself a typical indicator of the increase in world tourism. Naturally, many of these visitors stay only one day (in 1958, 35 per cent of the total,) and the total figure counts separately many who return several times.

Furthermore, 83 per cent in 1963 were Swedes (74 per cent in 1961; of them, 96 per cent came by car); but all the same, the figures give a good impression of the flood of foreign visitors and thereby of

423

stimuli from the world community which Norwegians are being exposed to.

However, we are dealing with a very limited part of the world community, even when we have corrected for the high percentage of Swedes (Table XXII).

Sweden's position has at all times been the leading one, which is not in the least unusual when we remember geography. World War II put Denmark in second place, and then follow Great Britain and the USA. Germany's position is interesting: that the country sank immediately after the war is hardly surprising, but it is only since around 1957 that Germany has re-attained, more or less, her position as number four. Since German currency and the standard of living were quite strong in the early 1950s, it may be well to interpret this as an incidence of a mutual feeling of what is 'fitting': which again may be interpreted as an incidence of Norwegian moralism.

These nine countries are all among the top 12 in the reference group, and the internal order by number of tourists in 1963 is practically the same. The USA and Great Britain, great powers that they are, rank a bit higher on the comparison list than on the tourist list. Otherwise, this high correlation is hardly coincidental, but indicates the importance the pressure from tourists can have in creating standards for comparison. In general, then, there is harmony between the various sources of world images.

At the same time, Norwegians are great travellers. This was investigated by the International Peace Research Institute, Oslo, by asking a sample of Norwegians: 'Have you ever been abroad? If so, where?' Only 27 per cent answered 'No'; 38 per cent have visited Norway's neighbours; 20 per cent have been to countries in Western

Table XXII. *Ranking of countries by number of visitors to Norway*

Rank 1930	1937	1947	1957	1960	1963
1. Sweden	Sweden	Sweden	Sweden	Sweden	Sweden
2. America*	Denmark	Great Britain	Denmark	Denmark	Denmark
3. Great Britain	Germany	Denmark	Great Britain	Germany	Great Britain
4. Germany	America	Germany	America	USA	USA
5. Denmark	Great Britain	America	France	Great Britain	Finland
6. France	Finland	Finland	Finland	Finland	Germany
7. Netherlands	France	Netherlands	Netherlands	France	France
8. Finland	Netherlands	France	Switzerland	Netherlands	Netherlands
9. Switzerland	Switzerland	Switzerland	Germany	Switzerland	Switzerland

Sources: *Landslaget for reiselivet i Norge* ('Norwegian Travel Association') 1964, and NOS XII, 100.

* Until 1955 all Western Hemisphere countries were designated 'America'; by far the majority of these visitors were from the USA.

Europe, only 2 per cent to countries in Eastern Europe, USSR included, 5 per cent to the USA, and 5 per cent to Asia, Africa, or Latin America. Such high figures as these can be explained only by the great numbers of Norwegians who, at one time or another, and probably for short periods, have taken jobs aboard Norwegian ships calling at foreign ports.

But having been abroad is not the same as having developed international attitudes. The reason is not so much the brief time spent abroad as it is the type of contact most often made: with the lower, highly commercialized levels of the tertiary sector. Such contact can easily form the basis for contempt and generalizations that the foreigners are all out to make money, barter, and cheat.

Only seldom does tourist contact go further than to this superficial level which most countries show to foreigners. It is easier to give an impression of dignity and integrity when one is not dependent on some kind of trade with the tourists – but these levels in the population are hard for the tourist to find or have contact with.

15. NORWAY IN THE INTERNATIONAL SPORTS PICTURE

Let us conclude our survey of Norway's international interaction with data from a rather different field: international sports (see Table XXIII). Norway's imbalance – or leitmotif – turns up again here: she is low in the Summer Olympics, high in the Winter ones. A main factor for high position in the Winter Olympics is the amount of snow in the country, but still, Norway's position is quite incontestable. If we were to calculate position per inhabitant, Norway would move up on the list for Summer Olympics as well as on the total score.

However, the statistics are somewhat misleading, because Norway's high position in the Winter Olympics seems to be declining. In 1924 she won 83 per cent of the total points awarded in the Nordic branches of the Winter Olympics, but in 1956 only 15 per cent. In speed skating Norway reached a top in 1928, with 53 per cent of total points, but received only 16 per cent in 1956 (Andersen 1957). It is not so much that Norway is receding as such, but that the other countries are advancing. Moreover, the results of the 1968 Olympics tend to modify the picture.

We have given so many statistics on this point because sports is a form of placement in the world community and a form of international dealing which for many is highly important, perhaps most important, in that much personal experience and feeling are connected with it. The image of the world community is also formed on this basis, and there are many important impressions to be gained from such com-

Table XXIII. *Ranking of countries in Olympic Games, by scores achieved*

Summer Games 1896-1960	Winter Games 1924-1960	Total 1896-1960
1. USA	1. Norway	1. USA
2. USSR	2. USA	2. USSR
3. Great Britain	3. Finland	3. Sweden
4. Sweden	4. Sweden	4. Great Britain
5. Germany	5. Austria	5. Germany
6. France	6. USSR	6. Finland
7. Italy	7. Switzerland	7. France
8. Hungary	8. Germany	8. Italy
9. Finland	9. Canada	9. Hungary
10. Australia	10. France	10. Norway

Source: Andersen 1957.

parisons. First, that a small country such as Norway can do so very well, even become the world's best. World rank order is *not* constant; it *can* be changed, Norway *can* come at the top – ahead of the great powers, even ahead of all the 'countries it is natural for us to compare ourselves with'. Second, that such a position must be protected and defended, and that natural advantages (snow, long winter, mountains) do not represent any guarantee in a development-oriented world. Third, that people become accustomed to rank disequilibrium as characteristic of Norway, typical of the country. People become accustomed to the idea of being able to compensate for low performance in one field by high performance in another, and people may well become frequent users of mechanisms (of the type 'Well, what really counts are the Winter Olympics') which attach interest especially to those variables where Norway ranks high. Fourth, that a whole set of new countries is brought to the public consciousness through sports relations. The developing countries are still missing, but we see that the socialist countries have come quite far. Norway is thereby put in a slightly different connection than the purely Western, put in a framework where the competition is regulated according to international norms – and this probably helps increase openness towards such countries.

16. CONCLUSION

At this point we stop. The reason is not that we place so much importance on the international sport picture as such, but rather because this picture indicates new possibilities in the international pattern. Norway's position in the world community is not a given quantity; nor

426

is any other nation's. Her position may be changed by her own growth and efforts – it may be strengthened, and it may be weakened if her resources are used without talent and imagination.

But Norway's position may also be changed in quite different ways: if the very criteria for a nation's position are changed, or if the importance of nations as actors in the international game is changed. Until now, nations have mostly been ranked according to political and economic power – a great power has been and is a country which ranks high on both these dimensions. But there is no reason to believe that the future may not bring new patterns. Koestler once wrote a play where the leitmotif was a ranking of nations according to average degree of happiness per inhabitant. Now, it is perhaps not so clear just what this happiness is, and definitely not clear how it is to be measured for use in international statistics. But it is hardly improbable that, in the not too distant future, well-being among a nation's inhabitants will be more emphasized than the nation's military and economic potential in the world society. Nor it is so improbable that we, in the not too distant future, will witness the decline of nations and the rise of international organizations as main actors in the international game. We have seen this develop – on the national level – where the local districts have gradually been overshadowed by organizations – and there is little reason to believe that the communications revolution will not have similar consequences on the international level.

And with that, everything in this article will seem a voice from the past – with its emphasis on political and economic variables, its emphasis on Norway as a unit. But the future has not yet begun on this point; and in the meantime this survey may perhaps provide a picture of Norway's position – from a bird's-eye view.

NOTES

[1] PRIO-publication no. 21-8 from the International Peace Research Institute, Oslo. The original article was written in 1967 and the data have not been updated.

Bibliography

Aarseth, Bjørn: «Status og framtids-perspektiver i norsk reindrift». *Sameliv VI. Samisk Selskaps Årbok 1964/ 66*, Oslo 1967, pp. 114–147.

Aarflot, Andres: *Norske kirkehistorie.* Oslo 1967.

Åhman, Egon: *Sekulariseringsprosessen och kyrkan.* Stockholm 1966. *Årbok for Den norske kirke.* Oslo 1967.

Albrechtsen, Carl Severin and Einar Kringlen: «En analyse av 466 sykebe-søk i Oslo», *Tidsskrift for Den Norske Lægeforening*, Vol. 85, no. 1, 1965, pp. 8–17.

Alstad, Bjørn (ed.): *Norske Meninger* I–III, Oslo 1969.

Anchersen, Per: «Psykiatriske proble-mer i indremedisinen», *Tidsskrift for Den Norske Lægeforening*, Vol. 73, no. 4, 1953, pp. 135–138.

Andenæs, Johs.: *Alminnelig strafferett.* Oslo 1956.

Andenæs, Johs.: «Straff og almenpre-vensjon», *Tidsskrift for rettsvitenskap*, Vol. 79, 1966, pp. 1–47.

Andenæs, Johs., O. Aukrust and I. Hauge: *Samfunnskunnskap for gymnaset.* Oslo 1966.

Andersen, Helge et al.: 'Sport and Games in Denmark in the Light of Sociology', *Acta Sociologica*, Vol. 2, no. 1, 1957.

Andersen, P. Chr.: *Olympiaboken.* Oslo 1957.

Arensberg, Conrad: 'The American family in perspective', in R. Winch (ed.), *Selected Studies in Marriage and the Family.* New York 1962.

Arner, Oddvar and Ole W. Tenfjord: «Sykdom, ulykker og død blant norske sjømenn», *Tidsskrift for den Norske Lægeforening*, Vol. 84, no. 18, 1964, pp. 1228–1236.

Arnholm, Carl Jakob: *Lærebok i Familierett.* Oslo 1969.

Årsberetning 1967, Landslaget for Reiselivet i Norge. Oslo 1967.

Ås, Berit: «Ulykkesfugler og trygge barn. En undersøkelse av 14-åringers innstilling til sikkerhet og fare», *Tidsskrift for samfunnsforskning*, Vol. 3, 1962, pp. 1–16.

Ås, Dagfinn: «En spørreskjemaunder-søkelse om barnehager», *Sosialt Arbeid*, no. 5, 1966.

Ås, Dagfinn: *Tannleger 1946–1957. En studie av mobilitet og karrieremønster*, Supplement II. Innstilling fra Norges Tannlægeforenings folketannrøkt-komité. Oslo 1962.

Aubert, Vilhelm: «Fattigdommen i Norge», *Kontrast*, Vol. 3, 1967, pp. 10–20.

Aubert, Vilhelm: «Kvinner i akademiske yrker», *Tidsskrift for samfunnsforsk-ning*, Vol. 2, no. 4, 1961, pp. 239–242.

Aubert, Vilhelm: *Norske jurister fra 1814 til den annen verdenskrig.* Mimeo, Institute for Social Research. Oslo 1960.

Aubert, Vilhelm: «Norske sakførere 1932–50», *Norsk Sakførerblad*, no. 26, 1959, pp. 73–82.

Aubert, Vilhelm: *Om straffens sosiale funksjon.* Oslo 1954.

Aubert, Vilhelm: *Priskontroll og rasjo-nering.* Mimeo, Institute for Social Research. Oslo 1950.

Aubert, Vilhelm: *Straff og lagdeling.* Institute for Social Research.

Oslo 1963.

Aubert, Vilhelm and Harrison White: 'Sleep: A Sociological Interpretation', *Acta Sociologica*, Vol. 4, nos. 2 and 3, 1959.

Aubert, Vilhelm, Torstein Eckhoff and Knut Sveri, with Per Norseng: *En lov i søkelyset*. Oslo 1952.

Aubert, Vilhelm, G. Haldorsen and P. O. Tiller: «Lærernes holdning til yrkesrollen og oppdragelsesspørsmål», *Norsk pedagogisk tidsskrift*, Vol. 40, no. 3, 1956, pp. 81–113.

Aubert, Vilhelm et al.: «Akademikere i norsk samfunnsstruktur», *Tidsskrift for samfunnsforskning*, Vol. 1, 1960, pp. 185–204.

Aubert, Vilhelm et al.: *The Professions in Norwegian Social Structure, 1720–1955*. Institute for Social Research. Oslo 1961–1962.

Augedal, Egil: *Eksponering for massmedia blant Oslo-folk*. Mimeo No. 13, Institute for Press Research. Oslo 1970.

Aukrust, Tor: *Mennesket i kulturen*. Oslo 1968.

Backer, Julie E.: *Dødeligheten og dens årsaker i Norge*. Statistisk Sentralbyrå, Oslo 1961.

Backer, Julie E.: *Ekteskap, fødsler og vandringer i Norge 1856–1960*. Statistisk Sentralbyrå, 1965.

Baker, Elsworth F.: *Man in the Trap*. New York 1967.

Bakke, Marit: *Utenrikstelegrammer fra NTB: en analyse av nyhetskriteriet*. Mimeo No. 14, Institute for Press Research. Oslo 1970.

Barth, Fredrik: 'Family Life in a Central Norwegian Mountain Community', in Eliot and Hillman (eds.), *Norway's Families*. Philadelphia 1959.

Barth, Fredrik: 'Subsistence and Institutional System in a Norwegian Mountain Valley', *Rural Sociology*, Vol. 17, no. 1, March 1952.

Bay, Christian et al.: *Nationalism*. Mimeo, Institute for Social Research. Oslo 1953.

Becker, Howard S.: 'The Professional Dance Musician and His Audience', *American Journal of Sociology*, Vol. 57, no. 2, 1951.

Bendiksen, Bjørnulf: «Bosetningen i Norge 1960–1980: En regional befolkningsprognose», *Sosialøkonomen* no. 5–6, May–June 1963, pp. 10–14.

Bendix, Reinhard: *Max Weber: An Intellectual Portrait*. New York 1960.

Bentsen, Bent Guttorm: «Legepraksis og sykelighet», *Tidsskrift for den Norske Lægeforening*, Vol. 85, no. 13, 1965, pp. 1086–1095.

Bentsen, Bent Guttorm: «Sykelighet i en landbefolkning», *Tidsskrift for den Norske Lægeforening*, Vol. 86, no. 4, 1966, pp. 245–254.

Berge, Marit: *Norsk skolepolitikk*. Oslo 1960.

Berle, A. A. and G. C. Means: *The Modern Corporation and Private Property*. New York 1932.

Bernstein, B.: 'Social Class and Linguistic Development', in A. H. Halsey et al. (eds.), *Education, Economy, and Society*. Glencoe 1962, pp. 288–314.

Bjartveidt, Kjell and Hans Waaler: 'Some Evidence of the Efficacy of Mass BCG Vaccination', *Bulletin of the World Health Organization*, no. 33, 1965, pp. 289–319.

Bjerve, Petter Jakob: *Planning in Norway 1947–1956*. Amsterdam 1959.

Bjørnson, Jon: «Legesituasjonen i Norge», *Sosialt Arbeid*, Vol. 39, no. 2, 1965, pp. 34–45.

Bladcentralen 25 år. Oslo 1958.

Blitsen, Dorothy: *The World and the Family*. New York 1963.

Boalt, G. and T. Husén: *Skolans sociologi*. Stockholm 1964.

Bødal, Kåre: *Arbeidsskolen og dens behandlingsresultater*. Oslo 1962.

Börjeson, Bengt: *Om påföljders verkningar*. Stockholm 1966.

Bolling, Reidar: *Norske prester og teologiske kandidater*. Oslo 1958.

Bondeson, Ulla: 'Argot Terminology as Innovation of Socialization into the Reformatory', *Scandinavian Studies in Criminology*, Vol. 2. Oslo 1968.

Bonnevie, Margarethe: *Patriarkatets siste sjanse*. Oslo 1948.

Bott, Elizabeth: *Family and Social Network.* London 1957.

Braatøy, Trygve: *Livets cirkel.* Oslo 1929.

Braatøy, Trygve: *Pasienten og lægen.* Oslo 1952.

Brastad, Arvid: Article in *Dagbladet,* no. 241, 18 October 1965, p. 12.

Bratland, Per: *Hvem har makt i Norge?* Oslo 1965.

Bremer, Johan: 'A Social Psychiatric Investigation of a Small Community in Northern Norway', *Acta Psychiatrica et Neurologica,* Vol. XII, 1951.

Brøgger, Jan: «Om gjengstruktur i et ungdomsmiljø», *Tidsskrift for samfunnsforskning,* Vol. 4, no. 3, 1963.

Brofoss, E.: *Distriktsutbyggingspolitikk.* Mimeo, Lectures at the University of Oslo, Fall 1965.

Broom, Leonard and Philip Selznick: *Sociology,* 3rd ed. New York 1963.

Brun-Gulbrandsen, Sverre: «Alkoholforbrukets mørketall», *Tidsskrift for samfunnsforskning,* Vol. 8, no. 1, 1967.

Brun-Gulbrandsen, Sverre: *Kjønnsrolle og ungdomskriminalitet.* Oslo 1958.

Brun-Gulbrandsen, Sverre and Berit Ås: «Kjønnsroller og ulykker», *Tidsskrift for samfunnsforskning,* Vol. 1, 1960, pp. 65–79.

Brun-Gulbrandsen, Sverre and Olav Irgens-Jensen: *Alkoholmisbruk blant unge norske sjømenn.* Oslo 1964.

Bull, Edvard: «Etter valget», *Det 20de Århundre,* no. 4, 1927.

Bull, Trygve: *Mot dag og Erling Falk.* Oslo 1955.

Burgess, Ernest W.: *The Family – from Institution to Companionship.* New York 1955.

Bye, Lillian: *The Mother's Status in Different Cultural Groups and its Implications for Case Work Treatment.* Master's Thesis, Boston University School of Social Work. Boston 1947.

Carlsson, Gösta: 'The Decline of Fertility: Innovation or Adjustment Process?' *Population Studies,* no. 20, November 1966, pp. 149–174.

Castberg, Frede: «Utviklingslinjer i den juridiske tenkning i Norge siden 1814», *Tidsskrift for rettsvitenskap,* no. 77, 1964, pp. 115–135.

Centers, R.: 'Attitude and Belief in Relation to Occupational Stratification', in D. Katz et al. (eds.), *Public Opinion and Propaganda,* New York 1954, pp. 132–151.

Christie, Nils: Discussion on Lødrup: «Domstolene og alkoholproblemet», *Medlemsblad for Den Norske Dommerforening,* 1961, pp. 108–112.

Christie, Nils: «Edruelighetsnemndene. Analyse av en velferdslov», *Nordisk tidsskrift for kriminalvitenskap,* Vol. 52, 1964, pp. 89–118.

Christie, Nils: «De fratagbare goder», *Tidsskrift for samfunnsforskning,* Vol. 7, 1966, pp. 119–130.

Christie, Nils: *Tvangsarbeid og alkoholbruk.* Oslo 1960(a).

Christie, Nils: *Unge norske lovovertredere.* Oslo 1960(b).

Christie, Nils and Ragnar Hauge: *Alkoholvaner blant storbyungdom.* Oslo/Bergen 1962.

Christie, Nils, Johs. Andenæs and Sigurd Skirbekk: 'A Study of Self-reported Crime', *Scandinavian Studies in Criminology,* Vol. 1. Oslo 1965.

Christoffersen, Tor: «Søkelyset på økonomisk svakstilte områder i Troms og Finnmark», *Arbeidsmarkedet,* Vol. 7. Oslo 1963, pp. 6–11.

Cohen, J.: 'The Scientific Revolution and Leisure', *Nature,* Vol. 198, no. 4885, 15 June 1963.

Coleman, James: 'Academic Achievement and the Structure of Competition', in A. H. Halsey et al., op. cit., pp. 367–387.

Coleman, James: *The Adolescent Society.* New York 1962.

Coucheron-Jarl, Vidkunn: «De unge menns utdannelse», *Norsk pedagogisk tidsskrift,* Vol. 37, no. 3, 1953, pp. 67–93.

Cyert, R. M. and J. G. March: *A Behavioral Theory of the Firm.* Englewood Cliffs, N. J. 1964.

Dag & Tid 8 May 1965.

Dahl Jacobsen, Knut: *Teknisk hjelp og politisk struktur.* Oslo 1964.

Dahlström, Edmund et al. *Kvinnors liv och arbete*. Stockholm 1962.

Davis, Allison: 'Socialization and Adolescent Personality', in T. M. Newcomb and E. L. Hartley (eds.), *Readings in Social Psychology*. New York 1958, pp. 139–150.

Davis, Kingsley and Judith Blake: 'Social Structure and Fertility: An Analytic Framework', *Economic Development and Cultural Change*, no. 4; also published in S. M. Lipset and N. J. Smelser (eds.), *Sociology*. Englewood Cliffs, N. J., 1961, pp. 356–77.

Department of Youth Authority, State of California: *Annual Report: The Status of Current Research in the Californian Youth Authority*. Sacramento, July 1967.

Dewhurst, J. F. et al.: *Europe's Needs and Resources*. New York 1961.

Dill, E. and J. Coleman: 'High School Status, College Plans, and Interest in Academic Achievement', *American Sociological Review*, Vol. 28, no. 6, 1963, pp. 905–912.

Durkheim, Emile: *Les formes élémentaires de la vie religieuse*. Paris 1912.

Easton, David: *The Political System*. New York 1953.

Eckhoff, Torstein: 'Justice, Efficiency and Self-made Rules in Public Administration' in Torstein Eckhoff: *Rettferdighet og Rettssikkerhet*. Oslo 1966, pp. 66–90.

Eckhoff, Torstein: «Noen bemerkninger om domstolenes uavhengighet», *Jussens Venner*, no. 1, 1965, pp. 1–30. Also published in *Festskrift tillägnad Karl Olivencrona*. Stockholm 1964.

Eckstein, Harry: *Division and Cohesion in Democracy, a Study of Norway*. Princeton 1966.

Eisenstadt, S. N.: *From Generation to Generation*. Glencoe 1956, Chapters 1 and 2.

Ekonomen 1965.

Ekteskapsloven av 1915. (The Law Concerning Marriage, 1915).

Eliassen, Rønnaug: «Skjevheter i trygde- og skattesystemet», *Familiepolitikk i dag og i morgen*. Oslo 1967.

Eliot, Thomas and Arthur Hillman (eds.): *Norway's Families*. Philadelphia 1959.

Ericson, M. C.: 'Social Status and Child-rearing Practices', in Newcomb and Hartley (eds.), op. cit., pp. 494–502.

Euler, Roland v.: *Idrottsrörelsen av idag*. Malmö 1953; reprinted from *Svensk Idrott 1903–1953*.

Europa Publications: *The Europa Year Book 1965*. London 1965.

Europa Publications: *The Middle East and North Africa 1964—65*. London 1965.

Evang, Karl: *Health Services in Norway*. Oslo 1960, pp. 73–75.

Evang, Karl: «Noen administrative problemer i Norge i dag belyst ved eksempler fra helsesektoren», *Nordisk administrativt Tidsskrift*, Vol. 42, 1961, pp. 81–111.

Evans, K. M.: *Sociometry and Education*. London 1962.

Fivelsdal, Egil: *Funksjonærenes syn på faglige og politiske spørsmål*. Oslo 1964.

Flint, John T.: 'The Church in Relation to Family Life', in T. Eliot & A. Hillman op. cit.

Flint, John T.: 'The Secularization of Norwegian Society', *Comparative Studies in Society and History*, Vol. 6, no. 3. The Hague.

Floud, Jean and A. H. Halsey: 'English Secondary Schools and the Supply of Labour', in Halsey et. al., op. cit. pp. 80–92.

Ford, Clellans & Frank A. Beach: *Sexualitet hos människor och djur*. Stockholm 1962.

Foreløpig innstilling fra arbeidskomiteen av 1964. Oslo 1966.

Forskningsnytt 1967.

Foss, Øivind (ed.): *Seksualitet og frihet*. Oslo 1966.

Furhoff, Lars. *Pressens förräderi*. Stockholm 1964.

Galbraith, J. K.: *The Affluent Society.* London 1959.

Galtung, Johan: *Fengselssamfunnet.* Oslo 1959.

Galtung, Johan: 'Foreign Policy Opinion as a Function of Social Position', *Journal of Peace Research,* Vol. 1, 1964, pp. 206–231.

Galtung, Johan: *Verdiorientering og sosial posisjon.* Mimeo, Institutt for samfunnsforskning. Oslo 1961.

Galtung, Johan and Mari Holmboe Ruge: 'Patterns of Diplomacy', *Journal of Peace Research,* Vol. 2, 1965, pp. 101–135.

Galtung, Johan and Ståle Seierstad: *Utenrikspolitikk og norsk opinion.* Mimeo, Institutt for samfunnsforskning. Oslo 1962.

Galtung-Hansen, Otto: 'The Tuberculosis Programme in the Developed Countries', *Excerpta Medica International Congress Series No. 119,* Proceedings of the XVIIIth International Conference on Tuberculosis, 1965, pp. 25–35.

Galtung-Hansen, Otto and Leif Riddervold: «Skjermbildefotografering i Norge», *Nordisk Medicin,* Vol. 61, no. 5, 1959, pp. 169–174.

Gavron, Hannah: *The Captive Wife.* London 1966.

Gjestland, Trygve and T. Mork: «En regional undersøkelse av dødeligheten i Oslo 1890–1939. Tuberkulose, andre infeksjonssykdomme og åndedrettsorganenes sykdommer», *Festskriftet til helsedirektør Karl Evang på 60-årsdagen,* Oslo 1962, pp. 111–120.

Glass, D. V. (ed.): *Social Mobility in Britain.* London 1954.

Gluckman, Max: *The Judicial Process among the Barotse of Northern Rhodesia.* Manchester 1956.

Gough, E. K.: 'The Nayars and the Definition of Marriage', *Journal of the Royal Anthropological Institute,* Vol. 89, 1959.

Grønseth, Bjørg: *Husmødres sosiale situasjon og veiledningsbehov.* Institute for Social Research. Oslo 1965.

Grønseth, Erik: *The Dysfunctionality of the Husband Provider Role in Industrialized Societies.* Mimeo, Institute of Sociology. Oslo 1970.

Grønseth, Erik: *Early Marriage in Norway.* Mimeo, Institute for Social Research. Oslo 1963.

Grønseth, Erik: 'Economic Family Policy and its Guiding Images in Norway, – Inconsistencies and Consequences', in deBie and Reslevov (eds.), *National Family Guiding Images and Policies.* International Scientific Commission on the Family. Louvain 1967 (a).

Grønseth, Erik: *Ekteskap og familie – demografiske data.* Mimeo, Institute for Social Research. Oslo 1963.

Grønseth, Erik: *Ekteskap og familie: Sosiologiske synspunkter og tilnærminger.* Mimeo, Institute for Sociology. Oslo 1965 (a).

Grønseth, Erik: *Familie, seksualitet og samfunn.* Oslo 1966 (a).

Grønseth, Erik. 'The Husband Provider Role: – A Critical Appraisal'; in Andrée Michel, (ed.), *Family Issues of Working Women in Europe and America.* Leyden 1971.

Grønseth, Erik: 'Notes on the Historical Development of the Relation between Nuclear Family, Kinship System and the Wider Social Structure in Norway', in Reuben Hill and René König (eds.), *Families East and West.* Paris 1970.

Grønseth, Erik: 'Research on Socialization in Norway', *Family Process,* Vol. 4, 1963.

Grønseth, Erik: «Samfunnets ansvar for barnas underhold og stell», *Familiepolitikk i dag og i morgen.* Oslo 1967 (b).

Grønseth, Erik: «Seksualitet og samfunn», in Foss (ed.) op. cit., 1966 (b).

Grønseth, Erik: *Sjøfolks familieforhold og mannsatskilte mødre.* Mimeo, Institute for Social Research, Oslo 1961.

Grønseth, Erik: «Sjømannshustruers reaksjon på frustrasjon ved mannens fravær til sjøs», *Nordisk Psykologi,* no. 1–2, 1960.

Grønseth, Erik: *Strategic Variables in Family and Sex Research and Policies.* Mimeo, Institute of Sociology. Oslo 1969.

Grønseth, Erik: *Virkninger av sjøfolks fravær til sjøs*, *Nordisk Psykologi, tilpasning og sosiale relasjoner*. Manuscript, Institute for Social Research. Oslo 1956.

Gurvin, Olav: *Fartein Valen*. Oslo 1962.

Gustafsson, Berndt: *Religionssociologi*. Stockholm 1965.

Haakonsen, Daniel: *Den katolske kirke i norske lærebøker*. Oslo 1951.

Hacker, Helen: 'The New Burden of Masculinity'; *Marriage and Family Living*, Vol 4. 1957.

Halsey, A. H., J. Floud and A. Anderson (eds.): *Education, Economy, and Society*. Glencoe, Ill., 1961.

Hanssen, Eivind: «Rekrutteringen til dommerembetene», *Medlemsblad for Den Norske Dommerforening*, No. 165, 1954, pp. 1296–1299.

Harbo, Torstein: *Målsetting og læreplan i den 9-årige skole*. Oslo 1960.

Hauge, Ragnar: «Gjengkriminalitet», *Nordisk tidsskrift for kriminalvitenskap*, No. 51, 1963, pp. 74–81.

Hauge, Ragnar: «Gjengkriminalitet og gruppestatus», *Tidsskrift for samfunnsforskning*, Vol. 5, 1964, pp. 117–131.

Havighurst, R. and B. L. Neugarten: *Society and Education*. Boston 1962.

Heiestad, Sigurd: *Fra folkelesningens saga*. Oslo 1946.

Hendin, Herbert: *Suicide and Scandinavia*. New York 1965.

Hermansson, C. H.: *Monopol och storfinans – de 15 familjerna*. Stockholm 1965.

Herzberg, Alfhild and Hans Georg Lindblom: *Familiens økonomiske stilling*. Department of Family and Consumer Affairs. Oslo 1956.

Himmelweit, Hilde: 'Social Status and Secondary Education since the 1944 Act', in Glass (ed.), op. cit., pp. 145—151.

Hirsch, Johs. «Oslo Helseråds avdeling for psykiatri 1958–1962», *Tidsskrift for den Norske Legeforening*, Vol. 84, no. 8, 1964, pp. 673–675.

Hoem, Anton: «Samenes skolegang.

Realiseres skolens mål i samedistriktene?» *Sameliv VI*, Samisk Selskaps Årbok 1964/66, Oslo 1967, pp. 60–72.

Hoem, Anton: *Undervisningssystem i etnisk marginalområde*. Mimeo, Master's Thesis in Education. Oslo 1963.

Høyer, Svennik: *Enkelte trekk ved avisenes lederartikler foran tre stortingsvalg*, Mimeo, Institute for Social Research.

Høyer, Svennik: 'The Norwegian Political Press', *Scandinavian Political Studies*, Vol. III. Oslo 1968.

Høyer, Svennik: «Pressens økonomiske og politiske struktur», *Tidsskrift for samfunnsforskning*, Vol. 5, 1964, pp. 221–242.

Holbæk-Hanssen, Leif: «Konkurranseformer – struktur og utvikling», *Sosialøkonomen*, no. 2, 1963, pp. 19–26.

Holbæk-Hansen, Leif: «Litt om velgerne ved Stortingsvalget i 1949», *Sak og samfunn*, Vol. 24. Bergen 1951.

Holm, Sverre et al.: *Industrireisinga og samfunnet*. Mo-stensil (Mimeographs on Mo i Rana) no. 1, Institute for Sociology. 1958.

Holmberg, Per. «Om de ekonomiske konsekvenserna av de nuvarande kjønsroller», *Kynne eller kön*. Stockholm 1966.

Holmsen, Andreas: *Norges Historie*, Vol. I. Oslo/Bergen 1961.

Holter, Harriet: «Husmoren: En sosial rolle i omforming», *Tidsskrift for samfunnsforskning*, Vol. 7, no. 4, 1966.

Holter, Harriet: 'Rebellion Against the Family', *Acta Sociologica*, 1963.

Holter, Harriet: *Sex Roles and Social Structure*. Oslo 1970.

Holter, Harriet: «Sosialarbeidernes yrkesrolle», *Tidsskrift for samfunnsforskning*, Vol. 1, 1960, pp. 28–49.

Holter, Harriet, Willy Martinussen and Bjørg Grønseth: *Heimen som arbeidsplass*. Oslo 1967.

Horn, J. «Hyppigheten av psykiske sykdommer i en indremedisinsk avdeling», *Nordisk Medicin*, Vol. 48, no. 41, 1952, pp. 1411–1413.

Hornslien, John: «Generasjonsskifte på Vestlandet», *Tidsskrift for det norske landbruk*, nos. 8–9, 1957.

Huizinga, J.: *Homo Ludens.* Boston 1955.

I L O: *Yearbook of Labour Statistics.* Geneva 1966.

Innstilling fra Utredningsutvalget for Inntektsoppgjørene 1966. January 1966.

Innstilling II fra Utredningsutvalget for Inntektsoppgjørene 1966. October 1966.

Innstilling om gjennomføringen av 4 ukers ferien. Oslo: Ferielovutvalget av 1963, 1964.

Innstilling om organisering av og støtte til det frivillige opplysnings- og kulturarbeid. Kirke- og undervisningsdepartementet. Oslo 1964.

Iversen, Olav Hilmar: «Erfaringer fra privat praksis i et herred i Nordland», *Tidsskrift for den Norske Lægeforening*, Vol. 79, no. 8, 1959, pp. 441–452.

Jackson, B. and Dennis Marsden: *Education and the Working Class.* London 1962.

Jacobsen, P. and A. Mathney: 'Mate Selection in Open Marriage Systems', *International Journal of Comparative Sociology*, Vol. 3, no. 1, 1962.

Jahn, Gunnar: «Befolkningsspørsmål og familiens størrelse». *Statistiske meldinger*, no. 7, 1952.

Jensen, Magnus: *Norges historie under eneveldet – 1660–1814.* Oslo 1962.

Johansen, Leif: *Offentlig økonomikk.* Oslo 1964, Part 2.

Johnsen, Arne Odd: *Fra ættesamfunn til statssamfunn.* Oslo 1948.

Johns-Heine, P. and H. H. Gerth: 'Values in Mass Periodical Fiction, 1921–1940', *Public Opinion Quarterly*, Vol. 13, 1949, pp. 105–113.

Jonassen, Øyvind: «Dødfødsler og dødsfall i 1. leveår og det lys de kaster over de sosiale forhold». *Tidsskrift for Den norske Lægeforening*, Vol. 84, no. 20, 1964, pp. 1396–1404.

Kendall, M. G.: *The Advanced Theory of Statistics*, 4th ed., Vol. I. London 1948.

Kiær, A. N.: *Indtægts og formuesforhold i Norge*, Christiania (Oslo) 1892 –1893.

Kierulfs Håndbok 1957.

Kirke- og undervisningsdepartementet: *Undervisningsplaner for den høgre almenskole*, Oslo 1959.

Kjeldstadli, Sverre: *Verdenshistorie for gymnaset.* Oslo 1959.

Kjønstad, O.: «Lønnsutviklingen i forskjellige næringer 1910–1950», *Statistiske Meldinger*, no. 6. Oslo 1951.

Klausen, Arne Martin: «Sosial organisasjon i et norsk dissentersamfunn», *Tidsskrift for samfunnsforskning* Vol. 1, 1960, pp. 153–176.

Klunde, Trygve: *Vi og vårt land.* Oslo 1963.

Kooy, Gerriet A.: *Rural Nuclear Family Life in Contemporary Western Society.* Mimeo, The Agricultural University, Wageningen, Netherlands, 1965.

Kreyberg, Hans Jacob: «En undersøkelse av norske røykevaner», *Tidsskrift for den Norske Lægeforening*, Vol. 74, no. 17, pp. 549–554, 1954.

Kringlen, Einar: «Sykdom i et landdistrikt på Vestlandet», *Tidsskrift for den Norske Lægeforening*, Vol. 85, no. 1, 1965, pp. 18–19.

Kristiansen, Oskar: *De fattige i Norge 1914–1945.* Oslo 1934.

Landbruksdepartementet: *Utkast til lov om reindriften.* Oslo 1966.

Landsforeningen mot kreft: *Røking blant barn og unge.* Oslo 1957.

Landslaget for reiselivet i Norge: *«Antall utenlandske reisende til Norge.* Oslo 1967.

Langfeldt, Knut: *Moskvatesene i norsk politikk.* Oslo/Bergen 1961.

Larsen, Øivind: «Vanerøking blant 19-årige men ni Østfold», *Tidsskrift for Den Norske Lægeforening,* Vol. 85, no. 5, 1965, pp. 443—449.

Le Play, L.: «Fondeur des Usines à Cobalt du Buskerud», *Les Ouvriers*

Européens. Vol. III, *Les Ouvriers du Nord,* Paris 1877.

Lettenstrøm, Gerd Skoe and Gisle Skancke: *De yrkesaktive i Norge, 1875–1960 og prognosen for utviklingen fram til 1970.* Oslo 1964.

Lie, Hildegunn and Bergljot Egge: «Behovet for dagsinstitusjoner for barn», *Sosialt Arbeid,* no. 10, 1965, and no. 1, 1966.

Likelønnsrådet: *Om enslige mødres økonomi og arbeidsmuligheter.* Oslo 1967.

Lindbekk, Tore: «Embedseksamenshyppighet blant etterkrigs-artianere», *Tidsskrift for samfunnsforskning,* Vol. 5, 1964, pp. 132–145.

Lindbekk, Tore: *De lærde profesjoner i Norge.* Mimeo, Institute for Social Research. Oslo 1962 (a).

Lindbekk, Tore: *Mobilitets og stillingsstruktur innenfor tre akademiske profesjoner 1910–63.* Oslo 1967 (a).

Lindbekk, Tore: *Rekrutteringen av leger til de norske utkantområder.* (Expanded and revised edition), Mimeo, Institute for Social Research. Oslo 1967 (b).

Lindbekk, Tore: «Den sosiale rekruttering til de akademiske profesjoner i vår tid», *Tidsskrift for samfunnsforskning,* Vol. 3, 1962 (b), pp. 231–254.

Lippe, Anni von der: *Femundundersøkelsen.* (Unpublished manuscript), Institute for Social Research. Oslo 1967.

Lipset, S. M.: *The First New Nation.* London 1964.

Lipset, S. M.: 'Opinion Formation in a Crisis Situation', in D. Katz et al., *Public Opinion and Propaganda.* New York, pp. 584–598.

Lipset, S. M.: *Political Man.* New York 1960.

Littlewood, Joan: 'A Laboratory of Fun', *New Scientist,* Vol. 199, no. 391, 1964.

Løchen, Yngvar: *Idealer og realiteter i et psykiatrisk sykehus.* Oslo 1965.

Løchen, Yngvar: «Om utvikling og virkemåte i et sosialt tiltak, lovene om attføringshjelp og uføretrygd», *Tidsskrift for samfunnsforskning,* Vol. 7,

no. 1, 1966, pp. 1–18.

Løchen, Yngvar and Arne Martinsen: «Samarbeidsproblemer ved gjennomføringen av lovene om attføringshjelp og uføretrygd», *Tidsskrift for samfunnsforskning,* Vol. 3, 1962, pp. 133–168.

Lov om folkeskolen. 10. april 1959.

Lund, Bernt H.: *Utdanning av sosialarbeidere i Norge, utredning og forslag.* Kirke- og undervisningsdepartementet. Oslo 1963.

Lundar, Johan: «Tobakksrøkning og lungesykdommer», *Tidsskrift for den Norske Lægeforening,* Vol. 85, no. 5, 1965, pp. 437–446.

Lunde, Anders Steen: *Norway: A Population Study.* Doctoral dissertation, Columbia University, New York 1955.

Lysgaard, Sverre: *Arbeidernes syn på faglige og politiske spørsmål.* Oslo 1965.

Lysgaard, Sverre: *Arbeiderkollektivet.* Oslo 1960.

Lysgaard, Sverre: «Dyden og belønningen», *Tidsskrift for samfunnsforskning,* Vol. 1, 1960, pp. 80–93.

Lysgaard, Sverre: «Organisasjonsgraden blant norske arbeidere», *Tidsskrift for samfunnsforskning,* Vol. 5, 1964, pp. 70–84.

McClelland, David: *The Achieving Society.* Princeton 1961.

McClelland, David et al.: *The Achievement Motive.* New York 1953.

McMahan, C. A.: 'An Empirical Test of Three Hypotheses Concerning the Human Sex Ratio at Birth in the United States 1915–1948', *Milbank Memorial Fund Quarterly,* Vol. 29, no. 3, 1951, pp. 273–293.

Manniche, Erik and Kaare Svalastoga: *La Famille en Scandinavie.* Mimeo, Copenhagen 1965.

Mannsåker, Dagfinn: *Det norske presteskapet i det 19. århundre.* Oslo 1954.

Marshall, T. H.: *Class, Citizenship and Social Development.* New York 1965.

Martel, M. U. and G. J. McCall: 'Reality-Orientation and the Pleasure Principle: A Study of American Mass

Periodical Fiction (1890–1955)', in Dexter and White (eds.), *People, Society and Mass Communication.* Glencoe, Ill., 1964.

Martin, F. M.: 'An Inquiry into Parents' Preferences in Secondary Education', in Glass (ed.), op. cit., pp. 160—174.

Martinussen, Karl: «Kristendomsfaget i den linjedelte ungdomsskole», *Prismet,* Vol. 9, no. 1, 1958, pp. 22–26.

Maslow, Abraham: *Motivation and Personality.* New York 1955.

Mathiesen, Thomas: *The Defences of the Weak.* London 1965.

Mathiesen, Thomas: «Generasjonskontakt og sosial klasse», *Tidsskrift for samfunnsforskning,* Vol. 7, 1966, pp. 155–174.

Mathiesen, Thomas: *Tiltak mot ungdomskriminalitet: En opinionsundersøkelse.* Oslo 1965.

Maurseth, P.: «Næringsliv: Bidrag til en beskrivelse av norsk næringsliv», *Det norske samfunnet.* Mimeo, Instituttet for sosiologi, Oslo 1961.

Midbøe, Finn Backer: *Bøtestraff og subsidiær fengselsstraff.* Oslo 1960.

Mills, C. Wright: *The Power Elite,* New York 1956.

Moe, Ole Henrik: Article in *Aftenposten,* no. 239, 28 May 1964, p. 3.

Møglestue, Idar: *Kriminalitet og sosial bakgrunn.* Oslo 1962.

Mogey, John: 'Family and Community in Urban Industrial Societies', in H. Christensen (ed.), *Handbook of Marriage and the Family.* Chicago 1964.

Mogey, John: 'Social Aspects of English Housing', *Studies of the Family,* Vol. 3. Göttingen 1958.

Molne, Kåre and Peter F. Hjort: «Utnyttelsen av liggedagene i en indremedisinsk avdeling», *Tidsskrift for den Norske Lægeforening,* Vol. 85, no. 5, 1965, pp. 298–307.

Moser, C. A. and J. R. Hall: 'The Social Grading of Occupations', in Glass (ed)., op. cit., pp. 29—50.

Moss, J. Joel: 'Teenage Marriage: Gross National Trends and Sociological Factors in the Decision of When to Marry', *Acta Sociologica,* Vol. 8, 1964.

Moyes, A. and T. Hayter: *World III. A Handbook on Developing Countries.* London 1964.

Munch, Peter A.: 'The "Gard", in Eliot and Hillman (eds.), op. cit.

Murdock, George Peter: *Social Structure.* New York 1949.

Myklebust, Petter: «Personer med lave inntekter. Skattelikningen 1962». *Arbeidsnotater. Statistisk Sentralbyrå.* Oslo 1966.

Næss, Siri: «Behandling eller straff? Avgjør utdanningsnivået vår innstilling?» *Vernelagsnytt,* Vol. 7, no. 3, pp. 5–11.

NAVF (Norwegian Research Council for Science and the Humanities): *Elevfrekvens i gymnas og realskole høsten 1966.* Oslo 1967 (a).

NAVF: *Om tilgangen og behovet for akademisk arbeidskraft.* Oslo 1957.

NAVF: *Tilgangen på nye studenter og samlet antall studenter ved norske og utenlandske læresteder. Melding 3.* Oslo 1967 (b).

Nesheim, Asbjørn: *Innstilling fra samekomitéen,* Kirke- og undervisningsdepartementet. Oslo 1959.

Nesheim, Asbjørn: «Samene og deres kultur», *Sameliv IV,* Samisk Selskaps Årbok 1959/60. Oslo 1961, pp. 48–84.

Ness, Einar: «Hva leser folk i en mellomstor norsk by?», *Vinduet,* no. 1, 1953.

Newcomb, T. M.: 'Some Patterned Consequences of Membership in a College Community', in Newcomb and Hartley (eds.), op. cit., pp. 345–357.

Newcomb, T. M. and E. L. Hartley (eds.): *Readings in Social Psychology.* New York 1958.

Neymark, Einar: *Selektiv rörlighet.* Stockholm 1961.

Nilsen, Egil: *Interesser hos voksne.* Oslo 1958.

Nilsen, Egil: *Røykevaner og opplysningsarbeid,* Landsforeningen mot kreft. Oslo 1964.

Nisbet, J.: 'Family, Environment and Intelligence', in Halsey et al., op. cit., pp. 273–287.

Nissen, Ingjald: *Absolute Monogamy, the Attitude of Women and War.* Oslo 1961.

Nissen, Ingjald: *Seksualitet og disiplin.* Oslo 1934.

Nobel Foundation Calendar 1963–64. Uppsala 1963.

Nørstebø, G.: *Folkehøgskule, ei aktuell skuleform.* Mimeo, Master's Thesis, Oslo 1957.

Norges Lover 1682–1964. Oslo 1965.

Norsk Aviskatalog 1965–66.

Den Norske Lægeforening: *Årbøker 1954–1964.*

Norsk Presseforbund: *Norske Pressefolk 1967.* Oslo 1967.

Norsk Rikskringkasting: *Lyttervaner.* Result of NRKs surveys August 1953 –March 1954. Oslo 1955.

North, C. C. and P. K. Hatt: 'Jobs and Occupations: A Popular Evaluation', in L. Wilson and W. L. Kolb (eds.) *Sociological Analysis,* New York 1949, pp. 464–473.

NOS, *see* Statistisk Sentralbyrå.

The Observer, no. 218, 1964.

Odelstingsproposisjon no. 30. Oslo 1958.

OECD: *The Flow of Financial Resources to Less Developed Countries 1956–1962.* Paris 1964.

Ødegård, Ørnulf: 'The Incidence of Psychosis in Various Occupations', *International Journal of Social Psychiatry,* Vol. II, 1956, pp. 85–104.

Ødegård, Ørnulf: 'New Data on Marriage and Mental Disease. The Incidence of Psychosis in the Widowed and the Divorced', *Journal of Mental Science,* 1953, pp. 778–785.

Øidne, Gabriel: «Litt om motsetninga mellom Austlandet og Vestlandet», *Syn og Segn,* no. 7, 1957.

Østgaard, Einar: 'Factors Influencing the Flow of the News', *Journal of Peace Research,* no. 1, 1965, pp. 39–63.

Øyen, Else: «Ekteskap som problemløsning blant ugifte mødre», *Tidsskrift for samfunnsforskning,* no. 4, 1966 (a).

Øyen, Else: *Ugifte mødre.* Oslo 1966 (b).

Øyen, Ørjar: *Jernverksbyen tar form.*

Et økologisk studium av Mo i Rana pr. 1950. Mimeo, Instituttet for sosiologi. Oslo 1958.

Øyen, Ørjar: «Krake søker make», *Tidsskrift for samfunnsforskning,* Vol. 5, 1964, pp. 179–188.

Øyen, Ørjar and Else Øyen: *Prognoser for befolkningsveksten i Mo i Rana.* Mo-stensil no. 11. Institutt for sosiologi. Oslo 1959.

Ortmark, Åke: *Maktspelet i Sverige – ett samhällsreportage.* Malmö 1967.

Paine, Robert: *Coast Lapp Society I,* Tromsø Museums Skrifter. Oslo 1957.

Paine, Robert: *Coast Lapp Society II,* Tromsø Museums Skrifter. Oslo 1965.

Paine, Robert: «Læstadianismen og samfunnet», *Tidsskrift for samfunnsforskning,* Vol. 6, 1965, pp. 60–73.

Parsons, Talcott: *Family, Personality and Interaction Process.* New York 1955.

Parsons, Talcott: 'Voting and the Equilibrium of American Voting Behavior', in E. Burdick and A. Brodbeck, *American Voting Behavior,* Glencoe, Ill. 1959.

Pedersen, H. Winding: *Industriens struktur og dens sammenslutninger.* Copenhagen 1965.

Pollan, Sonja: «Prestetradisjon og presterekruttering 1720–1955», *Tidsskrift for samfunnsforskning,* Vol. 3, 1962, pp. 83–98.

Population Index, Vol. 33, *Population Size and Growth.* Population Reference Bureau, World Population Data Sheet, 1968, pp. 138–147.

Prisdirektoratet: *Oversikt nr. 3 over registeret for konkurransereguleringer og storbedrifter,* Bilag til *Pristidende.* Oslo 1963.

Radikal Familjpolitikk. Stockholm 1955.

Raknes, Ola: «Litt ekteskapspsykologi», *Fri vokster.* Oslo 1949.

Raknes, Ola: *Wilhelm Reich and Orgonomy.* Oslo/New York 1970.

Ramsøy, Natalie Rogoff: 'Assortative Mating and the Structure of Cities', *American Sociological Review,* Vol. 31, 1966(b), pp. 773–785.

Ramsøy, Natalie Rogoff: 'Changes in Rates and Forms of Mobility', in Smelser and Lipset (eds.), *Social Structure and Mobility in Economic Development.* Chicago 1966(a).

Ramsøy, Natalie Rogoff: «Evner, utdannelse og yrkesvalg i norsk samfunnsstruktur», *Tidsskrift for samfunnsforskning,* Vol. 2, 1961, pp. 217–237.

Ramsøy, Natalie Rogoff and Gunvor Iversen: «Sosiologisk kartlegging av Oslo», *Tidsskrift for samfunnsforskning,* Vol. 8, 1967, pp. 20–44.

Ramsøy, Odd: *Samfunnsbygning og skolesøkning.* Oslo 1957.

Ramsøy, Odd: *Trekk fra en saneringsprosess.* Oslo 1967.

Rasmussen, Egil: «Lægen i norsk litteratur», *Tidsskrift for den Norske Lægeforening,* Vol. 81, no. 11, 1961, pp. 710–777.

Read, Dick G.: *Natural Childbirth.* London 1956.

Read, Sir Herbert: 'Atrophied Muscles and Empty Art', *New Scientist,* no. 391, 1964.

Reich, Wilhelm: *The Function of the Orgasm.* New York 1945 and 1961.

Reich, Wilhelm: *The Sexual Revolution.* New York 1945 and 1961.

Rhenmann, E. and B. Stymne: *Företagsledning i en förenderlig värld.* Stockholm 1965.

Riesman, David: *The Lonely Crowd.* New Haven 1952.

Rikstrygdeverket: *Sosialtrygdene i Norge, en oversikt.* Oslo 1966.

Ritter, Paul and Jean Ritter: *The Free Family.* London 1959.

Rod, Jacob: *Folkereligion og kirke.* Copenhagen 1961.

Rodnick, David: *The Norwegians.* Washington, D. C., 1955.

Røstad, Helge: «Ungdomskriminalitetens omfang i vårt land», *Lov og rett,* no. 3, 1967, pp. 141–142.

Rokkan, Stein: *Citizens, Elections, Parties,* Oslo/New York 1970.

Rokkan, Stein: 'Norway: Numerical Democracy and Corporate Pluralism', in Dahl (ed.), *Political Oppositions in Western Democracies.* New Haven

1966, pp. 70–115.

Rokkan, Stein: *Presse, velgere og lesere.* Mimeo, Oslo 1960.

Rokkan, Stein: *Readers, viewers, voters.* Guildhall Lectures 1964, Manchester 1964.

Rokkan, Stein and Per Torsvik: «Der Leser, der Wähler und die Parteipresse», *Kölner Zeitschrift für Soziologie und Sozialpsychologie,* Vol. 12, 1960, pp. 278–302.

Rokkan, Stein and Henry Valen: 'Regional Contrasts in Norwegian Politics', in E. Allardt and Y. Littunen (eds.), *Cleavages, Ideologies and Party. System,* Helsinki 1964, pp. 162–238.

Rosen, B.: 'Family Structure and Achievement Motive', *American Sociological Review,* Vol. 26, no. 4, 1961, pp. 574–585.

Rummel, Rudolph: 'Dimensions of Conflict Behavior within and between Nations', *General Systems.* 1963, pp. 1–50.

Russett, Bruce et al.: *World Handbook of Political and Social Indicators.* New Haven 1964.

Ryder, N. B.: 'Fertility', in Philip M. Hauser and O. D. Duncan (eds.), *The Study of Population.* Chicago 1959.

Salomonsen, Per: *Religionssociologi.* Copenhagen 1966.

Schjelderup, Harald: *Nevrose og oppdragelse.* Oslo 1937.

Schjelderup, Harald: *Nevrosene og den nevrotiske karakter.* Oslo 1940.

Schjelderup, Harald: «Seksuell opplysning», *Sosialt Arbeid.* Oslo 1964.

Scholer, E. A.: *The Public Recreation System of Norway.* Unpublished manuscript, Urbana, Ill., 1960.

Schweigaard Selmer, Elisabeth: *Familiejus.* Oslo 1959.

Seierstad, Ståle: «En sammenlikning av budsjetterte og realiserte nasjonalregnskapsstørrelser.» Unpubl. statistical seminar work. Sosialøkonomisk Institutt, Oslo 1963.

Seip, Jens Arup: «Den norske Høyesterett som politisk organ», *Historisk*

Tidsskrift, Vol. 43, 1964, pp. 103–135.

Seip, Jens Arup: *Et regime foran under-gangen*. Oslo 1945.

Selid, Betty: *Women in Norway*. Mimeo, Oslo 1966.

Sims, V. M. and J. R. Patrick: 'Attitude towards the Negro of Northern and Southern College Students', in Newcomb and Hartley (eds.), op.cit., pp. 358–365.

Singer, J. David and Melvin Small: 'The Composition and Status Ordering of the International System 1815–1940', *World Politics* 1966, pp. 237–282.

Sivertsen, Dagfinn: *Goal-setting and Social Norms*. Mimeo (Master's Thesis), Institute of Sociology. Oslo 1952.

Skard, Åse Gruda: «Barn i et norsk miljø», *Nordisk Psykologi*. Oslo 1956.

Skard, Åse Gruda: *Ungene våre*. Oslo 1948.

Skard, Torild: «Gymnasiastenes sosiale bakgrunn», *Tidsskrift for samfunns-forskning*, Vol. 5, 1964, pp. 123–124.

SØS = *Samfunnsøkonomiske Studier*, series published by the Norwegian Central Bureau of Statistics.

Solstad, Karl: *Utkantungdom og flytting*. Mimeo, Institute for Educational Research, Oslo 1965.

Soltow, Lee: *Toward Income Equality in Norway*. Madison, Wisc. 1965.

Stangvik, S.: «Skolemodenhet og begynnerundervisning», *Norsk pedagogisk tidsskrift*, Vol. 51, no. 5, 1967, pp. 205–221.

Statistisk Sentralbyrå (Norwegian Central Bureau of Statistics). The publications of this bureau are identified by 'NOS' (Norway's Official Statistics) and numbered and dated.

Steen, Sverre: *Det gamle samfunn*. Oslo 1957.

Stenersen, Rolf: *Edvard Munch*. Oslo 1964.

Stensaasen, Svein: «Sosiale relasjoner i klasserommet», *Forskning og danning*, no. 7, Oslo 1962, pp. 71–138.

Stephenson, John C.: 'Family Life in an Industrial Community', in Eliot and Hillman (eds.), op. cit.

Strøm, Axel: «De eldres levevilkår og helsetilstand», *Norske Gerontologiske Skrifter*, Vol. 2, 1965.

Strøm, Axel: *Lærebok i sosialmedisin*. Oslo 1963.

Stub, Kjell: «Befolkningens innstilling til forskjellige nedrustnings- og forsvarsalternativer», *Norsk Militært Tidsskrift*, Vol. 121, 1962.

Sundby, Per and Per Nyhus: 'Major and Minor Psychiatric Disorders in Males in Oslo', *Acta psychiatrica Scandinavia*, Vol. 39, 1963, pp. 519–547.

Sundt, Eilert: *Om Dødeligheten i Norge*. Christiania (Oslo) 1855(a).

Sundt, Eilert: *Om Giftermaal i Norge*. Christiania 1855(b), reissued Oslo 1967.

Sundt, Eilert: *Om Piperviken og Ruseløkkbakken*. Christiania 1858.

Sussman, Marvin B.: 'The Help Pattern in the Middle-Class Family', *American Sociological Review*, Vol. 18, no. 1, 1953.

Sussman, Marvin B.: 'The Isolated Nuclear Family: Fact or Fiction?' *Social Problems*, 1959.

Sussman, Marvin B.: 'Kin Family Network: Unheralded Family Structure', *Marriage and Family Living*, Vol. 24, 1962.

Sussman, Marvin B.: 'The Urban Kin Network in the Formulation of Urban Theory', Paper for the Ninth International Seminar on Family Research, Tokyo 1965, in Hill and König (eds.): *Families East and West*. Paris 1970.

Svalastoga, K. and P. Wolf: *Social rang og mobilitet*. Copenhagen 1963.

Sweetser, Dorian Apple: 'The Effect of Industrialization on Intergenerational Solidarity', *Rural Sociology*, Vol. 31, no. 2, 1966.

Sweetser, Dorian Apple: 'Mother–Daughter Ties between Generations in Industrial Society', *Family Process*, Vol. 3, 1964.

Taranger, A.: *Norsk familierett*. Oslo 1926.

Thagaard Sem, Tove: *Kjønnsroller og studiemotivering*. Mimeo (Master's Thesis in Sociology), Oslo 1967.

Tiller, Per Olav: 'Father Absence and Personality Development in Sailor Families', *Nordisk Psykologi Monografi serie,* no. 9, 1958.

Tiller, Per Olav: «Kulturelle variasjoner i persepsjonen av foreldre», *Nordisk Psykologi,* nos. 1–2, 1960.

Tiller, Per Olav: «Når far er borte», *Tidsskrift for samfunnsforskning,* Vol. 1, no. 4., 1960.

Torgersen, Ulf: *Church Independence and Doctrinal Purity.* Mimeo, Institute for Social Research. Oslo 1966.

Torgersen, R. N. «Dommerutnevnelser», *Medlemsblad for Den Norske Dommerforening,* No. 164, 1954, pp. 1268–1273.

Torgersen, Ulf: «Høyesterettsrolle i norsk politikk», *Tidsskrift for samfunnsforskning,* Vol. 1, 1960, pp. 94–104.

Torgersen, Ulf: «Lederskiktet innenfor næringslivet: Stabilitet eller fornyelse?» *Tidsskrift for samfunnsforskning,* Vol. 4, Oslo 1963, pp. 43–55.

Torsvik, Per: *Fem år med fjernsyn.* Markedskommunikasjon, September 1966.

Torsvik, Per: «Folk og fjernsyn», *Minervas kvartalskrift,* no. 1, 1967(a), pp. 20–33.

Torsvik, Per: *International Guide to Mass Media Statistics, Norway* (Draft 1967). UNESCO. (1967b).

Torsvik, Per: 'Magazines in Norway', *Gazette,* Vol. 6, no. 2, 1960.

Torsvik, Per: *Norsk Ukepresse 1939–1964.* Mimeo, Working report, Institute for Press Research, Oslo 1965.

Torsvik, Per: «Valgkampen i fjernsyn og radio 1965», *Tidsskrift for samfunnsforskning,* Vol. 8, 1967(c), pp. 143–162.

Townsend, Peter: *The Family Life of Old People.* London 1957.

Trustkommisionens betænkning, no. 8. *Konkurrancebegrænsninger i dansk erhvervsliv.* Copenhagen 1960.

Ukepressekatalogen, Oslo 1954–1966.

Ullern, Ingrid: «Miljøplanlegging», *Familiepolitikk i dag og i morgen.* Oslo 1967.

UNECE: *Economic Survey of Europe in 1959.* Geneva 1960.

UNESCO: *World Communications.* Paris 1964.

UNESCO Courier, The, August/September 1967: 'Inquiry into Disarmed World. First Results of an International Poll', pp. 5–9.

UN Demographical Yearbook 1962, 14th ed. New York 1962.

UN Statistical Yearbook 1958. New York 1958.

U. S. Department of Health, Education, and Welfare: 'Infant Mortality Problems in Norway', in *Vital and Health Statistics,* October 1967.

Utenriksdepartementet: *Innstilling avgitt av den norsk-svenske reinbeitekommisjon av 1964.* Oslo 1967.

Utenriksdepartementet: *Innstilling om den videre utbygging av Norges bistand til utviklingslandene.* Oslo 1957.

Valen, Henry: «Partiforskyvninger ved stortingsvalget i 1965». *Tidsskrift for samfunnsforskning,* Vol. 8, 1967, pp. 113–142.

Valen, Henry: «Politisk lederskap», *Forskningsnytt,* no. 9, 1963, p. 9.

Valen, Henry: «Den sosiale og politiske bakgrunn for rekrutteringen av det politiske lederskap». *Tidsskrift for samfunnsforskning,* Vol. 7, 1966, pp. 175–198.

Valen, Henry and Daniel Katz: *Political Parties in Norway. A Community Study.* Oslo 1964.

Valen, Henry and Per Torsvik: «Øking i valgdeltakelsen i 1963 og 1965», *Tidsskrift for samfunnsforskning,* Vol. 8, 1967, pp. 187–218.

Valgundersøkelsen 1957 (Election Survey 1957). Basic Tables I–II. Mimeo, Chr. Michelsens Institute, Bergen 1960.

Vangsnes, Kari: *De gifte kvinners yrkesaktivitet.* Oslo 1965.

Vangsnes, Sigmund: *Rekruttering av artianere og karakter til examen artium. En undersøkelse av 4 artiumskull.* Melding no. 1, NAVF, Utredningsavdeling. Oslo 1967.

Vogt, Johan: «Kvinneoverskuddets tid i

Norge er forbi», *Samtaler på en for-stadsbane* (essays). Oslo 1953.

Vogt, Johan: «Det smertefulle tilbake-blikk», *Arbeiderbladet,* 28 February 1967.

Vorren, Ørnulf and Ernst Manker: *Samekulturen.* Tromsø 1958.

Waal, Nic.: *Vi og smårollingene våre.* Oslo 1948.

Wach, Joachim: *The Sociology of Religion.* Chicago 1944.

Werner, Anita: «Norske Journalister», *Tidsskrift for samfunnsforskning,* Vol. 7, no. 1, 1966, pp. 37–71.

Werner, Anita: *Norske Pressefolk.* Oslo 1967.

Westerståhl, Jørgen and Carl Gunnar Jansson: *Politisk Press.* Gothenburg 1958.

Westrup, C.: *Kvinde og Mand,* Vol. II of *Talt og skrevet.* Copenhagen 1943.

Wheeler, Stanton: *A Preliminary Report on the Scandinavian Prison Study.* Mimeo, Cambridge, Mass., 1962.

Wilkenfeld, Jonathan: 'Domestic and Foreign Conflict Behavior of Nations', *Journal of Peace Research,* 1968, pp. 56–69.

Winsnes, Hanna: *For tjenestepiger,* 2 ed. Christiania 1868.

Wisløff, Carl Fr.: «Et år av kirkens liv», *Aftenposten* 31 December 1964.

World Health Organization: *Annual Epidemiological and Vital Statistics 1960.* Geneva 1963.

Wyller, Thomas: *Frigjøringspolitikk.* Oslo 1963.

Yearbook of Nordic Statistics. Nordic Council, Stockholm.

Yinger, J. Milton: *Riligion, Society and the Individual.* New York 1957.

Young, Michael: *Intelligensen som over-klasse,* Oslo 1966. Translated from the English *The Rise of the Meritocracy* (Penguin Books).

Young, Michael and Peter Willmot: *Family and Kinship in East London.* New York 1957.

Zelditch, Morris: 'Family, Marriage and Kinship', in R. Paris, (ed.), *Handbook of Modern Sociology.* Chicago 1964.

Zylberg, Turid: «De enslige forsørgere og deres barn», *Familiepolitikk idag og imorgen.* Oslo 1967.

Subject Index

423–24; UN voting 414; working situation 328, 403
Switzerland 249, 415

Teaching see Education
Television see Radio/TV
Temperance: t. boards 359; t. movement 135
Thranite movement 113
Tourism 336, 423–25
Trade 77–78, 86, 87, 92, 93, 422, 23
Trade unions 91–92, 137, 139–40. See also Organization society
Tuberculosis 30, 263, 279, 280–81, 282. See also Health, Health services

Unemployment 91, 327
United Nations 150–51, 411–15, 418, 419
United States of America: attitudes to 411; education 167, 172, 173; kinship relations 51; marriage 66, 68; mass media 291; migration flows 35–39 *pass.*; mortality 261–63; Nobel Prizes 405, politics 203; reference country 387, 388; religion 249–54 *pass.*; tourism 424, 425; UN voting 414, 415
Union of Soviet Socialist Republics 68, 411, 414, 425

Venereal disease 281
Venstre see Liberal Party
Voting: v. patterns 134–37, 198, 201, 202, 215–17, 394–95. See also specific population groups and parties.

Wages see Income distribution
Weekly press 310–16; circulation 311, 323n; content 313–16; popular culture 310, 316; readership 143, 311–13, 332
Welfare state 78–84, 114, 395; definition 78–79; family aid 80–83; Labour Party policies 82; pensions 81–84 *pass.*, 284; social assistance 80–84. See also Health service, Leisure
Women: childbirth 74; economic dependence 62–64; education 181, 188; mother–child relations 70–72, 74; position in marriage 65; reading habits 302–3, 311–12; religion 248, 249, 251; unwed mothers 59–60; working women 56–58, 68–70, 91, 116–17, 118. See also Children, Marriage
Workers: attitudinal patterns 147–53; blue-collar w. 87–92, 116–17, 121–26, 13440; consumption patterns 140–46; white-collar w. 84, 88, 106, 116–18, 121–26, 134–40
Working population 77, 85
Work-period 328–30

Name Index

449

450

Contributors

Natalie Rogoff Ramsøy, Director, Institute of Applied Social Research, Oslo.

Ørjar Øyen, Professor of Sociology, University of Bergen.

Erik Grønseth, Associate Professor of Sociology, University of Oslo.

Ståle Seierstad, Research Associate, Work Research Institute, Oslo.

Vilhelm Aubert, Professor of Sociology, University of Oslo.

Tore Lindbekk, Professor of Social Sciences, University of Trondheim.

Ulf Torgersen, Professor of Political Science, University of Oslo.

Thomas Mathiesen, Professor of the Sociology of Law, University of Oslo.

Otto Hauglin, Principal of the Lay Deacons' School of Social Work; Member of Parliament (Socialist People's Party).

Yngvar Løchen, Professor of Social Sciences, University of Tromsø.

Per Torsvik, Research Director, Norwegian Centre for Media Research, University of Bergen.

Odd Ramsøy, Professor of Sociology, University of Oslo.

Nils Christie, Professor of Law, University of Oslo.

Johan Galtung, Professor of Peace and Conflict Research, University of Oslo.